# NATIONAL SYSTEMS OF INNOVATION IN COMPARISON

T0223933

# National Systems of Innovation in Comparison

## Structure and Performance Indicators for Knowledge Societies

*Edited by*

ULRICH SCHMOCH
*Fraunhofer Institute for Systems and Innovation Research,*
*Karlsruhe, Germany*

CHRISTIAN RAMMER
*Centre for European Economic Research,*
*Mannheim, Germany*

*and*

HARALD LEGLER
*Lower Saxony Institute for Economic Research (NIW)*
*Hannover, Germany*

 Springer

A C.I.P. Catalogue record for this book is available from the Library of Congress.

ISBN-13  978-90-481-7226-9
ISBN-10  1-4020-4949-1 (e-book)
ISBN-13  978-1-4020-4949-1 (e-book)

Published by Springer,
P.O. Box 17, 3300 AA Dordrecht, The Netherlands.

*www.springer.com*

*Printed on acid-free paper*

Printed in the Netherlands.

# Contents

# Preface

This book evolved in the context of an annual report on Germany's technological performance prepared on behalf of the German government. This report is primarily based on a broad set of innovation indicators reflecting different aspects of the innovation system. One characteristic of the report is the systematic benchmarking of the German structures by indicators for a variety of other countries, and a broad international dataset was developed as a result. The report is prepared by a consortium of eight research institutes, each of which is responsible for specific subjects and indicators. These sub-reports are critically discussed by the whole group, so that a profound expertise on appropriate innovation indicators and their interpretation is arrived at.

With this book, we respond to the request of many of our international partners who are interested in the methodology and the results of our research, as the report and the more detailed partial reports are published in German, and an English version of the summary report was available for some individual years only. The interest centres on the specific situation in Germany, on the one hand, but also on the broad documentation of data for many other countries, on the other hand. Of course, we cannot cover every facet of the last decades, but we selected some focal activities which should be of special interest to a non-German readership.

Many people at the institutes of the three editors contributed to the successful preparation of the book. At Fraunhofer ISI, we have to thank Renate Klein and Sabine Wurst in particular for their meticulous work in the layout and checking of all contributions, including the generation of joint reference and abbreviation lists, and Christine Mahler-Johnstone for the language editing. At the Centre of European Economic Research (ZEW), we would like to thank Vladimir Dzharkalov for carefully formatting all the figures and tables, at the Lower Saxony Institute for Economic Research (NIW), we are grateful to Mark Leidmann for technical assistance.

We are most grateful to all contributors for their considerable commitment in preparing interesting contributions within very narrow time limits. We hope that the outcome will be helpful to a broad readership.

Karlsruhe, Mannheim, Hanover
January 2006

Ulrich Schmoch, Christian Rammer, and Harald Legler

# Part 1. Introduction and Summary

# 1.1 Technological Performance – Concept and Practice

Harald Legler, Christian Rammer, Ulrich Schmoch

The contributions in this book are based on the activities of a group of nine German research institutes which annually produce the 'Report on the Technological Performance of Germany' on behalf of the German Federal Ministry of Education and Research (BMBF). This report informs about indicators of the status quo and developments in science, research, and technology which are conceived to be of high importance for Germany's international performance, and to be major determinants for economic growth and employment in the long run.

The report is based on a set of core indicators which are annually updated and which also allow for long-term observations, plus additional theoretical and empirical studies on new indicators, specific technologies or sectors, specific regions or countries of interest, etc. So this book reflects only a small part of the total activities in this context. The indicators compiled in the report refer to a variety of national or international sources such as R&D, industry, foreign trade, employment, or education statistics, but these data are analysed from the specific perspective of technological performance, for instance, the focus is on employment in technology-intensive sectors, foreign trade of technology-intensive goods and so on. In addition, specific primary statistics of patents, publications, trade marks, technology start-ups and the like are generated.

The approach followed by the German system of reporting on technological performance differs from those found in many other countries or in most international organisations. While the scoreboard activities of the OECD and the European Commission (see OECD 2005; European Commission 2005) as well as the US Science and Engineering Indicators Report (NSF 2004), or a recent study on Switzerland (Arvanitis et al. 2005) follow a similar indicator approach, economic interpretation and policy recommendations are fairly restricted in these publications. By contrast, in some other countries such as Great Britain (DTI 2003), Australia (DEST 2003), New Zealand (MED 2003) or Austria (BMBWK et al. 2005), technology reporting is much more focussed on the contribution of innovation policy to the national innovation system performance, restricting the empirical analysis to a smaller number of key indicators.

A specific feature of the German report on technological performance is the steadfast endeavour to provide indicators on various aspects of the innovation system on a sound methodological basis, on the one hand, and supporting explanations of the indicators, on the other hand, so that the reader is enabled to interpret the findings in an appropriate way. As the group of participating institutes does not belong to a public authority, the analyses can keep a critical, but still solidary distance to official German innovation policy.

The reporting system was established in 1985 by two of the institutes still participating today and focussed on industrial innovation activities according to the perception of that time. Since then, the awareness has steadily grown that the understanding of innovation processes has to include other factors, as expressed in the growing

*U. Schmoch, C. Rammer and H. Legler (eds.), National Systems of Innovation in Comparison, 3–14.*
© 2006 Springer. Printed in the Netherlands.

interest in the concept of national systems of innovation (NSI), reflected in various publications, e.g. Nelson (1988; 1993), Freeman (1988), Lundvall (1988; 1992), Amable et al. (1997) or Edquist (1997). As a direct consequence, the number of topics considered has been enlarged continuously, and the number of participating research institutes has also increased.

Today, the system reporting on technological performance is guided by five principles:

- First, technological performance is captured by a comprehensive indicator approach that attempts to consider a variety of dimensions which may be classified into four groups: Education and human capital, knowledge generation (R&D in the public and private sector), implementation of knowledge (patents, innovations, firm startups), and market success and diffusion (productivity, production, employment, foreign trade).

- Secondly, indicators are differentiated by sectors, or fields and technology as far as possible, paying special attention to those sectors that rely particularly on new knowledge and new technologies. This thematic differentiation allows specialisation patterns to be identified, as well as sectoral strengths, weaknesses and dynamics.

- Thirdly, indicators are used to analyse both current trends as well as long-term changes in economic and technological structures.

- Fourthly, international benchmarking is at the very centre of the reporting system, taking those countries into consideration which are Germany's main competitors in world markets. In the course of time, the number of countries systematically considered increased from five in 1985 to about 12 to 20 presently, depending on the indicator considered. In recent years, particular attention has been paid to emerging economies.

- Finally, indicator analysis and interpretation attempt to identify and address critical factors for NSI performance, such as the interaction between industry and science, financing of innovation and new firms, the legal framework, the policy support system, and sectoral and technology shifts.

Consequently, the analyses are based on a large dataset covering various aspects of national systems of innovation (NSI) whereof major elements are illustrated in Fig. 1. In our work, we consider the NSI as a heuristic concept, guiding the research in specific elements and linkages between them. With regard to this concept, the report primarily addresses various dimensions of the industrial, the education, and the research system. Some elements of the infrastructure, such as the provision of venture capital, the conception of intellectual property legislation or the role of norms and standards, are analysed in special focus reports. The same applies to the role of intermediaries between the industrial and the research system or public research and innovation policies.

Some attempts have been made to look at the linkages between these different elements in more detail, as a basic assumption of the NSI concept is the co-evolution of the various elements depicted in Fig. 1. This project proved to be extremely complex, as the indicators on different aspects of innovation systems are classified in different ways (disciplines, sectors, technologies, goods, services etc.) and are often linked, but indirectly, and with different time lags. Some relationships found for some countries do not apply to others. So a satisfactory 'final' solution has not been achieved yet. But in any case, the report shows the different dimensions of technological performance for various countries and allows specific national profiles to be drawn.

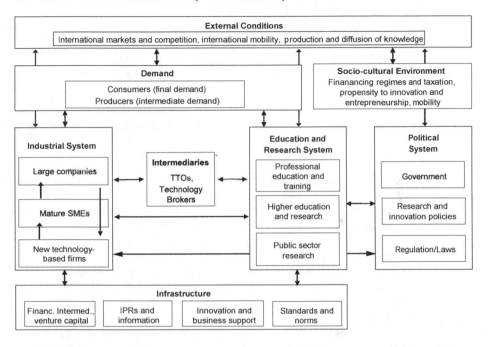

Source: Based on Kuhlmann and Arnold (2001: 26) – own supplements

**Fig. 1.** Illustration of major elements of the heuristic model of national systems of innovation

In view of the enormous extent of globalisation, the analysis of innovation systems on a purely national basis is not sufficient. Therefore, we enlarged the illustration of NSIs in Fig. 1 by the introduction of external conditions such as international markets, international competition and so on. The aspect of international relations is addressed in most parts of the performance report by looking at international trade flows or comparing countries, and in special reports, the globalisation strategies of enterprises are examined in more detail. In any case, this topic will receive increased attention in the next years.

To satisfy the concept of systems of innovation in a more comprehensive way, framework conditions such as the financial environment, mobility issues, the demand of enterprises and private consumers, the general attitudes towards new technologies or the various elements of the political system need more attention. A further interesting aspect is a more detailed analysis of the impact of socio-cultural indicators on tolerance, willingness to take risks, political interest etc. on innovation performance. Nevertheless, the existing dataset already provides a broad spectrum of information showing relevant structures for international performance and changes of key elements, not only for Germany, but also for many other countries. All in all, the report on technological performance and the contributions to this book already cover a broad set of elements which are generally linked to the NSI concept, but could be complemented by topics in particular with regard to the socio-political framework. However, the introduction of these aspects will be limited for two reasons: first, many parts of the socio-political framework cannot be described by indicators in an appropriate way, but the focus of our work is on indicators. Second, we must concentrate on a limited set of indicators in order to maintain the clarity of the report.

The next section resumes some major findings of recent years for Germany, and linked to that, the general international structures are addressed as well.

## Technological Performance of Germany – Indicators and Empirical Findings

Industrial R&D activities represent the core investment in new technical knowledge and therefore mark the beginning of technological innovation processes. R&D plays a decisive role in the functional chain of education and training, science, research and technology, inventions, investment and innovations, international performance, productivity, growth and employment in economies. It is the centre-piece of industrial activities aiming at innovation, restructuring and growth (see Chapter 2.1).

With its share of 2.5 per cent of GDP in R&D expenditure, Germany ranks high in R&D competition with other economies (2.2). But the international competition in R&D has increased during the last decades. Other large industrialised countries (USA in the 1990s, Japan) as well as countries from northern Europe and, in particular, threshold countries from Asia are exhibiting considerably greater dynamics in the expansion of R&D capacities than Germany. As a result of this catching-up process, they managed to secure a continuously rising share of scientific research results (3.1) as well as of technological inventions (3.2).

Recently, industrial R&D in Germany is no longer the driving force behind economic growth; it just runs along with the business cycle (2.1). On the other hand, in the USA industrial R&D has been in a particularly weak position since 2001 (2.2). Given the high weight of the US economy in global R&D and its enormous linkages with other economies (2.3), this should turn out to be a big negative impact on innovative power worldwide.

Industries that invest very strongly in R&D have been winners in structural change (Pharmaceuticals, Electronics, ICT Industry and more recently, Services). Germany's R&D specialisation has slightly shifted in favour of these 'leading-edge technologies' also, but R&D activities are still concentrated on high-level technology and production engineering. The nucleus of the German R&D increase is the automobile industry. About one-quarter of its worldwide R&D capacities are located in Germany, compared to about 10 per cent of total business sector (2.1).

R&D in Germany is shifting more and more towards large firms, whereas the R&D participation of SMEs seems to be decreasing slightly. This has to be seen as a warning sign, because firms without own R&D activities are going to become rarer among the group of innovating firms (3.3). 'Innovators' are firms introducing new products and/or new processes; they are the key linkage between science, research and technology and its final output measured by international performance, productivity and employment. In this respect, it must be remembered that the German economy used to show a nearly unequalled high share of innovating firms. This, in particular, is due to the strong participation of SMEs in innovative activities (3.3). This advantage must not get lost. But first we find some problems in recruiting young technology-oriented firms (4.2), and secondly the participation rate of newly founded firms in R&D is diminishing.

**Box 1.**

It is useful to focus the analysis of an economy's technological performance on those sectors in which science, knowledge, research and technology play a decisive role in entrepreneurial activities. Therefore the branches of economic activity are classified according to their 'technology intensity'.

In manufacturing industry the R&D intensity (share of R&D expenditure in turnover or value added) is the most critical indicator in this respect. The cutting rule is: Any sector or product group with an above average R&D intensity (what means at least 3.5 per cent in 1995–1997) is called 'R&D-intensive'. The enumeration of R&D-intensive products alone, however, would still conceal considerable intensity differences among this group. Therefore, a further differentiation is made between 'high-level technology' (3.5 to 8.5 per cent) and 'leading-edge technology' (more than 8.5 per cent in 1995–1997). 'Leading-edge technologies' on the one hand are cross-sectional technologies (e.g. Biotechnology, Electronics) and the key factors for related product groups such as Pharmaceuticals, Computers, Telecommunication Equipment, and Scientific Instruments, but also for users in other branches. On the other hand, they are often subject to protectionism, such as in Aircraft and Aerospace or Weapons Technology. In 'high-level technology' industries, there is still a need for above average R&D activities, too. But they concentrate less on research and more on experimental development.

In the service sector, however, technological R&D is not an adequate indicator for the generation and use of new knowledge, as investment in R&D is not that important. Rather, we can assume that the innovative potential is embodied in the skills of workers. 'Knowledge-intensive services' are defined by an intensive employment of academically trained workers, natural scientists and engineers in particular, or by selected occupational characteristics (such as high shares of workers in planning, construction, development, research, consulting). Therefore, in this sector we mainly find knowledge-intensive business services (e.g. telecommunication services, software development, economic and technical consulting), but also some other services with a high affinity to technology (Health, Media, Transport).

To some extent this decrease has to do with the rising demand for academic qualifications in the industrial R&D process, on the one hand (2.1), and pressure on the markets for highly qualified employees on the other hand. SMEs in particular are suffering from the scarcity of skilled personnel. Therefore tertiary education has to be stepped up/intensified (5.3).

In the long run, the governmental share of financing industrial R&D has been decreasing worldwide (2.1 and 2.2). At the same time, R&D capacities in higher education and in extra-university institutions have shown weak dynamics. But since 2000 we find that governments are re-assuming more responsibility for science and technology, for research and development. Most countries report an increasing share of governmental and/or higher education R&D (2.2). In Germany, too, there has been a positive turnaround since the end of the 1990s, even if dynamics cannot keep pace with important competitive economies, the USA and northern Europe in particular.

The reversal of German governments towards supporting R&D is very important. Publicly conducted basic and applied basic research open up new technological options to the business sector (3.1) that itself is more and more reliant on R&D co-operations. SMEs especially prefer public science and research institutions as co-operation partners as well as R&D services of specialised firms. Big firms, however, used to co-operate in R&D more intensively with other (associated) firms at home and to an increasing extent with linked firms abroad (2.1). Co-operation not only in R&D but also in day-to-day-innovative activities is gaining in importance (2.1, 3.3), but compared to other countries, co-operation potentials in Germany are not being sufficiently exploited (3.3).

**Box 2.**

---

No economy is able to be top in every technological branch. For economic reasons, countries have to participate in the international division of labour and use their 'comparative advantages'. This means that every country has a 'profile of specialisation': There are sectors where its share or position is clearly above average. On the other hand, we find sectors where it is not outstanding or hardly visible. The profile of specialisation therefore measures strengths and weaknesses of a country. Ideally, you find a very sharp profile, but in reality this only applies to small countries. The concept of specialisation has its origin in the theory of international division of labour regarding international trade flows (see also Chapter 4.1).

As an example: export (x) specialisation patterns of a country (j) according to product groups (i) are measured by comparing the shares of this country in world trade by product group with the share of this country in total world trade ('relative shares in exports', RXS). Expressing these relations in logarithms (ln), positive figures reveal 'comparative advantages' (or strengths) of this country in trade with these markets, while negative figures show a weaker position of this country on the commodity markets than on average:

$$RXS_{ij} = \ln [(x_{ij}/\Sigma_j x_{ij})/(\Sigma_i x_{ij}/\Sigma_{ij} x_{ij})]. \tag{1}$$

This concept is also used to analyse the strengths of the countries in patents, publications, sectoral patterns of the economy, R&D structures and so on.

---

Business sectors value export market exploitation strategies (2.3), thus the business sector is massively intensifying global market exploitation strategies (2.3). The need for investment and production abroad is rising, as a consequence the globalisation of industrial R&D capacities is accelerating. In addition, German firms have increased their international activities in 'knowledge seeking'. Therefore industrial R&D abroad is mainly located in very R&D-intensive branches and science-based technology fields (2.3). This is also reflected in a rising share of cross-border scientific research (3.1) and inventions (patents) (3.2). But foreign companies in Germany invest in R&D capacities to the same extent, focussed on industries where they find favourable market, production and R&D conditions (2.3). Improving these three criteria should blaze the trail for innovation policy.

Science is the basis for the technological performance of economies and is gaining in importance for the development of new technologies. On the one hand, the results of scientific research enhance existing innovative potentials. On the other hand, public science and research act as technological pioneers in some neuralgic generic fields. The research of German scientists is highly regarded, but their contribution to global science is decreasing. To some extent, this is due to the fact that German scientists in some of the main focuses of the German science and technology system (with affinity to Mechanical Engineering, and Process Engineering) are still publishing in journals of only national scope. They should address their research results more to the international scientific community (3.1).

Another aspect of globalisation is the fact that German firms are getting their impulses for innovations more and more from foreign markets (3.3). This becomes apparent when regarding Germany's dynamics in the field of patents destined for the global market ('triadic patent families', 3.2). Technological inventions are a first indication of market-oriented results from science, research and experimental development. Patents should give protection so that inventors can appropriate economic earnings from technological inventions. Germany's good position in the international patent markets on the one hand reflects the fact that Germany is one of the most innovation-oriented countries worldwide (3.3). Additionally, it depends on the weak dynamics of the home market. Firms necessarily orient themselves to foreign markets (4.1). In this sense the German system of innovation can be classified as very (export) market-oriented.

The structure of Germany's inventions mirrors its technological focuses: it is top in the sector of high-level technologies, but it has only a low rank in the sector of leading-edge technologies. Small and highly specialised, export-oriented economies with a high affinity to leading-edge technologies - such as northern Europe and Switzerland, but also Japan - show the highest intensities in patent protected inventions. But the sharp cutback of R&D in ICT and associated branches since 2000 brought a lot of problems to those economies which did not have any noteworthy alternative to this technological path (3.2). Germany's good position in the high-level technology sector has to do with the high share of small and medium-sized firms integrated in innovative processes (3.3) and patenting their inventions.

New products and new processes mark the output of innovative activities in the business sector. In hardly any other country are SMEs integrated so intensively in innovation processes as in Germany. This is true for R&D activities, too, and for nearly every branch of the business sector, in production engineering in particular. In the service sector as well as in Electronics and associated sectors, the situation must be assessed less favourably. Compared to other countries, the German economy could realise higher economic outcomes from innovative activities, e.g. the mix of goods and services used to be refreshed very fast (high share of new-to-market products). But in the new decade innovative dynamics stagnated in Germany, many firms abstained from innovative activities and just recently resumed them (3.3). Additionally, a significant lack of 'fresh blood' in the technology-intensive sector became apparent (4.2).

In economies with very intensive and varying innovative activities, firms inevitably meet with impediments and barriers standing in their way. You can find this more often in an innovation-oriented business sector such as in Germany than in other economics (3.3). In the year 2000 - from the innovation point of view marking nearly a 'boom year' - the lack of skilled personnel has been reported as the most important bottleneck. This may give a foretaste of the future: in the light of inevitable shortages in the field of highly qualified personnel, it cannot be exclude that a strong innovative upswing could be limited by a lack of sufficiently qualified workers (5.1, 5.2, 5.3).

Highly qualified people, academically trained natural scientists and engineers in particular, form the pool of technology-oriented start-ups. This 'structural change from the bottom' is one of the most important factors in renewing and modernising sectoral economic structures and in transferring newest knowledge from science and research into innovative products and services. In R&D-intensive and knowledge-intensive sectors of the economy, Germany indeed shows rates of firm foundations which are comparable to other big countries. But there is only a low rate of regeneration concerning the stock of all firms. Moreover, the dynamics of firm foundations is diminishing. In the R&D-intensive manufacturing industry, this is the case worldwide, being just another expression of the secular trend of structural change in favour of services. But in the knowledge-intensive service sector which is the sector of the future, Germany has clearly been outrun by many economies in terms of firm foundations (4.2).

Cross-section or generic leading-edge technologies have a particular relevance and pioneering consequences for economic structure and dynamics. *Pars pro toto*, the diffusion of IC technologies in Germany has been analysed. In similar fashion to Biotechnology or Nanotechnology, the diffusion of ICT enables a diversity of new products and efficient production processes. At the same time, it is accompanied by strong interventions into the (internal) structures of firms and into the traditional interrelationships between economic subjects. Intensive use of ICT is said to be connected with big gains in productivity. One example is the stormy development of e-commerce worldwide. Particularly in this field, Germany is participating to a large extent, thanks to the close connections between firms (4.3). But with respect to nearly every other ICT indicator, Germany ranks in the middle field and in most cases is far from initiating rapid catching-up processes. Typically, exactly those economies have top ranking which also take a leading position according to other indicators (e.g. see R&D, 2.2, or education and qualification, 5.1). They come from North America and from northern Europe as well as from Switzerland.

That Germany will not be able to catch up rapidly is partly due to the fact that IC-related technological infrastructure (broadband, cable, UMTS) is lagging behind a lot of countries. In addition, the use of ICT in the public sector could be more intensive, as the pioneering function of government fosters the diffusion of new technologies into the private sector. An essential contribution to a more rapid and thorough diffusion of ICT within the economy, however, can be seen in an improved education and training of workers (4.3).

The yardsticks for the technological performance of an economy are international performance, production structures and employment. Above all, it has to prove itself in the international markets of research and knowledge-intensive goods and services. International trade flows in particular reveal Germany's position, giving a direct comparison with its competitors.

According to these criteria, Germany shows two faces: on the one hand, it exhibits favourable sectoral patterns. In manufacturing industry in particular, the large section of high-level technologies stands out, the share of knowledge-intensive services is average. However, there are two problems: first, Germany's contribution to world production of leading-edge technologies is low. Secondly, there is a lack of macro-economic dynamics in the domestic market. In the international markets, the reverse applies: a nearly unbroken export dynamic diminishes the adjustment pressure which results from the weakness of the home market. On the other hand, specialisation in research-intensive goods is clearly decreasing and Germany's comparative advantages are gradually disappearing (4.1).

Education is the basis of the technological performance of an economy. Economic structural change (4.1) and the pressure to generate innovations continuously increase the demand for highly qualified and skilled people. The 'knowledge economy' in particular needs natural scientists and engineers and their key competence for technical innovations. This trend is true for every economy, with some countries being more successful than Germany to satisfy this demand (5.1). In Europe, an additional pressure on education policy comes from demography: in the (near) future, many highly skilled personnel will leave the labour market due to old age. They may be replaced, but then there will be not enough potential to meet the rising need for natural scientists and engineers of a growing information and knowledge economy. In Germany, this gap is the result of a hesitant education policy during the last 25 years (5.4). We have to expect a shortage of skilled people (5.1).

Germany's structural strengths in the sector of high-level technology are reflected in the qualification of labour force: Germany shows skill advantages at the 'secondary' level of qualification caused by its 'dual system' of vocational and educational training based on joint efforts of employers and government. Ten years ago, a strong need for modernisation became obvious, especially in the field of technical occupations which induced a careful and extensive reform process. Consequently, the system now seems to meet the sharply rising skill demands of the business sector better. But knowledge requirements are increasing further, particularly in the new and modernised technical occupations. So this system is competing more and more for young people who are qualified to start a university education. Recently, serious problems relating to the lack of training places emerged, with the high cost of training, especially in the field of technical occupations, as well as unsure growth expectations, as the main reasons. As in most other cases, many firms are reacting with a view only towards the immediate future. This could turn out to be a threat to the German skill basis in its middle section (5.2).

This rather unfavourable development and perspective for Germany's dual system is not compensated by a corresponding expansion in the field of higher education at the 'tertiary level'. This is clearly a disadvantage, because the 'knowledge economy' is based on academically trained people. Up to now, Germany's education system does not provide a sufficient number of school leavers with the right to start a tertiary education (5.3) - in contrast to other countries. At every level, education and qualification of workers in Germany has to be upgraded (5.4). From the viewpoint of the technological performance, there is one specific bias: only seven out of thousand young people in Germany get a university degree in natural science or engineering, in many other countries there are twice as many. Young people's interest in the fields of science and engineering is rather diminishing (5.3).

In principle, there are not enough students in higher education in Germany, most courses of study are not organised efficiently, thus taking too long as well as being very expensive. Government's investment in higher education is not sufficient (5.4). Universities need drastic structural and financial reforms as well as more effectiveness. First steps have been taken, and these efforts must be intensified (5.3).

## Conclusions for Innovation Policy

The empirical analysis of Germany's technological performance is ultimately designed to inform policy about current trends, coming challenges and possible policy answers. While the link between indicator-based international comparisons and innovation policy recommendations is strongly emphasised, the German reporting system is not meant as a tool to evaluate policy activities. Its main contribution to policymaking is to offer a regularly updated and adequately disaggregated (by sector and field of technology) monitoring system, the results of which are interpreted from an economic perspective, including conclusions on potential policy interventions to react to identified challenges. Analyses of the role and impact of particular policy initiatives in research, technology and innovation on Germany's technological performance are, however, beyond the scope of the present reporting system. Likewise, the reporting system refrains from describing in detail relevant policy actions, since such information is available from governmental publications (e.g. Federal Report on Research, see BMBF 2004a; or the Annual Economic Report, see BMWA 2004).

A main finding of the studies presented in this book, and a starting point for policy conclusions, is that Germany's technological performance is still strong, but slowly decreasing vis-à-vis other countries. Many of the areas of strong performance tend to rest on investment made in previous years or even decades, however, such as the educational level of the workforce or the science system. In order to maintain the present status and keep pace with other countries, considerable efforts, in particular in education, science and the emergence of new cutting-edge technologies, are needed. This involves, among others, increasing public investment. In particular, the following five issues should be dealt with most urgently:

*More dynamics in research and innovation*: for about 15 years, the German innovation system has been characterised by low dynamics with respect to investment in skills, R&D expenditures and market growth. At the same time, many other industrial countries, and especially a large number of catching-up economies, have experienced strong increases in the resources devoted to research and new technologies, and show high rates of growth in the demand for new products and services. R&D activities of firms, as well as career decisions of researchers, are likely to be attracted by such dynamic environments. These differences in system dynamics substantially weaken Germany's position in competing for scarce resources such as highly qualified personnel, talented researchers or R&D investment. So far, low dynamics of inputs and market stimuli had only limited effects on output indicators such as average qualification level of the workforce, scientific publications, patent applications, or export success with high-technology goods. This may reflect to some extent higher efficiency in using increasingly scarce inputs, but first of all it shows that time lags between changes in inputs and associated changes in output indicators of technological performance are long.

In order to avoid long-term lasting drawbacks to Germany's technological performance, the most urgent task is to re-introduce dynamic development into its innovation system. This means considerably higher public investment in education, science and R&D. While many other countries have significantly increased their budgets for public research in recent years, spending for research in universities and public research labs has stagnated in real terms. What is more, the German economy as a whole has to return to a growth path. Increasing demand for new products and services is a main prerequisite for investment in R&D and innovation. While export-oriented firms could benefit from high growth of the world economy, small firms are much more dependent on domestic demand.

*Investing in skills*: rather low dynamics are also to be seen in the area of skills. For many decades, one of Germany's most prominent comparative advantages was a high qualification level among the majority of the workforce. Though qualification levels have further risen in recent years, other countries caught up rapidly and left Germany behind with respect to the skill level of the younger generation. At the same time, the trend towards increasing demand for highly qualified labour is expected to accelerate as a result of ongoing structural and technological changes, and demographic developments in industrial countries. From this perspective, decreasing shares of Science and Engineering (S&E) graduates among younger cohorts are particularly alarming. Although this challenge has been addressed in public debates for many years, it still seems too little understood that education is one of the most important factors for technology advance. Improving learning conditions at all levels of education, broadening further and continuing education, stronger inter-linking of vocational education and tertiary education, and bringing more young people to university, especially to S&E studies, are the most urgent tasks to improve the education base for innovation.

*Sectoral change towards leading-edge technologies*: Germany's still strong performance in technology and innovation heavily rests on fields of high-level technology, such as Automobiles, Machinery, Chemicals and Electric Machinery. While these are still important sources for technological progress and productivity gains, their worldwide dynamics are rather restricted. In the most dynamic fields of technology, which typically belong to the sector of leading-edge technologies such as Computers and Electronics, Instruments and Pharmaceuticals, Germany's position is rather weak compared to other advanced industrial countries. Consequently, strengthening leading-edge technologies was and is a main objective of innovation policy in Germany. Policy instruments in place include funding for collaborative research and supporting technology transfer from science to commercial application. A challenge that remains is a somewhat low propensity in Germany to adopt new leading-edge technologies quickly, which can be seen most prominently in the field of ICT, where Germany is clearly lagging behind most other industrial countries. In other fields such as Biotechnology and Pharmaceuticals, industry sees regulatory requirements and bureaucratic procedures as the main obstacles for innovation and the diffusion of new technologies.

*Responding to globalisation*: R&D activities are spreading throughout the world and catching-up economies such as China and India are becoming important R&D locations. While most of this R&D is targeted towards opening up the large and dynamically evolving national markets, global R&D networks among large corporations and between suppliers, producers and users become more important. Since German enterprises are highly internationally oriented, they fully participate in this trend and increasingly establish global networks of R&D and innovation. While this certainly strengthens their position in world markets and contributes to increasing export surplus, there is a fear in Germany that this process will result in a loss of innovative potential at home. In order to fully profit from increased internationalisation of R&D and innovation, Germany has to be more open to impulses and resources from abroad in order to guarantee a mutual flow of knowledge and people. This could include, among others, dismantling immigration barriers to skilled non-EU citizens, offering foreign students job opportunities in Germany, opening national technology and innovation programmes to foreign participants, and further facilitating international exchange in science and technology.

*Improving conditions for innovation in SMEs*: SMEs in Germany are traditionally highly innovation-oriented, but currently suffer from low domestic demand, market domination by large enterprises, and difficulties in finding financing sources for innovation. As a result, R&D and innovation activities tend to decrease in the SME sector, and the number of technology start-ups remains rather low. Policy measures to improve innovation conditions for SMEs may cover, among others, the introduction of an indirect R&D support scheme (such as tax credits), measures to increase venture capital supply for seed and start-up stages (a public high-tech venture capital fund was introduced in summer 2005), preventing potential shortage in supply of highly qualified labour (from which SMEs suffer in particular), and introducing new instruments for financing innovation in SMEs, such as subordinate capital. The effectiveness of such measures will be restricted, however, as long as the macroeconomic environment remains unfavourable, and demand prospects of SMEs remain low.


**Final Remark**

The German Report on Technological Performance is based on a carefully developed methodology of analysing indicators of various aspects of the innovation system with reference to benchmarks from a variety of other countries. On this basis, it is possible to derive sound conclusions for policy-makers and a broader public. The report deliberately avoids the reduction of the results to one composite indicator, because concrete starting points for policy-making can be determined only from a multi-dimensional perspective. For some non-German readers, the focus of some contributions to this book may be too German. In some cases, we try to respond to an explicit request from foreign experts to explain typically German structures. In other cases, the interpretation of the indicators with regard to the German situation may be considered as a model of how indicators can be analysed within a context of innovation policy. In any case, we hope to provide interesting and useful information for many readers far beyond the German borders.

# Part 2. The Origin of Knowledge: Research and Development

# 2.1 R&D Activities in the German Business Sector

Harald Legler, Christian Rammer, Christoph Grenzmann

**Abstract.** Research and experimental development (R&D) activities represent an investment in new technical knowledge and therefore mark the beginning of technological innovation processes. It is the centre-piece of industrial activities aiming at innovation, restructuring and growth. Germany's business sector ranks highly regarding R&D intensity. However, industrial R&D behaviour is becoming increasingly dependent on business cycles and growth expectations. Also, Germany's technology structure is unbalanced: the gaps in leading-edge technologies are closing only very slowly, R&D in the automobile industry is extremely dominant. A high share of small and medium-sized enterprises performing R&D used to be one of Germany's outstanding features in business R&D. But Germany has to worry about the supply of new, R&D-performing enterprises. Science-business R&D interfaces become more important as well as R&D co-operations within the business sector at home and with (related) companies abroad. Governmental support of industrial R&D in Germany has diminished to a low level.

## Introduction

It has become more and more evident that investments in technical knowledge as well as the availability of highly qualified labour are crucial determinants of economic growth in the long run.[1] In particular, the modern theory of economic growth endogenized the factor technical progress. These models emphasise the need for enterprises and scientific institutions to invest in research and experimental development (R&D) as the basis for technical progress. Through R&D, new products and new production techniques are created and existing products and processes are improved. These innovations allow progress in product quality as well as a reduction of production costs and product prices. These are strategic entrepreneurial parameters strongly influencing competitiveness and growth of firms. Therefore the ability to develop and implement technological advance is regarded as a main factor to explain differences in growth between enterprises as well as between national economies.

R&D is in a way a 'linchpin' in the national system of innovation, since science and research represent the knowledge base of its technological performance. Technological knowledge is created by different actors: enterprises in Germany account for about 70 per cent of total R&D expenditures, the sectors higher education and government (other publicly financed or assisted research institutes, private non-profit foundations) perform 17 and 13 per cent, respectively. This chapter analyses R&D activities of the German business sector over time, taking particular attention of sectoral shifts.

---

[1] See the summarising article by the European Commission (1997) as well as the references quoted there.

*U. Schmoch, C. Rammer and H. Legler (eds.), National Systems of Innovation in Comparison, 17–30.*

The prominent use of R&D data in the analysis of national systems of innovation is based on the assumption that in the medium and long run there are stable relations between:

- the input of R&D personnel and of specific R&D capital goods (intramural R&D) as well as of additional knowledge bought from research institutes or from industrial co-operation partners (extramural R&D), on the one hand; and
- the success of innovations (new products, new production processes, cost reduction, increasing competitiveness, growth and employment), on the other hand.

## Definitions and Data

According to internationally accepted definitions ('Frascati Manual'), R&D is characterised as systematic creative work in order to increase the stock of knowledge. Statistical measurement of R&D includes financial input in terms of R&D expenditures and the input of human resources in terms of R&D personnel (Grenzmann 2004). Both indicators are essential criteria for estimating the 'innovative potential' of economies and their industries, respectively. Constitutive elements to distinguish R&D from other components of the innovation process are the creation as well as the use of new technological knowledge.

However, the concept of measuring R&D is closely oriented to innovation activities of manufacturing industry. Activities to create new knowledge in the service sector can hardly be recorded in a systematic way, despite manifold efforts in statistical practice to dissolve this 'manufacturing industry bias'. In many cases, these activities are not yet considered as R&D (Revermann & Schmidt 1999), because innovative activities in the service sector depend less on technological R&D than in Manufacturing:

- In Germany, statistical data on R&D in firms are to be collected in self responsibility of the business sector. For the subsequent analysis, data compilations of the SV Wissenschaftsstatistik are primarily used, which conducts an annual survey on R&D in the business sector in Germany, based on internationally harmonised concepts as laid down in the Frascati Manual.
- The second source is the Mannheim Innovation Panel (MIP). This annual survey collects data on innovative activities of enterprises in Germany, following the recommendations of the Oslo Manual (see Janz et al. 2001, Rammer & Schmidt 2003).

Both surveys are part of international statistical compilations of the OECD and of the EU, respectively. While Chapter 2.2 presents an analysis of the R&D behaviour in Germany in an international comparison, this chapter looks at R&D of the German business sector from the national point of view. It covers R&D activities during the last two decades. The most important indicator is the R&D intensity of the business sector and its different branches. First of all, selected key data on R&D activities of the business sector in the last 20 years are reported. Subsequently, some indicators for the development of important structural components have to be derived for a more detailed analysis: this reveals sectoral concentration and intensities in R&D, participation of small and medium-sized enterprises (SMEs), co-operation behaviour in R&D as well as the contribution of government to funding industrial R&D.

## R&D Activities and Business Cycles

Germany belonged for a long time to the economies with the highest R&D intensities in the world (see Chapter 2.2). However, the trends and cycles of industrial R&D in the medium run indicate a significant change in R&D behaviour over time (Fig. 1):

- On one hand, R&D was in good shape in the 1980s. Even in recessive periods, the accumulation of knowledge was pursued continuously.
- On the other hand, long periods of the 1990s show a certain reservation in performing R&D intensively or even enlarging R&D capacities. Towards the end of the 1990s, industrial R&D in Germany experienced a remarkable revival, but in the new millennium R&D has once again been affected by economic recession.

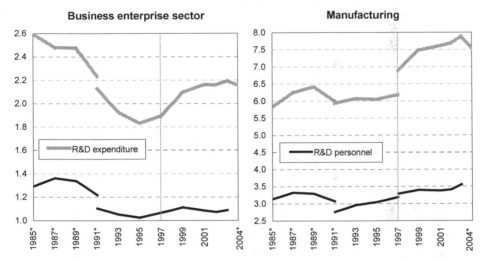

\* Data prior to 1990 applies to former West Germany only and for both territories starting 1991 – \*\* Planned
Break in the time series 1997 due to a change in the classification system for economic activities
Source: Wissenschaftsstatistik – Federal Statistical Office, National Accounts – NIW calculations and estimates

**Fig. 1.** Intramural R&D expenditure of business sector as a percentage of gross value added and R&D personnel as a percentage of total employment in Germany 1985–2004

Industrial R&D behaviour has changed substantially: Whereas in the 1980s R&D was performed as anticyclical investments for the future, this attitude changed more and more to a market-oriented behaviour in the 1990s, towards short-term trends and changes of demand as well as growth prospects in the near future: industrial R&D was performed increasingly under the aspect of short-term utilization and it was adjusted upwards and downwards accordingly.

Expenditures for new knowledge, R&D and highly qualified personnel are by and large fixed costs. The propensity of enterprises to carry such fixed costs will increase with a stable macroeconomic environment and expectations of high and increasing market volumes for their products. Consequently, the business sector has reacted very sensitively to cyclical changes and, in reaction to the reduced growth potential of the German economy in the first half of the 1990s, scaled down its strategic research in particular. In this period, R&D-intensive producers of capital goods have been affected by recessive tendencies in the global economy. At the same time, the boom in consumer goods as a result of the German reunification gave only very few incentives for additional R&D.

However, figures on R&D behaviour in Germany at the end of the 1990s show intensified R&D efforts again. A lot of (large) enterprises stopped the cut back of research and re-introduced more continuousness and medium-term and strategic perspectives into their R&D activities. In this respect, the situation of business R&D in Germany at the beginning of the new millennium has to be seen in a slightly brighter light than at the beginning of the recession in the 1990s. R&D gained in importance for the business sector again.


## Sectoral Distribution of R&D

The partial comeback of R&D in the strategies of the business sector were accompanied by enormous structural changes. The German economy attaches more and more importance to R&D in high-value services. Nevertheless, Germany still shows substantial gaps in R&D in the service sector compared to other developed economies (see also Chapter 2.2). The trend that high-value services emerge as 'mothers of invention' is recognised. This affects R&D in manufacturing industry, too. High-value services are closely connected in particular with those industries that conduct highly ambitious R&D ('leading-edge technologies' such as Biotechnology and Pharmacy, Electronics and Communications Technology, Aircraft and Aerospace etc., see Fig. 2).

Industrial research in Germany was not among the top performers of the world in most fields of leading-edge technology (for definition see Chapter 1) for a long time. For decades, the German economy focussed very strongly on competent implementation of (to a large extent imported) results of research in leading-edge technologies. They were applied in sectors that perform high-value R&D ('advanced technology'), but not as intensively as in the leading-edge technology sectors. For a long period, the economic success justified this strategy. Income and employment grew, particularly in branches of medium-/high-technology. These branches combined highly qualified labour and creative traditional competencies with new leading-edge technologies (Chemicals, Electrical Equipment, Machinery, Automobiles). However, this strategy does not seem to work any more. Structural changes took place at increasing speed, and the product life cycles have shortened: Growth is especially fast in sectors where R&D intensity and dynamics are high and the invention and application of new knowledge is crucial. So the available time to integrate basic generic technologies into a firm's own spectrum of competencies shortened and the scope to imitate got closer. If the German economy really wants to climb in the technological hierarchy, it cannot wait any longer until other economies provide new technologies. Rather, it has to engage more extensively in basic leading-edge technologies. This has been neglected for years.

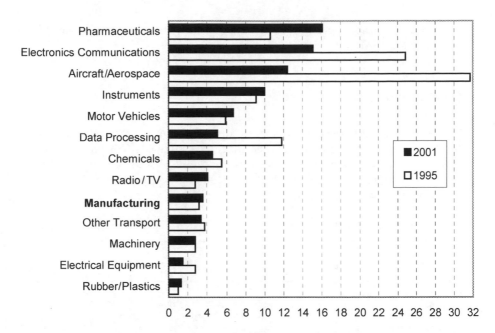

Source: Wissenschaftsstatistik – Federal Statistical Office, FS 4, Reihe 4.1.1 and 4.3 – NIW calculations and estimates

**Fig. 2.** Total R&D expenditure as a percentage of turnover from own products in German manufacturing industry 1995 and 2001

The R&D upswing in the German economy from the second half of the 1990s onwards was indeed closely connected to a rapid structural change in favour of leading-edge technologies. In so far, Germany made a remarkable change in its R&D focuses. In particular, Pharmaceuticals and Telecommunications caught up to a considerable degree. But even leading-edge technologies are by no means resistant to trend changes and breaks in the business cycle: ICT suffered a cutback in R&D intensity since 2000 in connection with the crisis of the 'new economy'. Aircraft and Aerospace have reduced their R&D activities massively; in many cases R&D in this sector is inspired by government aid and demand.

However, rapid structural changes in Germany also mean that branches outside leading-edge technology sectors, which had a traditionally strong R&D position in Germany obviously fall behind (Chemicals, Machinery, Electrical Equipment, Instruments), except for Automobiles. This branch expanded its share in R&D capacities in the German business sector by more than a third. Since the second half of the 1990s, the automobile industry has written a success story with respect to most performance indicators such as exports, value added, and employment (see also Chapter 4.1).

Once again a view from a different perspective: in the 1980s, the German economy as a whole participated in the R&D upswing: Nearly every branch expanded R&D considerably, even more than employment and value added. However, in recent years this process has been rather selective, first of all in direction of leading-edge technologies and Automobiles. But structural changes in R&D in favour of (large) enterprises in leading-edge industries in Germany have consequences for the participation of SMEs in German industrial R&D.

## R&D Participation of SMEs

In Germany, R&D is overwhelmingly conducted by big companies (Table 1). Only about 18 per cent of industrial R&D personnel are employed in SMEs, while the share in total industrial employment is about 50 per cent. SMEs as well as big companies play specific roles in innovation processes, resulting in a division of labour in R&D between certain types of enterprises (Fig. 3).

**Table 1.** Structure of R&D Activities in German Business Sector 1997 to 2001

| | West Germany | | | | | | | Germany | | | | | |
|---|---|---|---|---|---|---|---|---|---|---|---|---|---|
| | | | | | | | Shares as percentage | | | | | | |
| | 1979 | 1981 | 1983 | 1985 | 1987 | 1989 | 1991 | 1991 | 1993 | 1995 | 1997 | 1999 | 2001 |
| *Funding of Total R&D in Business Sector* | | | | | | | | | | | | | |
| Industry | 83.3 | 85.2 | 85.2 | 85.9 | 88.2 | 86.8 | 88.4 | 88.2 | 90.6 | 90.3 | 88.0 | 90.7 | 92.9 |
| Government | 14.2 | 13.0 | 12.9 | 12.5 | 10.1 | 10.1 | 8.6 | 8.8 | 7.3 | 7.5 | 8.3 | 6.4 | 4.1 |
| *thereof* SME | 7.5 | 7.8 | 18.0 | 15.1 | 7.6 | 6.5 | – | 8.2 | 6.1 | 7.4 | 9.2 | 7.2 | 5.5 |
| Enterprises > 500 | 14.1 | 13.0 | 11.0 | 12.0 | 9.9 | 10.1 | – | 8.3 | 6.8 | 7.0 | 7.7 | 6.3 | 3.3 |
| Abroad | 2.2 | 1.5 | 1.6 | 1.4 | 1.5 | 2.9 | 2.8 | 2.7 | 2.0 | 2.1 | 3.6 | 2.7 | 2.9 |
| *Distribution of enterprise R&D personnel* | | | | | | | | | | | | | |
| Less than 100 employees | 4.1 | 6.0 | 9.0 | 10.2 | 8.7 | 7.7 | 4.9 | 5.7 | 7.7 | 8.1 | 8.6 | 7.1 | 6.3 |
| 100 to less than 500 employees | 9.5 | 10.1 | 10.3 | 10.4 | 9.3 | 9.1 | 9.7 | 12.1 | 11.0 | 11.7 | 11.4 | 11.2 | 11.6 |
| 500 to less than 1,000 employees | 6.8 | 4.6 | 4.5 | 4.5 | 4.9 | 4.9 | 5.0 | 6.1 | 5.8 | 6.2 | 6.9 | 7.1 | 6.8 |
| 1,000 and more employees | 79.6 | 79.3 | 76.2 | 74.9 | 77.1 | 78.3 | 80.4 | 76.1 | 75.6 | 74.1 | 73.1 | 74.6 | 75.3 |
| *Share of extramural R&D expenditure in total R&D expenditure* | | | | | | | | | | | | | |
| All enterprises | 5.7 | 7.7 | 10.1 | 9.3 | 8.6 | 9.2 | 10.1 | 10.2 | 12.2 | 10.5 | 13.3 | 14.9 | 17.0 |
| SME | 6.0 | 6.9 | 18.4 | 14.3 | 11.1 | 8.1 | 9.8 | – | 8.5 | 8.1 | 8.4 | 8.2 | 11.9 |
| Enterprises > 500 | 4.7 | 7.1 | 7.9 | 7.9 | 8.0 | 9.3 | 10.1 | – | 12.4 | 10.5 | 14.1 | 15.5 | 17.5 |
| *Extramural R&D of business sector* | | | | | | | | | | | | | |
| *Sector of performance* | | | | | | | | | | | | | |
| Industry | 70.3 | 63.6 | 70.5 | 69.5 | 67.1 | 64.6 | 62.6 | 62.9 | 65.4 | 59.9 | 64.0 | 68.3 | 71.0 |
| Higher education | | | | 8.5 | 10.6 | 9.1 | | 10.4 | 9.0 | 13.1 | 9.3 | 7.4 | 7.7 |
| Extra-R&D | 20.7 | 25.6 | 20.0 | 9.4 | 10.9 | 10.0 | 20.8 | 8.8 | 8.6 | 8.6 | 5.6 | 4.1 | 4.0 |
| Other (at home) | | | | 0.0 | 0.4 | 0.5 | | 1.5 | 1.3 | 3.3 | 2.1 | 1.4 | 0.9 |
| Abroad | 9.4 | 10.8 | 9.5 | 12.6 | 11.0 | 15.8 | 16.6 | 16.4 | 17.4 | 15.2 | 18.9 | 18.7 | 16.4 |
| *Composition of intramural enterprise R&D expenditure* | | | | | | | | | | | | | |
| Personnel | 60.1 | 58.8 | 58.4 | 58.0 | 58.3 | 60.1 | 57.9 | 57.9 | 59.9 | 59.8 | 61.5 | 59.2 | 58.5 |
| Other current | 30.4 | 31.3 | 31.6 | 31.0 | 30.4 | 31.0 | 32.8 | 32.9 | 33.0 | 33.4 | 31.2 | 32.2 | 33.4 |
| Capital | 9.4 | 9.9 | 10.0 | 10.0 | 11.0 | 8.9 | 9.3 | 9.3 | 7.1 | 6.8 | 7.3 | 8.6 | 8.1 |
| *Structure of enterprise R&D personnel* | | | | | | | | | | | | | |
| Scientists, engineers | 30.9 | 31.8 | 32.8 | 34.0 | 36.3 | 38.2 | 41.4 | 43.8 | 43.9 | 45.7 | 46.2 | 48.7 | 51.3 |
| Technicians | 31.8 | 30.1 | 30.9 | 31.4 | 30.7 | 29.7 | 28.5 | 26.9 | 27.9 | 27.6 | 27.6 | 26.3 | 24.1 |
| Other occupations | 37.3 | 38.1 | 36.3 | 34.6 | 33.0 | 32.1 | 30.1 | 29.3 | 28.2 | 26.7 | 26.1 | 25.1 | 24.6 |

Source: Wissenschaftsstatistik – NIW calculations and compilations

It is to be expected that young enterprises are more likely to enter the market with new ideas and try to meet competition by successful R&D projects than old enterprises. Most typically, enterprises in technology sectors are founded in connection

with an innovation project. In many cases, they concentrate R&D activities on products of leading-edge technologies. Therefore the R&D share of employment in small
researching companies of manufacturing industry is more than 8.5 per cent on average.

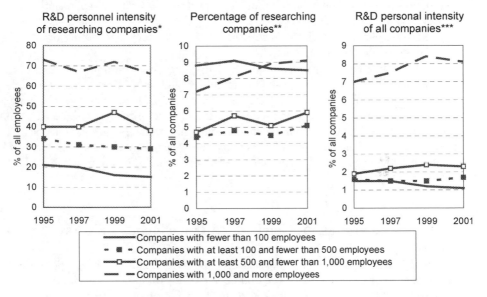

| | | |
|---|---|---|
| R&D personnel intensity of researching companies* | Percentage of researching companies** | R&D personal intensity of all companies*** |

────────Companies with fewer than 100 employees
– ■ – Companies with at least 100 and fewer than 500 employees
──□──Companies with at least 500 and fewer than 1,000 employees
── ── Companies with 1,000 and more employees

\*      R&D-personnel share, in per cent of all employees of researching companies
\*\*     Researching companies, as per cent of all companies
\*\*\*   R&D personnel, as per cent of employees of all companies
Source: SV Wissenschaftsstatistik – Federal Statistical Office, FS 4, R. 4.3 (cost-structure
survey, 1995–2001) – NIW calculations and estimates

**Fig. 3.** R&D personnel intensity and R&D participation in Germany's mining and manufacturing sectors, by employment size classes, 1995–2001

Medium-sized enterprises typically are technology users, i.e. they are rather engaged
in technology application and production than in generating new technologies. The
average R&D intensity of researching firms in this group thus is lower and amounts to
five to six per cent.

  Large companies have an advantage if R&D needs large budgets and if routinised
and formalised approaches are key factors for successful innovation. They typically
run large R&D departments, and their average R&D intensity attains nine per cent.

  Since the group of SMEs is not homogeneous, there are no uniform characteristics
of R&D attitudes in SMEs: the relevant statistics cover subsidiaries of large companies, technology-oriented start-ups, typical middle-class firms with a long term
tradition and market experience, university spin-offs etc. Generally, the *share* of
R&D-performing enterprises ('R&D participation ratio') increases according to the
company size class: 20 per cent of manufacturing enterprises conduct R&D on average. But there is a bandwidth from 15 per cent in the group of small enterprises (up to
100 employees) to 29 per cent (medium-sized enterprises), 38 per cent in the class
of larger companies (from 500 up to 1,000 employees) and 66 per cent in the class of
large enterprises employing 1,000 and more employees. The high R&D intensity of

small R&D-performing companies is thus contrasted by a low R&D participation ratio.

According to the German statistics, business R&D tends to concentrate on a lower number of firms over time: the *share* of R&D-performing firms among manufacturing SMEs has diminished:[2]

- On the one hand, especially those SMEs which conducted R&D discontinuously have withdrawn from R&D activities.
- On the other hand, R&D-performing SMEs have been assigned a central role worldwide as they enter more and more into research in leading-edge technologies.

Relative stability of continuously R&D-conducting firms (as indicated by the surveys) coexists with volatility in discontinuously R&D-conducting firms. On the one hand, this shows that R&D is becoming increasingly important (stability). On the other hand, there is evidence that most SMEs react very sensitively to the current economic situation and to the environment and expectations which are relevant for R&D decisions (volatility).

## Start-Ups Renewing the Stock of R&D-performing SMEs

Decreasing R&D participation in Germany has been for a certain period of time accompanied by a slow-down of the number of firm foundations in general. Young firms (up to five years old) represent 20 to 25 per cent of the total stock of firms. Therefore they strongly influence the total R&D participation ratio (see also Chapter 4.2). So the question arises if young firms have revised their R&D behaviour as a reaction to weak external impulses (e.g. domestic demand) and therefore contributed to the decreasing R&D participation of SMEs:

- The issue of performing R&D is a strategic business decision (Table 2). The innovation strategy of firms is often set during the start-up phase. At the same time it has to be decided if the firm is going to conduct R&D continuously or just according to current needs, i.e. spontaneously or occasionally. The likelihood that a firm that started business without any R&D activities and that this firm will decide to take up R&D at a later stage is quite small (20 to 30 per cent).
- A newly founded firm's decision whether to perform R&D or not depends, among others, on the business cycle situation at the time of start-up: The share of continuously R&D-conducting firms in relation to all newly founded firms increased sharply until the end of the 1990s, but decreased in the following cyclical downturn. Some of the young firms (30 per cent) that originally were devoted to continuous R&D refrained from R&D in following years.
- A further point is the positioning in the product life cycle: if an innovation project has been finished successfully, the firm can spend more resources on production and marketing activities, consequently R&D activities are reduced. During later

---

[2] It has to be assumed that the decline recorded in the R&D statistics is overstated to some extent. Despite a lot of efforts made, it is not possible to detect all newly founded firms conducting R&D. The MIP uses a different approach and indicates an increasing share of SMEs conducting R&D until 2000. In subsequent years this share remained constant and increased in 2003.

phases, i.e. growth or phasing-out of earnings from the 'old' innovation project, R&D comes to the fore again - after three or four years on average.

**Table 2.** Share of continuously researching young enterprises in Germany 1998–2003 according to age (percentage)

| Age | 1998 | 1999 | 2000 | 2001 | 2002 | 2003 |
|-----|------|------|------|------|------|------|
| 0 to below 1 year | 35 | 49 | 42 | 44 | 42 | 25 |
| 1 to below 2 year | 32 | 43 | 43 | 39 | 53 | 50 |
| 2 to below 3 year | 31 | 35 | 41 | 32 | 48 | 38 |
| 3 to below 4 year | 33 | 49 | 34 | 40 | 49 | 58 |
| 4 to below 5 year | 33 | 40 | 49 | 32 | 46 | 53 |
| 5 to below 6 year | 33 | 37 | 42 | 41 | 46 | 38 |

Explanation: In 1998 35 per cent of enterprises aged 0 or 1 year (i.e. founded this year) continuously performed R&D. In 1999 the quote of this formation cohort was 43 per cent (= enterprises aged between 1 and 2 years). In 2002 R&D participation of this cohort attained 46 per cent (= enterprises in 2002 aged between 4 and 5 years) and it decreased in 2003 to 38 per cent.

In particular, the start-up cohorts of 1999/2000 and 2002 added a significant number of R&D-performing firms to the total population of firms performing R&D, resulting in an increase in the R&D participation ratio in 2003. The currently still high R&D participation ratio of SMEs is mainly based on an environment that was particularly favourable to the formation of R&D-active firms until the end of the 1990s. But analysis of the behaviour of recent start-up cohorts, in particular the cohort of 2003, suggests no positive projection. Little by little, the share of R&D-conducting firms in the total number of newly founded firms has dropped. In 2003 – which, for statistical reasons, however cannot be finally assessed yet[3] – just one of four newly founded firms recorded R&D activities. At the end of the 1990s, this share still attained 35 to 50 per cent.

   This calls for attention, because R&D – at least in the medium run – is still the decisive cornerstone for industrial innovation activities: firms that generate innovations, that are busy in exports, and that create additional jobs without any R&D activities are rare. Firms without any intramural R&D activities are more likely to refrain from innovation activities than others (see also Chapter 4.2).

   A high participation of SMEs used to be one of Germany's advantages. So the lack of fresh supply of new R&D-performing enterprises is a challenge to innovation policy. The innovative ability of SMEs in the medium and long run is quite closely connected to participation in R&D and to the availability of suitable trained and experienced personnel. Furthermore the access to results of scientific research as well as to technology transfer will be difficult if SMEs cannot communicate at the same level with potential co-operation partners: The ability of SMEs to co-operate with research units and industrial firms increases to the extent that SMEs participate continuously in R&D. Co-operative innovation projects gain in importance. Germany in particular used to have a strong culture of business/science co-operation.

---

[3]   The very low R&D participation quota of newly founded firms in 2003 is caused to a certain extent by a rising number of 'one-man' firms fostered by labour market policy. Only a handful of such firms would be able to conduct their own R&D.

## Co-operation and Outsourcing

The requirements of innovation processes have grown sharply, with quality and efficiency becoming more important. Enterprises have to react to shortages of personnel and capital, on the one hand, and at the same time, to increasing demand for quality. Consequently, they concentrate on intramural R&D in their core competencies. They also defer R&D activities to external co-operation partners in the business sector, from universities or non-university research units, at home and abroad: whereas the share of extramural R&D attained just 6 per cent until the end of the 1970s, this share recently increased to 17 per cent (Fig. 4). Big companies in particular increasingly switch over to R&D performed by external specialists. On the other hand, in the group of SMEs the share of external R&D rose sharply by three percentage points just recently. But nevertheless it is still nearly six points below the share of external R&D among large companies.

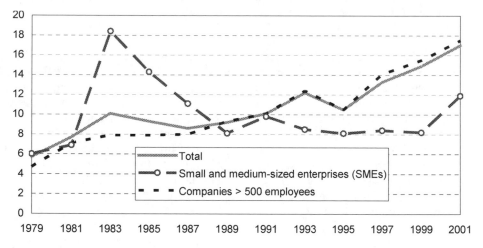

* Until 1991, Western Germany
Source: SV Wissenschaftsstatistik – NIW calculations and compilations

**Fig. 4.** Extramural R&D expenditures of the business enterprise sector in Germany*, 1979 to 2001, as a percentage of total R&D expenditures

The structure of external R&D clearly shows a growing intensification of R&D relationships within the business sector, thus e.g. between producers and component suppliers. Furthermore, partial outsourcing of R&D departments is leading to augmented extramural R&D.

Moreover, a closer R&D interaction with foreign countries is appearing: parallel to the increasing globalisation in the 1990s (see Chapter 2.3), the share of co-operation partners abroad rose from 17 to 19 per cent. Behind this dynamics are more contracts to R&D institutions and independent R&D service providers, on the one hand. On the other hand, it is also a result of the internationalisation of R&D activities of German enterprises, which follows a general increase in internationalisation of business activities.

Although science-based knowledge has become increasingly important for innovation processes, the share of science in extramural R&D has lost ground. Whereas its share in 1995 was still more than 22 per cent, it fell to half of this in 2001.

The quantitative amount of external R&D is largely defined by activities of large industrial corporations. But the following observations are of interest for innovation policy:

- The science sector is more significant for SMEs than for big companies. This may be ascribed to the noticeable public financial support for R&D co-operations between SMEs and scientific institutions and its cost-saving effects. Small firms tend to co-operate with other enterprises to a relatively large extent, primarily with specialised private R&D enterprises.

- Conducting innovation co-operations is usually is linked to a higher innovation success, compared to innovators who do not co-operate. It is particularly noticeable that firms which received impulses for innovations from science and research are able to attain higher shares of sales from new products and/or more cost reduction by new processes (Rammer & Schmidt 2004, see also Chapter 3.3).

## Governmental Support to Industrial R&D

No government in the world is watching private R&D activities inactively. In fact, governments actively support R&D processes in the business sector, using different instruments and incentives and varying intensity over the time. In order to assess governmental intervention, the financial contribution of governments to R&D in the business sector has to be observed in particular (for international comparison of government funding of R&D see Chapters 2.2 and 6).

According to the German R&D statistics in 2001, more than 93 per cent of total R&D expenditure of the business sector was funded by industry sources, government accounted for just about 4 per cent (Table 1). R&D financed from abroad (€1.2 billion, nearly 3 per cent) rose sharply. Indeed, this can be predominantly traced back to the increasing globalisation of the economy and of industrial R&D. But these figures also reflect rising R&D co-operation within the EU (framework programmes) and other supranational organisations (e.g. ESA, Eureka, NATO etc.). More and more of these organisations award R&D subsidies. In Germany about 10 per cent of R&D funds from abroad come from the EU.

German governmental bodies contribute €1.5 billion to industrial R&D. But government has reduced its share of R&D funding from more than 14 per cent at the end of the 1970s to nearly three-quarters (Fig. 5). Governmental contributions are directed steadily downwards, this trend was broken only for a short time (i.e. from 1993 to 1997).

Governmental funding of business enterprise R&D not only means subsidising R&D projects, but also directly awarding R&D commissions to enterprises based on independent government targets, i.e. for improved performance of public tasks by innovative goods and services ('public goods'):

- On the one hand, public funds find their way into industries with large R&D capacities and into industries producing notably R&D-intensive goods, respectively.

Aircraft and Aerospace alone attract more than 40 per cent of the entire government funding for business enterprise R&D. Nearly one-third of R&D activities in this sector is supported by government; these figures still exclude funding by supranational authorities such as ESA. Furthermore within the leading-edge technology sector, R&D is considerably subsidised in the electronic components industry (around 10 per cent of total R&D expenditure of this branch). But government has cutback somewhat on industrial R&D funding in Transport and Communications, as well as in Aircraft and Spacecraft.

- Large companies receive 80 per cent of total governmental R&D funding for the business sector. In the 1990s, however, it can no longer be asserted that governmental R&D intervention intensity in Germany was biased extremely in favour of large companies. Taking 500 employees as the line separating SMEs and large companies, the share of governmental support in total R&D expenditures is 5.5 per cent for SMEs and 3.5 per cent for large companies. In this context, it must be assumed that the intensive support of R&D in Eastern Germany plays a decisive role: SMEs predominate in Eastern Germany.

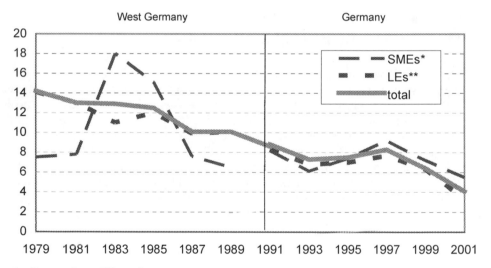

\* Companies < 500 employees
\*\* Companies > 500 employees
Source: Wissenschaftsstatistik – NIW calculations and compilations

**Fig. 5.** Governmental funding of R&D in SMEs and large enterprises in Germany 1979 to 2001 as percentage of total R&D expenditure

For a long time federal and regional ('*Länder*') governments clearly reduced their contributions to R&D funding in the business sector. This enormous decrease overstepped a critical point considering the 'leverage effect' of governmental support to private R&D. For each € in financial aid from public funds, enterprises spend approximately the same amount for R&D. These funds mainly benefit pre-competitive research and therefore enhance the technological options of the economy. In addition, enterprises have to spend internal resources for experimental development and to transfer R&D results into innovations and capital investment.

## Outlook

Until 2000/2001, German enterprises invested strongly in R&D. At that time, this must be seen as a signal for considerably improved expectations of future market development. They were focussed on expansion. But after the decrease in economic prospects, R&D growth became flat.

2003 showed a moderate increase in intramural R&D expenditure of the German business sector, which was better than initially expected. The planned R&D expenditures for 2004 were less than in 2003, in real terms as well as in nominal terms. This indicates that the positive attitudes of the business sector towards R&D are still not sustainable. Firms wait and see. And it is not clear if this is just a temporary restraint or if it is a reaction to the continuous stagnation of the German economy. But from today's point of view, it can nearly be ruled out that the current weakening dynamics of industrial R&D will again end in deep cutbacks in R&D capacities. This might be partly seen as a success, but it is not enough in the longer run. More dynamics might be more appropriate!

The business sector does not assess R&D projects by their technological feasiblity, but with respect to the acceptance of new products by consumers. In most cases R&D cannot be performed without a relation to the market. Though continuousness in R&D has increased, the 'black box' uncertainty of growth still remains: The weaker the growth expectations, the sooner R&D projects will be cancelled, broken off or delayed. SMEs in particular are susceptible to this. A number of enterprises tend to use profits to improve their financial background rather than invest in R&D. This is because real interest rates are high in international comparison. In no case can the profit situation of major companies be held responsible for the cautious R&D expansion.

The increasing globalisation of R&D leads to a sharp worldwide competition within large, globally active corporations. German R&D sites are not really favourised here. One reason is that R&D and innovation in Germany are more expensive than in other European economies. As R&D activities are labour-intensive and require high skills, R&D in Germany is therefore is affected by the high labour costs. Furthermore R&D ties up capital, which is sparsely available and therefore also relatively expensive in Germany. The costs of R&D gain in importance in times of cyclical downswings and increased uncertainty about the likely returns on R&D activities. R&D in the USA is expensive, too. But industrial R&D in the USA tends to be more efficient, through outsourcing to specialised R&D services as well as to SMEs. This fact explains both the R&D boom in the service sector and the increasing R&D activities in SMEs in the USA, especially in the leading-edge technology sector (see European Commission 2003a). SMEs in the USA are well integrated into supply chains and R&D networks. In Germany, this kind of R&D division of labour between large and small firms does not have the same tradition. As a consequence, large companies tend to expand their R&D capacities mostly in foreign and less cost-intensive economies, because Germany's advantage in having a highly skilled work force dwindles, too (OECD [ed.] 2004a). In Europe, mainly central and eastern transitional countries are focussed in the R&D considerations of the companies (DIHK 2005). On the other hand, in some cases Germany benefits through the still higher R&D costs in the USA. In some branches (Pharmaceuticals and medical devices industry), R&D sites were relocated from the USA to Germany – also for cost reasons.

But not only costs are important for the choice of R&D locations. Above all, market perspectives as well as the conditions for research in the science sector and the outcomes of the education system are of significance, too (see also Chapter 2.3). Expectations seem to be limited with a view to market conditions. Growth perspectives of high-value markets in Germany as 'crowd-pullers' for international companies are disappointing. One major exception is the market for automobiles, but no other new 'lead markets' are visible. The creation of such lead markets not only needs a high technological performance, but also a higher dynamics of domestic demand.

Regarding R&D in leading-edge technologies – and not only with the USA in mind – it should be noticed that focal points of invention activities of German multinational firms in highly science-based and mostly cross-sectional technologies with a broad economic impact (Biotechnology, Pharmacy, Semiconductors, Organic Chemistry) have been shifted abroad in the 1990s (Edler et al. 2003). It therefore does not seem that leading-edge-technologies could advance faster than in other countries.

## Conclusions for Innovation Policy

R&D in the business sector plays a key role in the entire chain of education and training, science, research and technology, inventions, investment and innovation, international competitiveness, productivity, growth and employment: on the whole, empirical studies indicate a positive impact of R&D on macroeconomic targets. So the question is whether Germany's R&D level can lead to satisfactory results in the medium term. If Germany wants to come close to the goals of achieving *both* a high employment level *and* an appropriate economic growth, it cannot be satisfied with the share of R&D in GDP stagnating at a level of 2.5 per cent.

An improved environment in education and science, research and technology could create necessary prerequisites for an expansion of R&D and innovation capacities of the business sector (see also Chapters 5 and 6). Above all, public support for innovation should not be adjusted in a pro-cyclical way. There is a great temptation to adjust pro-cyclically, as the figures on government funding of private R&D recently showed. In fact, innovation policy should be 'potential oriented'; this could automatically contribute to stabilising R&D activities.

Essential points for a policy to expand R&D in the business sector are a further sharpening of the technological profile in the direction of leading-edge technologies, based on a competitive science and research infrastructure, as well as broadening the R&D base by an intensified participation of SMEs. But this would not be sufficient without a marked improvement of macroeconomic conditions in Germany in order to get better market and sales expectations that promise higher returns on innovation: The German business sector is likely to hold back in the field of risky innovations.

# 2.2 The Global Distribution of R&D Activities

Harald Legler, Olaf Krawczyk

**Abstract.** Research and development (R&D) play a decisive role in the innovation system. Germany ranks high in comparison to other countries, with its share of 2.5 per cent of GDP in R&D expenditure. The international competition in building up new R&D facilities has increased during the last decades. Other large industrialised countries (USA, Japan) as well as smaller European countries and threshold countries from Asia are exhibiting considerably greater dynamics in the expansion of R&D capacity than Germany. Industries that invest very strongly in R&D have been winners in structural change (Pharmaceuticals, Electronics, the ICT industry). Germany's R&D specialisation has shifted slightly in favour of leading-edge technologies, too, but R&D activities are increasingly concentrated on Motor Vehicles. The public sector assumes more responsibility in fostering R&D worldwide. However, in most countres the budgetary priorities are targeted more specifically, faster and more intensively towards R&D than in Germany.

## Introduction

Following the analysis of the R&D activities in Germany in Chapter 2.1, this chapter gives a combined time-series/cross-section analysis[1] of the German R&D performance in global benchmarking. Based on selected key data, this chapter informs about the R&D activities in the economy as a whole and particularly in the business sector. Furthermore, it analyses the R&D division of labour between the business and the public sector. Finally, it examines sectoral focuses and R&D intensities in the business sector.

This international comparison uses data compilations provided by the OECD,[2] which ensure comparability of the data. National data sources may provide more actual and, to some extent, revised data, but they are not comparable at all.

## Trends in International Distribution of R&D Expenditure

### Industrialised Countries

The international comparison of R&D intensities (R&D expenditure as a percentage of GDP) shows Sweden leading in the OECD at 4.3 per cent, followed by Finland at 3.5 per cent, Japan (3.1 per cent), Korea (2.9 per cent), the United States (2.6 per cent) and Switzerland (2.6 per cent). Germany and Denmark follow at 2.5 per cent, just ahead of

---

[1] For the theoretical and methodological background of R&D and its impact on macroeconomic performance and international competitiveness, see Chapter 2.1.

[2] The OECD publication 'Main Science and Technology Indicators' presents R&D data at a glance. Furthermore the OECD databases ANBERD and STAN provide general economic as well as R&D data on a deeply sectoral, disaggregated level.

*U. Schmoch, C. Rammer and H. Legler (eds.), National Systems of Innovation in Comparison, 31–45.*

France and Belgium (2.2 per cent), the Netherlands, Austria, the United Kingdom and Canada (each at 1.9 per cent; see Fig. 1). After belonging to the top group at the end of the 1980s, Germany nowadays is maintaining a middle-rank position.

Since the mid-1990s, R&D has become more important again in most countries. But only the USA and Japan pursue R&D in the new millennium with the same intensity as at the beginning of the 1990s. The big European countries did not keep up with them (see Fig. 1).

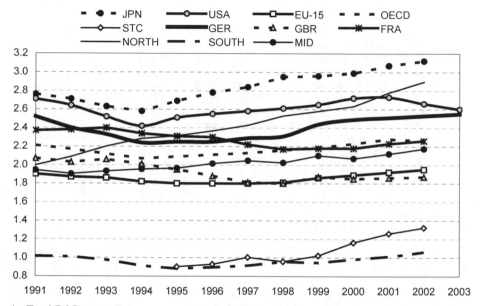

* Total R&D expenditure as a percentage of GDP
*NORTH*: SWE, FIN, NOR, DEN, IRL, ISL – *MID*: BEL, NED, AUT, SUI – *SOUTH*: ITA, POR, ESP, GRE – *STC* (selected threshold countries): CHN, KOR, IND, RUS, TPE, ISR, SIN
Source: OECD, Main Science and Technology Indicators (2004/2) – IMD World Competitiveness Yearbook – Federal Statistical Office Germany, Statistical Yearbook – Wissenschaftsstatistik – NIW calculations and estimates

**Fig. 1.** R&D intensity* in selected world regions 1991–2003

In the process of international R&D expansion, the activities are shifting significantly to overseas countries, namely to North America, Japan, Korea and to some big threshold countries (see Fig. 2 and 3). With a share of 45 per cent in the OECD's R&D capacity, the USA has been the country mainly responsible for the R&D revival in the western developed countries in the second half of the 1990s. Germany belongs to the group of countries with an R&D intensity above the OECD's average. However, R&D capacity growth fell below the average there. The Nordic countries achieved the largest increase, and even southern Europe as well as the central European countries bordering on Germany gained relatively more weight in R&D than Germany, France and the United Kingdom. As investment in new technological knowledge is crucial for economic growth in the long run, it is not surprising that the ranking of economic growth corresponds with the ranking of R&D capacity growth in the last decade – except for Japan, which faced a poor economic growth despite a large real R&D increase.

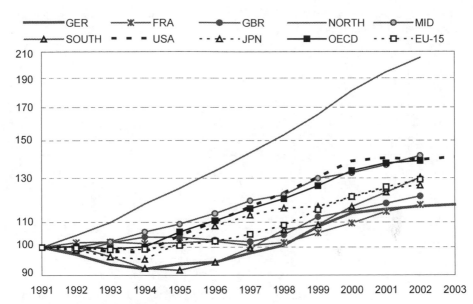

*NORTH*: SWE, FIN, NOR, DEN, IRL, ISL – *MID*: BEL, NED, AUT, SUI – *SOUTH*: ITA, POR, ESP, GRE
Source: OECD, Main Science and Technology Indicators (2004/2) – Wissenschaftsstatistik – NIW calculations and estimates

**Fig. 2.** Trends of gross domestic expenditure on R&D (GERD in constant prices) 1991–2003 in selected world regions (1991 = 100)

The economic downturn at the beginning of the new millennium did not lead to correspondingly less investment in science, technology and innovation in all western developed countries. The reaction concerning R&D behaviour varied and changed considerably in some countries. R&D behaviour has to be re-evaluated, but the short observation period permits only a provisional statement.

In particular, the United States decreased its R&D expenditure notably since the year 2000. From 2000 to 2002, R&D expenditure in the US business sector slumped as never before (see Table 1). This was caused by structural turbulences: in some branches the R&D capacities were simply oversized (e.g. in the ICT sector) and have been shortened for cyclical reasons or as a consequence of regulations (Telecommunication). It is now a moot point whether the R&D expenditure will re-increase from this lower level or stagnate in the near future. It is also a doubtful question whether the US automobile industry will be able to extend its R&D capacity again. Whereas the pharmaceutical industry considerably increased its R&D capacity, other sectors with less importance for the US economy rose on the international average. On the other hand, there is a massive expansion of R&D in the public sector. For 2003 and 2004, the projection of R&D dynamics in the US economy indicates stagnation rather than expansion.[3]

---

[3] See OECD (ed.) (2004b).

**Table 1.** Annual percentage change of real R&D expenditure in regions and sectors 1994–2000, 2000–2002 and 1994–2002

|  | OECD | USA | JPN | EU-15 | GER | GBR | FRA | North | South | MID |
|---|---|---|---|---|---|---|---|---|---|---|
| *Business sector* | | | | | | | | | | |
| 1994–2000 | 5.7 | 7.1 | 4.0 | 4.1 | 4.6 | 1.9 | 1.5 | 9.0 | 4.0 | 5.2 |
| 2000–2002 | 0.6 | –3.1 | 4.7 | 3.4 | 0.5 | 3.9 | 1.8 | 6.8 | 4.8 | 3.0 |
| 1994–2002 | 4.4 | 4.4 | 4.2 | 3.9 | 3.5 | 2.4 | 1.6 | 8.4 | 4.2 | 4.6 |
| *Public sector** | | | | | | | | | | |
| 1994–2000 | 3.3 | 2.9 | 4.1 | 2.1 | 1.6 | 1.2 | 1.0 | 4.2 | 4.0 | 1.4 |
| 2000–2002 | 4.9 | 9.9 | –4.1 | 3.2 | 3.1 | 0.7 | 2.5 | 5.8 | 6.6 | 4.5 |
| 1994–2002 | 3.7 | 4.6 | 2.0 | 2.4 | 2.0 | 1.1 | 1.4 | 4.6 | 4.7 | 2.2 |
| *Total* | | | | | | | | | | |
| 1994–2000 | 4.9 | 5.9 | 4.0 | 3.4 | 3.6 | 1.7 | 1.3 | 7.4 | 4.0 | 3.8 |
| 2000–2002 | 1.9 | 0.3 | 2.2 | 3.3 | 1.2 | 2.8 | 3.5 | 6.5 | 5.7 | 3.5 |
| 1994–2002 | 4.2 | 4.5 | 3.6 | 3.4 | 3.0 | 1.9 | 1.8 | 7.2 | 4.4 | 3.7 |

* Higher education and governmental R&D facilities
*NORTH*: SWE, FIN, NOR, DEN, IRL, ISL – *MID*: BEL, NED, AUT, SUI – *SOUTH*: ITA, POR, ESP, GRE
Source: OECD, Main Science and Technology Indicators (2004/2) – NIW calculations and estimates

In the period of R&D revival in the second half of the 1990s, the R&D actors in France, United Kingdom and southern Europe did not reach German growth rates. But since 2000 they realised higher R&D dynamics than Germany and caught up. This might have been partly due to increased efforts for interior and exterior security in those countries, which led to a higher governmental share in R&D expenditure, also in the USA. On the other hand, several countries set explicit national R&D goals and enhanced their R&D efforts accordingly. These endeavours reflect the confidence of government and the business sector in the (positive) interrelation in the functional chain of R&D, innovation, competitiveness, growth and employment.

Germany is increasing its R&D capacity also, but it is still a long way back to the top. The deep decline of R&D at the beginning of the 1990s has not yet been overcome. After a short burst in the second half of the 1990s, Germany is again losing ground in R&D performance. In fact, its international position in R&D at the beginning of the new millennium ranks below that held at the beginning of the 1990s. Currently Germany's R&D expenditure is expanding almost at the same speed as the economy grows. The current R&D intensity of 2.5 per cent seems to be a level which Germany cannot exceed without massively intensified efforts in the innovation system and without sustained economic growth. Generally, the current propensity to invest is highly insufficient in Germany.

## Challenges Through Emerging Threshold Countries

The industrialised countries[4] compete more and more against ambitious, populous and enormously growing threshold countries. In terms of aggregated R&D volume these countries accessed top ranks in the world. These countries discover high technological performance as a basis to accelerate economic growth and they upgrade their innovation systems consequently:

---

[4] Due to the availability of data, an in-depth analysis has to be focussed mainly on those countries.

- China for example quadrupled its R&D expenditure since the middle of the 1990s. With a total amount of US $72 billion, China ranks third in the world, just ahead of Germany at US $54 billion.[5] Even India belongs to the top ten in the world with US $24 billion.
- Amongst the smaller non-OECD countries, Israel stands out with an R&D intensity of 4.7 per cent (with a high share in non-civil R&D), as well as Taiwan (2.3 per cent) and Singapore (2.1 per cent). The total R&D of these countries exceeds e.g. Canada.
- The dynamic of R&D expansion in these countries is considerably high. While the nominal expenditure on R&D in the European Nordic countries increased at about 80 per cent since the mid-1990s (50 per cent in the USA and on the OECD average, 35 per cent in Germany), the selected threshold countries realised a growth rate of about 180 per cent.
- Since 1995 the average R&D intensity of the most important threshold countries increased at about half a percentage point to 1.4 per cent and clearly exceeds the South European countries.

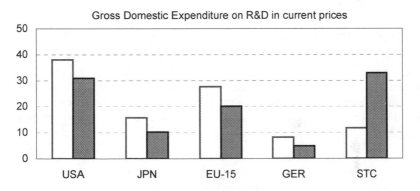

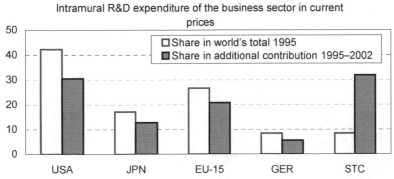

*STC* (selected threshold countries): CHN, KOR, IND, RUS, TPE, ISR, SIN
Source: OECD, Main Science and Technology Indicators (2004/2) – IMD World Competitiveness Yearbook – Federal Statistical Office Germany, Statistical Yearbook – Wissenschaftsstatistik – NIW calculations and estimates

**Fig. 3.** Share of the world regions in the expansion/growth of R&D capacities 1995 until 2002

---

[5]   The relation in R&D personnel between China and Germany is 1 million to 480,000.

The prominent role of the USA in the world's R&D growth in the recent decade weakens when considering the threshold countries, which have spent more than a third of the additional R&D expenditure between 1995 and 2002 in the world (see Fig. 3). As a result, they have made an even larger contribution to global R&D growth than either the USA (31 per cent), the EU (19 per cent, thereof Germany 4 per cent) or Japan (11 per cent). In the middle of the 1990s the threshold countries contributed a share of 12 per cent to the world's R&D spending, in the meanwhile already 20 per cent.

Big indigenous firms as well as multinational enterprises in particular are driving the increase in R&D activities in these countries, expanding their international production into them. Local market and growth perspectives are no longer the only factors in these companies' considerations. The markedly lower R&D costs also play a decisive role now (DIHK 2005). Despite the enormous and still above averagely increasing R&D growth in the threshold countries, Germany can still compete in knowledge and innovation. But this requires ongoing efforts, because Germany cannot compete in costs.

## Structural Changes in Private R&D

The business sector accounts for about 70 per cent of the world's R&D expenditure. Germany's business does not come off badly in an international comparison. However, it has been absent from the top ranks it held at the end of the 1980s for some time now (see Fig. 4). Furthermore, its R&D intensity has been stagnating since the beginning of the new millennium (see Fig. 5).

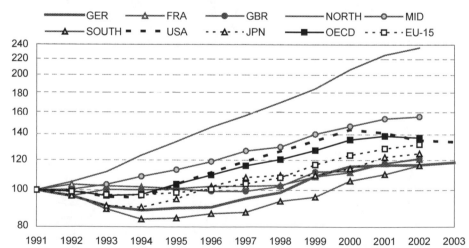

*NORTH*: SWE, FIN, NOR, DEN, IRL, ISL – *MID*: BEL, NED, AUT, SUI – *SOUTH*: ITA, POR, ESP, GRE
Source: OECD, Main Science and Technology Indicators (2004/2) – Wissenschaftsstatistik – NIW calculations and estimates

**Fig. 4.** Trends in intramural R&D expenditure in the business sector at constant prices 1991–2003 in world regions (1991 = 100)

The changes shown in Fig. 5 reveal the extreme turbulences in the R&D performance since the beginning of the new millennium in most countries. In the middle-term analysis, only a two years' extension of the considered period causes a displacement of the coordinates.

Including the new millennium, the annual R&D growth rate since 1994 declined in Germany, in the USA and in the North European countries. The increasing R&D-intensity of the business sector in the North European countries appears in a different light. The GDP growth until 2002 in this region is even weaker than R&D growth. Japan works the other way round: increasing R&D growth and further decline of GDP lead to an excursive boost of R&D intensity. In Germany, the decline of R&D and GDP

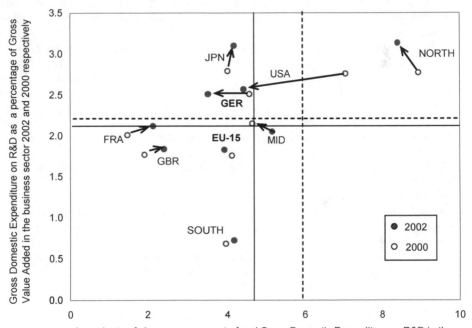

The time periods in this figure describe once the upswing period 1994–2000 and the extended period until 2002, which integrate the R&D stagnation in the new millennium. A divided presentation in two following time periods is not educible.

The lines mark the respective value of the OECD's average: the continuous line marks the year 2002 (ordinate) and 1994–2002 (abscissa) respectively, the dashed line marks the year 2000 (ordinate) and 1994–2000 (abscissa) respectively.

Interpretation: 1994–2002 (1994–2000) the real gross domestic expenditure on R&D in Germany increased about 3.5 (4.6) per cent p.a., whereas the R&D intensity stayed at about 2.5 per cent.

*NORTH*: SWE, FIN, NOR, DEN, IRL, ISL – *MID*: BEL, NED, AUT, SUI – *SOUTH*: ITA, POR, ESP, GRE

Source: OECD, Main Science and Technology Indicators (2004/2) – NIW calculations and estimates

**Fig. 5.** R&D intensity and change of real R&D expenditure in the business sector in world regions 1994–2002

growth run parallel and in the USA the business sector collapse in R&D activities is accompanied by a further increase in GDP growth.

Everywhere throughout the world, R&D in the business sector is more and more aligned to short-term market trends on demand and to medium-term growth perspective. The short-term realisation of R&D outcomes becomes more important, thus impacting firms' R&D behaviour. Therefore particularly in the first half of the 1990s, the business sector responded to the cyclical trend and to reduced growth perspectives through the decline of R&D, especially with medium-term and strategic objectives. The present data on R&D illustrate that those perspectives and continuity gain slightly in importance. Expecting growth, German industry expanded its R&D activities until the year 2000; subsequently R&D is just following the demands of the economic trend. This development was not at least caused by structural changes in the economy (see also Chapter 2.1).

R&D in the business sector plays a decisive role in the functional chain of education and training, science, research and technology, inventions, investment and innovations, international competitiveness, productivity, growth and employment (see Voßkamp 2005). Correspondingly, production and employment are growing more vigorously in those industries that invest considerably in R&D.

The sectoral focuses of business R&D activities in Germany are noticeably different from other western developed countries. However, relating to R&D growth, structural R&D patterns are getting closer to international trends (see Fig. 6). Also in Germany R&D is becoming increasingly important for services in the innovation process.

Services give more and more impulses to industrial R&D. They are often closely connected to leading-edge-technology branches (Biotechnology/Pharmaceuticals, Electronics, ICT, Aircraft and Aerospace). Furthermore, global R&D expenditure in the service sector increased due to a greater use of knowledge of specialised R&D services by manufacturing for quality and efficiency reasons. The revival of R&D activities in the German business sector since the mid-1990s is followed by a structural change in which leading-edge sectors become more important (Pharmaceuticals and ICT in particular). But the nucleus of the German R&D increase is still located in the automobile industry. Nearly 50 per cent of additional R&D expenditure in the business sector between 1995 and 2000 was incurred here (see also Chapter 2.1).

The differences in R&D patterns between Germany and its main competitors persist. These differences become obvious in particular in the automobile sector, on the one hand, as well as in the ICT sector and related branches (Electronical Equipment, Instruments) and also still in the service sector, on the other hand. Furthermore, the change of the R&D structures run in an opposite direction:[6]

- Germany as well shows increasing expenditure in these branches, which are the winners of R&D structural change, such as the ICT and the service sector: 12 and 18 per cent respectively of the expansion of R&D is accounted for by these sectors. However, this increase is well below the OECD average growth of 32 per cent in the ICT sector and of 43 per cent in the service sector from 1995 until 2000.
- The enormous R&D engagement in the automobile sector compensated for this lack. Moreover, the pharmaceutical industry contributed positively to Germany's R&D balance.

---

[6] Caused by enormous data lags, the analysis includes only the upswing period of R&D expenditure until 2000.

- In most other branches (in particular Machinery and Chemical Industry) business R&D developed at the global average, to some extent even above. However, the volume of world increase in R&D expenditure in these branches is more likely to show a stagnation of R&D and innovation potential.

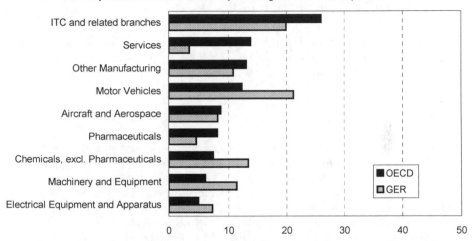

R&D expenditure of branches as a percentage of total R&D expenditure 1995

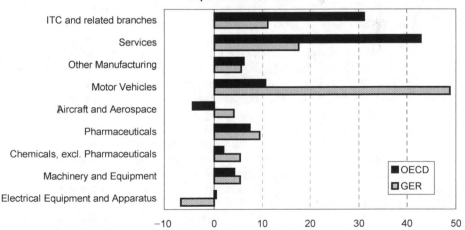

Change of R&D expenditure of branches as a percentage change of total R&D expenditure 1995–2000

Source: OECD ANBERD Database – NIW calculations

**Fig. 6.** Focus of R&D activities in Germany and the main OECD countries (OECD) 1995 and its change 1995–2000

Compared to the international R&D performance in Machinery and Chemicals, the German activities in these branches were even properly dynamic. Reciprocally, the above-average growth in the ICT and service sector from the national point of view was marginal in comparison to the growth in competitors' countries. In brief: in sectors which did not benefit from the world's structural change in R&D, Germany performed above average – and *vice versa*. Germany's business sector goes its own way in R&D performance.

## Governmental Contribution to R&D

Governments play an important role in the R&D systems, both by performing R&D in universities and non-university institutes and by providing financial aid to private R&D (see also Chapter 6).

### The Governmental Funding of R&D

But in nearly every developed country the share of governmental[7] contribution to R&D funding has decreased during the last two decades. The OECD average slipped below 30 per cent of the gross domestic expenditure on R&D. Relative to GDP, it declined from 0.85 per cent to 0.63 per cent since the beginning of the 1990s to 2002. Governmental funding of R&D decreased particularly in those countries where the non-civil section required a lot of R&D capabilities (USA, France, United Kingdom).

However, in some countries the current R&D budget plans of public authorities show a significant deviation from the long-term trend. Increasing R&D budgets indicate a regained confidence in public and private R&D as a crucial factor for growth. The USA, Sweden and Korea have a nominal annual growth between 10 and 14 per cent from 2000 to 2004 respectively 2003, in Norway governmental R&D expenditure increased by about 8 per cent p.a. in the same period. It still remains to be seen to what extent the budget plans have actually been realised and which effects they will have had on R&D capacities. Anyway, this fact shows that R&D has gained greater priority in public budgets – even in Germany. The annual growth rate of governmental R&D expenditure is about 2 per cent, which is still moderate, but, compared to the downward trend until 1998, at least a positive change. This indicates a higher priority for innovation policy. The public sector assumes more responsibility both through the increase of financial aid for business sector R&D and through extending R&D capacities in universities and non-university public R&D institutions. The signals for the private business sector are evident. However, in most countries the budgetary priorities have been targeted more specifically, faster and more intensively to R&D than in Germany.

A precondition for increasing R&D and innovation activities in the business sector is an improved environment of education, science, research and technology. This is essential both for a higher participation of SMEs and for an extension and restructuring of private R&D towards more R&D-intensive products and more market innovations. Above all, pro-cyclical governmental policies have to be avoided. Public funding of R&D through subsidies or procurement act rather as 'leverage' to R&D in the business

---

[7] 'Governmental' includes all levels of public authorities as well as special assets. In the broader sense, supranational organisations belong here too, as far as the bodies responsible for innovation policy confer competence to these organisations (e.g. the EU). But the contribution of these organisations are entered into the statistics as 'abroad'.

sector. Among the OECD countries, indirect financial R&D aid through tax credits became more popular. Especially in order to reach an increasing participation in R&D, indirect R&D assistance is particularly suitable (Rammer et al. 2004). Numerous countries among the 18 OECD nations that allow R&D tax credits have special conditions for SMEs as well. Especially the United States use preferences, respectively quotas, for SMEs in placing public R&D in connection with governmental procurement.


### 'Mission-Orientated' Strategies in Governmental R&D

The US government in particular has been able to compensate the R&D decline in the business sector arising since 2000 through an enormous increase in public R&D (see Table 2). This process was stimulated by a massive extension of R&D for military and security purposes (see also Chapter 6). Its monetary impulse is considerable. The budget for US military R&D was about one-third larger than Germany's total intra-mural corporate R&D expenditure in 2000, in 2003 even 70 per cent. Another main emphasis of governmental R&D in the USA is research in Life Sciences. This is an essential backing of the excellent US position in global biotechnological and pharmaceutical research and in the development of medical devices.

**Box 1.** Non-civil and life sciences research in the USA

Concerning innovation policy, Germany should be neither easily impressed nor motivated by the increasing military research in the USA. Just the opposite: the fast increasing R&D in the US business sector in the second half of the 1990s – a period, when government rapidly diminished its funding of non-civil research – is an indicator for the crowding-out effects of military research. Enterprises which are involved in non-civil R&D and production are usually involved in civil projects of Machinery, Transport, Electrical Engineering, Metals, Chemicals etc. at the same time. Direct spillovers from non-civil to civil projects mostly arise in the case of multi-purpose products only. Furthermore, the direction of the innovation is dedicated to the requirements of security and military, and not to social productivity and growth.

A substantial reason for the prominent position of the USA in Biotechnology is the governmental assistance for life sciences research with currently a share of 0.2 per cent in GDP (EU average: 0.05 per cent). The main beneficiaries are the National Institutes of Health, whose budget doubled since 1998. Despite difficulties in demarcation from the health sector, it is to be assumed that the US share of life science R&D in GDP is twice as much as in Germany. The health care branch is said to have enormous growth perspectives. On the other hand, an extremely strong orientation towards Life Sciences implies risks like crowding-out effects and rising R&D cost inefficiency.

Altogether, governmental impulses on the innovation system in the USA have had much more power than in Germany. However, the question is: how can such extensive R&D projects be implemented in such a short time without impacts on prices of R&D personnel or without even withdrawing R&D capacities from the private sector?

**Table 2.** Structure of governmental R&D expenditure* in selected countries 1991 until 2003

| | 1991 | 1995 | 1997 | 1999 | 2001 | 2002 | 2003 |
|---|---|---|---|---|---|---|---|
| **GER    Civil (as a share of total)** | **89.0 a** | **90.9** | **90.4 a** | **91.7** | **92.6** | **94.5** | **93.5 b** |
| containing**: Economic development | 25.5 a | 23.0 | 22.9 a | 22.6 | 20.3 | 20.5 | 20.5 b |
| Health and environment | 13.0 a | 12.6 | 12.5 a | 13.0 | 14.5 | 14.5 | 15.2 b |
| Space programmes | 6.1 a | 5.7 | 5.3 a | 4.9 | 5.3 | 5.4 | 5.4 b |
| Non-oriented research | 17.0 a | 16.5 | 17.1 a | 17.4 | 18.5 | 18.0 | 17.4 b |
| General university funds | 37.3 a | 41.5 | 42.6 a | 41.8 | 41.4 b | 42.0 | 41.7 b |
| **GBR    Civil (as a share of total)** | **56.1** | **63.5** | **60.8** | **62.1** | **69.5** | **65.9** | |
| containing**: Economic development | 28.8 | 16.6 | 14.3 | 11.7 | 13.6 | 14.9 | |
| Health and environment | 22.3 | 31.7 a | 32.9 | 35.7 | 32.3 | 30.6 | |
| Space programmes | 4.8 | 4.3 | 4.6 | 3.7 | 3.0 | 2.9 | |
| Non-oriented research | 9.1 | 18.3 | 18.7 | 18.2 | 19.5 | 20.2 | |
| General university funds | 33.7 | 28.5 | 28.9 | 30.1 | 31.3 | 30.7 | |
| **FRA    Civil (as a share of total)** | **63.9** | **70.0** | **74.8 a** | **77.3** | **77.2 a** | **77.0** | **77.2 b** |
| containing**: Economic development | 32.8 | 20.7 | 18.7 | 18.9 | 16.5 a | 16.1 | 16.7 b |
| Health and environment | 9.8 | 12.1 | 12.5 | 11.3 | 13.0 a | 13.3 | 12.8 b |
| Space programmes | 13.5 | 15.0 | 15.6 | 14.2 | 12.5 a | 11.7 | 10.6 b |
| Non-oriented research | 23.9 | 27.4 | 26.7 | 28.2 | 25.0 a | 26.9 | 28.4 b |
| General university funds | 19.5 | 22.2 | 23.2 | 23.6 | 30.1 | 30.0 | 29.5 |
| **USA    Civil (as a share of total)** | **40.3** | **45.9** | **44.8** | **46.8** | **49.5** | **47.9** | **46.3 c** |
| containing**: Economic development | 22.1 | 22.2 | 19.7 | 14.4 | 13.1 | 12.8 | 12.0 c |
| Health and environment | 43.5 | 43.9 | 46.6 | 50.0 | 53.0 | 55.1 | 56.9 c |
| Space programmes | 24.5 | 25.1 | 24.5 | 22.7 | 19.8 | 18.7 | 18.2 c |
| Non-oriented research | 9.9 | 8.9 | 9.2 | 12.9 | 14.0 | 13.4 | 12.9 c |
| General university funds | | | | n/a | | | |
| **JPN    Civil (as a share of total)** | **94.3** | **93.8** | **94.2** | **95.4** | **95.7** | **96.0 b** | **95.5 b** |
| containing**: Economic development | 33.5 | 31.4 | 34.8 | 34.4 | 34.3 | 33.8 b | 33.4 b |
| Health and environment | 5.7 | 6.2 | 7.3 | 7.1 | 7.9 | 7.7 b | 7.6 b |
| Space programmes | 7.2 | 7.9 | 6.7 | 6.6 | 7.0 | 6.3 b | 7.0 b |
| Non-oriented research | 8.5 | 10.3 | 11.5 | 13.5 | 14.5 | 16.0 b | 16.0 b |
| General university funds | 45.1 | 44.2 | 39.7 | 38.4 | 36.3 | 36.3 b | 36.1 b |
| **OECD  Civil (as a share of total)** | **63.6 a** | **68.8 a** | **69.2** | **70.6** | **71.4** | | |
| containing**: Economic development | 28.1 a | 24.4 a | 24.6 | 23.3 | 22.1 | | |
| Health and environment | 21.7 a | 22.6 a | 22.9 | 24.5 | 26.2 | | |
| Space programmes | 11.8 a | 12.2 a | 11.4 | 10.7 | 10.0 | | |
| Non-oriented research | 12.9 a | 12.3 a | 12.8 | 14.3 | 14.9 | | |
| General university funds | 24.3 a | 25.9 a | 26.0 | 24.9 | 24.8 | | |

\*  GBAORD: total government budget appropriations or outlays for R&D means the governmental budget's debit amount for R&D
\*\* In per cent of total civil R&D expenditure
a)  Break in series for reasons of statistical/methodical change – b) Provisional – c) Estimate
Source: OECD, Main Science and Technology Indicators (2004/2) – NIW compilation

The structure of business R&D is not independent of governmental commitment.
Especially in the USA, the United Kingdom and France the leading-edge technology
sector benefits particularly from the massive public engagement in non-civil and life
science research. In Germany and Japan, governmental R&D mainly focuses on civil
objectives with about 95 per cent of total spending (Table 2). In most European

countries, the goal of government involvement is to provide (civil) 'public goods' as well as assistance in the industrial development of technologies and the diffusion of new technologies.

### R&D in Universities and Governmental Institutes

In the OECD countries about 31 per cent of R&D capacities are located in universities and non-university public research institutes. But during the last two decades, the business sector increased its R&D capacities faster than the public sector. Since 2000 the relation between business and public sector is shifting again. Over this short period, it cannot be predicted if this development is only temporary or if it indicates a sustained increase of R&D capacities in the public sector.

Due to the fact that companies tend to orient their R&D policy towards short-term market and sales prospects rather than medium-term strategic objectives, it may be expected that public R&D institutes gain more importance, not only temporarily. Enterprises complete their technological knowledge more and more through contracts with R&D partners, such as public institutions, and co-operate with partners in the business sector to keep and develop their technological abilities. The supply of pre-competitional public basic research broadens the technological options of the economy in the long run.

Especially in Germany many companies – and SMEs in particular – rely on collaborative arrangements with (publicly funded) science and research for their innovation projects. These co-operations are well established and form a German advantage in technological competitiveness. About 12 per cent of R&D expenditure obtained by universities in Germany are financed by the business sector – with an increasing tendency. The OECD average is still below 6 per cent.

In the 1990s, public R&D spending in Germany increased (in real terms) to about 17 per cent. However, this falls behind the growth rate of the northern and southern European countries and the USA (each at 50 per cent), as well as Japan (30 per cent) and the United Kingdom (20 per cent; see Fig. 7). Nevertheless, it is a positive signal that the German public sector has been expanding its own R&D activities again since the beginning of the new millennium. The same holds for France, the United Kingdom in contrast did not.[8]

Currently almost everywhere in the world public R&D expenditure was pushed ahead more forcefully than in the late 1990s, although the economic environment was even better at that time (in detail see Chapter 6). Especially in the USA it seems that the governmental contribution wants to compensate for the losses in the business sector.[9] In contrast, in most European countries, the political goal to increase private and public R&D spending to a level of 3 per cent of GDP by the year 2010, may have stimulated the growth of public R&D activities. However, this goal is greatly ambitious and requires great efforts by both private and public sector.

---

[8]  In Japan, a considerable decline of R&D activities since 2000 is statistically noticed as a consequence of the privatisation of public R&D institutions.

[9]  Apparently the process in the USA stopped recently. On the one hand, the Federal government faces considerable budget problems. On the other hand, even the USA suffer a lack of qualified R&D personnel now. The more restrictive immigration policy greatly hampers the inflow of foreign scientists.

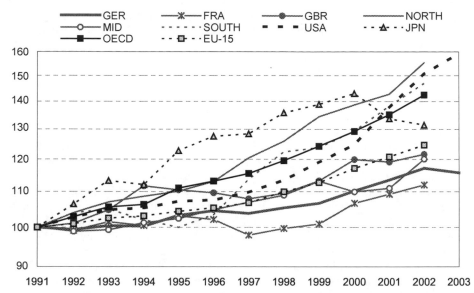

NORTH: SWE, FIN, NOR, DEN, IRL, ISL – MID: BEL, NED, AUT, SUI – SOUTH: ITA, POR, ESP, GRE
Source: OECD, Main Science and Technology Indicators (2004/2) – NIW calculations

**Fig. 7.** Trends of intramural R&D expenditure of higher education and governmental public research institutes in constant prices 1991–2003 in selected world regions (1991 = 100)

## Conclusion

With respect to the effects of investments in new technological knowledge on economic growth, it is not surprising that those economies have grown faster during the last decade whose R&D capacities increased the most. From this point of view it seems distressing that R&D in Germany developed quite unevenly in the last twenty years. In the new century R&D capacities were enlarged considerably in nearly all regions of the world. However, Germany could not keep up with this dynamic. As a consequence – with an almost unchanged R&D intensity of 2.5 per cent – Germany slipped from third position in the year 1991 to ninth position in 2003 in the world ranking.

International comparisons of R&D performance are important for self-assessment. Regarding R&D indicators, there is only little evidence of any significant improvement in the German position during the last decade. The recent considerable decrease of R&D activities in the US business sector may neither be a comfort nor a benchmark at all. Other countries in northern and central Europe as well as China and India are expanding their investments in R&D at an extraordinarily fast rate. Additional investments in R&D are necessary if Germany wants to keep a leading position in global markets. This seems even more important to overcome the current economic and social problems in Germany. An R&D share in GDP of 2.5 per cent might not be enough to achieve objectives such as a high level of employment and appropriate economic growth.

It is recognised that public engagement in science, research and education as well as the creation of interfaces to the business sector have become more important. The downward trend of the public sector has been stopped, but governmental funding of R&D did not increase as much as in other countries. Furthermore, the establishment of R&D tax credits should be contemplated, in order to achieve a more intensive participation of SMEs in the innovation process. R&D in Germany's business sector is slanted towards the automobile industry, while there are gaps in leading-edge technology fields which offer enormous potential for growth and the opportunity to implement lead markets of international standing. To enter these fields, an assessment of the relevance of innovation factors is required. These factors range from excellent science and technology in the public sector to innovation-friendly regulations fostering demand and procurement that stimulates innovation.

# 2.3 Internationalisation of Industrial R&D

Heike Belitz, Jakob Edler, Christoph Grenzmann

**Abstract.** The internationalisation of industrial R&D has been an increasingly debated and analysed topic since the early 1990s. A series of studies analysed this internationalisation from a German perspective. On that basis, this paper shows that while German firms have increased their international activities both in market exploitation and knowledge seeking, this cannot be interpreted as a loss of attractiveness of Germany as a research location. Rather, internationalisation is a two-way street for Germany, and the activity of foreign companies in the country has not only increased, but has also been conducted in knowledge-intensive, future-oriented technological areas. Thus, while differences between sectors and technologies will remain, it will be important in the future to further adjust the innovation system in order to better exploit the potential offered by the internationally dispersed generation and transnational diffusion of know-ledge.

## Introduction

In the 1990s, in Germany as well as in other industrialised countries, the internationalisation of R&D in multinational companies became an important issue of scientific and political discussions. The tendency of German multinational enterprises (MNEs) to internationalise R&D was partly seen as a relocation of R&D resources abroad and therefore as a threat to the long-term technological performance of Germany. The growing importance of research done by foreign affiliates was interpreted as evidence of weakness on the part of domestic conditions for industrial research. Similarly, the R&D activities of foreign companies in Germany has for a long time been interpreted as rather weak, signalling a low attractiveness of Germany as host country. On the other hand, from the perspective of Germany as a host country, the acquisition of German firms with high R&D intensity by foreign-owned companies was sometimes interpreted as a weakening of the domestic R&D basis.

There are several ways to improve the understanding of the dynamics of internationalisation of R&D by multinational companies. First, one can implement the ownership concept in conventional national R&D statistics and in special company surveys. Second, one can use firm specific micro data on R&D output (i.e. patents, publications). *We use both kinds of data to analyse the internationalisation of R&D in MNEs and the impact on Germany as a location for R&D.*

Since the mid-1990s, DIW Berlin and SV Wissenschaftsstatistik[1] have examined the international integration of R&D in MNEs, using separate analyses of the surveys

---

[1] SV Wissenschaftsstatistik GmbH is the R&D statistics branch of the Donors' Association for German Research (Stifterverband für die Deutsche Wissenschaft).

*U. Schmoch, C. Rammer and H. Legler (eds.), National Systems of Innovation in Comparison, 47–66.*

of business R&D in Germany.[2] The internationalisation of R&D activities is considered on the basis of sector-specific data on R&D expenditure by German companies abroad (outward) and by foreign companies in Germany (inward). Additional data from the OECD and the US Department of Commerce permit an international comparison.[3] In addition to these regular analyses, a one-off focus study has analysed both the inward and the outward internationalisation from the German perspective based on patent analysis, publication analysis and surveys of a German sample of 88 and a foreign company sample of 47 companies (Edler et al. 2003; Edler 2003; 2004). The study covers the period from 1990 to 1998. The companies were selected for their size and R&D capacity and were drawn from four industrial sectors (Chemistry, Electronics, Mechanical Engineering, Motor Vehicles). Thus, this focal study enabled a more differentiated analysis for a significant share of MNEs.

This chapter begins with a short overview of theoretical concepts of the internationalisation of multinational firms. We then discuss the advantages and disadvantages of R&D expenditure und output indicators (with a focus on patents) as two measures to analyse the internationalisation of R&D in multinationals. In the following section we present the main results of our studies of the R&D behaviour of multinational companies from the German perspective – both inward and outward – based on the German R&D survey and on the focus study by Edler et al. (2003), partly complemented by the analysis of the patent behaviour of multinationals by Les Bas and Sierra (2002). After a summary of our results we close with some conclusions for national technology policy.


## Theoretical Background

What are the motivations of multinationals in expanding R&D and other knowledge-based activities in their affiliates abroad? The question has prompted much debate in recent years. In the existing literature a 'dichotomous set of motives' for the internationalisation of R&D can be found, namely, that firms invest in R&D abroad either to exploit their existing stock of knowledge in foreign environments (Cantwell & Janne 1999; Cantwell & Kosmopoulou 2001; Patel & Vega 1999; Patel & Pavitt 2000; Dalton & Serapio 1999) or to augment their knowledge base by gaining access to foreign centres of excellence (Edler et al. 2003; Florida 1997; Koopmann & Münnich 1999; Boutellier et al. 1999; Cantwell 1995; Edler et al. 2001; Dunning & Wymbs 1999; Grandstrand 1999; Pearce & Singh 1997; Pearce 1999; Criscuolo et al. 2001; Narula 2002; Les Bas & Sierra 2002).

The answer should be consistent with a microeconomic theory of the multinational firm, which yields clear predictions as to how we should expect multinational activity

[2] Findings from earlier studies published in English can be found in Beise & Belitz (1998; 1999), Belitz (2000; 2002; 2004a and 2004b).

[3] Multinational companies are assigned to the home countries from which they are controlled. As a rule, this is also where companies' majority ownership is based. In this process, national and international statistics on foreign direct investment usually apply lower threshold values in terms of share ownership; in the case of the German Central Bank (Bundesbank), for example, this value stands at 10 per cent. However, different threshold values in the statistics influence findings of analyses on the cross-border activity of multinational companies only marginally and are therefore not taken into account here.

to relate to country characteristics, industry characteristics, and trade and investment costs.

One useful starting point for theory is the conceptual framework proposed by Dunning (1979). He suggested that there are three conditions needed for a company to become international:

- The company must have a product or a production process such that the company enjoys some market power or cost advantage abroad (ownership advantage).
- The company must have a reason to want to locate production abroad rather than concentrate it in the home country (location advantage).
- The company must have a reason to want to own a foreign subsidiary rather than simply license to or sub-contract with a foreign firm (internalisation advantage).

In more recent microeconomic models the ownership advantage is modelled by the existence of firm-level scale economies (Markusen 2001/2002). The general idea is that there are knowledge-based activities such as R&D, management, marketing and finance that are at least partially joint inputs across separate production facilities.

Within one company the knowledge generated at one location can be exploited in production at various sites at the same time without reducing its potential benefit at the point of origin. Jointness is the key feature which gives rise to horizontal multi-nationals, firms that produce roughly the same goods and services in multiple locations. For these firms, broadly defined trade costs constitute a location advantage, encouraging production abroad. Horizontal motivations for foreign activities are the need to place production close to customers and to avoid trade costs. Skill differences between the countries are relatively small.

Fragmentation and skilled-labour intensity are key features which give rise to vertical multinationals where the activities are fragmented geographically, so that headquarters and plants can be located in different countries. Vertical motivations for foreign activities are the desire to carry out unskilled-labour-intensive production activities in locations with relatively abundant unskilled labour when trade costs are low.

More recent theoretical and empirical studies on the internationalisation of multi-national firms in industrialised countries assume the dominance of the horizontal model of international division of labour, in which companies conduct similar activities and produce similar products in different locations with the same factor endowment.[4] This is consistent with the fact of large volumes of cross foreign direct investment among the rich countries of the world.

What can we expect to be the dominant motivation for conducting R&D abroad in a world of horizontal multinationals? Since joint use of knowledge within one company is one of the main features of the horizontal model, exploiting their existing home-based stock of knowledge in foreign environments should be the predominant strategy of multinationals. These companies produce similar goods and services in multiple locations with similar factor endowments and therefore should to a growing extent demonstrate similar R&D behaviour in their R&D locations in both home and host countries. In the horizontal model, market size and demand in the host country provide strong incentives for multinational activity. Accordingly, the innovation impulses generated by the market in particular should determine companies' R&D. This holds true for both domestically owned and foreign-owned companies. Thus, one

---

[4]  See, for example Markusen (2001/2002) and the literature cited there (Bloningen et al. 2002).

consequence for R&D is that it may be dispersed globally as well and done near to different production sites if local market adaptations are needed, because of different local preferences or local regulations.

However, if knowledge generation is very much specialised or if there are locations with clear competitive advantages as to knowledge generation (excellence, costs) R&D even in the horizontal mode may be done at *one* location (e.g. at headquarters or at the site with the best knowledge assets) and then transferred to the global production sites. Such a capability-augmenting mode in 'globally learning companies' (Meyer-Krahmer & Reger 1997) is becoming more and more important in those areas that are very knowledge-intensive and where a global specialisation needs to be exploited.

Therefore market-seeking and exploiting and – to a growing extent – capability augmenting are expected to be the most important motives for R&D abroad. This means, in consequence, that in the host countries domestic and foreign firms should demonstrate similar R&D behaviour to an increasing degree.

# How to Measure the Internationalisation of R&D

It is difficult to measure the internationalisation of companies and, by extension, the integration of R&D at the international level. Studies in this field are mainly based on two sets of measures:

- R&D expenditures (input); and
- patent statistics and – to a much lesser extent – publications (output).

### R&D Expenditures

National statistics record company activities primarily with regard to their location in a given national economy, but often provide only insufficient information on the cross-border integration of multinational enterprises and the internal exchange of capital, goods, services and knowledge.

The statistical concept has to be changed to describe the activities of MNEs. In the ownership concept, economic activities of home countries comprise domestic and foreign activities of the domestically owned firms (parent companies and their affiliates at home and abroad). In the host country we distinguish between the activities of domestically owned firms and foreign-owned affiliates.

### German Data on R&D Expenditures of Multinationals

The statistical System for Research and Development, based on the international standards (OECD 2002) defines the statistical requirement to provide international comparability of the national R&D activities. Two main indicators are established, the one reporting on the monetary input (R&D expenditure), the other reporting on human resources (R&D personnel).

Based on these OECD standards, the R&D activities which are performed on the territory of the respective country have to be compiled. So the Frascati Manual argues in §38: 'The main aggregate used for international comparison is gross domestic expenditure on R&D, which covers all expenditures for R&D performed on national territory [...]' and respectively for the human resources: 'It covers total personnel working on R&D on national territory [...].' This international standard for the R&D survey assures that the intramural R&D in different countries does not include any overlapping. It cannot be denied that this requirement can cause problems for multinationals, performing R&D in different national territories, because the enterprises are expected to distribute their R&D engagement into different national territories, depending on the localisation of performance and report to different national statistical services.

On the other hand, for the management of the global players the national borders are of decreasing importance (Edler et al. 2003). MNEs generally inform about their global R&D in their business reports, frequently split into different branches or divisions. But in general the business reports do not provide R&D broken down by regions or countries. The R&D statistics must be tailored in order to take into account this obvious change in the demand of the statistical user. The OECD has articulated the importance of R&D globalisation in the Frascati Manual (§39–41), not giving detailed regulations how globalisation should be surveyed. The subject of economic globalisation has been treated in depth in a separate OECD Handbook (OECD 2005), which also deals with global indicators for science and technology.

New indicators are required to report about the global activities of multinationals and to measure the degree of R&D globalisation. Therefore the German R&D statistic deals with the question how to provide statistical information about R&D globalisation. Two 'directions' have to be distinguished:

• Germany as R&D host for foreign-controlled enterprises (inward);
• German-controlled enterprises as R&D guest abroad (outward).

In the first case, it has to be established to what extent R&D in Germany is performed in foreign-owned enterprises. In the second case, the statistic has to report about the amount of R&D multinationals with their headquarters in Germany are performing abroad. According to this concept, the R&D activities of foreign enterprises in Germany and respectively of German enterprises abroad are compiled.

For the first question, the national R&D activities are evaluated by country of control. The aggregate for all countries is identical with the corresponding national R&D total. The classification of the statistical unit to the nationality of the country of owner follows the 'ultimate beneficial owner concept' (BPM5 1993). Following this concept the affiliates in the compiling country, Germany, are classified to the country of control located abroad. This concept assures that, for instance, non-European multinationals with intermediate European holdings are classified to their ultimate headquarters outside Europe.

Because the German R&D survey does not include questions about the country of control, this information was added from external sources, especially from publicly accessible data files.

For the opposite question, answers have to be found about the outward activities of German multinationals in terms of R&D. For practical reasons, an enterprise has been regarded as German if its headquarters are in Germany. For the years 1995, 1997 and 1999 the national R&D survey included additional questions, concerning the global R&D activities of the multinational to which the surveyed unit belonged. Based on the experiences from the three surveys, the approach was revised for 2001. This was caused by two observations:

* The person responsible for the reporting of the national R&D data for the National R&D survey did not have access to information about worldwide R&D expenditures of the whole group. In other cases it was not his responsibility to forward the international R&D data to the statistical service.

* As the additional 'global' questions became part of the national R&D survey, basically the same global data had been reported by various statistical units representing different affiliates of the same multinational company. This meant a certain risk of duplication. The presentation of qualified data for 1995 till 1999 therefore required a high and uneconomical amount of individual checks.

For the year 2001, the procedure was modified: based on business reports and internet information a data file had been built up with global R&D data of multinationals, including – if available – a classification to their different branches. Principal condition to include the data in the file was that they could be taken from business reports or equivalent publications. In the next step, the reporting units of the national statistical R&D survey were linked to the international parent unit. To arrive at the R&D activity abroad, the national R&D data was subtracted from the global R&D expenditure of the corresponding multinational company.

## Output Indicators: Patents and Publications

Patents can be assigned to the firm which owns them and the inventor's address given in each published patent is used as a proxy measure for the geographical location of R&D activities. But not every innovating activity leads to a patent (see also Chapter 3.3). Often foreign R&D is devoted to adapting existing products or processes to local demand or to exploratory research of 'listening posts' with no patentable outcome. R&D expenditures tend to include all activities ranging from basic research to adapting existing products to local demands, while patents only refer to R&D activities leading to patentable outcomes. Another disadvantage of using patent data to describe the internalisation of R&D is the time lag between the R&D activities, the date of the application for a patent and the date of publication. On the other hand, one advantage of using patents is that they indicate the output of corporate research activities with a demonstrated market potential ('applied'). The main advantages of patent-based data – however – are that innovation activity can be analysed in much greater detail regarding the individual firm's intellectual property, the technological fields, the geographical location of R&D activities and – in principle – co-operation patterns via co-inventors.

One shortcoming of using patents as potential indicators for R&D activities abroad is that the propensity to patent varies considerably between industries and nations – and changes over time due to changing patent strategies (Blind et al. 2004). An important prerequisite for the patent analysis is a firm register with complete information on worldwide majority equity holdings of multinational firms. Most affiliates apply for patents under their own names which are often different from the group's name. In order to consolidate the entire multinational enterprise in the patent database, all names of assignees belonging to the multinational group have to be identified. As a result of this time-consuming method, only samples of multinationals can be included in the analysis.

Another output indicator for international R&D are scientific publications (see also Chapter 3.1). They indicate the scope and scale of research activities at an earlier stage, farther away from the market application. As with patents, publication analysis can differentiate much better as to different (scientific) areas and via co-publications enables the analysis of co-operation patterns across countries. A publication analysis accompanied the patent analysis for the sample of foreign companies in order to better characterise the attractiveness of Germany as a host of industrial R&D.[5]

One specific problem in using patent and publication analysis is the question of attribution of patents to companies. This has to do with the many changes occurring in multinational firm structure. Thus databases for equity holdings of the multinational firms monitored have to be updated frequently. Because this is an expensive procedure, many studies use samples of firms where they are consolidated for one year only. In most cases time trend analysis based on patents does not reflect the changes due to mergers and acquisitions. The focus study in the context of the German reporting on technological competitiveness has controlled for the changes due to mergers and acquisitions in its sample and has thus – at least for the outward activities – has been able to detect patterns over time (Edler et al. 2003, see below).

## R&D of German Multinationals Abroad

The internationalisation of R&D must be interpreted in the context of internationalisation in general. The internationalisation of production is most advanced in the research-intensive sectors (Chemical Industry, Motor Vehicles, Computer, Electrical, Electronic and Precision Engineering). In these sectors, in 2001 for every 100 people employed by German companies in Germany,[6] on average another 75 were employed in German subsidiaries abroad, whereas German manufacturing as a whole only employed 53 abroad.

The pioneers of internationalisation, and not only in Germany, are the chemical and pharmaceutical firms. In 2001 they were already employing one-fifth more staff abroad in production than in Germany. They may only be in second place in research abroad, but on average they spend nearly one-half of their total R&D expenditures there (see Table 1).

Since 1998 the German motor vehicle companies have also employed more workers abroad than in Germany. This sector now has the highest amount of R&D expenditures abroad.

---

[5] The database used for publication analysis was the Science Citation Index.
[6] Persons employed in all companies minus the number employed in foreign-owned companies.

**Table 1.** R&D activities of German firms in 2001, by economic sector

| Economic sectors | Total domestic R&D expenditure[1] | R&D expenditure at home | | R&D expenditure abroad | | Worldwide R&D expenditure |
|---|---|---|---|---|---|---|
| | million € | million € | % | million € | % | million € |
| Manufacturing | 29.490 | 20.210 | 69 | 11.589 | 36 | 31.799 |
| Chemicals | 5.070 | 3.948 | 78 | 3.649 | 48 | 7.597 |
| Mechanical Engineering | 3.441 | 680 | 20 | 444 | 40 | 1.124 |
| Computer, Electrical, Electronic, Instruments | 6.586 | 4.627 | 70 | 2.801 | 38 | 7.428 |
| Vehicles | 12.351 | 10.618 | 86 | 4.568 | 30 | 15.186 |
| Other sectors | 3.330 | 2.264 | 68 | 360 | 14 | 2.624 |
| Total | 32.820 | 22.474 | 68 | 11.949 | 35 | 34.423 |

[1]    Total domestic R&D business expenditure minus foreign firms' R&D expenditure
Sources: SV Wissenschaftsstatistik – DIW Berlin calculations and estimates

**Table 2.** Total R&D expenditure by companies in Germany and abroad, 1995 and 2001

| | 1995 | 2001 | Change 1995–2001 |
|---|---|---|---|
| | billion € | billion € | % |
| In Germany | 30.0 | 43.8 | 46 |
|   Foreign firms | 5.0 | 11.5 | 130 |
|   German firms | | | |
|     Without R&D abroad | 8.0 | 9.8 | 23 |
|     With R&D abroad | 17.0 | 22.5 | 32 |
|      German companies abroad | 5.1 | 11.9 | 133 |
|   German companies worldwide | 22.1 | 34.4 | 56 |
| As % of R&D in Germany | | | |
| In Germany | 100 | 100 | – |
|   Foreign firms | 17 | 26 | – |
|   German firms | | | |
|     Without R&D abroad | 27 | 22 | – |
|     With R&D abroad | 57 | 51 | – |
| As % of German R&D worldwide | | | |
| German firms with R&D abroad | 100 | 100 | – |
|   In Germany | 77 | 65 | – |
|   Abroad | 23 | 35 | – |

Sources: SV Wissenschaftsstatistik – DIW Berlin calculations and estimates

Against this background, after stagnating for a long time in the first half of the 1990s, total expenditures by companies on R&D in Germany have risen by nearly half, from €30 billion in 1995 to a good €44 billion in 2001.[7] The greater part of these expenditures is by MNEs, whose production, and increasingly research locations as well, are spread internationally.

---

[7]  Cf. Stifterverband für die Deutsche Wissenschaft (2004).

R&D expenditures by German subsidiaries abroad are estimated at about €11.9 billion for 2001. In 1995 they were presumably €5.1 billion (see Table 2).

R&D expenditure of German companies abroad rose by a good 130 per cent in nominal terms from 1995 to 2001; it grew significantly more rapidly than total R&D expenditure in Germany (46 per cent; see Table 2). This increase in foreign R&D involvement is very probably due primarily to M&As rather than to an expansion in R&D in existing German companies abroad. Between 1995 and 2001 there was a strong worldwide increase in M&As, which fell sharply after 2000. Between 1995 and 2001 Germany was the fourth-largest investor in cross-border M&As,[8] after the United States, the United Kingdom and France (OECD [ed.] 2003a).

The R&D intensity in Germany of German companies which are also active abroad is, on average, higher than that of those companies who have no foreign involvement (see Fig. 1).[9]

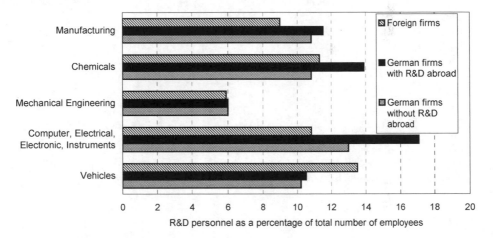

Sources: SV Wissenschaftsstatistik – DIW Berlin calculations

**Fig. 1.** R&D personnel intensity in Germany in 2001, by sector (in per cent)

German companies spent one-third of their overall R&D expenditure abroad. For comparison: subsidiaries of US American concerns spent US $19.7 billion on R&D abroad in 2001. This was 12 per cent of total R&D expenditures by US MNEs (Mataloni 2004). German multinationals are thus on average already far more internationalised than their US counterparts. MNEs in smaller countries have to locate more of their production and R&D abroad if they are to make use of the advantages of scale and the many stimuli to innovation in international markets. Another factor affecting the higher internationalisation degree of multinationals from smaller countries is the need

---

[8] The most prominent example of this expansion was the fusion of Daimler-Benz AG with the US Chrysler Corporation, which in 1998 became DaimlerChrysler – with a strong effect on the number of patents held and applied for by German companies. The acquisition of Rover by BMW in the United Kingdom has had similar effects on the United Kingdom patents of German firms (Edler et al. 2003)

[9] R&D intensity is measured as R&D personnel as a share of all employees, or R&D expenditure as a share of turnover.

to master an increasing range of potentially useful technologies (Granstrand et al. 1997), not all of which may be available in the home country. The degree of internationalisation of R&D activities is thus particularly high for Swiss and Dutch firms, as is evident from the relation of their R&D expenditures in the United States to their domestic R&D potential (see Table 3).

**Table 3.** Internationalisation of R&D and production in selected industrialised countries, 2001

| | R&D expenditure | | | | Level of foreign direct investment | |
| | Total | Share of foreign firms | by subsidiaries in the United States | | by foreign countries | in foreign countries |
| Country | million PPP $ | % share | million US $ | % share | % of GDP | |
| --- | --- | --- | --- | --- | --- | --- |
| USA | 209,955 | 14.9 | 19,402[3] | 9.4 | 13.1 | 13.7 |
| EU | 120,127 | 9.4[4] | 17,657 | 14.7 | – | – |
| JPN | 6,455 | 3.9[1] | 3,474 | 4.5 | 1.2 | 7.2 |
| GER | 38,036 | 26.5 | 6,010 | 15.8 | 22.3 | 29.8 |
| FRA | 21,920 | 16.4[2] | 3,215 | 14.7 | 22.0 | 37.3 |
| GBR | 19,796 | 39.4 | 4,762 | 24.1 | 38.6 | 63.4 |
| CAN | 10,007 | 31.6 | 2,218 | 22.2 | 29.7 | 34.7 |
| SWE | 7,680 | 34.1[1] | 408 | 5.3 | 42.0 | 55.6 |
| NED | 5,078 | 21.5[1] | 1,627 | 32.0 | 74.2 | 85.7 |
| SUI | 4,140[1] | – | 4,162 | 100.5 | 36.1 | 100.3 |
| FIN | 3,325 | 14.2 | 162 | 4.9 | 21.6 | 46.1 |

[1]1999 – [2]1998 – [3]R&D expenditure of US companies abroad – [4]US companies in the EU
Sources: SV Wissenschaftsstatistik – DIW Berlin calculations and estimates

### The United States as the Most Important Foreign Research Location

The United States is the most important foreign location for R&D by German firms. Their R&D expenditures in the United States increased approximately 3.4-fold in nominal terms from 1990 to 2001, while their turnover increased only 2.9-fold. In total, foreign companies operating in the United States increased R&D spending 2.6-fold over this period, at the same time doubling their turnover.[10] Thus, foreign companies expanded their R&D activities in the United States more quickly than their production and sales. With their R&D expenditure of approximately $6 billion, and with some 26,000 people employed in R&D, German companies demonstrate the largest R&D capacities of all foreign firms in the United States, followed by British, Swiss and Japanese companies. At the same time, on average German companies have the highest R&D intensity of all foreign firms in the United States. The patent-based analysis of foreign research activities of 88 firms confirms that throughout the 1990s the USA remained by far the most important R&D location of German companies, although its relative importance has slightly decreased (Fig. 2, Edler et al. 2003).

---

[10] US Department of Commerce: US Affiliates of Foreign Companies, various years. Data cover all companies in which Germans hold at least ten per cent of the shares.

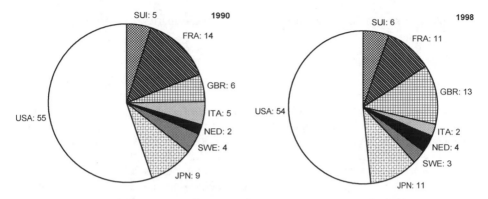

Source: Edler et al. (2003), PCTPAT, EPAT – Fraunhofer ISI calculations

**Fig. 2.** Host country distribution of foreig patents (German companies, N = 88)

The 88 companies analysed in depth have registered about half of their patents in the USA, followed by a group of medium countries France, Japan and the United Kingdom. The USA has about half the patents, having decreased only slightly from its share in 1990 (see Fig. 2), while the United Kingdom especially has apparently had the highest gains.[11]

The main sectors of R&D activities by German firms in the United States changed due to massive merger activities. In 1999, after the merger between Daimler and Chrysler, around 41 per cent of the R&D expenditures by German firms in the United States were in Vehicle Construction. The pharmaceuticals sector, long the leader in German R&D expenditures abroad, now has a share of 19 per cent. But for some time now R&D expenditures by foreign firms in the United States have been concentrated on the pharmaceutical industry; clearly the US market for pharmaceutical products displays characteristics of a lead market.[12]

Foreign companies also adapt products that have been successful worldwide to the US market, and they concentrate their US R&D activities in the corresponding sectors:

- Japanese companies: Electrical Engineering, Computer and Communications Technology, Automobile Construction;
- Swiss companies: Pharmaceuticals and Foodstuffs;
- British companies: Pharmaceuticals, Foodstuffs, Mechanical Engineering;
- French companies: Communications Technology;
- German companies: Automobile Construction.

But MNEs also maintain many independent research centres in the United States that are not directly linked to production units. Japanese companies in particular choose this path, and at the end of the 1990s they had the highest number of these centres. German companies were in second place (Dalton & Serapio 1999). This suggests that

---

[11] The high share of the United Kingdom in 1998 is mainly due to the acquisition of Rover by BMW that is history already and that was, moreover, not motivated by the R&D potential of the British car company.

[12] The concept of lead markets and their role in R&D location decisions of multinationals is described in detail by Beise (2001).

both the research environment and the appropriate markets in the United States are highly attractive.

## Strategies of German Multinationals-Insights from Patent-based Analyses

By analysing the foreign technological activities of German companies utilising patent analysis, the technological specification can be depicted. On that basis, differences in technological patterns can be discerned that allow interpretation as to the basic motivation for foreign R&D. Moreover, through a comparison over time it is possible to see how technological focuses of activities abroad have changed.

While the 88 companies of the sample used in Edler et al. (2003) have not changed their regional pattern of foreign activity very much, they have somewhat changed their technological patterns and strategies abroad. First of all, the German companies investigated broadened their technological activities across the technological fields as the share of international patents in all patents of the sample has grown in all but two technological fields.[13] Still, the growth of international activities developed very unevenly across the technological fields. To illustrate this, Table 4 indicates the six technological fields with the highest and the lowest share of foreign patents in all patents in 1998 and in 1990. Three technological fields stand out; almost half of the patents in the biotechnology sector and more than a third in the fields Medical Technology and Pharmaceuticals were registered abroad. Although starting from a relatively high level already in the 1990s, the companies even intensified their international activities in these fields in the 1990s. By far the highest dynamic, however, can be registered in the semiconductor field, in which foreign R&D activities of the German MNEs of the sample in 1990 were almost non-existent.

**Table 4.** Most and least internationalised technological fields of German MNEs 1990 and 1998 (N = 88)

| Highest foreign share | 1998 | 1990 | Diff. | Lowest foreign share | 1998 | 1990 | Diff. |
|---|---|---|---|---|---|---|---|
| Biotechnology | 43.6 | 30.7 | 12.9 | Telecommunications | 9.2 | 12.7 | −3.5 |
| Medical Technology | 38.4 | 33.8 | 4.6 | Construction/Building | 8.9 | 3.2 | 5.7 |
| Pharmaceuticals | 33.3 | 18.7 | 14.6 | Transport/Aircraft/Weapons | 8.1 | 3.6 | 4.5 |
| Food Processing | 28.6 | 10.0 | 18.5 | Environmental Technologies | 8.1 | 3.2 | 4.9 |
| Organic Chemistry | 24.2 | 13.2 | 11.0 | Audio-Visual Technologies | 6.7 | 16.1 | −9.5 |
| Semiconductors | 24.0 | 4.4 | 19.7 | Consumer Goods | 5.3 | 1.4 | 3.9 |

Source: PCTPAT, EPAT – Fraunhofer ISI calculations

The patent analysis furthermore allows us to compare the technological profiles of the foreign activities of company samples to their domestic profile.[14] This shows that in the course of the 1990s the activities of the companies abroad have converged to the pattern at home.

---

[13] Internationalisation has decreased in the two technological fields Telecommunications and Audio-Visual Technology, both from the electronics area.
[14] See Edler (2003; 2004) for details of the methodology used here.

This finding can be further specified by the comparison of the foreign profile of the sample with the profile of the host countries of their research. The premise behind this comparison is that a high correlation of the foreign profile of the sample with the profile of a given host country indicates that the international R&D strategies of the companies are focused on the technological strengths of a host country. Edler et al. have conducted such a comparison for the USA as a research location, showing that across the board the 88 companies have not specialised their activities in the USA according to the technological strengths and weaknesses of the USA as research location (Edler et al. 2003; Edler 2004). Across the board it seems that the internationalisation of R&D has remained a production-related, adaptation-oriented activity that accompanies local production and marketing activities.

However, important deviations of this pattern are to be seen, as those technological fields in which the share of international patents was high and even grew further in the 1990s show one important common characteristic: they are all highly knowledge-intensive.[15] The more knowledge-intensive a technological field is, the closer the related research is to the scientific forefront of knowledge. The analysis shows that there is a positive – and growing – relationship between the knowledge intensity of a technological field and its share of foreign activities. Among the six most highly internationalised technological fields (see Table 4) are the four most knowledge-intensive ones (Biotechnology, Pharmaceuticals, Organic Chemistry and Semiconductors). Apparently, although the companies have broadened their international R&D activities across the board, they have intensified their foreign activities even more in fields in which they need access to forefront knowledge, and therefore their presence in the global centres of excellence is important. This clearly indicates a growing specialisation of knowledge production that companies need to exploit.

This is in line with other findings on the knowledge-seeking motivation for international R&D. It is, for example, confirmed by Les Bas and Sierra (2002) in a study of 345 multinationals with the biggest patenting activity in Europe (patent applications registered in the EPO between 1988–1990 and 1994–1996). 42 of these firms are German multinationals. 47 per cent of the patenting of the whole sample and 55 per cent of the patenting of the German companies can be assigned to a strategy labelled 'home-base-augmenting' R&D investment abroad. Such R&D activities are aimed at monitoring or acquiring competitive advantages in countries with similar fields of competence. Firms gain access to foreign technological assets and can capture externalities created by local firms and research institutions.

All in all, our analysis shows a more and more similar R&D behaviour of German MNEs at home and abroad. This is in line with the assumption of the dominance of the horizontal motivations for foreign activities.

---

[15] Knowledge intensity is here defined as the number of cited publications within a patent document (Grupp & Schmoch 1992; Schmoch 2003a). Grupp & Schmoch determined the knowledge intensity by analysing patent documents for the 28 technological areas and calculating knowledge indexes for each technological area. While the average index across all technological fields is 0.88 citations per patent, at the high end it is 2.65 for Biotechnology, 1.87 for Pharmaceuticals, at the low end 0.18 for Construction/Building and 0.22 for Consumer Goods.

## Foreign R&D in Germany

In 2001, every fourth €invested in R&D in Germany was spent by foreign firms, and one-quarter of those employed in R&D were working in these companies (see Table 5). In manufacturing industry – the area in which business R&D is concentrated – only about one-fifth of all employees were employed in foreign companies. Between 1995 and 2001, the 130 per cent increase in R&D expenditure of foreign companies in Germany was roughly the same as that spent by German firms abroad. M&As[16] led to a sharp increase in foreign firms' share of total German R&D capacity, increasing it from one-sixth to one-quarter (see Table 2 above). This expansion of R&D activity was stronger than the increase in the turnover of foreign companies conducting R&D.[17] Just as in the United States, foreign companies in Germany expanded their R&D activities more quickly than sales and production.

**Table 5.** Total R&D expenditure and R&D employees in foreign firms in Germany in 2001, by economic sector[1]

|  | Total R&D expenditure | | | R&D staff | | |
|---|---|---|---|---|---|---|
|  | All Firms | Foreign firms | | All Firms | Foreign firms | |
|  | € million | | % | Full-time equivalents | | % |
| All Sectors | 43,239 | 11,478 | 26.5 | 302,519 | 73,173 | 24.2 |
| Of which: | | | | | | |
| Manufacturing | 39,326 | 10,744 | 27.3 | 270,546 | 68,279 | 25.2 |
| Of which: | | | | | | |
| Chemicals | 7,029 | 2,037 | 29.0 | 42,001 | 11,254 | 26.8 |
| Mechanical Engineering | 4,058 | 817 | 20.1 | 36,730 | 7,499 | 20.4 |
| Computers, Electrical, Electronic, Instruments | 8,837 | 2,540 | 28.7 | 79,651 | 20,325 | 25.5 |
| Vehicles | 16,750 | 4,438 | 26.5 | 88,272 | 21,720 | 24.6 |
| Business Services | 2,361 | 550 | 23.3 | 20,277 | 4,177 | 20.6 |

[1] Extrapolated on the basis of a company panel that comprises 91 per cent of total domestic R&D expenditure and 85 per cent of companies R&D staff
Sources: SV Wissenschaftsstatistik – DIW Berlin calculations

The cross-border integration of companies' R&D locations and knowledge exchange occurs primarily within and between the knowledge-intensive regions of the United States and Western Europe. In Germany, western European and US companies are involved in R&D to more or less the same extent; for German firms the most important foreign research location is the United States. The role of Japan, China and

---

[16] Between 1995 and 2001 Germany was in third place in terms of the purchase of companies by foreign buyers, after the United States and the United Kingdom (cf. Science, Technology and Industry Scoreboard, op. cit.).
[17] The increase in turnover between 1995 and 2001 was 83 per cent in companies with majority foreign ownership conducting R&D (calculated on the basis of SV Wissenschaftsstatistik data), or 58 per cent in all companies in which foreign firms had a share of at least 10 per cent in terms of voting rights/capital (calculated on the basis of data from the German Bundesbank on international capital integration, various years)

other East Asian countries as a destination of foreign R&D of German multinationals is low until now – although, given the combined potential of their markets and skilled workforce, there is scope for expansion.

With the expansion of R&D by foreign companies in Germany, the sector-specific structures of R&D expenditure in domestic and foreign firms have become more closely aligned (see Fig. 3). An analysis of the patenting of 29 foreign companies[18] in Germany in 1998 reveals a similar result (Edler et al. 2003). Foreign firms are increasingly prioritising the same key areas as their German competitors in their R&D activities. This is in line with the theoretical expectation in the horizontal model of internationalisation, namely that competitors in the same location demonstrate similar R&D traits. Accordingly, the innovation impulses generated by the market in particular determine companies' R&D.

The economic significance of foreign companies in a given country can be measured by foreign direct investment as a share of gross domestic product (GDP). Countries with a high weighting of foreign direct investment often also demonstrate a high share of R&D expenditure on foreign multinational firms (see Table 3 above). In the case of Germany, measured against the weighting of foreign direct investment, the share of research activities by foreign companies is relatively high.

In Germany, too, internationalisation takes the form of shareholdings in companies by foreign investors, and M&As. The percentage of foreign-controlled firms in German industry – measured by their share of the total workforce – has risen only slightly, to over 20 per cent at present. But while the number employed in foreign manufacturing firms increased slightly at 1.2 million in 2001, their R&D personnel rose by about one-half from 1997 to 2001, most recently reaching nearly 73,000. But it is not possible to establish whether this growth was mainly due to new R&D sites or the acquisition of firms in research-intensive branches.

The average research intensity per sector – measured by the share of R&D personnel in the total number employed – for foreign firms in Germany that engage in R&D is comparable to the figures for the big German companies (see Fig. 1).[19] By contrast, the figures are much lower for the small and medium-sized firms that operate in other markets. This supports the thesis that companies competing in the same market also invest in R&D to a similar extent.

Vehicle Manufacturing accounts for by far the biggest amount of R&D expenditures by foreign firms at more than €4.4 billion, and the R&D capacities of this sector in Germany have been particularly expanded in recent years.

The sector attracts nearly 40 per cent of total R&D expenditures by both foreign and German firms. This is due to the fact that some segments of the German market for cars and supplies are lead markets. A relatively large number of R&D activities are also to be found in Chemical Industry, Computer, Electrical Engineering and Media Technology.[20]

---

[18] For this analysis, the original sample of 47 companies had to be reduced due to lack of comprehensive data for all companies.

[19] The research intensity figures (R&D personnel in relation to number employed) were calculated for the most research-intensive companies in Germany (about 1,000) with German and foreign majority shareholders.

[20] These sectors each have higher shares of the total R&D expenditures by foreign companies in Germany than in those by German companies.

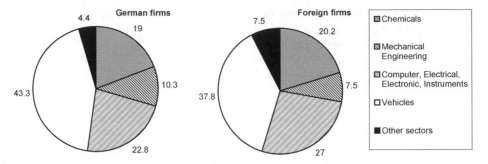

Sources: SV Wissenschaftsstatistik – DIW Berlin calculations

**Fig. 3.** Share of the R&D expenditures of the Manufacturing Industry in Germany in 2001 (in per cent)

## R&D by US American Companies in Germany

From 1995 to 1998 the annual R&D expenditures by US American firms in Germany remained almost unchanged at about US $3 billion; in 1999 they rose to US $3.4 billion (€3.2 billion); in 2001 they reached US $3.2 billion (€3.6 billion). After Germany had remained in first place for a long time in the list of research locations abroad for the United States, it was overtaken in 1999 by Great Britain with R&D expenditures totalling US $4.1 billion. Great Britain and Germany together account for more than one-third of expenditures on R&D abroad by US American firms. The share of R&D expenditures in value added by US American subsidiaries is highest in Germany at 5.6 per cent compared with the other big foreign locations, and is only exceeded by multinationals from smaller countries, like Israel at 23.1 per cent and Sweden at 10.0 per cent. The R&D propensity of US subsidiaries, measured by their share of value added in subsidiaries engaging in R&D compared with value added by all US subsidiaries in a host country, is highest in Germany (Mataloni & Yorgason 2002).

## Basic and Applied Research of Foreign MNEs

Further to a sectoral differentiation presented above, the activities of MNEs in Germany can also be analysed for technological fields (patent analysis) and scientific fields (publication analysis). For a set of technological and scientific fields the relative attractiveness of Germany as host for more applied (patents) and more basic-oriented (publications) research can be depicted. For doing so, a concordance of 19 patent fields and 19 science fields has been constructed. For each of these fields, the relative importance of the activities in Germany in relation to the global activities of the set of companies was calculated.[21]

---

[21] Technically, this was done by subtracting the so-called Relative Technological Advantage (RTA) of the global activities (overall patents of the sample) in a given field from the RTA of the activities in Germany (German patents) of the sample of foreign MNEs. For methodological details, see Edler et al. (2003), as well as Chapter 1 ('specialisation').

Table 6 below summarises the results of this analysis. It shows in which technological and scientific fields the set of foreign MNEs are significantly more ('positive') or less ('negative') active in Germany, in relation to their global activities in these fields. 'Neutral' are those fields in which the relative importance of the activities in Germany is about the same as for the global activities.

**Table 6.** Specialisation of foreign MNEs in Germany (N = 47): Applied vs. basic research, 1998–1999

| | | Basic research* | | |
|---|---|---|---|---|
| | | Positive | Neutral | Negative |
| *Applied research **| Positive | Biotechnology Environmental Tech. | Polymers; Materials Thermal Processes | Analysis/Measurement/Nuclear Energy; Organic Chemistry; Pharmaceuticals Mechanical Engineering Civil Engineering |
| | Neutral | | Basic Materials Chemistry | |
| | Negative | Medical Technology Chemical Processing | Telecommunications Optics | Information Technologies Electrical Engineering; Food Chemistry |

\* The profile of the publication activities of the foreign MNEs in Germany, resulting from the relative importance of the German activities in a given field (relative scientific advantage of a given field in Germany) *minus* relative importance of the global activities in that field (relative scientific advantage globally). Positive (negative) German activities are more (less) important than global activities, neutral: difference is marginal.
\*\* The profile of the patent activities of the foreign MNEs in Germany, resulting from the relative importance of the German activities in a given field (relative technological advantage of a given field in Germany) *minus* relative importance of the global activities in that field (relative technological advantage globally). Positive (negative): German activities more (less) important than global activities, neutral: difference is marginal.
Source: PCTPAT/EPA – Science Citation Index – Fraunhofer ISI calculations

First, the companies differentiate between focuses in Germany in applied vis-à-vis basic research. There is no strong link between applied and basic research in one given field, only 5 out of 19 fields have identical classifications, i.e. only in five fields do the set of companies show the same relative importance in basic and in applied research. Secondly, for the foreign MNEs, Germany is more attractive in market-related, applied research (as indicated by patent activities) than in basic research (publication activities). While in Table 6 nine technological fields show a positive German specialisation vis-à-vis the global specialisation for their patenting activities (classified as 'positive' in Table 6 in 'applied research'), only five science fields do so for publication activities (basic). Thirdly, like the German MNEs, the foreign MNEs are more active in applied research in knowledge-intensive areas, such as Biotechnology, Pharmaceuticals and Organic Chemistry. Fourthly, there are only two technological fields in which Germany has a distinct attractiveness both for applied and basic research. While this was to be expected for Environmental Technologies, given the high level of environmental regulation and the resulting take-off of Environmental Technologies in Germany some years ago (lead market), it is somewhat surprising for Biotechnology, since the general perception has been that in this area there was a drain of brains and R&D resources to other countries, especially the

USA. Apparently, this learning abroad has not harmed the German innovation and research system in Biotechnology.

To sum up, foreign firms operating in Germany increased their R&D activities in Germany in the second half of the 1990s. At the same time, their R&D behaviour (distribution of R&D expenditures on industries, R&D intensities) converged to that of German firms. In Germany foreign firms are more specialised in applied or market-related research in relation to their global and therefore also home-based activities. Hence the European und German markets for new products and services and the local production seem to determine the attractiveness of the R&D location for MNEs. However, in some areas specialisation and excellence of knowledge production are the key to attractiveness.

# Summary

Germany is one of the leading home and host countries for R&D activities by MNEs. The cross-border activities of R&D locations by companies and the exchange of knowledge are mainly within and between the knowledge-intensive regions in the United States and Western Europe.

In 2001, expenditure on R&D by German companies abroad of €11.9 billion, only marginally exceeded the €11.5 billion spent on R&D by foreign firms in Germany.

In Germany, approximately three-quarters of total domestic R&D spending is on companies linked into the international exchange of knowledge through capital integration (see Table 2 above): on the one hand, these are R&D expenditures by foreign companies in Germany (26 per cent of all R&D research in Germany);[22] on the other, this is R&D spending by German companies also involved in R&D abroad (51 per cent). For the most part, therefore, Germany's 'research laboratories' are to be found in international companies.

As an indicator of the degree of internationalisation of R&D in MNEs, it is possible to apply the share of R&D expenditure of the companies in the country with the largest R&D volume worldwide – the United States – in relation to total R&D expenditure in the respective home country. According to this, in an international comparison German companies were found to invest the highest amount in the United States; however, the value of this indicator is only marginally higher than the average for European Union member states – which are often 'small' countries. Compared with other large industrialised countries, the internationalisation of R&D in MNEs in Germany has progressed considerably in both directions. The growing international integration of national research potential is also shown in increasing shares of the respective foreign firms in terms of R&D expenditure in industrialised countries such as the United States, the United Kingdom, Germany, Sweden and Japan.[23] For Germany and the United States the R&D intensity in domestically owned companies

---

[22] This is based on the assumption that companies with foreign majority ownership also have research locations abroad, which exchange knowledge with their plants in Germany. This does not apply, however, when, for example, freign financial investors own an independent company in Germany that conducts research.

[23] Cf. OECD (ed.) (2003b: Table 64).

is slightly higher than in foreign-owned companies conducting research. In 2001, research by foreign firms in Germany was more intensive than that of their domestic competitors in the vehicle manufacturing and nutrition sectors, and equally intensive in Mechanical Engineering. In earlier years, for which more detailed sector-specific data is available, foreign companies also demonstrated a slightly higher R&D intensity in Electrical Engineering (Belitz 2002).

The internationalisation of activities developed very differently also when differentiated for technologies. In some areas the increase in international activities is very modest (Construction, Consumer Goods) or even negative (Telecommunications, Audio-Visual Technologies), in other areas the share of foreign patents out of all patents grew considerably (Semiconductors, Biotechnology, Food Processing).

Moreover, there is a dual trend to be observed as regards the motivation to do R&D abroad: while the market motive – that always played a major role – remains important, the knowledge-seeking motive to do R&D abroad has become more important over the last decade, whereby R&D activities are not accompanying production or marketing activities, but are stand-alone activities in order to generate knowledge and make it useful for the whole international company.

Thus, in the course of the 1990s the German MNEs have become extremely active in those areas that are knowledge-intensive and that need a strong linkage to specialised forefront knowledge (such as Biotechnology, Pharmaceuticals and Organic Chemistry). This does not mean, however, that Germany is not competitive in these important areas, as at the same time foreign companies are more active in applied research in these areas than on average. Rather, this reflects a growing international division of labour in knowledge-intensive areas to which both German companies and Germany as research location contribute. Finally, across the board of all technologies and science areas, Germany as host to foreign industrial R&D is more attractive in applied, market-oriented research than in basic research.

## Implications for Innovation Policy

The progressive internationalisation of R&D in Germany, both outward and inward, is an expression of the increasing overall commercial internationalisation. In a co-evolutionary process, the generation and exploitation of knowledge has also become 'more international'. This has given rise to the fear in Germany that the importance of Germany as an R&D and innovation location is becoming undermined, given the expansion of German companies' R&D capacities abroad. However, the analyses conducted in the last couple of years have shown the contrary. Foreign firms are demonstrating their interest in high quality production and R&D in Germany. Foreign MNEs have contributed to the evident expansion of the R&D and innovation potential of the economy in Germany in recent years. Foreign firms operating in Germany are increasing their R&D activities to approximately the same extent as German companies abroad. Foreign companies are involved in R&D – just as their domestic competitors are – particularly in those business areas that they consider to provide new market opportunities in the medium term, based on the competitive advantages still prevalent in their home countries. Furthermore, they tap into highly specialised pockets of excellence in Germany and thus contribute to further improvements of capacities in Germany. At the same time, German companies need to go abroad with their own R&D activities, both to adjust to these markets and to exploit specialised forefront knowledge. This in particular is true in 'neuralgic', i.e. knowledge-intensive areas such as Biotechnology, Pharmaceuticals, Organic Chemistry and Electronics. As this is a reciprocal process, Germany has won rather than lost from internationalisation of industrial R&D. It is the challenge of national innovation systems, and thus also of innovation and research policy, to constantly improve the conditions under which German MNEs (outward) and the German innovation system as such (inward) can take most advantage of international knowledge production and cross-national knowledge transfer.

The ability of MNEs to plan and organise their various activities internationally, that is, under different regulatory regimes as well, is seen as an essential advantage for these firms compared with those operating only on a national or on a more limited international basis (Ietto-Gillies 2000). Therefore more foreign firms engaging in research and more domestic companies that are more internationalised should have a positive influence on a country's technological performance. Furthermore, all actors of the national innovation system – including domestic public research institutes and funding organisations – need to adjust to the growing presence of international actors conducting R&D and strive to exploit co-operation and transfer opportunities.

Policy must react to the demands made on the national innovation system through the progressive internationalisation of knowledge generation and innovation. That includes shaping a social framework that will remove barriers to cross-frontier innovation activities in both directions and support attractive demand conditions for new products in the domestic market. It will, for example, include measures:

- in education to increase competence in languages and make occupational qualifications comparable;
- to promote mobility in skilled personnel (work and residence permits, regulation of immigration);
- to help shape and implement international technical standards and norms;
- to give foreign firms located in this country equal access to national research promotion and pre-competitive research associations;
- to prepare publicly funded research facilities for joint research ventures with MNEs and for international competition between suppliers of research;
- to ensure internationally compatible protection of intellectual property.

Altogether, the German system of innovation has largely been adequate to meet the demands of the internationalisation of R&D by MNEs. In the years to come it will be essential for the country to better link the on-going dynamic of international industrial R&D – both inward and outward – to the international dynamic of public research activities and the development from distinct national innovation systems to more globally integrated innovation systems. A starting point for a more globally oriented policy in this direction – and by far not the only path to proceed – may be an active involvement in the creation of a European Research Area (Edler & Kuhlmann 2005).

# Part 3. Performance Indicators of NSI

# 3.1 Scientific Performance in an International Comparison

Ulrich Schmoch

**Abstract.** The scientific performance of countries is generally compared on the basis of analyses in the Science Citation Index. This chapter does not only provide a snapshot of the recent performance, but also shows long-term developments of more than ten years, highlighting for example the growing relevance of catch-up countries in recent years or the restructuring of the science system after the German unification. By splitting citations into two elements, International Alignment and Scientific Regard, it can be shown that the high citation scores of the United States are largely linked to publications in highly visible journals, whereas in terms of Scientific Regard, they are only slightly better than German authors. The examination of international co-publications reveals that the European Research Area has high relevance and has already become reality. An analysis of patent applications shows an important direct contribution of science to technology in science-based fields, so the role of scientific institutions is not limited to indirect effects, as often assumed.

## Introduction

The scientific performance of a country is an essential basis for its technological performance; therefore this topic is regularly analysed in the context of the reporting on technological competitiveness of Germany. A major contribution of science to technological development is the education of well-trained staff, the quality of education substantially depending on the performance of scientific research. The results of scientific research are also an important direct input for technological development. However, the linkages between science and technology are often indirect and less obvious, as in many cases a distinct lag between activities in science and their effect on technology can be observed.

The performance of science is difficult to measure, the more so as the structures in specific disciplines often differ considerably. The statistical analysis of scientific publications has proved to be meaningful, as long as they are conducted with a careful methodology. The analyses of this contribution do not only refer to scientific areas with close relation to technology, but to the natural, medical, life, and engineering sciences in total.

Country comparisons in science are generally conducted with the database Science Citation Index. Whereas the quality of the referring results is highly acknowledged for the natural and life sciences, the findings in fields of engineering often do not meet the expectations. In a special section, the methodological reasons for this phenomenon are examined in more detail by the example of Mechanical Engineering.

*U. Schmoch, C. Rammer and H. Legler (eds.), National Systems of Innovation in Comparison, 69–87.*

In addition to the performance measures, we analyse international scientific co-operation, as it plays an increasing role in recent years. Again, bibliometric methods are used for this purpose.

The contribution of scientific institutions to technology is primarily seen in indirect mechanisms such as the provision of information on new scientific trends to enterprises. In the last section, the direct contribution of scientific institutions to technology is investigated by analysing their patent applications with reference to science-based technology fields.

## Methodology

The statistical analyses of scientific publications were conducted in the database Science Citation Index (SCI), a multi-disciplinary database with a broad coverage of fields. The searches refer to the natural and engineering sciences as well as the medical and life sciences. The database primarily covers English language journals which is unproblematic for most fields. However, the German engineering sciences which mostly publish in German language are covered insufficiently. In general, the SCI includes journals which are frequently cited and thus have a high visibility, so that publications of higher value are considered. Already the fact of a registration in the SCI can be taken as a first indication of quality.

Apart of the absolute number of publications recorded until the year 2003, citations are used as specific performance indicators. For calculating annual citation rates, the citations of the particular publication year and the two following years are included, so that for every year, a citation window of three years is considered. In consequence, citation rates can be calculated only until the publication year 2001. For the citation analysis, the broadly accepted quality standards were applied,[1] for instance self-citations were excluded.

For a more detailed analysis of citation scores, the calculation of two additional indicators, the 'journal-standardized Scientific Regard' (SR) and the 'International Alignment' (IA) prove to be useful (Grupp et al. 2001). The Scientific Regard indicates whether the publications of a country/region are more or less frequently cited than the publications in the journals which they are published in. Positive indices point to citations scores above average; values of zero correspond to the world average. The relation to the specific journals compensates the disadvantages of countries which have a less good access to highly visible English language journals. The indicator of Scientific Regard is defined as follows:

$$SR_i = 100 \tanh \ln (OBS_i / EXP_i). \tag{1}$$

Therein, $EXP_i$ is the number of expected citations for publications of a country i, and $OBS_i$ the observed citation of this country. The number of expected citations $EXP_i$ has to be determined on an article-by-article base and measures the average citation frequency of the selected journals. We use the natural logarithm and the *tangens hyperpolicus* (and a multiplication by 100) in order to transform the results into a measure that ranges between +100 and −100.

---

[1]  See for instance Moed (2005) or van Raan (2004).

Differently from the Scientific Regard, the International Alignment shows whether the authors of a country publish in internationally visible or less visible journals, again with relation to the world average. By a high share of publications in internationally visible journals, an intensive participation in international scientific discourses is documented. Similar to the SR index, positive IA indices shows an International Alignment above average. The IA index is calculated as follows:

$$IA_i = 100 \tanh \ln (EXP_i / OBS_w). \qquad (2)$$

The notions quoted have the same meaning as above. The Index w refers to all countries worldwide.

For compensating possible distortions of the database coverage with regard to the analysis of absolute publication numbers, we introduce the specialisation index RLA (Relative Literature Advantage) which is calculated in the following way (for the concept of specialisation see Chapter 1):

$$RLA_{ij} = 100 \tanh \ln [(Publ_{ij} / ._i Publ_{ij}) / (._j Publ_{ij} / ._{ij} Publ_{ij})]. \qquad (3)$$

In this formula, i refers to the country and j to the field analysed. Positive values indicate a specialisation above average, negative ones a specialisation below average with the world average as reference.

## International Comparison of Publications

Analysing the development in time of publication numbers, it is less meaningful to consider absolute values, because the journal coverage of the SCI steadily changes. Therefore we document in Table 1 the share of selected countries with reference to all SCI publications.

The high shares of the United Kingdom and Canada in relation to Germany stand out, a fact which can be explained by the strong presence of these countries in English language journals. As to Germany, a steady increase of its share since the beginning of the 1990s can be noted which is primarily due to increasing activities of research institutions from East Germany. However, at the recent edge, a slight decrease can be observed which also applies to the United States and the United Kingdom in a similar way. This effect documents an increased scientific activity of East European, Asiatic, and South American countries which appears in the table in the growing shares of new member countries of the European Union (EU new).[2] In any case, the rollback of long established countries by catch-up countries is a relevant trend.

As to the citation rates, good positions of the United States, Switzerland and the Netherlands appear (Table 2). As to the German figures, a distinct drop at the beginning of the 1990s emerges, followed by a continuous heightening until the end of the 1990s. This observation can be ascribed to the restructuring of science in the eastern federal states which has been concluded meanwhile and has no further effect on the recent figures. Remarkably, the citation scores of countries with absolutely moderate

---

[2] Including the candidate countries Romania, Bulgaria, and Turkey.

citation levels improve in recent years, in particular the scores of France, Italy, the new EU countries and Japan.

**Table 1.** Shares of selected countries and regions within all SCI publications (in per cent)

| Country/region | 1989 | 1990 | 1991 | 1992 | 1993 | 1994 | 1995 | 1996 | 1997 | 1998 | 1999 | 2000 | 2001 | 2002 | 2003 |
|---|---|---|---|---|---|---|---|---|---|---|---|---|---|---|---|
| USA | 36.2 | 36.5 | 36.7 | 35.7 | 36.0 | 35.1 | 35.1 | 34.3 | 33.7 | 32.9 | 32.3 | 31.9 | 32.1 | 31.9 | 31.7 |
| JPN | 7.9 | 8.1 | 8.3 | 8.7 | 8.8 | 9.0 | 9.1 | 9.5 | 9.5 | 10.0 | 10.2 | 10.2 | 10.2 | 10.1 | 10.0 |
| GER | 6.3 | 6.4 | 7.3 | 7.5 | 7.4 | 7.8 | 7.9 | 8.2 | 8.6 | 9.0 | 9.0 | 9.0 | 9.0 | 8.8 | 8.7 |
| GBR | 9.0 | 8.9 | 9.1 | 9.1 | 9.3 | 9.5 | 9.5 | 9.6 | 9.3 | 9.4 | 9.3 | 9.4 | 9.1 | 8.8 | 8.6 |
| FRA | 5.4 | 5.4 | 5.5 | 5.9 | 6.0 | 6.1 | 6.3 | 6.4 | 6.6 | 6.7 | 6.7 | 6.6 | 6.6 | 6.4 | 6.4 |
| SUI | 1.4 | 1.5 | 1.6 | 1.6 | 1.7 | 1.8 | 1.8 | 1.8 | 1.9 | 1.9 | 1.9 | 1.9 | 1.9 | 1.9 | 1.9 |
| CAN | 4.7 | 4.7 | 4.8 | 4.8 | 4.8 | 4.8 | 4.7 | 4.7 | 4.4 | 4.3 | 4.3 | 4.3 | 4.1 | 4.2 | 4.3 |
| SWE | 1.9 | 1.9 | 1.9 | 1.8 | 1.9 | 1.9 | 2.0 | 2.1 | 2.1 | 2.1 | 2.1 | 2.0 | 2.1 | 2.1 | 2.0 |
| ITA | 3.0 | 3.1 | 3.2 | 3.5 | 3.5 | 3.7 | 3.9 | 4.2 | 4.2 | 4.3 | 4.4 | 4.4 | 4.6 | 4.7 | 4.8 |
| NED | 2.2 | 2.3 | 2.3 | 2.3 | 2.5 | 2.5 | 2.6 | 2.6 | 2.7 | 2.6 | 2.5 | 2.5 | 2.5 | 2.5 | 2.5 |
| FIN | – | – | – | – | – | – | – | – | – | – | 1.0 | 1.0 | 1.0 | 1.0 | 1.0 |
| KOR | – | – | – | – | – | – | – | – | – | – | 1.7 | 1.9 | 2.1 | 2.3 | 2.6 |
| EU-15 | – | – | – | – | – | – | – | – | – | – | 40.9 | 40.7 | 40.6 | 39.9 | 39.4 |
| EU new | – | – | – | – | – | – | – | – | – | – | – | – | 4.6 | 4.9 | 5.0 |
| World | 100 | 100 | 100 | 100 | 100 | 100 | 100 | 100 | 100 | 100 | 100 | 100 | 100 | 100 | 100 |

Sources: SCI – searches and calculations of the Leiden University (CWTS) – calculations of Fraunhofer ISI

**Table 2.** Citation rates (three years window) of selected countries and regions with regard to SCI publication (without self-citations)

| Country/region | 1989 | 1990 | 1991 | 1992 | 1993 | 1994 | 1995 | 1996 | 1997 | 1998 | 1999 | 2000 | 2001 |
|---|---|---|---|---|---|---|---|---|---|---|---|---|---|
| USA | 4.3 | 4.4 | 4.5 | 4.5 | 4.8 | 4.8 | 4.8 | 4.8 | 5.0 | 4.7 | 5.1 | 4.9 | 4.9 |
| JPN | 2.4 | 2.4 | 2.4 | 2.4 | 2.5 | 2.5 | 2.5 | 2.4 | 2.6 | 2.5 | 2.6 | 2.4 | 2.6 |
| GER | 3.0 | 3.2 | 2.9 | 3.1 | 3.4 | 3.4 | 3.4 | 3.5 | 3.6 | 3.3 | 3.6 | 3.6 | 3.6 |
| GBR | 3.1 | 3.3 | 3.2 | 3.4 | 3.6 | 3.5 | 3.6 | 3.5 | 3.9 | 3.6 | 3.7 | 3.6 | 3.8 |
| FRA | 2.7 | 2.9 | 3.0 | 3.0 | 3.2 | 3.1 | 3.2 | 3.2 | 3.3 | 3.1 | 3.2 | 3.2 | 3.4 |
| SUI | 4.5 | 4.7 | 4.7 | 4.7 | 5.0 | 5.2 | 5.0 | 5.1 | 5.4 | 4.7 | 5.1 | 5.0 | 5.0 |
| CAN | 2.8 | 3.0 | 3.0 | 3.2 | 3.3 | 3.5 | 3.4 | 3.6 | 3.8 | 3.6 | 3.8 | 3.4 | 3.8 |
| SWE | 3.1 | 3.2 | 3.2 | 3.4 | 3.5 | 3.6 | 3.6 | 3.5 | 3.7 | 3.4 | 3.7 | 3.8 | 3.9 |
| ITA | 2.3 | 2.4 | 2.6 | 2.6 | 2.8 | 2.9 | 2.9 | 2.9 | 3.1 | 2.9 | 3.2 | 2.7 | 3.0 |
| NED | 3.3 | 3.5 | 3.6 | 3.7 | 3.8 | 3.9 | 4.0 | 3.8 | 4.2 | 3.9 | 4.4 | 4.1 | 4.3 |
| FIN | – | – | – | – | – | – | – | – | – | – | 3.2 | 3.7 | 3.6 |
| KOR | – | – | – | – | – | – | – | – | – | – | 1.7 | 1.9 | 1.9 |
| EU-15 | – | – | – | – | – | – | – | – | – | – | 3.3 | 3.3 | 3.3 |
| EU new | – | – | – | – | – | – | – | – | – | – | 1.5 | 1.4 | 1.7 |
| World | 2.7 | 2.8 | 2.9 | 2.9 | 3.1 | 3.0 | 3.0 | 3.0 | 3.2 | 2.9 | 3.1 | 3.0 | 3.2 |

Sources: SCI – searches and calculations of the Leiden University (CWTS) – calculations of Fraunhofer ISI

The journal-standardised Scientific Regard of Germany slightly decreases since the middle of the 1990s, but at the recent edge, the level is still respectable. It is comparable to that of other industrialised countries, such as the United States, the United Kingdom, Sweden, or Finland. In the long term perspective, the quite low value for the United Kingdom in the period of 1996 to 1998 is striking which is probably linked to the substantial university reform of that time. As to the Scientific Regard, the values for Japan, South Korea but also the new EU member states are less favourable, however, the performance of the new EU members considerably improves in recent years. The index of the old EU member countries (EU-15) is only slightly above the world average. This is due to the fact that the above average values of the Netherlands, the United Kingdom, Denmark, Sweden, or Germany are counter-balanced by below average values of Italy, Spain, Portugal, or Greece.

As to the second derived citation index, the International Alignment (IA index), Germany demonstrates, in contrast to the Scientific Regard, a steady improvement since mid 1999 (Tables 3 and 4). In recent years, a stabilisation at the level reached becomes apparent. All in all, German authors succeeded increasingly in publishing their articles in internationally well reputed journals. Also with regard to the International Alignment, Japan and South Korea have a less favourable position. Furthermore, the extremely low International Alignment of the new EU member countries has to be mentioned. In contrast, the IA indices of Switzerland and the Netherlands are extremely positive similar to their good values of the Scientific Regard. With reference to the IA index, the United States are in the first position as expected. Thus, the high citation scores of the United States are primarily due to their presence in journals of broad international visibility, whereas the Scientific Regard is nearly equivalent to that of Germany. Nevertheless, it is striking that the non-English speaking country Switzerland nearly reaches the level of the International Alignment of the United States.

**Table 3.** Journal-standardised Scientific Regard of selected countries and regions of SCI publications (without self-citations)

| Country/region | 1989 | 1990 | 1991 | 1992 | 1993 | 1994 | 1995 | 1996 | 1997 | 1998 | 1999 | 2000 | 2001 |
|---|---|---|---|---|---|---|---|---|---|---|---|---|---|
| USA | 9 | 9 | 9 | 10 | 10 | 10 | 10 | 11 | 11 | 11 | 9 | 9 | 9 |
| JPN | –6 | –7 | –7 | –7 | –9 | –7 | –7 | –8 | –7 | –4 | –7 | –6 | –7 |
| GER | 9 | 11 | 6 | 8 | 10 | 10 | 9 | 9 | 7 | 8 | 7 | 7 | 8 |
| GBR | 8 | 10 | 8 | 9 | 10 | 10 | 9 | 5 | 4 | 3 | 8 | 9 | 9 |
| FRA | –1 | 2 | 1 | 2 | 3 | 2 | 4 | 4 | 3 | 2 | 1 | 3 | 2 |
| SUI | 17 | 20 | 17 | 19 | 18 | 24 | 20 | 23 | 22 | 17 | 15 | 17 | 17 |
| CAN | –2 | 0 | –1 | 2 | 1 | 5 | 5 | 6 | 5 | 9 | 5 | 9 | 3 |
| SWE | 15 | 10 | 10 | 12 | 12 | 15 | 12 | 13 | 14 | 12 | 15 | 9 | 8 |
| ITA | –11 | –10 | –8 | –7 | –8 | –4 | –4 | –5 | –5 | –4 | –3 | –2 | –4 |
| NED | 10 | 12 | 11 | 13 | 11 | 12 | 13 | 10 | 15 | 14 | 10 | 7 | 11 |
| FIN | – | – | – | – | – | – | – | – | – | – | 2 | 7 | 8 |
| KOR | – | – | – | – | – | – | – | – | – | – | –16 | –11 | –11 |
| EU-15 | – | – | – | – | – | – | – | – | – | – | 2 | 2 | 2 |
| EU new | – | – | – | – | – | – | – | – | – | – | –20 | –19 | –15 |
| World | 0 | 0 | 0 | 0 | 0 | 0 | 0 | 0 | 0 | 0 | 0 | 0 | 0 |

Sources: SCI – searches and calculations of the Leiden University (CWTS) – calculations of Fraunhofer ISI

All in all, Germany should not only strive for high values of Scientific Regard, but also of International Alignment for getting good access to the international scientific discourse. In this context, it is not realistic to achieve the very high indices of the United States, as in the Science Citation Index, American journals are very strongly

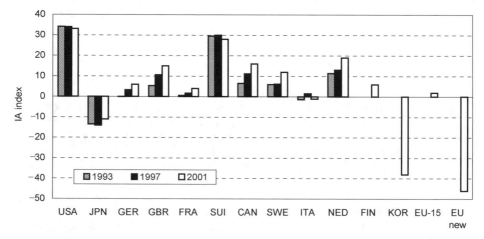

Sources: SCI – searches and calculations of the Leiden University (CWTS) – calculations of Fraunhofer ISI

**Fig. 1.** International Alignment of selected countries and regions as to SCI publications (without self-citations)

**Table 4.** International Alignment of selected countries and regions as to SCI publications (without self-citations)

| Country/region | 1989 | 1990 | 1991 | 1992 | 1993 | 1994 | 1995 | 1996 | 1997 | 1998 | 1999 | 2000 | 2001 |
|---|---|---|---|---|---|---|---|---|---|---|---|---|---|
| USA | 36 | 35 | 35 | 35 | 34 | 35 | 35 | 35 | 34 | 36 | 36 | 34 | 33 |
| JPN | −8 | −10 | −11 | −11 | −13 | −13 | 15 | −17 | −14 | −14 | −14 | −18 | −11 |
| GER | 2 | 3 | −3 | −2 | 0 | 0 | 3 | 4 | 3 | 3 | 5 | 7 | 6 |
| GBR | 4 | 7 | 4 | 7 | 5 | 5 | 7 | 6 | 11 | 10 | 12 | 15 | 15 |
| FRA | 1 | 1 | 4 | 1 | 1 | 0 | −1 | 0 | 2 | 2 | 0 | 3 | 4 |
| SUI | 34 | 31 | 32 | 29 | 30 | 29 | 29 | 29 | 30 | 29 | 30 | 29 | 28 |
| CAN | 5 | 5 | 5 | 7 | 7 | 8 | 7 | 10 | 11 | 11 | 13 | 11 | 16 |
| SWE | 4 | 8 | 5 | 8 | 6 | 8 | 8 | 7 | 6 | 8 | 8 | 11 | 12 |
| ITA | −2 | −3 | −3 | −2 | −1 | 0 | 0 | 0 | 2 | 1 | 2 | 1 | −1 |
| NED | 11 | 11 | 12 | 12 | 11 | 12 | 14 | 13 | 13 | 14 | 21 | 20 | 19 |
| FIN | – | – | – | – | – | – | – | – | – | – | 8 | 10 | 6 |
| KOR | – | – | – | – | – | – | – | – | – | – | −45 | −38 | −38 |
| EU-15 | – | – | – | – | – | – | – | – | – | – | 1 | 3 | 2 |
| EU new | – | – | – | – | – | – | – | – | – | – | −50 | −47 | −46 |
| World | 0 | 0 | 0 | 0 | 0 | 0 | 0 | 0 | 0 | 0 | 0 | 0 | 0 |

Sources: SCI – searches and calculations of the Leiden University (CWTS) – calculations of Fraunhofer ISI

represented. The graphical representation according to Fig. 1 shows that the International Alignment of Germany should be further improved in comparison to other countries.

## Profiles of Industrialised Countries

For a more detailed analysis, the calculation of the SR and IA indices were differentiated by 26 scientific fields whereof 18 show up close relations to technology, the other 8 having a more general character. As to the SR index for Germany, all fields reach values above the world average (Fig. 2). In particular, the values for Optics, Nuclear Technology, Polymers, and Food are excellent. The quite positive indices in Process Technology, Environmental Technology, Thermal Processes, and Civil Engineering may have a bias link to the limited coverage of these fields in the SCI.[3]

For an appropriate assessment of the German data, the comparison to the profile of Switzerland may be helpful, as this country has a relevant German-speaking part. Furthermore, it is interesting to see which specific structures are linked to the very high average values of this country. Similar to Germany, the Swiss profile is far from being homogeneous. But in all fields, the indices are significantly above the international average, and in nearly all cases, they are also above the German values. Finally, the high indices in large areas such as Electrical Engineering, Nuclear Engineering, Basic Chemistry, Physics, or Medicine are primarily relevant for the high total value.

As to the International Alignment of German publications, the structures are much more heterogeneous as those for the Scientific Regard, although a similar total index is reached on average. But distinctively positive indices in fields such as Multi-disciplinary Journals, Basic Chemistry, or Control Technology are contrasted with negative ones in Food or Process Technology (Fig. 3). But the negative indices are primarily linked to fields of the engineering sciences where the adequate coverage of German contributions in the SCI is doubtable (Schmoch 2005: 25ff). The positive index for Biotechnology and the at least average index for Data Processing have to be highlighted. In the perspective of a leading industrialised country such as Germany, IA indices between five and ten points above the world average should be aimed at. With reference to this level, the situation in many fields such as Organic Chemistry, Medicine, Ecology/Climate, Electrical Engineering, or Mathematics may be improved. Again, the comparison with Switzerland is interesting. The high average value of this country is linked to high indices in nearly all fields with values between ten and twenty. This is even valid for most fields of the engineering sciences. This example shows that even for a non-American country it is possible to achieve high indices of International Alignment. Obviously, Swiss authors publish their articles in different journals than German ones do.

---

[3] See further below.

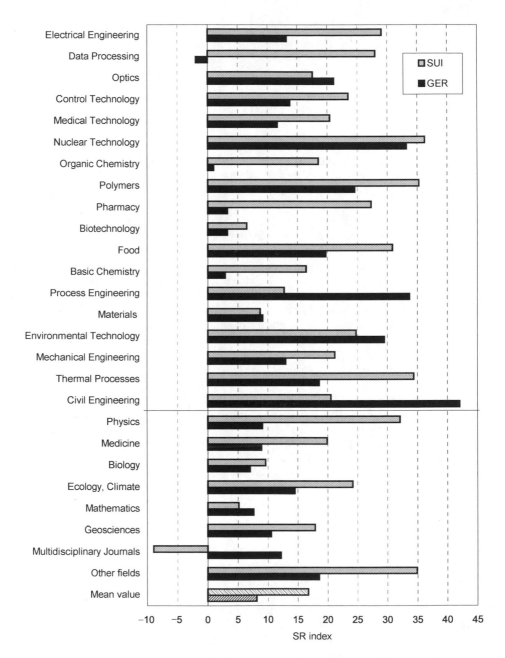

Sources: SCI – searches and calculations of the Leiden University (CWTS) – calculations of Fraunhofer ISI

**Fig. 2.** Scientific Regard of Germany and Switzerland as to SCI publications (without self citations) broken down by scientific fields, 2001

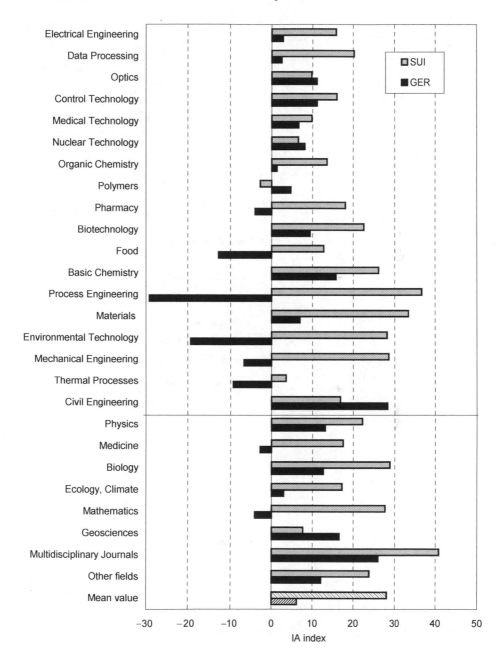

Sources: SCI – searches and calculations of the University of Leiden (CWTS) – calculations of Fraunhofer ISI

**Fig. 3.** International Alignment of Germany and Switzerland as to SCI publications (without self citations) broken down by scientific fields, 2001

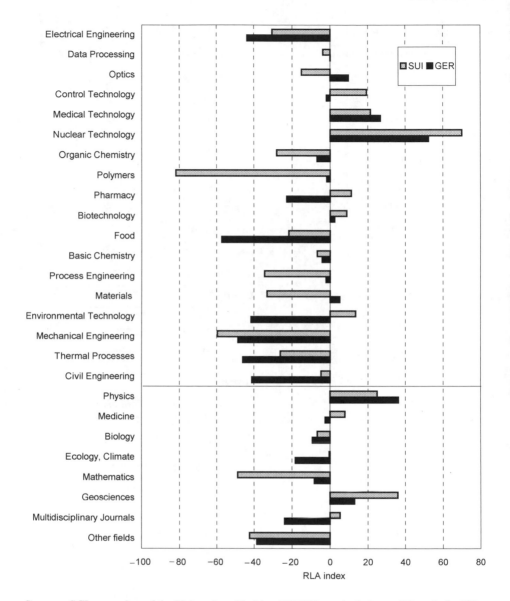

Sources: SCI – searches of the University of Leiden (CWTS) – calculations of Fraunhofer ISI

**Fig. 4.** Specialisation profile of Germany and Switzerland as to SCI publications broken down by scientific fields, 2003

Up to now, the analysis of scientific structures was made on the basis of the indices for Scientific Regard and International Alignment. A further important aspect is the number of publications in different fields in comparison to other countries, represented in terms of specialisation. In analogy to the Revealed Patent Advantage (RPA) for patents, we have calculated an RLA index, explained in the methodological section above. The profile for Germany is shown in Fig. 4, showing an above average specialisation in the fields Optics, Medical Technology, Nuclear Technology, Polymers, Basic Chemistry, Process Technology, Materials, and Physics. At first sight, the German profile is quite similar to the Swiss one; however, a closer look reveals various differences, in particular a higher specialisation of Germany in Optics, Organic Chemistry, Polymers, Process Engineering, Materials, Physics, and Mathematics, and *vice versa* a higher specialisation of Switzerland in Control Technology, Pharmacy, Food, Environmental Technology, Geosciences, or Multidisciplinary Journals. So the country profiles prove to be quite characteristic, and a comparison with former years reveals a high stability in time, also for smaller countries. On the basis of these profiles, it is possible to generate, by the so-called multidimensional scaling, a kind of maps where the local proximity indicates a proximity of profiles.[4]

A remarkable point are the low German indices in the engineering fields Environmental Technology, Mechanical Engineering, Thermal Processes, and Civil Engineering, and for Switzerland these indices are also low in Mechanical Engineering and Thermal Processes. We will discuss the reason for this finding in the following section.

## Coverage of Mechanical Engineering in the Science Citation Index

In the German specialisation profile according to Fig. 4, the strong negative specialisation in Mechanical Engineering is striking, as according to the general perception that scientific performance of Germany in this field is quite strong. Against this background, we analysed in more detail whether German publications in Mechanical Engineering are covered adequately in the Science Citation Index. The case of Mechanical Engineering may be considered as an example for other fields of engineering such as Environmental Technology, Thermal Processes, or Civil Engineering. A decisive criterion of such an analysis is the verification of the journal coverage of a database. For this purpose, we analysed the structures of the SCI category code Mechanical Engineering in the publication year 2003. Looking at the journals with the highest number of publications in SCI, the top 20 are English language journals with a focus on American ones. As to the journals with the highest number of articles by German authors, a similar picture appears, as illustrated in Table 5. Among the ten most relevant journals, only one has a German basis (BWK).

For assessing this finding, we analysed the structures in the database COMPENDEX, an international database with a focus on engineering sciences, in parallel. Again, we examined the most frequently appearing journals of German authors in Mechanical Engineering for the year 2003, leading to a fair mix of German and English language journals (Table 5).[5] This obvious difference in the coverage of journals implies a different relative position of Germany compared to other countries. In the Science Citation Index, the share of authors from Germany in Mechanical Engineering is 3.4 per cent, in COMPENDEX, it is much higher with 4.5 per cent. In addition to this comparison of the SCI and COMPENDEX, we considered the database DOMA (TEMA) which covers Mechanical and Process Engineering with an explicit focus on German institutions. In this case, the ten most frequently appearing journals of

---

[4] Such a map for twelve countries has been realised in Schmoch (2005)

[5] A similar structure appears, if the set of the top journals is enlarged to 20 or 30.

German authors in Mechanical Engineering are German ones; so the set is totally different to the coverage in the SCI and also COMPEDEX.

This different journal coverage of the three databases implies a completely different ranking of the most relevant institutions, as documented in Table 6. For instance,

**Table 5.** Top 10 Journals where German authors published most frequently in Mechanical Engineering as to different databases

| Rank | SCI | COMPENDEX | DOMA |
|------|-----|-----------|------|
| 1 | Proceedings of the Combustion Institute | VDI Berichte | O + P – Ölhydraulik und Pneumatik |
| 2 | WEAR | ZWF – Zeitschrift für wirtschaftlichen Fabrikbetrieb | Antriebstechnik |
| 3 | Journal of Aerosol Science | Industrial Diamond Review | Drei R International |
| 4 | BWK – Das Energie-Fachmagazin | CIRP Annals – Manufacturing Technology | Tribologie und Schmierungstechnik |
| 5 | Journal of Sound and Vibration | ThyssenKrupp Techforum | bbr, Wasser und Rohrbau |
| 6 | International Journal of Heat and Mass Transfer | Kunststoffe Plast Europe | Fluid |
| 7 | International Journal of Plasticity | WEAR | ATZ – Automobiltechnische Zeitschrift |
| 8 | Computer Methods in Applied Mechanics and Engineering | ZEV Rail Glasers Annalen | SMM – Schweizer Maschinenmarkt |
| 9 | Mechanical Systems and Signal Processing | Aufbereitungstechnik/ Mineral Processing | MM – Maschinenmarkt. Das IndustrieMagazin |
| 10 | Applied Thermal Engineering | Surface and Coatings Technology | Materialwissenschaft und Werkstofftechnik |

Sources: SCISEARCH (STN), COMPENDEX (STN), DOMA (FIZ Technik) – calculations of Fraunhofer ISI

**Table 6.** Top 10 German institutions in Mechanical Engineering as to different databases

| Rank | SCI | COMPENDEX | DOMA |
|------|-----|-----------|------|
| 1 | Univ. Karlsruhe | TU Hannover | RWTH Aachen |
| 2 | RWTH Aachen | RWTH Aachen | Univ. Karlsruhe |
| 3 | Univ. Stuttgart | TU Berlin | TU München |
| 4 | TU Darmstadt | Univ. Karlsruhe | Univ. Stuttgart |
| 5 | TU München | Fraunhofer Gesellschaft | TU Dresden |
| 6 | Univ. Erlangen-Nürnberg | Univ. Bremen | Univ. Bochum |
| 7 | TU Berlin | TU Braunschweig | TU Braunschweig |
| 8 | Univ. Bochum | Max-Planck-Gesellschaft | TU Darmstadt |
| 9 | DLR | TU Dresden | Univ. Bremen |
| 10 | TU Braunschweig | TU Darmstadt | Univ. Hannover |

Sources: SCISEARCH (STN), COMPENDEX (STN), DOMA (FIZ Technik) – calculations of Fraunhofer ISI

the University of Karlsruhe appears in all three lists, but on different ranks, or the University of Breme is only in two lists among the top institutions.

To summarise, the structures in a field such as Mechanical Engineering considerably depend on the choice of the database. In this context, we have to be aware that the structures in the engineering sciences are quite different to those of the natural and life sciences. The engineering sciences have a general orientation as to theories and concepts on the one hand. But as their major subjects refer to technology, they have a distinct local orientation on the other hand (Rip 1992: 257; Fuchs 1994). This means in particular that scientists in engineering have to interact with enterprises to get access to technology, and a large part of their articles are published in local journals which are also read by engineers in enterprises. This distinct orientation on local journals implies that countries with a large domestic language area such as Germany, France, Italy or Spain are not adequately represented in the Science Citation Index. Of course, the different results for the Science Citation Index, COMPENDEX, and DOMA are partly due to differences in the definition of Mechanical Engineering. However, the latter can not explain the enormous differences in the journal coverage and in the ranking of leading institutions. In addition, there is no systematic research which type of publications should be considered for appropriately assessing the scientific performance in engineering. In this section, we exclusively examined publications in journals. Furthermore, contributions to conferences or to books might be relevant. As to German authors, the SCI does not include any conference contributions for the year 2003, as the focus of the SCI is again on English language conferences. In contrast, COMPENDEX includes a relevant number of conference contributions of German authors, but the database does not cover contributions to books. In DOMA all types of publications are included, but with a distinct German focus. All in all, the standard SCI indicators can not be used for the engineering sciences in countries with large own language areas.

## International Co-operation in Science

In the present world with improved communication and transport facilities, the international exchange between scientists is important. This phenomenon can be analysed systematically by means of joint publications by authors located in different countries. There is still no clear consensus which types of co-operations are reflected by co-publications (Laudel 2002; Katz & Martin 1997), but this approach has proved to be valid to reflect the basic structures of international co-operation (Glänzel & Schubert 2004). We define each publication with authors from at least two countries as international co-publication. If several authors from the same countries are involved, this publication will be counted only once. However, in the case of several authors from several countries, double counting may happen, as we do not apply fractional counts. This approach is methodologically justified by the fact that the investment in an international co-publication is much higher than in publications with authors of one institution or of one country. Glänzel and de Lange (2002) have shown that in particular in the life sciences, international co-publications are more highly cited than purely national publications. The analyses presented below were conducted on the level of all publications and differentiated according to four segments defined by category codes of the SCI.

The increased relevance of international co-operation for science is impressively illustrated in Fig. 5 where the share of international publications of German authors

has increased from hardly 20 to 40 per cent between 1990 and 2003. This very high
level is probably not representative for all scientific publications, as the SCI reflects a
selection of journals with high international visibility where a higher share of international publications can be expected. At the same time, the SCI publications make
up an important part of the scientific output, so that the increasing internationalisation
obviously is a highly relevant phenomenon of present science, the more so as the end
of the development is obviously not reached yet.

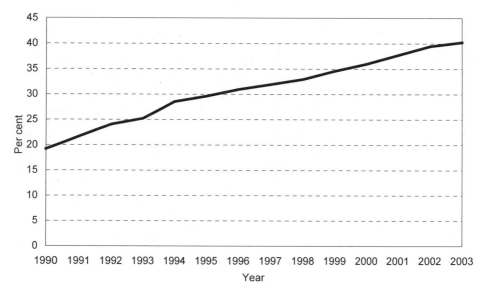

Sources: SCISEARCH (STN) – calculations of Fraunhofer ISI

**Fig. 5.** Share of SCI publications of German authors with at least one foreign partner

The present share of 40 per cent for Germany seems to be very high, however, other
countries, such as France, the United Kingdom, Italy, Canada, the Netherlands, or
Finland display similar shares; Sweden and Switzerland even demonstrate a higher
level. In conclusion, the high level of internationalisation of science is not a specific
feature of Germany, but applies to nearly all other advanced countries. Only the co-
publication shares of the United States, Japan and South Korea are distinctly lower
with 20 to 25 per cent. In the case of Japan and South Korea, their geographical
isolation may play a role. In the case of the United States, it may be assumed that the
number of US scientists is so large that external co-operations are less necessary.

Looking at broad segments of science, the share of co-publications of German
authors in the natural sciences is the highest with a present level of almost 50 per cent.
In contrast, the co-publication level in medicine is relatively moderate with 30 per
cent. In all segments the increase between 1995 and 2003 is considerable.

For analysing the co-publications in more detail, their absolute number was trans-
formed into an index allowing for a joint representation with their growth rates in one
figure. Looking at the partner countries of German authors, the co-publications increased
in all cases. In particular, the co-publications with European partners intensified
considerably. At the recent edge illustrated in Fig. 6, the number of co-publications with

European countries has reached a distinctly higher level than co-publications with the United States, and also the growth rates since 1995 are higher with regard to EU countries. Thus the empirical results support the assumption of an emergence of a European research area.

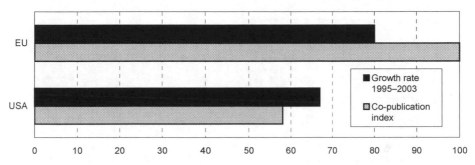

Sources: SCISEARCH (STN) – calculations of Fraunhofer ISI

**Fig. 6.** Co-publications of German authors in SCI journals with partners of EU countries and the United States by frequency (index for the largest region = 100) and growth rate

With regard to the absolute number of co-publications by country, the United States are the most important co-operation partner of Germany, as expected. But this does not mean that German scientists have a special preference for a co-operation with their American colleagues. This statement can only hold on the basis of a normalised ranking where the number of co-publications is referred to the country size which may be represented by the absolute number of publications of the analysed partner country. In this way, a preference index can be constructed where the worldwide co-operations define the average value 1, and preference indexes above 1 indicate co-operations above the expectation level. According to this specific index, documented in Fig. 7, German scientists have a specific preference for co-operations with their colleagues from Austria and Switzerland. The language affinity obviously plays a considerable role in scientific co-operation. The Netherlands as neighbour country follow in the third position. But then the neighbour country France does not follow, but the Scandinavian countries Denmark, Sweden, Norway, and Finland. Nevertheless, local proximity plays a role with regard to France as reflected in the higher preference for France compared to that for the United Kingdom, although the knowledge of the English language in Germany is higher than of the French one.

Similar to the preference index in the perspective of German scientists, it is possible to reciprocally calculate a preference index in the perspective of the partner countries. Also in this perspective, Austria and Switzerland have a special preference for co-operations with Germany and the Netherlands, Denmark and Sweden follow in a similar way; again, the United States, Japan, Canada and South Korea have a lower relevance.

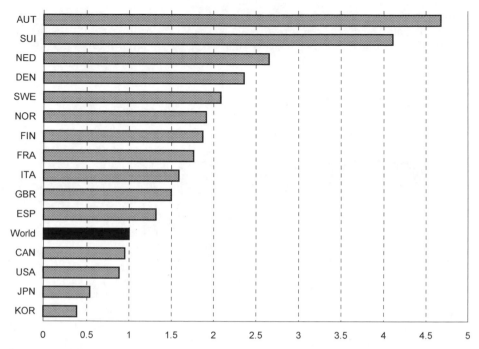

Sources: SCISEARCH (STN) – calculations of Fraunhofer IS

**Fig. 7.** Country preferences of German scientists for co-publications in SCI journals, 2003[6]


## Direct Contribution of Public Research Institutions to Technology

Public research institutions, in particular universities, contribute to the technological competitiveness primarily by the education of qualified staff. As to research, their focus is on the generation of new knowledge without the direct intention to achieve results relevant for application. However, in recent years, there is an increased expectation that public research institutions should directly contribute to technology, as reflected in the growing patent activities of universities (OECD [ed.] 2003c).

It can not be assumed that scientific research contributes to all areas of technology in the same way, but a focus on science-based technology fields can be expected. In this context, the term 'science-based fields' means that proximity between basic research and applied research exists, so that the results of basic research are quickly transferred into application. In this context, we examined the patent activities of non-profit research organisations from Germany at the German Patent and Trade Mark Office (DPMA), that is, domestic applications. The analysis refers to the period of 1990 to 2001 where German universities rarely were active as patent applicants, and in most cases the university researchers applied their inventions either privately or transferred their rights to firms and appeared as inventors. In the German case, patent

---

[6] Index: Observed co-publication share in relation to the expected one, normalised by the world average.

applications with university origin can often be identified by the title 'Professor'. In Germany, the title 'Professor' exclusively refers to universities; and professors generally indicate their title in official documents such as patent applications. According to expert interviews, we know that the number of university-based patents without professors as inventors or applicants has increased in recent years and achieved a relevant level. Hence the number of universities' patents is underestimated in our sample, but still a large sample is covered.

The analysis of non-university institutions was performed by name searches in the applicant fields, because these institutions have been active applicants for many years. Non-university institutes represent about 35 per cent of all patent applications by scientific institutions in Germany.

The analyses focus on eleven technology fields which proved to be the most science-based ones according to the operationalisation described above. The definition of these fields is documented in Table 7; they cover about 40 per cent of all applications of German origin.

**Table 7.** Definition of selected science-based technology fields by codes of the International Patent Classification (IPC)

| Technology field | IPC definition |
|---|---|
| Biotechnology | C12M, C12N, C12P, C12Q, C12R, C12S |
| Semiconductors | H01L, B81, G11C |
| Organic Chemistry | C07 |
| Data Processing | G06, G10L |
| Optics | G02, G03B, G03C, G03D, G03F, G03G, G03H, H01S |
| Telecommunications | G08C, H01P, H01Q, H03, H04B, H04H, H04J, H04K, H04L, H04M, H04N, H04Q |
| Materials | C01, C03C, C04, C21, C22 |
| Measuring and Control | G01, G04F, G04G, G05B, G05D, G05F |
| Surface Technology | B05C, B05D, B82, C23, C25D |
| Medical Technology | A61B, A61F002, A61F009, A61F011, A61H031, A61H039, A61M, A61N |
| Polymers | C08B, C08F, C08G, C08H, C08K, C08L |

Looking at the shares of the public institutions within all domestic patents, they achieve an average level of 7 per cent. Compared to this, the value in Biotechnology is rather high with 39 per cent in the priority period 1998 to 2001, and it was even higher in the earlier period of 1994 to 1997 with 52 per cent (Fig. 8). However, these values for Biotechnology prove to be extreme cases, as the other science-based fields such as Organic Chemistry, Materials, Surface Technology, or Medical Technology reach levels of about 20 per cent. Nevertheless, all science-based fields exhibit shares distinctly above the average level of 7 per cent mentioned above. The major exceptions are Data Processing and Telecommunications, where the public German research infrastructure is rather weak compared to other countries such as Japan or France. All in all, the thesis of a relevant direct technology contribution of public research institutes to science-based fields is supported by the findings.

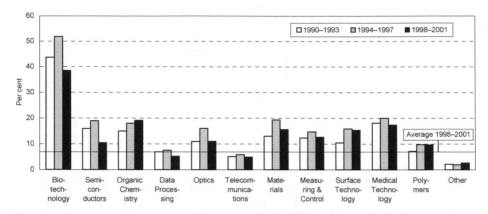

Sources: PATDPA (STN) – calculations of Fraunhofer ISI

**Fig. 8.** Share of German public research institutions within all domestic patent applications with German origin for selected science-based technology fields

The focus of scientific institutions on science-based fields is reflected in the low share of 3 per cent in other fields. 81 per cent of all applications of public institutions refer to science-based fields, compared to 47 per cent in the case of other patent applicants, in particular firms.

A further interesting observation is the decline of the public share in Biotechnology, Semiconductors, Optics and Materials between the periods 1994 to 1997 and 1998 to 2001, which reflects an increasing activity of firms in science-based fields. For the number of applications of public institutes still grows, but the applications by enterprises grow faster. Obviously, public research institutes played a pioneer role in these fields, and their knowledge is increasingly utilised by firms. Remarkably, the participation of public institutions in the 'traditional' field of Organic Chemistry is steadily increasing. This trend might be an indication of new emerging subfields with Organic Chemistry. This latter statement, however, is a reasonable assumption which needs further substantiation.

To summarise, it would be misleading to expect a contribution of public scientific institutions to all fields of technology. Their specific strength in mid- and long-term research implies a substantial contribution to science-based fields, whereas the participation in other fields is quite moderate. So in the context of scientific institutions, it is not sufficient to look at average shares, but major attention has to be paid to science-based fields.

## Conclusions

For recent years, the analysis of SCI publications reveals a slow decrease of the German share within in all publications worldwide, an observation applying to other large industrial countries as well. This development is linked to the strong increase of the activities of catch-up countries in Asia, eastern Europe, and South America. As to the citation scores of Germany and the derived indicators Scientific Regard and International Alignment, the stabilisation at the recent edge can be stated. The steady increase of the German indices in the second half of the 1990s is based on an improved scientific performance of the eastern federal states after the German unification. In the next years, a stronger orientation of German scientists to international visible journals, and linked to that, a stronger link to the international discourse should be aimed at. The example of Switzerland illustrates that the German mother tongue is not necessarily a limitation to the International Alignment of publications.

International co-publications have gained an increased relevance during the last fifteen years, an observation applying to all countries considered. In particular the co-operation between countries of the European Union has become much closer. As to Germany's partner countries, the specific preference for the German language neighbour countries Austria and Switzerland is striking. Furthermore, the co-operation level with Scandinavian countries is distinctly higher than expected. This preference in the German perspective is also reproduced in the perspective of the partner countries.

A comparison of the journal coverage of the Science Citation Index in Mechanical Engineering with that of the databases COMPENDEX and DOMA reveals a strong focus on English language journals. This implies a distorted ranking of leading institutions with respect to their real scientific capacity and performance, since a distinct focus on the local context is important in the engineering sciences. Therefore, the SCI-based analysis of the engineering sciences in countries with large domestic markets and language areas is generally misleading. Further research is necessary to what extent contributions to conferences and books have to be included in these fields for an appropriate assessment of the scientific performance.

The examination of patent applications of public scientific institutions leads to moderate participation shares on average. But in science-based fields these shares are quite high and document a direct relevant contribution of science to technology. In many fields, the scientific institutions play a pioneer role.

# 3.2 Technological Structures and Performance as Reflected by Patent Indicators

Rainer Frietsch, Ulrich Schmoch

**Abstract.** This chapter uses patent applications as an innovation indicator and compares the trends and structures of twelve countries, analysing so-called triadic patents as a first concept. According to this approach, the Scandinavian countries, the Netherlands, and Switzerland are the top countries in relative terms, whereas the USA, Japan, and Germany are the leading countries in absolute terms. As a second concept, applications at the European Patent Office (EPO) were investigated with regard to filings in R&D-intensive areas. At the EPO, an upsurge in the second half of the 1990s can be observed which is triggered by all countries in a similar way, but with some new players. This development caused the largest applicants to re-shape their portfolios. Finally, looking at international technology co-operations of German inventors, this mode of knowledge production proves to have gained importance. Common languages, local proximity, and technological competence of the partners distinctly support technology co-operation.

## Introduction

The system of intellectual property rights is multi-facetted and ranges from copyrights, trademarks, and design patents to utility patents for technical inventions. Further – less formal – mechanisms are often used in parallel or in advance of the protection by formal property rights. Among these are secrecy, head start into the market, complex design, or complex technical specifications. Beneath the mechanisms of protection, patents for technical innovations play a special and crucial role, as the formal requirements for patent applications are the most strict ones, and the assertion of patents is backed by a strong legal framework.

A patent application has to satisfy at least three criteria: novelty, inventive step and industrial applicability. The criterion of novelty implies not only novelty for a national system or for the applicant, but novelty on a worldwide scale. Furthermore, any publication – for example in a scientific paper or contribution to a conference – or any implementation of the invention in any product or process is considered prior art and inhibits patent protection. The second criterion – the inventive step[1] – means that an inventive act had to take place, which is defined by the fact that the new idea is not obvious to a person skilled in the art.[2] The third requirement of industrial applicability is generally fulfilled because of the considerable costs of patent applications which are only spent with a realistic market perspective.

---

[1] In US patent law, the correspondin requirement is called 'non-obviousness'.

[2] See Art. 56 of the European Patent Convention (EPC): http://www.european-patent-office. org/legal/epc/e/ar56.html#A56.

*U. Schmoch, C. Rammer and H. Legler (eds.), National Systems of Innovation in Comparison, 89–105.*

Starting from a simple legal perspective, patents give, for a limited period, an exclusive right of usage to the applicant for securing a *quasi* monopolistic revenue. From the perspective of analysing innovation systems, patents can be interpreted as an indicator of the codified knowledge of enterprises, and in a wider perspective of countries. Unlike trademarks, for example, that can be used as an innovation indicator for the service sector,[3] the focus of the statistical patent analysis is directed towards technological innovations, especially visible in the manufacturing sector.[4] It can be plausibly assumed that any patent application is preceded by mostly large investment in the research and development process (Grupp 1998: 145–147; Kash & Kingston 2001). From this point of view, patents can be seen as a success or output indicator of research and development (R&D) processes (Freeman 1982: 8). On the other hand, most – but not all – technological inventions will flow into a product or process that will then be offered on national or international markets. Thus, patents can also be interpreted as an input indicator (or throughput indicators) with regard to future market activities of enterprises, sectors or countries and therefore act as an early sign for future competitiveness.

The structure of this chapter is as follows. Section 2 compares the status and development of triadic patent applications in twelve industrialised countries and the EU-15, while Section 3 focuses on EPO applications in R&D-intensive fields. Next to these analyses of profiles, structures and developments, the co-patenting behaviour of German applicants is presented in Section 4.

# Triadic Patents

## Theoretical Concept and Data Basis

Triadic patents are inventions for which a patent has been applied in each of the three countries/regions (offices) of the Triad: USA (USPTO), Japan (JPO) and Europe (EPO)[5]. Applications at different national or regional offices that refer to the same invention are usually called a 'patent family'. Whereas this latter concept refers to any group of filings, the triadic approach is more restrictive. It is assumed that triadic patents are of higher economic as well as technological value than applications that are only

---

[3]  Trademarks as an innovation indicator are discussed in Schmoch (2003b) or Mendonca et al. (2004).

[4]  As to the appropriateness of patents as a technology indicator, see Schmoch and Hinze (2004) and the references cited there.

[5]  Sometimes the definition of Europe does not only include applications at the EPO, but at any national patent office within Europe as well. For reasons of simplicity and as the statistical effect is restricted, we focus on parallel applications at USPTO, JPO and EPO only. While non-European applicants almost always use the path of the EPO to get a European application, this might not be the case for all European applicants, who may submit make a national filing in their home country and subsequent filings at the JPO and USPTO – for example using the PCT path – without any EPO application, if they do not intend to file in any further European country. From an empirical perspective, this is only seldom the case, though especially the European applicants have a small 'disadvantage' with the approach used here and so their number of triadic patents might be underestimated in this respect.

**Box 1.**

This study uses patent applications rather than granted patents, as applications are published earlier than grants and reflect technological competitiveness in a more appropriate way. In former years, the USPTO only published granted patents, so that the standard triadic approach was distorted. To overcome these obstacles, we applied an alternative computation method, which takes the real patent flows between regions/offices into account: all applicants file the largest number of patents in their home country, of course. Furthermore, applicants from the USA file slightly more patents in Japan than in Europe, applicants from European countries apply for many more patents in the USA than in Japan. And Asian applicants file many more patents in the USA than in Europe (EPO et al. 2004). In consequence, the lowest number of filings for any country of origin is not at the USPTO; USA patent applications are not the limiting factor of triadic patents. From this perspective, we do not need USPTO data to compute them. It is sufficient to rely on applications at the EPO or the JPO, respectively. This method has proved its feasibility and validity in several analyses, since Fraunhofer ISI introduced the triadic approach in 1988 (Schmoch et al. 1988).

Since the second half of the 1990s, no database for Japanese applications exists anymore that allows for searching all relevant data necessary for this analysis. This – first of all – concerns the inventor or applicant country information, which is crucial for the determination of the country of origin. Therefore, we alternatively used PCT applications with Japan as a designated country. However, the PCT enjoys an increasing popularity, so that growth rates do not realistically reflect technological developments.

Against this background, the strategy for counting triadic patent applications applied in this study is as follows. First, the number of patent filings for any country at the European Patent Office and via PCT application designated to Japan is computed. In a second step, the numbers of these two procedures are compared and the lower number is taken as the number of triadic filings, based on the knowledge of the patent flows described above. Third, the trend of filings at the EPO is applied to the absolute number of PCT applications in the year 1998, tracking forward and backward. The results of this method have been compared to results published by the OECD as a triadic approach (Dernis & Kahn 2004; OECD [ed.] 2004b; 2004c; OECD 2005b).[6] The trend of the OECD data is rather similar to our approach, but we reach a higher absolute level, as our results are not limited by grants at the USPTO. For the same reason, we arrive at data that point to more recent years than with 'real' patent family counting. For the analysis of high-technology profiles, we use patent applications at the European Patent Office (EPO). Besides statistical and methodological advantages, the reasons for focusing on the European market are twofold. First, we aim to analyse the competitiveness of countries with a special focus on Germany; and for German companies, the European market – next to the German market, of course – is the most important one. Furthermore, Europe is one of the most important and largest markets in the world and therefore relevant for any internationally oriented company. Second, for European countries and companies it is their most relevant 'regional market' where they show their competitiveness – more or less – unvarnished. Besides, analysing European patent applications, we have to bear in mind that non-European countries like the USA or Japan only offer a selected set of technologies from their total technological potentials that is shaped by their export portfolio, expectations of the development of the European market and the strength of other countries serving this market. Non-European countries do not have a 'regional advantage' in statistical terms. In particular, low-technology goods with a distinct local orientation such as sanitary or lighting equipment are less represented in the EPO patent profile of non-European countries, whereas patents in high-technology fields are generally reflected in an adequate way.

---

[6] Direct comparisons of our results with the results published by the OECD (2005b) reveal that our approach leads to 50–80 per cent higher numbers of triadic patent applications for most European countries and about 140–160 per cent more filings for those countries, where the US data play a very prominent role (except US inventors themselves) e.g. GBR, CAN, SWE, FIN.

filed at one or two offices. Furthermore, from a methodological perspective, the home advantage of countries at their home office can be levelled by this approach (Schmoch & Hinze 2004: 225ff).

## Empirical Findings

Table 1 displays the total number of triadic patents in the year 2002, the patent intensity (patents per one million workforce) and the growth rate between 1991 and 2002. The United States are at the top of the list with nearly 30,000 filings. The EU-15 ranks second with almost the same number, followed by Japan with more than 21,000 triadic patents. Germany is responsible for more than one-third of all EU-15 applications. Great Britain, France and the Netherlands follow in the next places.

**Table 1.** Triadic patents; totals, intensities and growth rates, 2002

|        | Total  | Intensity (patents per 1 million workforce) | Growth rate (1991 = 100) |
|--------|--------|------------------------------------------|------------------------|
| FIN    | 1,217  | 516 | 312 |
| SWE    | 1,917  | 440 | 218 |
| NED    | 3,047  | 365 | 246 |
| SUI    | 1,443  | 346 | 179 |
| JPN    | 21,501 | 329 | 171 |
| GER    | 10,216 | 264 | 199 |
| USA    | 29,717 | 200 | 199 |
| GBR    | 5,137  | 174 | 181 |
| FRA    | 3,910  | 157 | 164 |
| CAN    | 1,912  | 122 | 372 |
| KOR    | 1,858  | 84  | 2,017 |
| ITA    | 1,603  | 67  | 194 |
| EU-15  | 29,103 | 171 | 196 |
| OECD   | 71,215 | 135 | 197 |
| Total  | 74,350 | –   | 201 |

Source: EPAPAT, WOPATENT, OECD (MSTI) – calculations by Fraunhofer ISI

As the absolute number of patent filings is first of all influenced by the size of a country in terms of inhabitants or workforce, the patent intensity indicator permits a better comparison of the international technological strengths of these countries. If this indicator is used, the smaller countries Finland, Sweden, the Netherlands and Switzerland appear at the top of the list, followed by Japan and Germany, whereas the United States only reach a medium position, reflecting their distinct orientation to their large domestic market and a relatively low engagement in exports. But the USA is still ahead of the EU-15 countries.

Looking at the growth rates, the ranking is quite different. South Korea is unrivalled at the top, reflecting its enormous upsurge in the world economy. Canada and the already mentioned Scandinavian countries Finland and Sweden follow. As for Sweden and

Finland, the figures underline their great success and unique development within the 1990s that shot them to the top of the innovative countries in the world. The Canadian growth mirrors its dissociation from a pure orientation to the US market and its increasing international engagement.

**Table 2.** Growth rates of triadic patents, 1991–2002

|       | 1991 | 1992 | 1993 | 1994 | 1995 | 1996 | 1997 | 1998 | 1999 | 2000 | 2001 | 2002 |
|-------|------|------|------|------|------|------|------|------|------|------|------|------|
| USA   | 0.1  | 2.1  | 2.3  | 5.6  | 10.2 | 6.0  | 11.0 | 11.2 | 6.7  | 11.0 | −4.2 | 10.1 |
| JPN   | −9.2 | −7.5 | 1.6  | −2.9 | 12.7 | 11.1 | 5.7  | 8.3  | 15.4 | 19.3 | −2.5 | 12.8 |
| GER   | −0.9 | 1.9  | 1.8  | 7.1  | 4.2  | 19.4 | 11.8 | 13.2 | 6.6  | 7.2  | −1.6 | 2.0  |
| GBR   | −1.8 | 0.2  | 1.3  | 4.9  | 5.1  | 9.7  | 8.1  | 14.6 | 10.1 | 7.1  | −1.8 | 4.4  |
| FRA   | 1.2  | 5.5  | 3.2  | 3.8  | 3.3  | 10.3 | 11.6 | 8.5  | 6.8  | 4.6  | 2.1  | 1.9  |
| SUI   | −4.3 | 8.6  | −2.8 | 3.3  | 0.1  | 12.0 | 11.8 | 11.6 | 6.6  | 11.9 | 2.6  | 0.3  |
| CAN   | 4.4  | 7.8  | 6.0  | 8.7  | 14.2 | 11.1 | 32.4 | 18.6 | 13.1 | 12.8 | 4.7  | 7.9  |
| SWE   | −1.5 | 15.8 | 5.0  | 19.6 | 12.9 | 19.1 | 13.6 | 2.0  | 5.8  | 10.8 | −11.0| −6.4 |
| ITA   | 2.9  | −5.6 | 4.1  | 3.8  | 6.2  | 16.2 | 9.2  | 5.8  | 11.1 | 9.1  | 1.1  | 5.7  |
| NED   | −4.4 | 1.4  | 1.4  | 4.8  | 15.2 | 18.8 | 11.9 | 10.5 | 12.3 | 17.7 | 14.5 | −6.6 |
| FIN   | −4.0 | 28.4 | 11.1 | 15.5 | 3.7  | 19.6 | 19.6 | 14.1 | 20.6 | 4.1  | 1.1  | −7.9 |
| KOR   | 41,9 | 17,0 | 46,1 | 25,2 | 26,5 | −1,0 | 32,6 | 47,4 | 13,3 | 53,6 | 15,6 | 34,7 |
| EU-15 | −0,2 | 0,6  | 3,1  | 6,1  | 4,8  | 15,7 | 12,3 | 10,5 | 8,6  | 7,4  | 0,1  | 1,4  |
| Total | −2.0 | −0.2 | 2.5  | 3.9  | 7.8  | 11.6 | 11.3 | 10.8 | 9.4  | 12.2 | −1.7 | 7.5  |
| OECD  | −2.1 | −0.4 | 2.5  | 3.9  | 7.9  | 11.5 | 11.0 | 10.5 | 9.4  | 11.4 | −1.4 | 7.1  |

Source: EPAPAT, WOPATENT — calculations by Fraunhofer ISI

This impressive change can also be traced in Table 2, where the growth rates of triadic patents are displayed separately for each year between 1991 and 2002. In the first half of the decade, the patent filings increase moderately for almost all countries. Only South Korea, Finland, and Sweden grow at a much higher speed. The second half of the 1990s is characterised by enormous growth rates in all countries, so that the total number of filings doubled within this decade. Several authors have examined and analysed the reasons for this massive expansion of patent filings. Apart from simplifications in the legal and administrative framework (Hall & Ziedonis 2001; Kortum & Lerner 1999) and an increased R&D efficiency (Janz et al. 2001), especially the strategic motivation to patent, particularly induced by very large companies, was identified as the main driving force behind this upsurge (Arundel & Patel 2003; Blind et al. 2003a; 2004; Cohen et al. 2002). However, this total upward trend was stopped after the year 2000. This was a result of the worldwide economic downturn, especially led by the ICT sector. As a consequence, the general decline did not hit all countries with the same force, but those above all, which are highly specialised in ICT and related sectors such as Sweden, Finland and to some extent also the Netherlands, whereas countries like the USA or Japan were affected only shortly. Canada and South Korea were more or less unaffected by this worldwide recession, though their speed was reduced for a while. The Japanese applicants performed badly in the first half of the decade, as they had to cope with the Asian crisis. But obviously there was a catching-up effect in the second half – also triggered by the weak national development – starting already in 1995, so that the Japanese applicants could nearly level the foregone total development of all OECD countries at the beginning of the new century. First estimates for the priority years 2003 and 2004 for all countries indicate a further and steady growth, but with a less steep slope than in the second half of the 1990s. It seems that the dramatic upsurge has come to an end and 'normality' gets the upper hand again.

## Patents in R&D-intensive Technologies

### Theoretical Concept and Data Basis

The international division of labour and competition implies the necessity for companies – and in consequence also for countries – to specialise in the production and provision of selected technologies. For each country, it is favourable to focus on its strength and buy other goods abroad, as already discussed in Ricardo's classic work (Ricardo 1996). Highly industrialised countries have other advantages such as qualified human capital, skills and knowledge that result in a technical and organisational lead, which they can offer to the world market embedded in profound and sound products.[7] These products meet these criteria are – first of all – high-technology goods (see Chapter 1 for definition and the concept of specialisation).[8] Therefore special attention is paid to the analysis of this part of national innovation systems (Edquist 1997; Lundvall 1992). However, the present situation is characterised by an increasing engagement of catching-up countries in high-technology, so that the boundaries with regard to the traditional industrialised countries are blurred.

### Empirical Findings

Table 3 displays the intensities and specialisation indices for the twelve countries in our analysis and the EU-15. The patent intensities allow for taking the different sizes of countries into account by setting the number of patent applications in relation to the size of the workforce. Looking at this indicator, Switzerland is at the top of the list, followed by Finland and Sweden, which both show enormous growth rates, especially in the second half of the 1990s. This result has already been observed in the analysis of triadic patents, but it can now be qualified further. The growth of applications from

---

[7] Cf. Amable and Verspagen (1995), Boskin and Lau (1992), Curzio et al. (1994), Dosi et al (1990), Fagerberg (1988; 1997), Freeman and Soete (1997), Gomulka (1990), Gustavsso et al. (1997), Mowery and Rosenberg (1989), Porter (1998), Wakelin (1997).

[8] With the definition or scope of this study, we focus on technical innovations. This does not mean that innovations only take place in the industrial sector; the opposite is true. Especially in the service sector, many creative and innovative novelties are invented and brought to the market. By definition and as a matter of fact, patents and patent statistics aim at technological inventions and innovations. The number of technical innovations originating in the service sector is restricted. For example, only 3–5 per cent of all patents are filed by service companies (Blind et al. 2003b; Blind & Frietsch 2003; Frietsch 2004a).

**Table 3.** Intensities and specialisation index for selected countries in the area of high-technology 1991–2000

| | 1991 | 1992 | 1993 | 1994 | 1995 | 1996 | 1997 | 1998 | 1999 | 2000 | 2001 | 2002 |
|---|---|---|---|---|---|---|---|---|---|---|---|---|
| | Patents per 1million workforce (intensities) | | | | | | | | | | | |
| USA | 92 | 93 | 94 | 99 | 108 | 114 | 124 | 136 | 144 | 148 | 133 | 131 |
| JPN | 117 | 106 | 105 | 103 | 115 | 127 | 137 | 142 | 169 | 198 | 196 | 214 |
| GER | 157 | 157 | 164 | 178 | 193 | 231 | 258 | 298 | 322 | 339 | 341 | 345 |
| GBR | 77 | 82 | 81 | 85 | 91 | 98 | 106 | 128 | 139 | 144 | 144 | 137 |
| FRA | 119 | 113 | 120 | 126 | 126 | 139 | 157 | 170 | 184 | 187 | 189 | 192 |
| SUI | 254 | 252 | 261 | 258 | 255 | 294 | 315 | 345 | 384 | 436 | 446 | 441 |
| CAN | 32 | 33 | 33 | 39 | 45 | 50 | 67 | 79 | 90 | 87 | 95 | 90 |
| SWE | 112 | 132 | 150 | 192 | 217 | 272 | 321 | 320 | 347 | 356 | 325 | 295 |
| ITA | 55 | 53 | 50 | 55 | 58 | 68 | 70 | 72 | 80 | 88 | 88 | 91 |
| NED | 124 | 126 | 123 | 125 | 147 | 177 | 190 | 214 | 225 | 270 | 304 | 271 |
| FIN | 98 | 155 | 180 | 224 | 235 | 287 | 353 | 379 | 455 | 435 | 451 | 386 |
| KOR | 6 | 8 | 9 | 11 | 15 | 14 | 20 | 33 | 35 | 40 | 48 | 64 |
| | Specialisation index (RPA) | | | | | | | | | | | |
| USA | 10 | 10 | 11 | 11 | 11 | 13 | 12 | 13 | 12 | 12 | 4 | 2 |
| JPN | 9 | 9 | 7 | 7 | 4 | 2 | 5 | 1 | 1 | 1 | 0 | 0 |
| GER | –12 | –15 | –13 | –13 | –10 | –11 | –11 | –10 | –9 | –9 | –8 | –8 |
| GBR | –2 | 3 | 1 | 0 | 1 | 0 | 1 | 7 | 5 | 5 | 2 | 2 |
| FRA | –10 | –9 | –7 | –7 | –11 | –10 | –10 | –10 | –8 | –8 | –9 | –8 |
| SUI | –4 | –12 | –5 | –10 | –13 | –10 | –15 | –17 | –14 | –9 | –10 | –9 |
| CAN | 11 | 7 | 3 | 11 | 12 | 12 | 14 | 16 | 18 | 13 | 16 | 13 |
| SWE | –13 | –15 | –11 | –7 | –6 | –3 | 0 | –2 | 0 | –1 | 3 | 4 |
| ITA | –10 | –8 | –18 | –16 | –17 | –17 | –22 | –26 | –26 | –24 | –24 | –21 |
| NED | –7 | –4 | –7 | –11 | –7 | –4 | –6 | –2 | –8 | –4 | –7 | –7 |
| FIN | –9 | 6 | 4 | 10 | 9 | 13 | 19 | 13 | 14 | 10 | 16 | 14 |
| KOR | 8 | 25 | 3 | –2 | 7 | 0 | 7 | 16 | 11 | 9 | 10 | 17 |
| EU-15 | –10 | –10 | –10 | –10 | –9 | –9 | –9 | –8 | –8 | –8 | –8 | –7 |

Source: EPAPAT, WOPATENT; OECD (MSTI) – calculations by Fraunhofer ISI

Finland and Sweden are especially driven by the R&D-intensive technologies (see also Chapter 2.2).

In the most recent year 2002, Germany ranks third among all countries considered and first among the large industrialised countries. The increase of the intensities in Germany is not only based on an expansion of the number of patents in high-level technologies – where Germany traditionally has its strength and ranks second behind Switzerland – but also on a strengthened position in the leading-edge technologies, where Germany reached a less prominent position for a long period. Thus, the absolute number of German EPO applications per year has tripled in the period of 1991 to 2002 in leading-edge technology, whereas the numbers in high-level technology 'only' doubled. A clear development in the direction of leading-edge technology is obvious. But a look at the specialisation index (RPA)[9] (lower panel of Table 3) does not reflect this change towards high-technology in Germany; only small increases in the position are visible.

This finding points to the fact that other economies also expanded their activities during the 1990s, and the enormous increase in the patent intensities in Germany could not be converted into clear advantages in the specialisation in leading-edge technologies. The total sum of patents for all countries nearly doubled in the observation period and even grew slightly more in the area of high-technology patents (see Table 4). So the minor shift in German specialisation reflects that other countries moved in the same direction as well; for a change of absolute numbers becomes visible in the specialisation index only if other countries do not alter their profiles.

**Table 4.** Growth rates of patent filings by technological areas, 1991–2002

|        | Total patent applications | High-technology | Leading-edge technology | High-level technology |
|--------|-----|--------|--------|--------|
| USA    | 165.4  | 166.8  | 190.2  | 148.8 |
| JPN    | 179.9  | 181.6  | 180.6  | 182.3 |
| GER    | 191.3  | 220.7  | 309.4  | 191.3 |
| GBR    | 166.8  | 190.6  | 249.3  | 154.8 |
| FRA    | 155.1  | 174.8  | 209.5  | 153.6 |
| SUI    | 175.2  | 183.6  | 266.7  | 156.6 |
| CAN    | 295.1  | 331.2  | 485.4  | 241.0 |
| SWE    | 196.9  | 256.1  | 317.9  | 216.8 |
| ITA    | 176.4  | 174.0  | 220.3  | 159.4 |
| NED    | 245.4  | 268.1  | 365.7  | 209.9 |
| FIN    | 283.3  | 393.4  | 666.0  | 196.7 |
| KOR    | 1055.7 | 1269.3 | 1778.6 | 963.7 |
| EU-15  | 183.8  | 208.2  | 278.7  | 176.9 |
| Total  | 181.3  | 199.2  | 246.0  | 172.0 |

Source: EPAPAT, WOPATENT – calculations by Fraunhofer ISI

The numbers in the leading-edge technologies grew by factor 2.5, whereas the patent applications in the area of high-level technologies 'only' grew by 1.7. In comparison to other large industrialised countries, the German development is at the top and is only surpassed by smaller countries such as Canada, South Korea, the Netherlands and especially Finland. So Germany does and can compete with these young technological nations, at least with respect to the growth rate of the patents in the area of high-technology. All in all, the patent data reflect a still competitive position of Germany in industrial R&D. (see Table 5).

---

[9] The specialisation index RPA (Revealed Patent Advantage) is defined as:

$$RPA_{kj} = 100 * \tanh \ln [(P_{kj}/\textstyle\sum_j P_{kj})/(\textstyle\sum_k P_{kj}/\textstyle\sum_{kj} P_{kj})]. \tag{1}$$

with $P_{kj}$ indicating the number of patent applications of country k in the technology field j (for further details cf. Nesta & Patel 2004 and Chapter 1).

**Table 5.** Specialisation index for selected countries by leading-edge and high-level technology, 1991–2002

| | 1991 | 1992 | 1993 | 1994 | 1995 | 1996 | 1997 | 1998 | 1999 | 2000 | 2001 | 2002 |
|---|---|---|---|---|---|---|---|---|---|---|---|---|
| | Leading-edge technology | | | | | | | | | | | |
| USA | 29 | 26 | 28 | 30 | 29 | 23 | 27 | 27 | 23 | 22 | 11 | 9 |
| JPN | 9 | 5 | 9 | –4 | 4 | –3 | –6 | –12 | –5 | 1 | –15 | –8 |
| GER | –47 | –43 | –47 | –46 | –49 | –34 | –39 | –36 | –39 | –36 | –34 | –34 |
| GBR | 1 | 11 | 5 | 15 | 10 | 14 | 11 | 20 | 20 | 15 | 11 | 7 |
| FRA | –4 | –10 | –3 | –5 | –15 | –19 | –11 | –14 | –12 | –14 | –7 | –9 |
| SUI | –44 | –34 | –43 | –39 | –50 | –40 | –51 | –46 | –39 | –28 | –25 | –35 |
| CAN | 18 | 23 | 12 | 33 | 40 | 34 | 46 | 40 | 41 | 25 | 35 | 28 |
| SWE | –7 | 7 | –11 | 21 | 12 | 21 | 16 | 14 | 16 | 19 | 2 | –3 |
| ITA | –45 | –50 | –48 | –44 | –48 | –44 | –60 | –65 | –63 | –58 | –64 | –55 |
| NED | –8 | 1 | 1 | –8 | 7 | 9 | 5 | 8 | 3 | 15 | 27 | –8 |
| FIN | 1 | 47 | 38 | 47 | 41 | 55 | 60 | 53 | 63 | 45 | 52 | 41 |
| KOR | 43 | 54 | 16 | –5 | 16 | –3 | 46 | 58 | 33 | 37 | 40 | 50 |
| EU-15 | –26 | –22 | –24 | –20 | –25 | –17 | –19 | –18 | –17 | –18 | –15 | –20 |
| | High-level technology | | | | | | | | | | | |
| USA | –1 | 1 | –1 | –1 | –1 | 0 | 0 | –1 | 0 | –1 | –5 | –6 |
| JPN | 4 | 7 | 6 | 9 | 7 | 6 | 8 | 7 | 9 | 8 | 11 | 10 |
| GER | 5 | 1 | 4 | 6 | 9 | 6 | 6 | 9 | 10 | 10 | 11 | 10 |
| GBR | –4 | –3 | –3 | –10 | –7 | –10 | –9 | –2 | –9 | –7 | –7 | –6 |
| FRA | –12 | –12 | –9 | –9 | –11 | –6 | –8 | –7 | –8 | –6 | –8 | –8 |
| SUI | 14 | 2 | 12 | 4 | 3 | 6 | 6 | 2 | 3 | 6 | 5 | 8 |
| CAN | 11 | 2 | –1 | –1 | –7 | –7 | 0 | –2 | –5 | –3 | 4 | –4 |
| SWE | –16 | –19 | –10 | –17 | –17 | –16 | –12 | –25 | –19 | –23 | –7 | –2 |
| ITA | 8 | 11 | –2 | –1 | 0 | 1 | 0 | –1 | 0 | 2 | 5 | 3 |
| NED | –8 | –6 | –12 | –12 | –13 | –9 | –13 | –11 | –15 | –14 | –26 | –18 |
| FIN | –17 | –9 | –18 | –17 | –23 | –29 | –30 | –35 | –54 | –48 | –43 | –45 |
| KOR | 7 | 12 | 15 | 9 | 11 | –6 | –11 | –6 | –9 | –11 | –6 | 3 |
| EU-15 | –1 | –3 | –2 | –2 | –1 | –2 | –2 | 0 | –1 | –1 | 0 | 0 |

Source: EPAPAT, WOPATENT – calculations by Fraunhofer ISI

In terms of growth rates, the USA and Japan are below the average, due to the high dynamics of smaller countries. South Korea and Canada reach impressive growth rates, because they started at a very low level in the early 1990s. At that time they were not very active in Europe and at the European Patent Office, respectively.

The development of the specialisation indices in leading-edge technologies throughout the 1990s shows constant and positive values for the USA, with a reduction in the most recent years. In contrast, the Japanese values have a negative trend during the whole 1990s that leads to a clear negative specialisation at the end of this decade.

**Table 6.** Specialisation indices of selected countries in high-technology product fields, 1998–2002

| | USA | JPN | GER | GBR | FRA | SUI | CAN | SWE | ITA | NED | FIN | KOR | EU |
|---|---|---|---|---|---|---|---|---|---|---|---|---|---|
| Leading-edge products | | | | | | | | | | | | | |
| Radioactive Substances | 9 | –1 | –58 | 55 | 63 | –77 | 18 | 66 | –71 | –64 | 100‾ | 84 | –3 |
| Plant Protective Agents | 24 | –48 | –17 | 10 | –7 | 36 | 39 | –59 | –31 | –41 | –96 | 60 | –18 |
| Pharmaceutical Agents | 43 | –41 | –39 | 45 | –7 | –11 | 62 | 5 | –44 | –24 | –57 | –14 | –15 |
| Nuclear Reactors | –27 | –66 | 19 | 15 | 20 | –45 | –23 | 30 | –23 | –37 | –48 | –44 | 23 |
| Weapons | –42 | –91 | 46 | –59 | 40 | 61 | 2 | 64 | –1 | –63 | –3 | 100‾ | 27 |
| Computers | 29 | 17 | –55 | 8 | –18 | –58 | –6 | –9 | –72 | 35 | 10 | 41 | –30 |
| Integrated Circuits | 12 | 45 | –20 | –68 | –8 | –59 | –86 | –86 | 25 | 47 | –95 | 25 | –21 |
| Communication Equip. | 5 | –4 | –29 | 6 | 2 | –60 | 45 | 52 | –69 | 13 | 89 | 61 | –5 |
| Medical Diagnosis | 39 | –26 | –48 | –17 | –61 | –42 | 24 | 35 | –74 | 33 | 28 | –39 | –32 |
| Top Instruments | 11 | 7 | –9 | 16 | –25 | 12 | –14 | –18 | –57 | 13 | –21 | –1 | –11 |
| Aircrafts | 26 | –65 | –8 | 31 | 56 | 30 | 33 | 6 | –78 | –94 | –92 | –100 | 2 |
| High-level products | | | | | | | | | | | | | |
| Organic Substances | 27 | –21 | –7 | 48 | 10 | 39 | 24 | –38 | –25 | –39 | –79 | 26 | –5 |
| Inorganic Substances | 0 | 22 | 4 | –28 | –8 | –10 | 53 | –62 | –70 | –16 | –43 | –8 | –14 |
| Polymers | 1 | 41 | 2 | –49 | –11 | –48 | 1 | –85 | –6 | –5 | –42 | 6 | –12 |
| Dyes | 7 | 37 | 15 | 16 | –42 | 52 | –81 | –84 | –74 | –3 | –88 | –41 | –12 |
| Pharmaceutical Products | 40 | –43 | –39 | 45 | –1 | 10 | 63 | 9 | –14 | –43 | –75 | –2 | –14 |
| Appl.-Oriented Chemicals | 22 | 1 | –12 | 20 | –10 | –12 | 18 | –8 | –51 | –20 | –17 | –56 | –10 |
| Engines | –23 | 10 | 51 | –22 | –22 | 26 | 24 | –44 | –20 | –99 | –85 | –99 | 12 |
| Pumps | –43 | 59 | –5 | –38 | –55 | –49 | –28 | 16 | 13 | –87 | –90 | 70 | –22 |
| Hydro-pneumatic Fittings | –31 | –41 | 29 | –13 | –1 | 0 | –21 | 15 | 59 | –70 | –68 | –52 | 21 |
| Conveyors | –57 | 22 | 37 | –55 | –17 | 43 | –74 | –4 | 52 | –13 | –4 | –82 | 18 |
| Heating & Cooling Equip. | –4 | –7 | 5 | –4 | 31 | –27 | –4 | –29 | –15 | –14 | –40 | –9 | 5 |
| Agricultural Machines | –50 | –82 | 44 | –25 | 48 | –83 | 5 | 5 | 51 | 52 | –31 | –98 | 40 |
| Machine Tools | –43 | 14 | 31 | –51 | –9 | 40 | –25 | 20 | 51 | –49 | –34 | –64 | 14 |
| Textile Machines | –58 | –33 | 30 | –21 | –21 | 73 | –98 | –77 | 87 | –52 | –97 | 72 | 26 |
| Special Purpose Machines | –24 | –38 | 26 | –10 | –16 | 12 | 35 | 29 | 57 | –16 | 66 | –72 | 22 |
| Office Machines | 5 | 69 | –53 | –37 | –47 | –97 | –69 | –87 | –91 | –50 | –92 | 42 | –54 |
| Electric Motors | –53 | 43 | 25 | –50 | –9 | 34 | –48 | –37 | 35 | –82 | –4 | 17 | 0 |
| Electric Transmission | –17 | –60 | 38 | 3 | 35 | –9 | –64 | –41 | 59 | –28 | –79 | –95 | 30 |
| Electric Lighting | –18 | 45 | –2 | –24 | –37 | –40 | 29 | –74 | –35 | 18 | –65 | 8 | –18 |
| Electronic Devices | 6 | 60 | –30 | –74 | –49 | –54 | –92 | –52 | –65 | 17 | –94 | –3 | –41 |
| Television Sets | –37 | 70 | –77 | –31 | –41 | –80 | –71 | –93 | –91 | 86 | –82 | 88 | –40 |
| Medical Devices | 45 | –81 | –38 | 4 | –23 | 57 | –17 | 26 | –7 | –61 | –73 | –61 | –22 |
| High Class Instruments | –19 | –35 | 31 | 6 | 17 | 61 | –54 | –10 | –9 | –53 | –7 | –56 | 15 |
| Optical Apparatus | 13 | 49 | –52 | –3 | –35 | –14 | 25 | –19 | –72 | –26 | –82 | 47 | –43 |
| Automobiles | –60 | 3 | 60 | –37 | 30 | –87 | –48 | 6 | –4 | –65 | –88 | –48 | 31 |
| Rail Vehicles | –78 | –88 | 67 | –26 | 47 | 57 | –51 | 1 | –45 | –81 | 5 | 33 | 47 |
| Other R&D-int. products | 26 | –4 | –41 | –32 | 20 | –94 | –48 | –22 | 6 | –14 | 32 | 48 | –10 |

Source: EPAPAT, WOPATENT – calculations by Fraunhofer ISI

Germany is still specialised below average in the area of leading-edge technologies accompanied by a slow upward trend in the second half of the period observed, although this trend can, at least to some extent, be explained by the weakening of the Japanese and US indices. The United Kingdom and the Netherlands display a positive advance in leading-edge technologies, but also small countries such as Canada, Finland and South Korea. France and Italy show a deterioration of their position, and the index for Switzerland improved, but is still distinctly below average.

As to high-level technology, especially Germany, Japan, but also Switzerland and Italy exhibit positive specialisation indices, while the USA and the EU-15 hold an average level. France still has a slightly negative specialisation, and Canada, Sweden, Finland and South Korea are under-specialised in this area.

By means of the high-technology concordance (Grupp et al. 2000), the profiles of the countries can be broken down further by 38 product fields, of which 11 represent the leading-edge technologies and 27 the high-level technologies, respectively.

We have already mentioned that the German strengths are more in the area of high-level technologies and less in leading-edge technologies. This general statement can now be qualified further. The German applicants have distinct advantages in the transport sector, including Engines, Automobiles, and Rail Vehicles, as well as in the sector of machinery (Machine Tools, Textile Machines, Agricultural Machines and Special Purpose Machines), and they have even been able to improve their position in these areas in the recent past. Furthermore, positive specialisations can be found in high class instruments as well as in 'classical' high-power electronic technology (Electric Motors, Electrical Transmission and Lighting). Most of these technologies belong to high-level technologies. In contrast, 'modern' electronics like ICT, Pharmaceutical Agents and Products, Medical Diagnosis, or Medical Devices are not among the German strengths. Despite this general profile, a positive overall trend in Germany's leading-edge technologies has been identified and is, first of all, linked to ICT, especially to Integrated Circuits, Communication Equipment, and Electronic Devices (see also Germany's R&D structure, Chapter 2.1)

US applicants reach a leading position in the medical fields (Pharmaceutical Agents and Products, Medical Diagnosis, Medical Devices) and in ICT (Computers, Semiconductors, and Electronic Engineering and Devices), but in Electronics, their position is still positive, but declining. They exhibit negative specialisation indices in Machinery and Transport (except Aircraft). All in all, the technology portfolio of the USA is stable, and the comparison of the US and the German specialisation profiles reveal that they rather complement one another.

In contrast, the Japanese activities at the EPO are much more similar to those of Germany, so that the frequent direct competition of these two countries in the European market is more obvious. In total, the specialisation of Japan shows many extremely positive as well as extremely negative values, a quite unusual observation for a large country – though besides the technological activities the non-European profiles are also guided by export possibilities and restrictions. Positive specialisations are visible in ICT – where clear competition exists with the USA and recently also with South Korea. Inorganic Substances and also Polymers and Dyes play an important role in the Japanese portfolio, while their specialisation is quite weak in Pharmaceutical Agents and Products. Further technological advantages refer to Optical Apparatus and Transport as well as Machine Tools. Within the observation period, the general Japanese orientation is rather constant.

British and French inventors both show only a few extreme specialisation indices. Great Britain is focused on Pharmaceuticals and Organic Substances. France is specialised in Nuclear Energy, Weapons, and Transport (Aircraft, Automobiles, Rail Vehicles). The smaller countries analysed generally display a more pronounced specialisation profile than the larger ones. Most of them focus on only a few technological areas, where they are able to reach a critical mass to be internationally competitive. Switzerland, for example, has stakes in Organic and Inorganic Substances, in Machinery and Instruments. Canada is active in areas like Organic and Inorganic Substances, and Pharmaceutical Agents and Products. Furthermore, they reach positive values in Engines, Special Machinery, Lighting, and recently also in Optics. Finland and Sweden are both highly specialised in Communication Equipment, Medical Diagnosis, and Sweden also in Medical Devices. Both countries have been able to increase their activities in Computers, where they now reach an average specialisation index. This might be a side effect of the technological fusion of computer systems and communication technologies. On the other hand, they show extreme negative values in Integrated Circuits and Electronic Devices. The Dutch portfolio has clear positive values in Electronics (Computers, Integrated Circuits, Electronic Devices, Communication Equipment) and Medical Diagnosis. Italy has a clear focus on Machinery (Pumps, Fittings, Conveyors etc.). A further positive orientation can be also found in Electric Motors and Transmission, as well as Integrated Circuits.

As already visible in the overall figures, South Korea plays a special role; it has made massive progress in various technical fields, where they now reach positive specialisation indices. In particular, this holds for Computers, Integrated Circuits, Communication Equipment and Television sets, which can be summarised under the heading of 'modern' electronics. It is interesting to look at the South Korean catching-up strategy in more detail. It started with copying innovations and with simple tasks in production and assembling that were off-shored by several electronic companies, in particular Japanese ones. The Koreans were able to use this impulse as a platform to start from and developed very quickly into a country with a gross domestic product per capita that is similar or beyond that of many western industrialised countries. This was possible due to various specific support measures that were adjusted towards this goal, e.g. by building up an educational system that is among the best in the world. The interesting fact about South Korea is that it took a similar path as Japan, namely by starting from imitation and then moving more and more towards innovation, where the switch to own innovations is visible in the tremendous increase of patents. Today, South Korea and Japan are competitors in many fields.

If the profiles of the United States and the EU-15 are compared, similar results to US and German activities can be found. The profiles are rather complementary than competitive. This is not only due to the fact that within Europe, Germany has great weight, but also that within Europe, the smaller countries like Sweden or the Netherlands that compete with the United States especially in the area of 'modern' electronics, only have a limited weight, when the totals are calculated for EU-15. But in sum, this means that the main areas of activity of the European Union and the United States – at least in the European market – are not the same and the US inventors seem to take advantage of the technological gaps that the European inventors do not cover with the same emphasis.

It is interesting to see that this result also applies when the EU-15 is compared to Japan, a result that was not that obvious in the comparison with Germany alone, where the overlap of the profiles is more pronounced. Obviously, the thresholds on the European market erected by European applicants are very high and foreign entrants have to adapt their portfolio to the profiles of the countries that are already active in this market. This also seems to be a good sign on the way to the European Research Area (ERA) (Edler & Kuhlmann 2005; European Commission 2000), as a strong 'home base' is an important prerequisite in heading for the goal to become the most important research area in the world.

To sum up, the development of technical innovations in the area of high-technology on the European market has been characterised by stability in the first half of the 1990s and enormous growth in the second half, with some turbulence after the year 2000. Some new players entered the market, among whom the Scandinavian countries and South Korea are the most prominent. While the large countries were able to keep their positions at least in part, the smaller countries caught up in some selected fields. Especially in the area of leading-edge technologies, first of all in the ICT sector (Computers, Semiconductors and Telecommunication Equipment), distinct changes have taken place. Smaller countries settled down and disputed the rights of the old-established applicants. Though the effect on the indices is of limited extent, the total system started to move. Against the background of a new international division of labour or technology production, everyone has to find his or her niche and defend it against a growing number of competitors.

## International Co-patents

### Theoretical Concept and Data Sources

In this section, we address the question which pattern of international technology co-operations exist and how it changed during the 1990s. For this purpose, co-patents at the European Patent Office are analysed, with a special focus on the German situation. We define a co-patent as any patent where at least one German inventor and at the same time at least one inventor from a foreign country is registered. This means that not only co-operations of German and foreign companies and research institutes are considered, but also such kinds of innovations are encompassed that arise from globally acting 'multinationals'(see also Chapter 2.3). For instance, if researchers from different international research sites of one company join in the production of a patent, this co-operation is included. One goal of this examination is to identify 'knowledge flows' for the assessment of the 'globalisation' of applied research and development. We performed the analysis on the basis of inventors instead of applicants, because in international co-operations, not all of the parties involved necessarily appear as applicants, whereas all the inventors have to be named according to legal requirements.

### Empirical Findings

In order to assess Germany's level of co-operations, an international comparison was carried out as the first step; in Figure 1, the shares of international co-patents of selected countries are displayed. They differ greatly, but for all countries, the statement applies that the number of international co-operations clearly increased in the 1990s. No rule without exceptions: Japan shows a constant lowering of co-operation, reflecting a re-orientation on the domestic market. But South Korea also has shrinking intensities, which can, at least for the recent past, be explained by the tremendous growth of their total number of patent applications. The absolute number of co-operations of South Korean inventors is – starting from a low level – about seven times higher in the year 2002 than at the beginning of the 1990s. Although both countries are located in the same region, the decrease of co-operation has to be interpreted differently. Japan has reached a high level of development, but has to cope with an economic crisis; South Korea is still in a catching-up process and need to co-operate for knowledge acquisition.

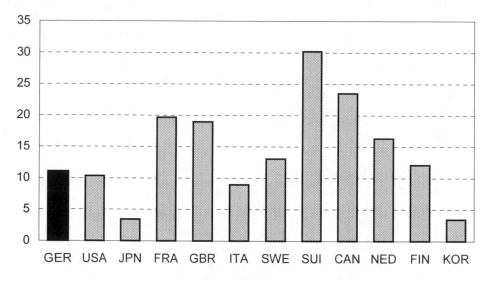

Source: EPAPAT, WOPATENT – Fraunhofer ISI computations

**Fig. 1.** Share (in per cent) of international co-patents on all patents of selected countries, 2002

Compared to other countries, the German share of international co-operation emerges at a medium level, at about 11 per cent. In the group of the larger countries, the USA and Italy display comparable shares, whereas Great Britain and France are more intensively engaged in international technology co-operation, with almost 20 per cent each. It seems obvious that the international linkages of smaller countries are more pronounced than those of larger ones, as they often need more international co-operation to achieve a critical mass in specific technology areas. Therefore, the international shares of Switzerland and Canada appear to be quite high. In this perspective, the international engagement of the Netherlands, Finland and Sweden prove to be quite modest. Compared to all other countries considered, the shares of Japan and South Korea are extremely low; both countries turn out to be quite isolated and do not participate in the process of internationalisation.

Table 7 displays the number of co-operations of German inventors with foreign colleagues in the years 1991–2002. First, it is noticeable that the absolute number of

**Table 7.** Number of German co-patents with international partners per 1,000 patent applications, 1991–2002

|     | 1991 | 1992 | 1993 | 1994 | 1995 | 1996 | 1997 | 1998 | 1999 | 2000 | 2001 | 2002 |
|-----|------|------|------|------|------|------|------|------|------|------|------|------|
| SUI | 15 | 15 | 15 | 15 | 18 | 17 | 16 | 17 | 18 | 18 | 18 | 19 |
| FRA | 7 | 9 | 9 | 7 | 8 | 10 | 11 | 11 | 12 | 14 | 14 | 15 |
| AUT | 6 | 6 | 5 | 6 | 6 | 7 | 7 | 7 | 9 | 9 | 10 | 11 |
| GBR | 6 | 6 | 5 | 5 | 7 | 6 | 6 | 7 | 7 | 7 | 8 | 9 |
| NED | 4 | 3 | 4 | 5 | 6 | 6 | 5 | 6 | 6 | 7 | 7 | 8 |
| BEL | 4 | 3 | 5 | 5 | 5 | 5 | 5 | 5 | 6 | 5 | 5 | 5 |
| ITA | 2 | 2 | 2 | 2 | 3 | 4 | 4 | 4 | 4 | 5 | 3 | 4 |
| USA | 14 | 17 | 16 | 24 | 25 | 25 | 28 | 32 | 32 | 36 | 31 | 32 |
| JPN | 4 | 5 | 2 | 3 | 4 | 3 | 3 | 3 | 4 | 4 | 3 | 5 |

Source: EPAPAT, WOPATENT – calculations by Fraunhofer ISI

co-operations per year has nearly quadrupled in the observation period. This alone shows that cross-national technology production has considerably gained in importance. But as the overall number of patent applications at the European Patent Office also clearly increased during this period, the increase of the co-operation frequency can be explained – at least in part – by this total growth. If the ratio of the number of international technology collaborations with reference to the total number of German patent filings is examined, as in Table 7, the statement of a clear and pronounced increase still holds.

At the beginning of the observation period, Swiss inventors were still the most frequent partners for Germany, and they still maintain a prominent position in the year 2002. But the frequency of co-operations with US inventors has developed in such a way that the already existing important position during the 1990s was noticeably expanded, and today about one-quarter of all international co-operations of German inventors are undertaken with US colleagues. Further important partners for international collaborations are foremost inventors from the European Union, in particular French, Austrian, British and Dutch ones. Even though the Japanese are also important partners in the technology production in the area of Electronics, they only take a lower position – together with Italy – in the group of countries compared.

It is obvious that the level of international co-operations with the USA, the largest technology producer in the world, is quite high. But it is interesting to compare the actual co-operation intensity with the expected one. For this purpose, we compared the distribution of countries within the German co-patents with their distribution within all EPO applications, and divided the co-operation share by the patent share, so that the resulting index shows at a value of 'one' that the expectations are met. In this perspective, the co-operation level with Austria and Switzerland are far above the expectation; thus geographical and language proximity have an important impact. The relevance of geographical proximity is underlined by the higher index of France compared to Great Britain. The co-operation with the USA and especially with Italy and Japan proves to be below the expectation level.

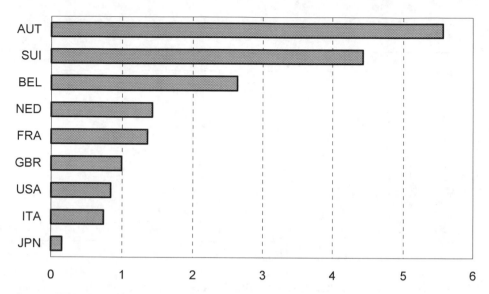

Source: EPAPAT, WOPATENT – Fraunhofer ISI computations

**Fig. 2.** Expectation index as to international co-operations of German EPO applications, 2001–2003

Table 8 displays the frequencies of co-operations of German inventors with partners from foreign countries in relation to 1,000 German patent applications, differentiated by six technological fields. Chemistry proves to be the most co-operation-intensive technological field. Whereas in the first half of the 1990s more than 13 per cent of all German chemistry patents at the European Patent Office emerged from international co-operations, this share increased in the late 1990s to nearly 23 per cent. Intensive collaborations can also be found in the area of Instruments, where nearly 12 per cent of the patents came into being in this way, first of all in collaboration with the USA and Switzerland. Furthermore, strong growth can also be found in Electrotechnology, including 'modern' and 'traditional' parts of this field. Bearing this in mind, international co-operations highly contribute to the relative increase in the position of Germany in Information and Communication Technologies (ICT), which became obvious in the previous section on high-technology patents.

Obviously, German inventors choose partners in fields where the respective countries have certain strengths. With France, co-operations take place in the areas of Chemistry and Machinery. Austria is a potential partner in Electrotechnology, Processing, and Machinery, whereas the USA are frequent co-operation partners in the areas Electrotechnology, Instruments, and, in the first half of the 1990s, also in Chemistry. In these fields, these countries exhibited clear technological advantages in the analysis of R&D-intensive fields. In absolute terms, the Japanese are at the lower end of the co-operation scale. But if any co-operations exist, they concentrate on Electrotechnology and Chemistry where also comparative advantages in the technology profile of Japan are evident. Switzerland, on the other hand, is an attractive partner in all technological fields, except Electrotechnology.

**Table 8.** Number of co-patents of German inventors with selected countries per 1,000 German patent applications at the EPO, differentiated by six technological fields

|  | Electro-technology | | Instruments | | Chemistry | | Processing | | Mechanical Engineering | | Consumer Goods | | Total* | |
|---|---|---|---|---|---|---|---|---|---|---|---|---|---|---|
|  | 91–95 | 98–02 | 91–95 | 98–02 | 91–95 | 98–02 | 91–95 | 98–02 | 91–95 | 98–02 | 91–95 | 98–02 | 91–95 | 98–02 |
| SUI | 5 | 9 | 14 | 20 | 28 | 39 | 13 | 16 | 7 | 11 | 6 | 8 | 12 | 18 |
| FRA | 4 | 10 | 5 | 9 | 14 | 28 | 6 | 9 | 4 | 9 | 3 | 7 | 6 | 14 |
| AUT | 4 | 12 | 4 | 7 | 8 | 11 | 6 | 9 | 4 | 7 | 3 | 8 | 5 | 11 |
| GBR | 4 | 7 | 4 | 7 | 9 | 15 | 3 | 6 | 3 | 5 | 4 | 4 | 5 | 8 |
| NED | 4 | 5 | 3 | 7 | 6 | 16 | 4 | 5 | 2 | 4 | 2 | 2 | 4 | 7 |
| BEL | 3 | 4 | 3 | 4 | 8 | 12 | 4 | 5 | 1 | 2 | 1 | 1 | 3 | 6 |
| ITA | 1 | 3 | 4 | 6 | 3 | 7 | 1 | 3 | 1 | 3 | 2 | 3 | 2 | 4 |
| USA | 12 | 32 | 19 | 39 | 38 | 63 | 11 | 26 | 5 | 15 | 4 | 10 | 17 | 36 |
| JPN | 2 | 4 | 3 | 3 | 9 | 9 | 2 | 2 | 1 | 2 | 0 | 0 | 3 | 5 |
| OECD | 43 | 103 | 64 | 117 | 134 | 228 | 55 | 91 | 32 | 66 | 31 | 50 | 63 | 125 |

\*   **Sum across all technological fields** (including multiple co-operations)
Source: EPAPAT, WOPATENT – calculations by Fraunhofer ISI

The level of international co-operations of Germany in Machinery and Mechanical Engineering is quite low, compared to the other technological fields. The most plausible explanation of this observation is the technological leadership of Germany in this area. Obviously, German inventors do not find enough international partners who bring complementary knowledge into the research process and – which might be even more plausible – a high importance of 'tacit knowledge' in this field reduces the number of international co-operations as inventors try to avoid knowledge transfer. Other reasons might be that German firms do not need knowledge from abroad, as sufficient national partners can be found.

To sum up, the analyses of co-patents of German inventors with international colleagues in the years 1991–2002 show that international collaboration has strongly increased, and therefore gained absolute relevance for technology production. The data show that globalisation has become an important aspect of industrial R&D, not only of scientific research, and it is gaining weight. The investigations presented in this section shed some light on the volume and structure of international co-operation in technology, but less on the underlying motives and directions of knowledge flows. As a fruitful approach, the differentiation by technological fields showed that the international co-operations are concentrated, first and foremost, on Chemistry and Electronics. Furthermore, the results sustain the thesis that geographical proximity, low language barriers, and the technological competence of the partners support international co-operation. Germany has profited from external knowledge in particular in Electrotechnology.

# 3.3 Innovation in Firms

Christian Rammer

**Abstract.** This chapter analyses major aspects of innovation activities of firms in Germany. The ability of firms to introduce new products and new processes may be viewed as a main determinant of a country's technological performance. Only when firms are able to transfer knowledge, R&D efforts and inventions into products that are accepted by the market, and to implement more efficient ways of production, will science and technology have real effects on productivity, competitiveness and wealth. Thus, innovation in firms is the key link between input and output indicators of technological performance. Using data from the annual German innovation survey as well as from the Community Innovation Survey and other national innovation surveys, four areas of innovation activities are analysed: share of innovating firms by type of innovation; input to and output of innovation activities; co-operation and information sourcing; and barriers to innovation. The results show that one of the main strengths of Germany's technological performance is the broad embodiment of innovation in the German enterprise sector, particularly in Manufacturing and in SMEs. For most innovation indicators, Germany ranks among the top performing countries. In most recent years, innovation performance deteriorated, however, caused by decreasing innovation activities of SMEs and falling direct economic returns from innovation efforts.

## Introduction

Innovation in firms refers to activities that are intended to gain an (at least temporary) absolute competitive advantage over competitors by either achieving a monopoly position in the product market (i.e. offering products that are clearly distinguished from other products in that market by quality characteristics) or by achieving marginal costs of production for a certain product that are clearly below those of competitors and thus result in a price advantage. While the former is associated with product innovation (the term 'product' covering both physical goods and services), the latter is typically linked to changes in production processes, although some changes in the organisation of business activities in a more broader sense (e.g. opening up new procurement markets, introducing new types of industrial relations) may fall under this category, too. This conceptualisation of innovation mainly follows the ideas of Schumpeter (1911).

The extent of monopoly profits will strongly depend on the type of innovation: radical innovations that clearly depart from existing technological solutions and/or open up totally new product markets, will promise longer lasting competitive advantages, although demanding high resources for successfully introducing such a type of innovations. Incremental innovations that adapt and further develop existing products may be much easier to introduce, but also much easier to copy, resulting in a shorter period of monopoly.

107

*U. Schmoch, C. Rammer and H. Legler (eds.), National Systems of Innovation in Comparison, 107–132.*

Two critical features distinguish innovation activities from other changes occurring in firms: uncertainty (in the sense of Knight 1920) about the outcome of innovative efforts, and spillovers to other firms through learning from the innovator's experiences and adopting its methods to gain competitive advantages (e.g. through copying new products or adopting new process technology). Both features may lead to private underinvestment in innovation as a result of financing restrictions and low private appropriability of returns.

This microeconomic view stresses the importance of absolute novelty, i.e. to be the very first in introducing a new product or process. It is thus linked to the concepts of research and experimental development (R&D) for generating new knowledge, and technological inventions and patenting as main outcomes of creative efforts. From this point of view, innovation is the commercialisation of R&D results. A macroeconomic perspective of innovation, however, places emphasis on the diffusion of innovation, too. For a country's technological performance, the rapid adoption of new technologies and the breadth of innovation activities in an economy are at least as equally important as R&D (see Chapter 2.2) and technological inventions (Chapter 3.2) for gaining productivity increases and improving competitiveness – both in terms of quality and price – in international markets. In this perspective, innovation is both the first-time introduction of a new product or process (which one may call 'original innovation'), and the copying, adopting and adapting of new products and processes introduced by other firms before (which one may term 'imitation'). The latter activity will be much less, if at all, linked to R&D and technological inventions, but rather demands skills and abilities that are often referred to as absorptive capacities (see Cohen & Levinthal 1989; 1990), such as learning and managing changes in organisations.

Innovation policy will have to balance both the incentives for firms to develop original innovations and accelerate the diffusion of innovations throughout the business sector. Balancing both goals is any thing but straightforward, however. While the former requires an effective system of property rights which allows the innovator to fully appropriate the returns of its innovative efforts over a reasonably long period, a rapid diffusion of innovation demands free or cheap access to new knowledge and technologies.

The particular relevance of indicators on innovation in firms for a system reporting on a country's technological performance is to provide information on both original innovations and the diffusion of technologies and new products. They thus far exceed a pure measure of successful marketing or implementation of the outcome of R&D activities and patents. Indicators on innovation in firms rather provide a crucial link between input and output indicators of technological performance and help to understand why performance in sciences, R&D and patenting may differ from performance in productivity, structural change and exports in high-technology goods.

In order to represent the different aspects of innovation in firms, the following groups of indicators are used:

- The share of innovating firms by type of innovation (specifically original innovations versus imitations, and product versus process innovations) informs about the breadth of innovative activities in the business sector and their orientation in terms of novelty and underlying firm strategies.
- The financial resources devoted to innovation, and the direct economic benefits from innovation (in terms of returns from innovative products and efficiency gains

from new processes) provide insight into the costs of innovating and the efficiency of innovation processes.

- Co-operation in innovation, and the use of different information sources for shaping innovation projects are two important aspects of interactions of firms with other actors in the innovation system (see Freeman 1987; Lundvall 1990; Edquist 1997; Nelson 1993).
- Barriers to innovation, as perceived by firms, are important hints as to market failures and other bottlenecks in the innovation system that may hinder the full exploitation of innovative potentials.

Analyses of innovation performance of the German business sector are based on an international comparison as well as on looking at developments over time. International comparisons are performed on a sector base for the most recent year available, which is 2000. The development of innovation indicators over time can only be investigated for German data, as most other countries do not conduct annual innovation surveys. When interpreting innovation data, one should note that all figures relating to the number of firms – which relates to most of the indicators used here – are determined by the behaviour of small and medium-sized enterprises (SMEs). Large companies, in contrast, dominate the figures on expenditure and revenue indicators.

## Data Sources

Data on innovation in firms has to be gathered through firm surveys. The OECD has developed a guideline for collecting and interpreting innovation data, the so-called Oslo Manual. The first edition was published in 1993, followed by a revised version, jointly edited by OECD and Eurostat in 1997. A third edition is expected to be published at the end of 2005. Based on the proposed methodology, a large number of countries conduct innovation surveys, although only a few on an annual base. Innovation as defined by the Oslo Manual has the following features:

- It is technology-oriented, i.e. it is based on new technological knowledge.
- It measures innovation at the level of a firm, and not at the level of individual projects.
- It is based on a subjective view, i.e. innovation has to be new to the firm, but not necessarily new to the market or the world, thus covering both original innovations and imitations.
- It distinguishes two types of innovations, new products (including services) and new processes (including distribution methods and methods for delivering services).
- It refers to successful innovations, i.e. new products that have been successfully introduced to the market, or new processes that have been successfully implemented in the firm.
- It measures innovation activities for a three-year reference period in order to cover discontinuous innovation (as a result of long product life cycles or machine life cycles), to take into account the often multi-annual character of innovation projects and to avoid little meaningful results on output indicators as effects of innovation tend to be low or almost zero in the year of introduction.

A main source for international comparison of innovation data are the Community Innovation Surveys (CIS), introduced by the European Commission and co-ordinated by Eurostat. The first CIS was conducted in 1993, followed by a four-year rhythm of surveys (1997; 2001; 2005). From 2007 on, core indicators on innovation in firms shall be collected bi-annually. For the current chapter, the data of CIS3 (2001) are available for international comparison. Comparison with the results of the first and second CIS is not advisable for most countries as a result of changes in survey methods and data processing. Due to some reasons, Eurostat did not officially publish sector data on innovation indicators for CIS3. Data from national sources as well as data from the CIS working group are used to perform sector analyses on innovation indicators.

Outside the EU, innovation surveys following the Oslo Manual have been conducted recently in Iceland and Norway (2001 as part of CIS3), Japan (2003; see Ijichi et al. 2004), Switzerland (2002; see Arvanitis et al. 2004), Canada (1999; see Schaan & Anderson 2001; 2003 only on ICT), Australia (2003; see Australian Bureau of Statistics 2005). South Korea (2002/2003; see Tae et al. 2002; Um 2004) and New Zealand (2003; see Statistics New Zealand 2004). For the USA, no national data on innovation in firms are available, though some states conduct surveys (e.g. Georgia; see Youtie et al. 2002). A number of non-OECD countries perform innovation surveys, too, e.g. most countries of Latin America as well as Russia (annually 2000–2002; see Gokhberg et al. 2004), Thailand (2000; 2002), South Africa (2001; see Oerlemans et al. 2003) and some others.

In Germany, the Centre for European Economic Research (ZEW) in Mannheim was commissioned by the Federal Ministry of Education and Research (BMBF) to conduct the CIS for Germany from 1993 on.[1] In contrast to the four-year rhythm of the CIS, it was decided to collect information on firm innovation activity on an annual base, using a panel sampling method. The same (stratified and random) sample of firms is surveyed each year, biannually refreshed by a stratified random sample of firms new to the population. The database is thus called the 'Mannheim Innovation Panel' (MIP). From 1993 to 2004, a total of 12 survey waves have been conducted, allowing for detailed analyses of firm innovation behaviour over time.

## Share of Innovating Firms

The German business sector is clearly one of the most innovation-oriented worldwide. In the reference period 1998 to 2000, 60 per cent of manufacturing firms (with 10 or more employees) and 65 per cent of firms in knowledge-intensive business services (KIBS) introduced at least one new product or new process (Fig. 1). In Manufacturing, only Swiss firms outperform German firms in terms of participation in innovation activities. In KIBS, only Austria and Portugal show higher shares of innovating firms.

---

[1] The survey is conducted in close co-operation with the Institute for Applied Social Science (infas). From 1995 to 1999, the survey in the service sectors was jointly performed by ZEW and the Fraunhofer Institute for Systems and Innovation Research (ISI).

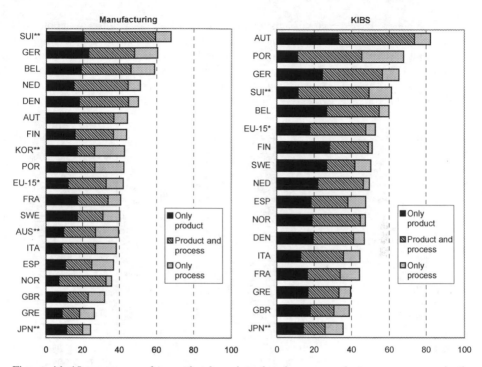

Firms with 10 or more employees that have introduced a new product or new process in the time period 1998 to 2000, as a percentage of all firms; Australia and KIBS in Switzerland: firms with 5 or more employees
* EU-15: excluding Ireland and Luxembourg, but including Norway
** Australia, Japan, Switzerland: 2000–2002; Korea: 2001–2002
Manufacturing: NACE 15–37; KIBS (knowledge-intensive business services): NACE 65–67, 72–73, 74.2–74.3; Finland: excluding 65–67
Sources: EU countries and Norway: Eurostat – CIS3 (New Cronos), Switzerland: Arvanitis et al. (2004), Japan: Ijichi et al. (2004), Australia: Australian Bureau of Statistics (2005), Korea: Tae et al. (2002) – calculation by ZEW

**Fig. 1.** Share of innovating firms in 2000 by product and process innovations (in per cent)

These results hold true both for product innovation and process innovation. 48 per cent of manufacturing firms and 56 per cent of firms in KIBS have introduced new products to the market in 1998 to 2000. The share of process innovators was 37 per cent and 41 per cent respectively. Higher shares of product innovators are reported only for Switzerland (Manufacturing) and Austria (KIBS). With respect to process innovation, Belgium and Switzerland in Manufacturing, and Switzerland, Austria and Portugal in KIBS show higher shares.

The country ranking for the share of innovating firms only partially corresponds to the ranking for other indicators on the innovative capacities of the business sector, such as R&D as a share of value added, or patents per employee. For instance, Finland, Sweden and Japan are typically to be found among the best performing countries for such indicators (see Chapter 2.2 and Chapter 3.2). Their share of innovating firms is, however, only around the EU average as far as Finland and Sweden are concerned, and extremely low concerning Japan. At the same time, some countries that are generally perceived to be specialised in medium or even low technology sectors – such as Belgium, Austria and Portugal – show high shares of innovating firms. This pattern is both valid for Manufacturing and Services, and it also holds for small, medium-sized and large firms (see Fig. 2). While the share of innovating firms tends to increase with firm size, the country ranking for the share of innovating firms is rather similar for each size class.

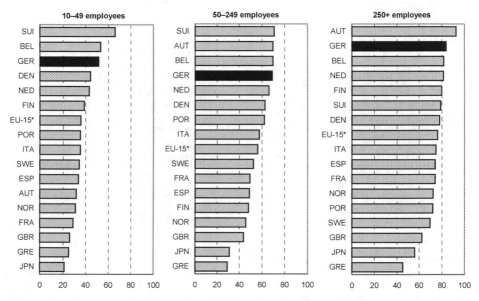

Firms with 10 or more employees that have introduced a new product or new process in the time period 1998–2000, as a percentage of all firms; Switzerland and Japan: 2000–2002; Switzerland: firms with 5 or more employees
Sources: EU countries and Norway: Eurostat – CIS3 (New Cronos), Switzerland: Arvanitis et al. (2004), Japan: Ijichi et al. (2004) – calculation by ZEW

**Fig. 2.** Share of innovating manufacturing firms in 2000 by size class 859

A high or low level of innovation orientation of firms tends to be prevalent for most sectors: Within a group of twelve countries for which sector data on innovation shares were made available,[2] for 12 out of 16 sectors Germany ranks among the three best performing countries (Table 1). High cross-sector innovation activities are also revealed for Switzerland, Belgium and Austria. At the same time, Japan is among the three countries with the lowest share of innovating firms for all 16 sectors, followed by Spain (11) and Italy (8). The Netherlands, Sweden, France and Finland tend to show medium-level innovation shares in most sectors. Denmark is the only country

---

[2]  Sector data on innovation indicators have not been officially released by Eurostat for CIS3 so far. Arvanitis et al. (2004) were able to gather sectoral data on some innovation indicators for some EU countries, however. The following analysis rests on these data, as well as on Japanese national data. Sector data on various innovation indicators for Germany can be found in Janz et al. (2002) and Rammer et al. (2005a; 2005b).

with high participation in innovation in a number of sectors, and a low propensity to innovate in a number of other sectors.

**Table 1.** Share of innovating firms in 2000 by sectors (in per cent)

| Sector (NACE) | SUI | GER | AUT | BEL | NED | DEN | SWE | FRA | FIN | ITA | ESP | JPN |
|---|---|---|---|---|---|---|---|---|---|---|---|---|
| Food/Beverages (15–16) | 74 | 58 | 53 | 49 | 48 | 57 | 44 | 47 | 35 | 40 | 36 | 23 |
| Textiles/Clothing (17–19) | 75 | 60 | 95 | 65 | 50 | 25 | 43 | 29 | 63 | 26 | 27 | 19 |
| Wood (20) | 63 | 52 | 49 | 51 | 49 | 44 | 31 | 44 | 38 | 41 | 36 | 15 |
| Pulp and Paper (21) | 64 | 67 | 75 | 48 | 67 | 41 | 46 | 46 | 56 | 39 | 32 | 18 |
| Publishing/Printing (22) | 68 | 67 | 36 | 58 | 40 | 40 | 45 | 31 | 42 | 36 | 41 | 32 |
| Chemicals/Oil (23–24) | 72 | 71 | 93 | 78 | 81 | 92 | 75 | 71 | 69 | 54 | 60 | 39 |
| Rubber/Plastics (25) | 71 | 67 | 82 | 59 | 66 | 52 | 65 | 57 | 61 | 57 | 45 | 31 |
| Glass/Clay/Stone (26) | 66 | 57 | 34 | 48 | 45 | 59 | 54 | 50 | 39 | 48 | 35 | 16 |
| Metal Production (27) | 69 | 56 | 85 | 45 | 58 | 29 | 62 | 46 | 53 | 48 | 40 | 22 |
| Metal Processing (28) | 65 | 59 | 33 | 57 | 45 | 32 | 36 | 34 | 44 | 41 | 32 | 20 |
| Mechanical Engineering (29) | 72 | 80 | 49 | 69 | 65 | 72 | 54 | 57 | 57 | 47 | 48 | 25 |
| Electrical Instruments (30–33) | 75 | 78 | 74 | 69 | 60 | 57 | 64 | 66 | 69 | 52 | 55 | 31 |
| Vehicles (34–35) | 71 | 72 | 69 | 71 | 53 | 62 | 48 | 55 | 37 | 39 | 41 | 24 |
| Furniture etc. (36–37) | 62 | 65 | 34 | 65 | 62 | 67 | 48 | 46 | 58 | 39 | 37 | 27 |
| Banking/Insurance (65–67) | 63 | 71 | 73 | 38 | 44 | 38 | 45 | 50 | n.a. | 40 | 47 | 27 |
| Techn. Services (72–73, 74.2, 74.3) | 70 | 64 | 90 | 71 | 52 | 51 | 52 | 43 | 51 | 46 | 48 | 37 |
| # Three highest values | 13 | 12 | 8 | 7 | 2 | 5 | 1 | 0 | 0 | 0 | 0 | 0 |
| # Three lowest values | 0 | 0 | 1 | 1 | 0 | 5 | 1 | 2 | 3 | 8 | 11 | 16 |

Firms with 10 or more employees that have introduced a new product or new process in the time period 1998–2000, as a percentage of all firms; Switzerland and Japan: 2000–2002
Three countries with the highest innovator share per sector are marked bold, three countries with the lowest share are marked italics; n.a.: not available
Source: Arvanitis et al. (2004), Ijichi et al. (2004), unpublished data of CIS3 working group – calculation by ZEW

Analyses of variance[3] show that nearly 70 per cent of the variance in innovator shares among countries and sectors can be explained by country and only 30 per cent by sector. The country-specific effects[4] on sectoral innovator shares are considerable for Switzerland (+18 percentage points higher than the average share), Germany (+14), Austria (+13), Belgium (+8), Japan (–26), Spain (–10) and Italy (–8) while for the other six countries considered here, no statistically significant country effects are to be observed. There are also sector-specific effects on the propensity to innovate, with Chemicals (+20), Rubber/Plastics (+8), Mechanical Engineering (+7) and Electrical/Instruments (+12) showing a significantly higher propensity across countries while Wood (–8), Publishing/Printing (–6) and Metal Processing (–10) show significantly lower innovator shares.

This result is rather striking as one would have expected a stronger sector influence on the propensity to innovate, and a lower influence of countries. All countries considered here are open economies that are strongly interlinked through trade and investment flows. They all may be perceived as mainly specialised in the production of knowledge-intensive goods, making innovation a main factor for competitiveness, and as competing amongst each other in international markets. Therefore incentives to innovate in order to maintain competitiveness should be rather similar within a certain

---

[3]  ANOVA analysis of the data shown in Table 1.
[4]  OLS regressions of country- and sector-specific innovator shares shown in Table 1 with country-specific and sector-specific indicators used as explanatory variables.

sector for each country. At the same time, sector differences in innovator shares are to be expected as a result of differences in technological opportunities and variations in the pace of innovation cycles caused by differing product lifetimes.

The strong country-specific influence upon innovation behaviour may be explained by several factors: first, there may be country-specific barriers or supporting factors for innovation that cause different shares of successfully innovating firms. This strongly relates to the concept of national innovation systems (see Nelson 1993; Lundvall 1990). However, those countries often regarded as having a particularly effective innovation system, such as Japan, Sweden or Finland do not show above average innovation rates. Secondly, innovation comprises a wide variety of activities involving the imitation of new products introduced by others previously, and the adoption of new processes. When looking at one moment in time only, some countries that are passing through a period of rapid technological modernisation and thus high activities of technology imitation and adoption will show high innovator shares, although the technological level of innovation with respect to uncertainty, risk, and the required knowledge and skills may be low.

Thirdly, there may be a strong separation in innovation activities between the majority of small and medium-sized enterprises – which determine the innovator share – and a few very large, internationally active companies who are the main bearer of innovation in their country. In such a case – which one may reckon for Japan – the majority of SMEs act in local or regional markets with little demand for innovation, while the development and commercialisation of new technology takes place in a few 'big players' only. Fourthly, one may suppose a country bias in firm responses on their innovation activities as survey procedures differ, and the term innovation may have different connotations in different languages. However, no systematic knowledge about the prevalence and scope of such biases exist.

The strong country effect is revealed by a comparison of sectoral innovator shares for Germany and the average of the twelve countries considered in the sectoral analysis (see Fig. 3): innovator shares are higher in Germany in each sector except Chemicals/ Oil, where the firms in the reference group show the same propensity to innovate as German firms do. A particularly high innovation share in Germany is shown by the sectors Publishing/Printing, Banking/Insurance, Metal Processing, Mechanical Engineering, Vehicles, and Pulp and Paper. In all these sectors, the difference of the share of innovating firms relative to the average innovation share in the German enterprise sector is higher than the respective difference in the total of the twelve countries. This means that these are sectors where the propensity to innovate is particularly high, i.e. there may be special incentives and supportive framework conditions that spur firms to engage in innovation. On the other hand, the sectors Chemicals/Oil, Metal Production, Rubber/Plastics and Technical Services perform relatively are less 'specialised' in innovation, i.e. their innovator shares are close to that in the reference group.

When looking at the share of innovating firms, a large variety of innovative activities are being mixed, ranging from pure imitation of product ideas implemented by others before to radical, new-to-the-world innovations. It is therefore useful to separate imitation and adoption from more ambitious forms of innovative work by regarding three types of innovation activities: the performance of research and experimental development (R&D), the application of patents, and the introduction of new products that were new to the market. The share of R&D-performing firms in Manufacturing is still highest in Switzerland, followed by Belgium and Germany (Fig. 4).

Scandinavian countries (Finland, Sweden) now show a level similar to that of Germany while southern European countries report only a small share of firms engaging in R&D. In KIBS, the picture is somewhat different, with Portugal showing the highest share, followed by Finland, Belgium and Germany. If one looks only at firms with continuous R&D activities, Germany ranks first in Manufacturing (although Switzerland may lead for this indicator, too, but no data are available) and fourth in KIBS, where Finland, Sweden and Belgium show higher shares. The high figure of Portugal for R&D-performing KIBS firms is driven by firms with occasional R&D, while the share of continuously researching firms is rather low.

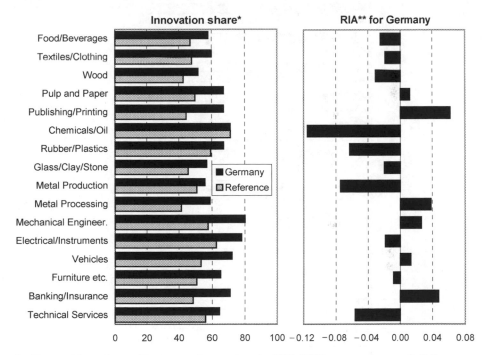

\*   Firms with product and/or process innovations in 1998–2000 as a percentage of all firms; reference: all countries listed in Table 1
\*\* RIA (Relative Innovation Advantage): relation of sector-specific innovator share in Germany to average innovation share in Germany in the 16 sectors considered, divided by the respective relation for the reference countries (including Germany); for ease of presentation, the *tangens hyperpolicus* of the log of this ratio (multiplied by 100) is depicted
Source: Arvanitis et al. (2004), Ijichi et al. (2004), unpublished data of CIS3 working group – calculation by ZEW

**Fig. 3.** Relative innovation share of Germany in 2000 by sectors

Closely related to in-house R&D are patent activities. Inventions are a typical outcome of own R&D efforts, and most inventions will be transferred to patent applications. However, a large portion of R&D may be devoted to other purposes than inventing a new technical solution, such as experimental development to adapt technical specifications of products to specific customer requirements, or the development of new software or new business methods which are by and large not patentable in

Europe. Consequently, the share of patenting firms is clearly below that of R&D-performing firms, and the country ranking clearly differs, too. In Manufacturing, Germany, France and Sweden show the highest share of patenting firms (17 per cent), while Switzerland (12 per cent) and Belgium (10 per cent) now rank in the midfield (Fig. 5). In KIBS, again Sweden, France and Germany rank first (for patent intensities see Chapter 3.2).

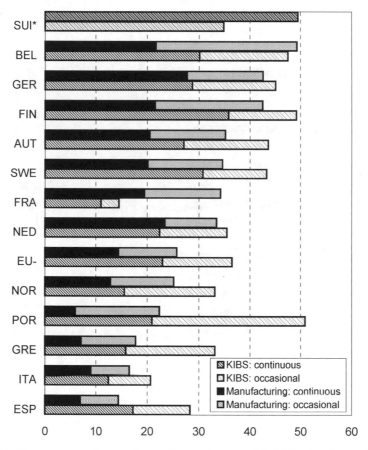

Firms with 10 or more employees that performed intramural R&D in the time period 1998–2000 either continuously or occasionally, as a percentage of all firms
*   EU-15: excluding Ireland, Luxembourg, Sweden, Great Britain, but including Norway
** Switzerland: firms with 5 or more employees, time period 2000–2002, no data on continuous vs. occasional R&D activities published
Finland, France: KIBS excluding NACE 65–67
Sources: EU countries and Norway: Eurostat – CIS3 (New Cronos), Switzerland: Arvanitis et al. (2004) – calculation by ZEW

**Fig. 4.** Share of R&D-performing firms in 2000 (in per cent)

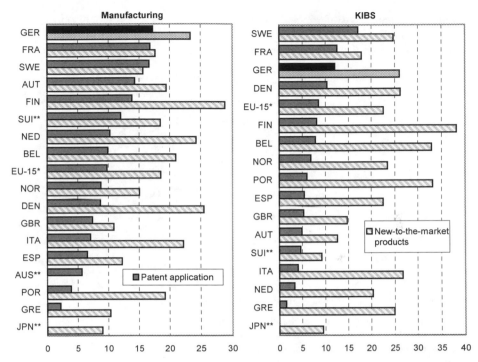

Firms with 10 or more employees that have applied for patents in the time period 1998–2000, and that have introduced new products that were new to their market, respectively, as a percentage of all firms; Australia, Switzerland: firms with 5 or more employees
*   EU-15: excluding Ireland, Luxembourg, Denmark and Great Britain, but including Norway
**  Australia, Japan, Switzerland: 2000–2002, data on patenting firms are missing for Japan, data on firms with new-to-the-market products are missing for Australia
Finland, France: KIBS excluding NACE 65–67
Sources: EU countries and Norway: Eurostat – CIS3 (New Cronos), Switzerland: Arvanitis et al. (2004), Japan: Ijichi et al. (2004), Australia: Australian Bureau of Statistics (2005) – calculation by ZEW

**Fig. 5.** Share of patenting firms and of original innovators in 2000 (in per cent)

A complementary indicator is the share of 'original innovators', i.e. firms that were the first to introduce a certain new product in their relevant market. As the relevant market is defined by the firm and may represent a regional market, new-to-the-market products are not automatically new-to-the-world products (i.e. absolute novelties), but may also represent some form of imitation and thus need not be connected to R&D and patenting. Nevertheless, introducing a new product to a market as first mover involves a particular degree of uncertainty and is thus a more ambitious innovation activity than simply imitating products of other firms already offered in a firm's market. Finland ranks first both in Manufacturing and KIBS concerning the share of original innovators. In Manufacturing, Denmark, the Netherlands, Germany and Italy also show high shares of such type of innovators, while in KIBS, Portugal and Belgium report very high shares (about one-third of all KIBS firms, see Fig. 5) of firms with new-to-the-market products. The German KIBS sector shows an original innovator share of 26 per cent, which is similar to the level of Italy, Denmark and Sweden and clearly above the EU average. The figures for Japan for this indicator are the lowest among the countries considered.

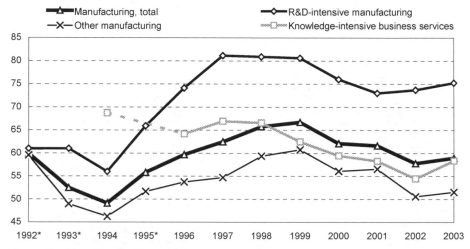

Firms with 5 or more employees that have introduced a new product or new process in the pre-vious three-year period, as a percentage of all firms
R&D-intensive manufacturing: NACE 24, 29–35; Other manufacturing: NACE 10–23, 25–28, 36–37
*   1992, 1993, 1995: no data available for KIBS
Source: ZEW, Mannheim Innovation Panel – calculation by ZEW

**Fig. 6.** Share of innovating firms in Germany 1992–2003 by sector groups (in per cent)

International comparison reveals a high innovation orientation of German firms. From the perspective of technological performance, the dynamics of the firm's participation in innovation activities is of particular interest, too, as this indicates changes in incen-tives and barriers to innovate. International data on this subject are missing, however, as only a very few countries perform annual innovation surveys. In analysing the dynamics of innovation shares, we restrict our analysis to German data. The second half of 1990s saw a rapid increase in the innovator share in German manufacturing, reaching a peak in 1999 with 67 per cent of manufacturing firms engaging in success-ful innovation activities (Fig. 6). High-tech sectors experienced a particularly marked increase from 56 per cent in 1994 to 81 per cent in 1997 to 1999.

The strong increase in innovation activities in the second half of the 1990s in German manufacturing was first caused by an increase in the number of firms that introduced new processes to cut costs. This share rose from 31 per cent in 1994 to 43 per cent in 1997 (Fig. 7). The further increase in the innovator share was strongly driven by firms that introduced original innovations, i.e. new-to-the-market products. Their share – remaining almost stable from 1994 to 1997 – climbed from 24 per cent in 1997 to 34 per cent in 1999. With respect to falling innovator shares after 1999, again cost-saving process innovations declined first (from 40 per cent in 1999 to 20 per cent in 2001), while the share of original innovators remained rather high until 2002, but fell back to the level of 1997 in 2003.

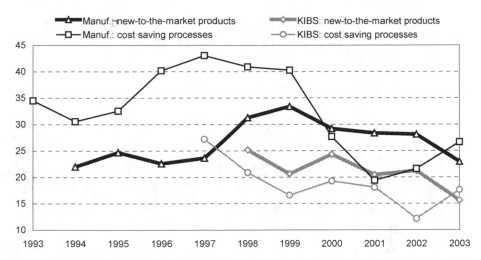

Firms with 5 or more employees that introduced new products that were new to their market, and firms with 5 or more employees that introduced new processes that lead to a reduction in unit costs of production, as a percentage of all firms
Source: ZEW: Mannheim Innovation Panel – calculation by ZEW

**Fig. 7.** Share of original product innovators and of rationalisation innovators in Germany 1993–2003 (in per cent)

In KIBS, a similar pattern emerges, although missing information prior to 1997/1998 restricts analysis over time. In 2003, a perfectly parallel development to that in Manufacturing occurs, with a strongly falling share of original product innovators and rising share of rationalisation innovators. If the latter is accepted as a type of 'leading indicator' on firms' propensity to innovate, one might expect increasing innovator shares for 2004 onwards. This is supported by firms' planned innovation activities in 2004 and 2005 as revealed by a respective question in the 2004 innovation survey (see Rammer et al. 2005b).

The observed pattern of increasing process innovation activities in the early upswing of a business cycle (which refers in particular to 1995–1998 after the 1993/1994 recession in Germany) and strongly decreasing activities in recession stages (i.e. 2000–2001) point to a strong link between process innovation and investment. The more lagging development of product innovations and new-to-the-market products in particular is partially a result of long project duration for such innovations. An unfavourable economic environment will also cause reduced product innovation activities, as low demand complicates market introduction of product novelties that are typically more expensive than competing products already in the market. At the same time, strong increases in demand – as experienced in Germany in 2000 – are likely to spur product innovation activities.

The high share of R&D-performing manufacturing firms in Germany as revealed by the international comparison is rather a structural feature of the German enterprise sector. While the innovator share declined after 1999, the share of R&D-performing firms remained stable and even increased in 2003 (Fig. 8). This means that the share of non-researching firms in all innovating firms is significantly falling.

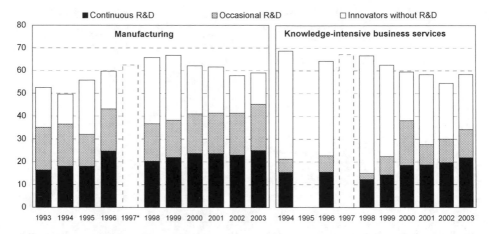

Firms with 5 or more employees that performed intramural R&D continuously or occasionally or that innovate without performing R&D, as a percentage of all firms
* No data on R&D activities in KIBS for 1995 and no data on R&D activities in Manufacturing and KIBS for 1997
Source: ZEW: Mannheim Innovation Panel – calculation by ZEW

**Fig. 8.** Share of R&D-performing firms in Germany 1993–2003 (in per cent)

This also holds true for KIBS, although some cyclical effects appear, such as a high share of occasionally R&D-performing service firms in 2000. This shows that stepping into and out of R&D is rather easy in services, as little fixed investment is associated with R&D in this sector, and the high average skill level of employees allows for shifting people from other firm functions to R&D and *vice versa*.


# Input and Output in Innovation Processes

The expenditures for innovation activities measure the financial resources that firms provide for developing and implementing new products and processes. These costs cover intramural and extramural expenditures for R&D, as well as a number of other categories, such as fixed investment for machinery, equipment and building for innovation, purchase of licensing of patents, non-patented inventions and other knowledge, expenditures for preparatory work, for training, and for market introduction of innovation. A useful indicator for the input to innovation is the ratio of expenditures for innovation to turnover ('innovation intensity'). Based on CIS3 data, innovation intensity for Manufacturing may be regarded as reliable, while data for services are less plausible for a number of countries.

In 2000, Sweden reports the highest expenditures for innovation as a percentage of total turnover in Manufacturing (considering both innovative and non-innovative firms for turnover) (Fig. 9). Germany ranks third, with an innovation intensity of 4.7 per cent, just behind Belgium (4.9 per cent) and in front of Switzerland (4.3 per cent) and Finland (3.9 per cent).

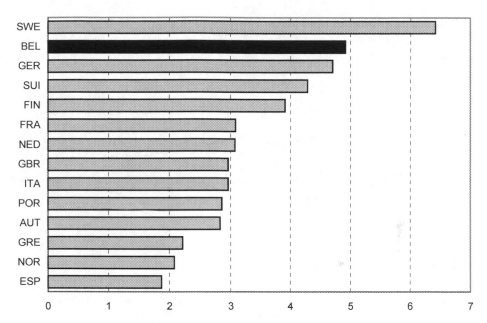

Total expenditures for innovation activities in 2000, as a percentage of total turnover of manu-
facturing firms (firms with 10 or more employees, except Switzerland: 5 or more)
Sources: EU countries and Norway: European Commission (Trendchart Website), Switzerland:
Arvanitis et al. (2004) – calculation by ZEW

**Fig. 9.** Innovation expenditures as a percentage of turnover in Manufacturing in 2000

The country ranking is very much in line with that for R&D expenditures as a percentage of production (see Chapter 2.2), though Finland shows rather low innovation
intensity compared to R&D, while that of Belgium is much higher than one would
expect from the country's R&D intensity in Manufacturing. Although differences in
the significance of non-R&D innovation expenditures (such as fixed investment,
training, preparatory work etc.) may account for some of the discrepancy, the differing survey methods and likely measurement errors should also be taken into account.

In German manufacturing, innovation intensity significantly declined from 1992 to
1995 as a result of the recession in 1993/1994, followed by a small increase until
1999 (see Fig. 10). The strong increase in turnover due to high economic growth in
2000 – associated with some shortages in factor supply, especially qualified labour –
caused the ratio to shrink in this year, despite further increasing expenditure figures.
Until 2003, innovation intensity significantly increased to about five per cent, despite
a weak macroeconomic environment since 2001.

This somewhat astonishing development may be attributed to a number of factors:
First, turnover figures grew only moderately in this period while innovation expenditures expanded at a more or less constant rate. Secondly, the main driver for increasing input in innovation is high-technology manufacturing. These sectors, dominated
in Germany by Automobiles, Mechanical Engineering, Electrical Engineering and
Electronics, and Chemicals, are increasingly export-oriented and tend to follow more
the world economic development rather than business cycles of the German domestic
economy. Since 2002 and 2003 have been years of high growth of the world economy,

these sectors were confronted primarily with expanding markets. On the contrary, innovation intensity in other manufacturing sectors has been stagnating at a low level since 2000 (see also Chapters 2.2 and 4.1).

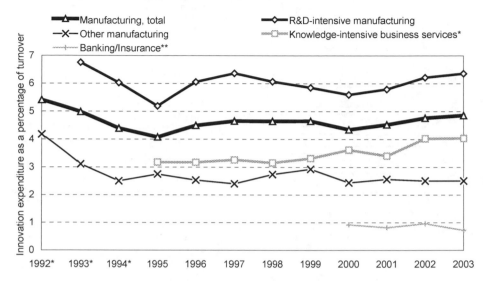

Firms with 5 or more employees
\* Knowledge-intensive business services exclude Banking/Insurance, data prior to 1995 not available
\*\* Banking/Insurance: NACE 65–67, turnover measured as gross income from interest, premiums and commissions
Source: ZEW: Mannheim Innovation Panel – calculation by ZEW

**Fig. 10.** Expenditures for innovation as a percentage of turnover in Germany 1992–2003 by sector groups

In KIBS, innovation expenditures grew faster than turnover in 1999 and 2000, but declined in 2001 and again in 2003, while 2002 saw a significant increase in expenditures for innovative projects. Innovation intensity in most KIBS – except Banking/Insurance – has reached 4 per cent in 2003 and is clearly above the level of non-high-tech manufacturing. The low level of Banking/Insurance may be associated with a different concept of turnover in this industry.

It is still more difficult to measure the output of innovation than input, as the result of innovation activities may take very different forms and thus yield different economic effects. The share of turnover with product innovations, i.e. products that have been introduced to the market within the previous three-year period, is a measure often used in innovation statistics to capture the direct economic impact of product innovations. It also allows differentiation by type of product innovation (new-to-the-market products vs. product imitations).

German manufacturing firms generated 45 per cent of their turnover in 2000 with products not older than three years (Fig. 11). This corresponds to the second highest value among the countries for which data is available, only one percentage point behind Finland. Manufacturing firms from Spain and Italy were also able to realise high shares with product innovation, while Belgium ranks last, despite a high share of product innovators, R&D-performers and firms with new-to-the-market products. This points to the fact that turnover share are strongly influenced by large companies, while innovator shares and the like are determined by SMEs.

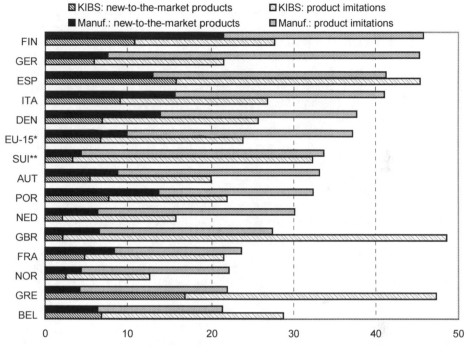

Turnover with new products in 2000 that have been introduced in 1998–2000, as a percentage of total turnover (firms with 10 or more employees, except Switzerland: 5 or more)
\* EU-15: excluding Ireland, Luxembourg and Sweden, but including Norway
\*\* Switzerland: new-to-the-market products refer to the world market
Finland, France: KIBS excluding NACE 65–67
Sources: EU countries and Norway: Eurostat – CIS3 (New Cronos), Switzerland: Arvanitis et al. (2004) – calculation by ZEW

**Fig. 11.** Turnover share with new products in 2000 by type of product innovation (in per cent)

Only 8 per cent of the total turnover of German manufacturing firms can be attributed to new-to-the-market products, which is less than EU average. High shares with such original innovations are obtained by Finland, Italy, Portugal, Denmark and Spain with 13 to 21 per cent. Since the market is defined from the perspective of the firm, one may assume that many firms apply a regional conceptualisation of market. Thus this measure also captures the geographical diffusion of new products to some extent. High values for this indicator may thus occur in the case of a high share of firms that focus on regional rather than worldwide markets. This may be the case for some southern European countries. If one considers R&D-oriented economies with a high export orientation and a strong world-market focus, such as Switzerland, the Netherlands, Belgium or Great Britain, indicator values are similar to the German ones. Still striking are, however, turnover shares from new-to-the-market products for Finland and Denmark, which both are world-market embedded economies, too.

A high sales share with new products in total, and a low sales share with new-to-the-market products in German manufacturing imply that industrial firms in Germany are notably strong in generating turnover with product imitations. This corresponds to a generally high innovation orientation of SMEs and points to a high pace of diffusion of innovation. One should note, however, that the turnover share with product imitations is also affected by factors not associated with innovation, such as the average lifetime or products in a certain market.

In KIBS, sales shares with new services are lower than sales shares with new products in Manufacturing for most countries. This is especially true for Germany. Just 21 per cent of total turnover in KIBS is generated by services introduced within the previous three-year period, while the EU average is 14 per cent. High figures for this indicator are reported for Great Britain, Greece, Spain and Switzerland. KIBS in Spain and Greece are also able to obtain high sales shares with new-to-the-market products (16–17 per cent), whereas Germany also ranks below EU average for this indicator (6 vs. 7 per cent).

Turnover with new products covers a certain aspect of innovation success only, i.e. the market acceptance of newly introduced products. Another important aspect is the economic effects of process innovation. Finding an appropriate measure here is complicated by the different potential effects of such innovation activities: first, process innovation may affect the efficiency of production, thus raising productivity by lowering unit costs of production. Secondly, it may also – or alternatively – increase the quality of products, thus increasing sales volume (both of new and old products). Finally, process innovations may also be associated with the introduction of new products and neither influence efficiency nor quality.

While international statistics on innovation do not cover innovation success on the side of process innovation, the German innovation survey applies a rough indicator for efficiency effects of process innovation: the share of unit costs that have been reduced as a result of process innovation in the previous three-year period. For this indicator, as well as for the turnover share with new-to-the-market products, annual figures for the last ten years are available. Success with process innovation tends to be pro-cyclical in Manufacturing: low level of process innovation driven unit cost reduction occur in 1994/1995 and again in 2002/2003, while high figures are reported for the second half of the 1990s (Fig. 12). This pattern may be explained by an associated development of factor costs, investment, and capacity utilisation: factor costs, especially labour costs, tend to increase slowly or even decrease (in real terms) in recession periods as a result of increasing unemployment, reducing the pressure to cut costs by innovative measures while opening up other alternatives, such as re-bargaining of wages or material supply costs. Low propensity to invest into fixed assets is likely to shift innovation expenditure away from investment in new machinery and equipment, reducing the likely efficiency gains of this type of expenditure. Falling rates of capacity utilisation due to decreasing demand finally diminish the opportunities to utilise scale economies, which is often a prerequisite for unit cost reduction.

In KIBS, such a pattern cannot be observed, partly because only data since 1997 are available. In 2001 and 2002, however, cost-saving effects of process innovation were particularly high, despite an unfavourable macroeconomic environment. Here one may assume lagged effects of investment in new ICT that took place in 1999 and 2000, producing unit cost reductions only some time later.

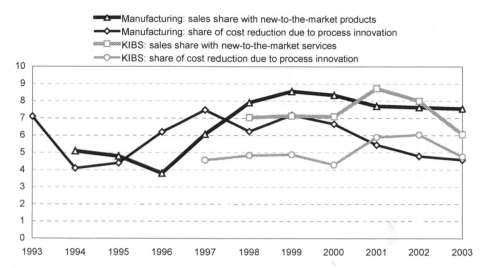

Firms with 5 or more employees
* Knowledge-intensive business services exclude Banking/Insurance
Source: ZEW: Mannheim Innovation Panel – calculation by ZEW

**Fig. 12.** Share of turnover with new-to-the-market products and share of cost reduction due to process innovation in Germany 1993–2003 (in per cent)

The share of turnover with new-to-the-market products follows a similar pattern (see Fig. 12). In Manufacturing, the highest level was reached in 1998–2000 with more than 8 per cent. Surprisingly, the economic downturn from 2001 to 2003 did not affect sales shares with original innovation significantly, the share remaining well above 7 per cent. This may be caused by different factors: first, decreasing demand may affect non-innovative products much more strongly than novelties, causing the sales share with novelties to rise even in the case of stagnating absolute sales. Secondly, new-to-the-market products often address customers with low price and income elasticity who keep on demanding such new products despite a general decline in demand. Thirdly, German manufacturers are highly and increasingly oriented to export markets and the business climate was more favourable in 2002 and 2003 in many export markets.

In KIBS, sales share with original innovations follow the same path as cost-saving shares, suggesting that a similar mechanism is at work, i.e. lagged effects of the introduction and use of new ICT such as computerisation, Internet applications, e-business etc. that were introduced in the late 1990s and especially in 2000.

Relating innovation success to innovation input – i.e. expenditures for innovation in the previous three-year period[5] – gives a crude measure for the 'efficiency' of innovation activities. In order to bring together both product- and process-related measures of innovation success, we calculate the contribution of new products sales and cost savings to value added, assuming that there is a rather stable relation between

---

[5] Since there is a certain time period between innovation activities (and associated expenditures) and the successful implementation of new products and processes, we use a 0.5 year time lag for innovation expenditures. The results are, however, not sensitive to the chosen time lag. For more details on the calculation, see Rammer and Schmidt (2003).

value added and profits for each sector in the period considered. Sales with new products are restricted to those made with new-to-the-market products, as these are most likely to generate extra profits while sales with product imitations will only rarely produce additional returns. Output–input relations are first calculated on a sector level and then aggregated to Manufacturing and KIBS.

The results indicate that 'efficiency' of innovation activities is strongly related to the business cycle in Manufacturing. There was a strong increase in the indicator until 1999, when it shrank successively until 2003, reaching the level of 1993/1994 (Fig. 13). In KIBS, the output–input relation arrived at its highest level in 2001, again indicating high returns from innovation projects carried out during the 'new economy' in 1999/2000. Since then, the indicator fell sharply until 2003, reaching a level below that of 1997.

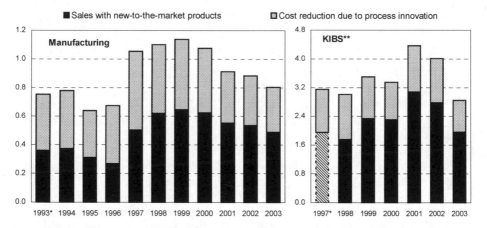

Value added effects of sales of new-to-the-market products, and cost savings through process innovation, related to innovation expenditures in the previous three year period, lagged by 0.5 years; firms with 5 or more employees
\* 1993: sales with new-to-the-market products in Manufacturing missing for 1993, figure estimated based on 1992 and 1994 shares and the change in total sales with new products 1992–1993; 1997: sales with new products missing, figure estimated based on the total sales with new products
\*\* Knowledge-intensive business services excluding Banking/Insurance
Source: ZEW: Mannheim Innovation Panel – calculation by ZEW

**Fig. 13.** Output-input relation of innovation activities in Germany 1993–2003

Fig. 13 also shows that the output–input relation is significantly higher in KIBS than in Manufacturing. This need not mean lower efficiency of innovation in Manufacturing, however. Although innovation is generally more costly in Manufacturing, innovations in this sector tend to generate extra profits for a longer period than new services do. One reason is that copying new products is much less easy than imitating new services. Secondly, industrial firms may make use of intellectual property rights (patents) to protect their novelties from imitation, while most services are not subject to patent protection. Moreover, one may assume that profit margins for new services are lower than those for new products as quality advantages of new products are easier to demonstrate and communicate to customers than higher quality associated with new services.

## Information Sources, Co-operation, Effects and Barriers

The previous analyses have shown a high innovation orientation of the German firm sector and high innovation success in German manufacturing. A special strength seems to be the high share of innovative SMEs and the rapid diffusion of new technologies and new products. This raises the question whether certain characteristics of the organisation of innovation processes may be accountable for this particular performance. The CIS3 provides indicators for several aspects of innovation processes: the sources used for gathering ideas and information for innovation activities, co-operation with external partners in innovation, effects of innovation, and barriers that hamper innovative activities.

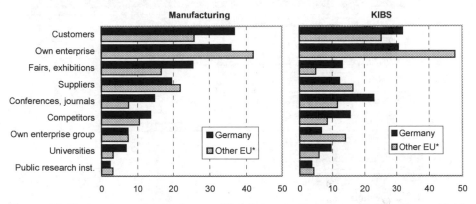

Firms with 10 or more employees that specified the respective source of information as highly important for supply of ideas and realisation of innovation projects in 1998–2000, as a percentage of all firms with innovation activities in 1998–2000
*   Other EU: Austria, Belgium, Finland, Greece, Iceland, Italy, Luxembourg, Netherlands, Norway, Portugal, Spain, Sweden (Manufacturing: excluding France)
Sources: EU countries and Norway: Eurostat – CIS3 (New Cronos) – calculation by ZEW

**Fig. 14.** Information sources for innovation activities in Germany and other European countries in 2000 (in per cent)

Innovative German firms more frequently use customers, fairs and exhibitions, conferences and journals, competitors, and universities as information sources for innovation activities than firms in other EU countries (Fig. 14). Contrarily, sources from within the own firm are used less often. This points to a more open-oriented design of innovation processes that particularly takes into account the needs and requirements of demand (directly through customers, or indirectly through fairs) and uses science sources (conferences, journals, universities) to develop technologically advanced solutions. This pattern holds true both for Manufacturing and Services. It reflects to some extent a particular advantage of the German innovation system, that is, innovation-demanding customers whose innovation preferences often turn out to lead global trends in innovation. Innovators can profit from such customer-driven innovation when attempting to push their new products in international markets (see Beise 2001).

The more intensive use of information sources is not accompanied, however, by more intensive active co-operation in innovation projects. In Germany, 17 per cent of manufacturing firms, and 23 per cent of KIBS firms with innovation activities in 1998–2000 had co-operation agreements with external partners, including customers, suppliers, competitors, consultants, universities, private R&D companies and public research institutes, as well as other firms within the own enterprise group (Fig. 15). This is among the lowest figures within EU countries. Only the southern European countries Spain, Italy and Portugal show a lower propensity of innovating firms to co-operate. As Spain and Italy, as well as Germany, show high rates of innovation success – at least when referring to turnover share with new products – this raises the questions whether a high level of co-operation in innovation is automatically a positive indicator for well-designed innovation processes.[6]

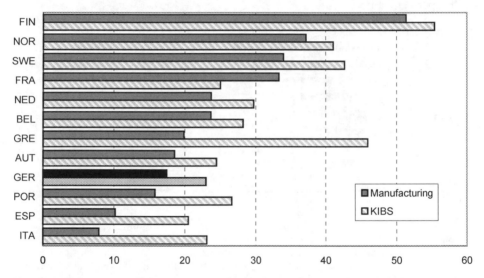

Firms with 10 or more employees that co-operated in innovation projects with external partners in 1998–2000, as a percentage of all firms with innovation activities in 1998–2000
Finland: KIBS excluding NACE 65–67
Sources: EU countries and Norway: Eurostat – CIS3 (New Cronos) – calculation by ZEW

**Fig. 15.** Co-operation in innovation projects in 2000 by countries (in per cent)

Nevertheless, multivariate analyses for German firms show that co-operation indeed positively contributes to innovation success in some sectors (see Rammer & Schmidt 2003): There is a positive effect on turnover with new products for innovating firms in KIBS. In Manufacturing, positive effects are to be observed for non-high-tech manufacturing, only where both turnover with new-to-the-market products and cost savings due to process innovation significantly increase in case of co-operations. In high-tech manufacturing, co-operation has almost no effect on innovation success. In the case of Germany one has to bear in mind that co-operation in innovation strongly interacts with the receipt of public financial support, as most innovation programmes demand co-operation.

---

[6] The latter is implicitly suggested by the European Innovation Scoreboard, for example, which uses the share of SMEs that co-operate in innovation as an indicator for the transmission and application of knowledge (see European Commission 2004).

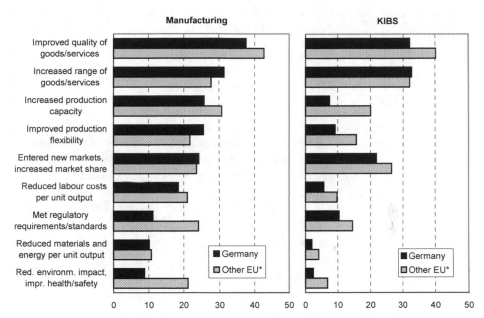

Firms with 10 or more employees that cited the respective effect as a highly important effect of their innovation activities 1998–2000, as a percentage of all firms with innovation activities in 1998–2000
* Other EU: Austria, Belgium, Finland, France, Greece, Iceland, Italy, Luxembourg, Netherlands, Norway, Portugal, Spain, Sweden (Manufacturing: excluding Luxembourg)
Sources: EU countries and Norway: Eurostat – CIS3 (New Cronos) – calculation by ZEW

**Fig. 16.** Effects of innovation activities in Germany and other European countries in 2000 (in per cent)

Another variable that informs about the design of innovation processes are the effects that emanate from innovation. German firms in general report less often highly important effects of innovation (Fig. 16). One exception is the increase in range of products where both Manufacturing and KIBS firms are slightly above the other EU countries. German manufacturers also more frequently report an increase in production flexibility as a main effect of innovation. A significantly lower share of firms in Germany compared to other EU countries mention an increase in capacity, the meeting of regulation and standards, and improving environment, health and safety as effects of innovation. As these outcomes are only indirectly if ever associated to economic success indicators of innovation, such as turnover shares or cost reduction, one may conclude that German innovators concentrate on competitive advantages as a main result of innovation activities.

With respect to barriers that hamper innovation activities, innovative firms in Germany more often cited a lack of qualified personnel, excessive economic risks and regulations, and regulations and standards as being highly important than innovative firms in other EU countries did (Fig. 17). This result holds for Manufacturing and KIBS, while German KIBS firms also perceived financial barriers (too high innovation costs, lack of appropriated financing sources) of higher significance. At the same time, customer responsiveness, market information and technological information are considerably less prominent for impeding innovation in German firms. Innovation in Germany thus seems to be more restricted by factor markets and inflexible regulation than by incomplete access to information or innovation-adverse preferences of customers. The higher importance of economic risks is likely to reflect the more ambitious scope of innovation in German firms with respect to technological scope and the need for R&D.

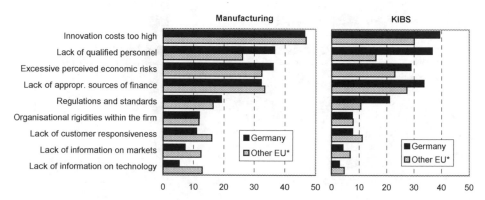

Firms with 10 or more employees that cited the respective effect as being highly important for hampering innovation activities in 1998–2000, as a percentage of all firms with innovation activities in 1998–2000
* Other EU: Austria, Belgium, Finland, France, Greece, Iceland, Italy, Luxembourg, Netherlands, Norway, Portugal, Spain, Sweden (Manufacturing: excluding Luxembourg)
Sources: EU countries and Norway: Eurostat – CIS3 (New Cronos) – calculation by ZEW

**Fig. 17.** Barriers to innovation in Germany and other European countries in 2000 (in per cent)

The significance of barriers to innovation changes, however, such as scarcity in factor supply, introduction of innovation-relevant regulations or the scope of innovation activities, may vary over time. Within the period 1994 to 2002, the relative importance of various barriers has changed quite markedly (Table 2):[7] Lack of qualified personnel was particularly relevant in the economic upswing of 1998 to 2000, but lost its dominating role in the stage of economic stagnation that followed that period.

In this 2000–2002 period, as well as in the mid of the 1990s, lack in financing sources was the most important barrier to innovation as perceived by German firms. Regulation and standards became particularly important in KIBS in periods of weak macroeconomic performance (1994–1996, 2000–2002). Lack in customer responsiveness has also gained in relevance in recent years, pointing to a possible anti-cyclical pattern. This may be associated with increasing price elasticity of demand in periods of regressing real household income and shrinking firm profits (which are typical for recession periods), resulting in decreasing demand for innovative products since these are often more expensive than comparable predecessor products. Lack of information

---

[7] We only look at barriers that are associated with some type of market failure, leaving 'high economic risks' and 'too high innovation costs' (since these barriers mainly refer to 'natural' characteristics of any innovation activity) as well as 'organisational rigidities within the firm' out of our analysis.

on markets and lack of information on technology are of very low importance throughout the whole period covered.

Table 2. Ranking of selected barriers to innovation in Germany 1994–2002

| | 1994–1996 | 1996–1998 | 1998–2000 | 2000–2002 |
|---|---|---|---|---|
| **Manufacturing** | | | | |
| Lack of appropriate sources of financing | 1 | 1 | 2 | 1 |
| Lack of qualified personnel | 2 | 2 | 1 | 2 |
| Lack of customer responsiveness | 5 | 4 | 5 | 3 |
| Regulation, standards, bureaucratic procedures | 3 | 3 | 3 | 4 |
| Lack of information on technology | 4 | 5 | 4 | 5 |
| Lack of information on markets | 6 | 6 | 6 | 6 |
| **KIBS** | | | | |
| Lack of appropriate sources of financing | 1 | 2 | 2 | 1 |
| Regulation, standards, bureaucratic procedures | 2 | 3 | 3 | 2 |
| Lack of qualified personnel | 3 | 1 | 1 | 3 |
| Lack of customer responsiveness | 4 | 4 | 5 | 4 |
| Lack of information on technology | 5 | 6 | 4 | 5 |
| Lack of information on markets | 6 | 5 | 6 | 6 |

Relative rank of the six barriers distinguished; data based on the share of innovative firms (with 5 or more employees) that cited the respective barrier as being highly important for hampering innovation activities in the respective time period; 1996–1998 and 2000–2002: importance of barriers measured with respect to serious delay, abandoning or stopping innovation projects
Source: ZEW: Mannheim Innovation Panel – calculation by ZEW

## Conclusions

The German business sector is highly innovation-oriented compared to most other industrial countries. This is due to a high propensity of SMEs to innovate and holds true for all sectors of Manufacturing and knowledge-intensive business services. A broad spread of innovation activities among the SME sector may be viewed as an important prerequisite for leveraging productivity and employment effects of innovation (see Acs & Audretsch 1990) and is a main source of the generally high international competitiveness of both high-technology and low-technology sectors, as revealed by surplus in international trade (see also Chapter 4.1) High innovation orientation of SMEs is accompanied by both high expenditures for innovation activities and high returns from innovation efforts, indicating high input and output innovation intensity among large companies.

Altogether, indicators on innovation in firms underpin the dependence of the German business sector on being a leader in technology development and diffusion, as most comparative advantages of Germany rest on being more innovative than others. From this perspective, low dynamics for many innovation indicators in recent years, including a declining share of innovating firms, are a source of concern. After a peak in many innovation indicators in the late 1990s, economic stagnation of the German domestic market resulted in a significant number of SMEs that retired from innovation, and falling returns from innovation activities. A still high level of innovation expenditures largely rests on export-oriented sectors and firms that benefit from high growth of the world economy and increasingly tend to orient their innovation efforts towards export markets.

In order to maintain a strong position of German firms in innovation, a revival of the German economy, as well as a removal of barriers to innovation, are the most urgent tasks. While a lack of qualified personnel was the most pressing hampering factor during the last boom period (1998–2000) – and is much likely to come back on the agenda as soon as economic stagnation will be overcome – a lack of financing sources was the most frequently cited barrier to innovation in 2000–2002, which particularly concerns SMEs (see Rammer et al. 2005c).

# Part 4. Structural Change and Performance of the NSI

# 4.1 Economic Performance of Technology Sectors

Dieter Schumacher

**Abstract.** In this chapter we analyse the performance in R&D-intensive goods and knowledge-intensive services in domestic and foreign markets in terms of production, employment and international trade flows. The empirical evidence on production suggests that the technological performance of the German economy is strong in terms of sectoral patterns, while it has fallen behind in terms of levels. On the other hand, the analysis of foreign trade flows suggests that the German position in R&D-intensive goods is strong in absolute terms whereas it weakened in terms of commodity patterns.

## Introduction

In this chapter, the technological performance of a national economy is to be assessed by output indicators. The analysis of innovations in Chapter 3.3 and the analysis of patent activities in Chapter 3.2 look at the output side as well. Here, the emphasis is on the success of R&D-intensive goods and knowledge-intensive services in domestic and foreign markets in terms of production, employment and international trade flows. From this point of view, the more a country produces and absorbs R&D and knowledge-intensive goods and services, the better the technological performance is evaluated (for definition see Chapter 1).

The chapter is organised as follows. To start with, we consider the position of Germany and other technologically important OECD countries in terms of total production of R&D-intensive and knowledge-intensive goods and services (human-capital-intensive production). The analysis refers to absolute levels as well as sectoral patterns of value-added, employment and productivity. Secondly, we provide detailed analysis of values and structures of exports and imports of these countries.

## Production

The most comprehensive indicator of the market success in leading technologies is the value of production in R&D-intensive manufacturing and in knowledge-intensive services. The efficiency of production is represented by the value-added per person engaged or per hour worked, respectively (labour productivity). Consequently, the main indicators for an international comparison of economic structures are value-added (in domestic currency and in PPP $) in terms of per capita levels, and sector patterns as well as labour productivity. The data are taken from OECD sources. The main body stems from the STAN database providing information at the sectoral level supplemented by economy-wide figures from the OECD Economic Outlook and by DIW estimates of some detailed data not originally reported. The R&D-intensive

*U. Schmoch, C. Rammer and H. Legler (eds.), National Systems of Innovation in Comparison, 135–151.*

industries here comprise the production of Chemicals, Machinery and Equipment; the knowledge-intensive services include Telecommunications, Finance, Insurance, Real Estate and Business Services as well as Health and Social Work.[1]

The ranking of countries according to their overall economic efficiency depends on the relation of value-added to population (per capita income), the number of persons engaged or the number of hours worked (labour productivity). The number of hours worked per capita can be very different among countries because the share of persons engaged in total population and the hours annually worked per person engaged may differ substantially. In western Europe, the hours annually worked per head range between 600 and 800, with the Netherlands, France and Italy at the lower end and Great Britain at the upper end, whereas it is significantly more in the USA, Canada and Japan, achieving 850 to 900 hours.

Table 1 presents relevant data for selected OECD countries in 2002. Relating total value-added, i.e. GDP, (at current PPP $) to population, the USA achieve the largest per capita income, Germany, Italy and the EU average achieving only 70 per cent of the US level. The value-added per person engaged in general differs less between the USA and the EU, per hour worked the difference diminishes considerably. In the Netherlands and France, the value-added per hour worked is even larger than in the USA, in Germany, Denmark and the EU as a whole it achieves 90 per cent of the US level.

Concentrating on human-capital-intensive production, the value-added in R&D-intensive manufacturing is highest in Germany amounting to some PPP $3,100 per capita in 2002.[2] In the USA, it is smaller and comparable to the level in Japan and Sweden. The per capita production of knowledge-intensive services, however, in the USA is by far the largest among all countries considered in the analysis. In Germany, it achieves some PPP $6,900 (excl. Real Estate), lagging behind the United States and also less than in most other OECD countries under consideration. Taking R&D-intensive manufacturing and knowledge-intensive services together, the human-capital-intensive production in Germany has a per capita value of some PPP $10,000, due to the large manufacturing sector. This is far behind the USA, but more than the EU average. It is somewhat lower than in Belgium, it compares with the Netherlands, Sweden and France and it is somewhat more than in Canada and Great Britain.

Compared to the beginning of the 1990s, the German position deteriorated considerably in relative terms. In 1991, the level of human capital production in Germany was significantly higher than in other OECD countries except for the USA. After 1995, due to low growth in Germany, other West European countries caught up with or overtook Germany in the production of knowledge-intensive services. Only at the beginning of the new decade did the (relative) German position not deteriorate further. In R&D-intensive manufacturing, the German advantage diminished in the

---

[1] Of which Pharmaceuticals; Office and Computing Machinery; Radio, Television and Communication Equipment as well as Aircraft and Spacecraft are defined as leading-edge technology. For the definition see Grupp et al. (2000: 99). Real estate activities account for some 8 to 12 per cent of value-added in OECD countries and only some 1 per cent of employment. They bias the comparison of productivity over sectors and are therefore excluded in some parts of the analysis.

[2] The value-added figures in the STAN database may refer to different pricing concepts. For Table 1 we recalculated the levels by industries according to the GDP concept (at market prices) in order to make the figures internationally comparable.

first half of the 1990s and increased again after 1995 as compared to most OECD countries. The setbacks in the IT sector after 2000 affected Germany less than countries such as the USA, Japan, Sweden and Finland. All in all, however, the lacking impetus for knowledge-intensive services in Germany could not be compensated by the improved position in R&D-intensive manufacturing.

**Table 1.** Production levels in selected OECD countries, 2002

| | GER | USA | JPN | FRA | ITA | GBR | NED | BEL | DEN | SWE | FIN | CAN | EU-15[1] |
|---|---|---|---|---|---|---|---|---|---|---|---|---|---|
| | Gross Domestic Product | | | | | | | | | | | | |
| Per head of population in thsd. PPP $ | 25.9 | 36.3 | 26.9 | 28.2 | 25.9 | 28.0 | 29.1 | 27.9 | 29.2 | 27.3 | 26.5 | 30.8 | 26.2 |
| USA = 100 | 71 | 100 | 74 | 78 | 71 | 77 | 80 | 77 | 81 | 75 | 73 | 85 | 72 |
| Per person engaged in thsd. PPP $ | 55.3 | 76.8 | 54.1 | 68.1 | 68.8 | 59.8 | 65.6 | 68.4 | 57.4 | 57.4 | 58.3 | 62.7 | 60.2 |
| USA = 100 | 72 | 100 | 70 | 89 | 90 | 78 | 85 | 89 | 75 | 75 | 76 | 82 | 78 |
| Per hour worked in PPP $ | 38.3 | 42.3 | 29.9 | 46.6 | 42.5 | 35.0 | 49.0 | 43.9 | 38.3 | 36.3 | 34.6 | 35.3 | 38.1 |
| USA = 100 | 90 | 100 | 71 | 110 | 100 | 83 | 116 | 104 | 90 | 86 | 82 | 83 | 90 |
| | R&D-intensive and knowledge-intensive value-added per head of the population in thousand PPP $[2] | | | | | | | | | | | | |
| Value-added in R&D-int. manufacturing (**A**) | 3.1 | 2.5 | 2.5 | 2.1 | 1.8 | 1.9 | 1.4 | 2.2 | 1.9 | 2.5 | 2.8 | 2.4 | 2.1 |
| USA = 100 | 126 | 100 | 101 | 85 | 71 | 74 | 58 | 88 | 76 | 101 | 113 | 95 | 82 |
| Of which: Leading-edge techn. | 0.4 | 0.9 | 0.8 | 0.5 | 0.4 | 0.6 | 0.3 | 0.6 | 0.5 | 0.5 | 1.3 | 0.7 | 0.4 |
| USA = 100 | 41 | 100 | 82 | 56 | 40 | 63 | 37 | 59 | 54 | 52 | 140 | 70 | 45 |
| High-level techn. | 2.7 | 1.5 | 1.7 | 1.6 | 1.4 | 1.3 | 1.1 | 1.6 | 1.4 | 2 | 1.5 | 1.7 | 1.6 |
| USA = 100 | 177 | 100 | 112 | 102 | 90 | 81 | 71 | 105 | 90 | 131 | 96 | 110 | 105 |
| Value-added in knowl-edge-int. services (excl. Real Estate) (**B**) | 6.9 | 10.5 | 4.6 | 7.8 | 5.9 | 7.8 | 8.6 | 8.3 | 7.5 | 7.4 | 5.9 | 7.3 | 6.7 |
| USA = 100 | 66 | 100 | 44 | 74 | 56 | 75 | 82 | 79 | 71 | 71 | 56 | 70 | 64 |
| (**A**) + (**B**) | 10 | 12.9 | 7.1 | 9.9 | 7.7 | 9.7 | 10.1 | 10.5 | 9.4 | 9.9 | 8.7 | 9.7 | 8.7 |
| USA = 100 | 78 | 100 | 55 | 76 | 59 | 75 | 78 | 81 | 72 | 76 | 67 | 75 | 68 |
| | for information | | | | | | | | | | | | |
| Hours annually worked per person engaged | 1444 | 1815 | 1805 | 1459 | 1619 | 1707 | 1340 | 1559 | 1499 | 1581 | 1686 | 1778 | 1581 |
| Per head of population | 677 | 858 | 897 | 605 | 609 | 800 | 594 | 635 | 764 | 751 | 766 | 874 | 687 |

[1] Excluding Ireland und Luxembourg; hours annually worked also excluding Austria
[2] Recalculated in line with the GDP pricing concept
Sources: OECD, STAN Database 2004 – OECD, Economic Outlook No. 75 – OECD, Employment Outlook, Paris 2004 – calculations and estimates of DIW Berlin

In structural terms, the German position appears much more favourable than in absolute values. The production patterns in the OECD countries covered by the analysis are presented in Fig. 1 in terms of percentage shares and in Table 2 in terms of relative shares, giving the differences between the country-specific patterns and the average

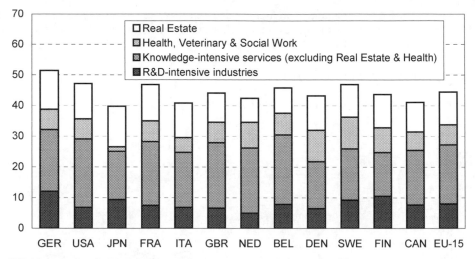

EU-15 excluding Ireland and Luxembourg
Sources: OECD, STAN Database 2004 – calculations and estimates of DIW Berlin

**Fig. 1.** Share of R&D and knowledge-intensive industries in value-added in selected OECD countries (in per cent), 2002

**Table 2.** Relative shares in value-added in selected OECD countries[1], 2002

|  | 6 coun- tries[2] | GER | USA | JPN | FRA | ITA | GBR | NED | BEL | DEN | SWE | FIN | CAN | EU- 15[3] |
|---|---|---|---|---|---|---|---|---|---|---|---|---|---|---|
| Manufacturing | 17 | 30 | –17 | 17 | 5 | 18 | –4 | –13 | 12 | –6 | 19 | 35 | 18 | 11 |
| R&D-intensive industr. | 8 | 44 | –13 | 18 | –5 | –13 | –17 | –45 | 0 | –19 | 17 | 30 | –2 | 0 |
| Leading-edge techn. | 2 | –45 | 9 | 19 | –23 | –50 | –11 | –69 | –17 | –31 | –28 | 74 | –10 | –38 |
| High-level techn. | 5 | 66 | –24 | 17 | 2 | –1 | –19 | –36 | 7 | –14 | 31 | 3 | 1 | 13 |
| Non-R&D-int. industr. | 9 | 15 | –21 | 17 | 14 | 39 | 6 | 10 | 21 | 5 | 21 | 39 | 34 | 20 |
| Services | 74 | –5 | 4 | –7 | 0 | –5 | –1 | 1 | –1 | –2 | –4 | –12 | –14 | –4 |
| Services excl. Real Estate | 62 | –8 | 5 | –11 | –1 | –5 | 3 | 5 | 5 | –1 | –3 | –13 | –13 | –2 |
| Knowledge-int. serv. | 38 | 4 | 6 | –22 | 4 | –11 | –1 | –1 | –1 | –3 | 0 | –13 | –12 | –4 |
| Excluding Real Estate | 26 | 2 | 10 | –41 | 6 | –13 | 7 | 13 | 13 | –2 | 4 | –16 | –9 | –2 |
| Telecommunications | 3 | –9 | 20 | –61 | –30 | –23 | 12 | –9 | –12 | –31 | –10 | 21 | –6 | –10 |
| Financial Services | 7 | –61 | 21 | –10 | –43 | –19 | –36 | –11 | –36 | –33 | –69 | –67 | –1 | –37 |
| Business Services | 10 | 27 | –5 | –30 | 30 | –7 | 23 | 16 | 37 | –26 | 1 | –40 | –26 | 10 |
| Health/Social Work | 6 | 16 | 16 | –131 | 19 | –13 | 18 | 40 | 23 | 61 | 61 | 38 | 8 | 14 |
| Non-knowl.-int. serv. | 36 | –15 | 1 | 7 | –6 | 1 | –1 | –1 | –2 | –1 | –8 | –11 | –15 | –3 |
| Other industries | 10 | –25 | –3 | 16 | –6 | 3 | 11 | 25 | –13 | 21 | –8 | 12 | 48 |  |
| Total | 100 | 0 | 0 | 0 | 0 | 0 | 0 | 0 | 0 | 0 | 0 | 0 | 0 | 0 |

[1]    A positive value indicates that the share is larger than the average in the six largest OECD countries. The figures are calculated analogously to the export specialisation RXA, see Box 1.
[2]    Percentage share on average in the six largest OECD countries
[3]    Excluding Ireland und Luxembourg
Sources:  OECD, STAN Database 2004 – calculations and estimates of DIW Berlin

pattern in the six largest countries combined. Taking R&D-intensive manufacturing and knowledge-intensive services together, the share in value-added is largest in Germany. In 2002, 39 per cent (excluding Real Estate) and 51 per cent (including Real Estate) of total value-added in Germany were human-capital-intensive. This is mainly due to the high share of R&D-intensive manufacturing (12 per cent) while the share of knowledge-intensive services (27 per cent excluding and 39 per cent including Real Estate) is some 1 to 2 percentage points lower than in the USA, France or Great Britain. Or to put it differently, Germany is characterised by a rather small share of non-knowledge-intensive services and a very high share of R&D-intensive manufacturing.

Relating the value-added in knowledge-intensive services (excluding Real Estate) to the value-added in R&D-intensive manufacturing, the ratio is smallest in Japan, amounting to less than two, whereas it is three to four times that in most of the other OECD countries and even six times in the Netherlands. According to this ratio, Germany and Finland – here it is slightly above two – are also lagging behind on the way to the services part within human-capital-intensive production. Due to the lack of international comparative studies we do not know, however, whether the production of services within manufacturing firms is more important in Germany than in other countries.

## Shifts Towards a Knowledge-based Economy

The structural changes in the OECD countries during the past decades followed the textbook model of the development of a knowledge-based economy. The share of knowledge-intensive services in value-added increased considerably, the share of other services remained more or less stable, whereas the share of Manufacturing decreased, in non-R&D-intensive industries more than in R&D-intensive industries. Thus, the weights have been shifting towards the knowledge-intensive segment of the growing services sector and towards the R&D-intensive part of the (relatively) shrinking manufacturing sector. This pattern is to be found in more or less pronounced form at different periods of time in nearly all OECD countries. On average in the six largest OECD countries, the share of Total Manufacturing in value-added was 16.6 per cent in 2002 and decreased by 4.4 percentage points as compared to 1991, the R&D-intensive manufacturing industries achieved 7.8 per cent in 2002 and diminished only by 1.8 percentage points. On the other hand, the knowledge-intensive services in 2002 accounted for 26 per cent or 5 percentage points more than 1991.

The shifts in production patterns are partly due to changes in preferences of private households which demand more knowledge-intensive services at higher incomes. They are also due to changes in the inputs of manufacturing firms which considerably increased their demand for knowledge-intensive services during the last two decades.[3] The competitiveness of manufacturing firms depends more and more on their ability to provide a package comprising the physical product and related services such as software, maintenance, training, logistics and planning. The result is a deepened national division of labour and a shift of value-added and employment from the

---

[3] See Schultz and Weise (1999) and Petersen et al. (1993) for an analysis of increasing shares of intermediate demand for services in the manufacturing sector in Germany.

manufacturing sector to the service sector, which is larger than the shift in the value of production. Moreover, product-related services, which are produced within the manu-facturing firms themselves, gain in importance. Thus, the production of manufactures becomes more service-intensive, but it does not mean de-industrialisation. Besides, however, production processes are relocated to other countries (international out-sourcing) replacing domestic value-added by imports of intermediate goods.

During the 1990s, the shift from the secondary to the tertiary sector was much stronger in Germany than in other OECD countries. The share of R&D-intensive and non-R&D-intensive manufacturing in value-added decreased considerably while the share of knowledge-intensive services significantly increased. The decline in Manu-facturing was concentrated in the years 1990 to 1993 when the share of R&D-intensive manufacturing decreased from 16 per cent (in West Germany) to 12 per cent (in Germany as a whole). After the mid 1990s, Germany specialised again more in R&D-intensive industries as compared with the overall trend in the six largest OECD countries (see Fig. 2). During the first years of the new decade, the share of R&D-intensive manufacturing in value-added even increased in Germany, as opposed to the general trend. On the other hand, the share of knowledge-intensive services recently increased only slightly, i.e. the shift towards the service economy in Germany has slowed down in terms of value-added.

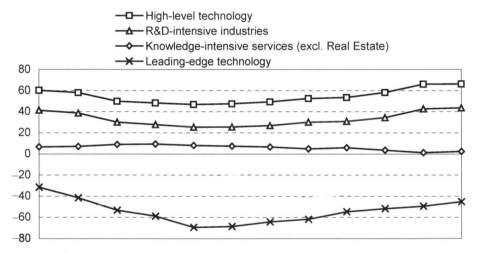

A positive value indicates that the share in Germany is larger than on average in the six largest OECD countries.
Sources: OECD, STAN Database 2004 – calculations and estimates of DIW Berlin

**Fig. 2.** Relative shares of R&D- and knowledge-intensive industries in Germany (measured in terms of value added), 1991 to 2002

In other large OECD countries we also observe different shifts in the production pat-terns, before 1995 at a high US $ value and after 1995 at a low US $ value. In the first half of the 1990s, the specialisation pattern in Germany and Japan changed to the disadvantage of Manufacturing, in the USA and Great Britain to the advantage of Manufacturing. After the mid 1990s, the changes were in the opposite direction. In Germany these shifts affected all technology segments similarly, in the other three countries they were restricted to high-level technology and ñon-R&D-intensive manufacturing. France and Italy specialised more in Manufacturing during both periods of time, France in all technology segments and Italy in high-level technology and non-R&D-intensive manufacturing. Thus, the French technological position in Manufacturing improved as compared to the beginning of the 1990s. This is also true for most of the six smaller countries considered here, which in general specialised more in R&D-intensive as well as non-R&D-intensive manufacturing. In Finland and Sweden the shift towards high-tech industries was stopped at the beginning of the new decade.

## Employment and Productivity

The shifts in the sectoral patterns of employment are similar to those in value-added. In terms of employment, the changes are in general more pronounced, the decrease in Manufacturing due to higher productivity is larger compared to the increase in Services due to lower productivity. In Germany, the changes in the employment pattern were relatively large during the 1990s.

In 2002, nearly 10 per cent of the labour force in Germany worked in R&D-intensive manufacturing (see Fig. 3). In most of the other OECD countries this was much less. The employment share of 26 per cent for knowledge-intensive services in Germany as well as France is somewhat lower than in the USA and significantly lower than in the Netherlands, Denmark and Sweden. Excluding Health and Social Services and concentrating on Communication, Financial and Business Services, the share in the Scandinavian countries as well is smaller than in Germany. The share of non-knowledge-intensive services in Germany amounts to some 43 per cent and is much lower than in the other large OECD countries.

Differences between sectoral patterns in terms of employment and in terms of value-added are due to the sectoral differences in labour productivity – calculated as value-added per person engaged.[4] In general, labour productivity is higher in Manufacturing and lower in Services. In R&D-intensive manufacturing – in leading-edge even more than in high-level technology – it is higher than in non-R&D-intensive manufacturing, in knowledge-intensive services it is higher than in non-knowledge-intensive services.[5] The productivity in knowledge-intensive services is relatively low, compared to R&D-intensive manufacturing. This is mainly due to Health and Social Services. Labour productivity in other knowledge-intensive services in Germany is even higher than in R&D-intensive manufacturing.

In Germany, the structural changes during the 1990s implied a large increase in relative labour productivity in R&D-intensive manufacturing and a large decrease in relative productivity in knowledge-intensive services. This trend continued in the first years of the new decade, providing a considerable increase in employment in knowledge-intensive services. Nevertheless, labour productivity in R&D-intensive manufacturing in Germany is still low in relation to the level in knowledge-intensive services, taking the relations in other OECD countries, in particular the USA and

---

[4] The calculations for this section exclude real estate activities.

[5] This corresponds to the definition of sectors by R&D and knowledge intensity. A higher share of highly qualified labour force implies a higher labour productivity in terms of value-added.

France, as a yardstick. The high employment share of R&D-intensive manufacturing in Germany, therefore, is not only due to a high value-added share. It is also due to a relatively low labour productivity. One reason is Germany's concentration on high-level technology and less on leading-edge technology. Another reason may be that in Germany many labour-intensive business-related services are produced within manufacturing firms and less in independent services firms because German manufacturers are specialised more in user-oriented tailored products and less in standardised mass production like US or Japanese firms. The significant changes towards the US pattern may indicate that German industry is relying more and more on standardisation. Thus, German exporters would face more price competition. This was not important in the period of a low-valued DM and €. It now becomes important, however, with a re-valued   providing the danger of significant reductions of export quantities.

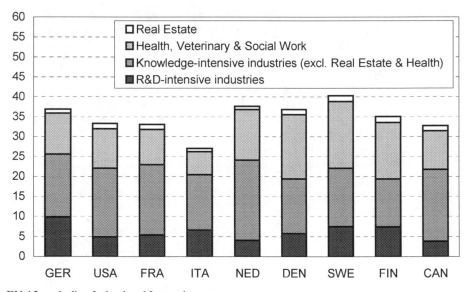

EU-15 excluding Ireland and Luxembourg
Sources: OECD, STAN Database 2004 – calculations and estimates of DIW Berlin

**Fig. 3.** Share of R&D- and knowledge-intensive industries in employment in selected OECD countries (in per cent), 2002

Macroeconomic growth and employment problems cannot be solved by an expansion of the R&D-intensive manufacturing industries. After 1995, additional employment in Germany did not appear in R&D-intensive manufacturing, except for the motor vehicles industry, it appeared only in the services sector. The contribution of high-tech production to employment is more indirect than direct. R&D-intensive products allow innovations and productivity increases in other sectors which then become more competitive and can extend production and employment. Achieving additional employment without reducing the economy-wide labour productivity would be possible through the expansion of knowledge-intensive services. The international comparison suggests for Germany that R&D-intensive manufacturing will reduce employment further, with high increases in productivity, whereas the demand for labour will grow in Services.

The structural changes towards R&D-intensive and knowledge-intensive production increase the average labour productivity of the economy. This increases the potential for growth and is positive in view of the demographic trend. If the labour force in Germany is shrinking in the long term, high productivity increases are necessary to maintain the present level of *per capita* income.

## International Trade in R&D-intensive Goods

The R&D-intensive industries are highly integrated into the world economy, leading-edge technology even more than high-level technology branches. Leading-edge industries, such as Office and Computing Machinery, Radio, Television and Communication Equipment as well as Aircraft, have the largest shares of exports in production and of imports in domestic consumption. After the mid 1990s, the increase in export and import ratios was by far the largest in Germany. Here both ratios in the R&D-intensive industries increased between 1995 and 2002 by 16 percentage points. In the other large OECD countries the export ratios increased by 5 to 7 and the import ratios by 7 to 10 percentage points. During this period, the foreign trade intensification in Germany was especially strong and appeared similarly on both the export and import side. In the other large countries the effect was weaker and more related to imports than exports. One reason for Germany's strong export performance surely is the difference in growth between Germany and other countries. Additionally, the weak € supported German exports, in particular to the USA.

Following international trade theory, every country gains from international trade because specialisation according to comparative advantage allows it to achieve higher productivity and higher real income. Exports are an indirect means of production and meet domestic demand more cheaply through imports instead of directly producing the good domestically. We already know from Ricardo's theory that labour productivity, and hence technology, determines the level of income. A country that uses its resources more efficiently due to better technologies also achieves a higher income. Such a country has a comparative advantage in goods whose production requires advanced technologies and, accordingly, needs a high expenditure on R&D. Thus, the technological performance of a country should be reflected in the pattern of its foreign trade by R&D intensity. The more R&D-intensive goods a country exports, the better its technological performance.

In this section we evaluate the position of the technologically most important OECD countries in international trade of R&D-intensive goods by analysing trade balances and indicators of specialisation based on trade patterns. The data are taken from the DIW trade database which comprises foreign trade data of all OECD countries by partner countries and is disaggregated by the International Standard Industrial Classification (ISIC Rev. 3).[6] Again, we arrange the industries according to the R&D

---

[6] The original data are from OECD, International Trade by Commodities Statistics, CD-ROM. The data at the most detailed level of classification according to product groups and partner countries have been recoded from the Standard International Trade Classification (SITC Rev. 3) to the industries of the ISIC Rev. 3, using a correspondence of the United Nations. We are only able to take into account the trade flows that are recorded at the most detailed level of classification according to SITC Rev. 3 and individual partner countries. Positions

expenditure per unit of output.[7] Here the group of R&D-intensive goods is more narrowly defined than in the analysis of production and employment, and the definition of leading-edge and high-level technology is slightly different.

The USA, Germany and Japan are the largest exporters of R&D-intensive goods. Until 1995 Japan was in first place and later lost in (relative) importance. The largest import market is by far provided by the USA, followed by Germany, while Japan still imports a relatively small number of R&D-intensive products. In terms of balances, Japan and Germany are still the leading net exporters of R&D-intensive goods, and the USA the largest net importer.

**Table 3.** Foreign-trade specialisation in R&D-intensive goods for selected OECD countries, 2002

| | 6 coun-tries[2] | GER | USA | JPN | FRA | ITA | GBR | NED | BEL | DEN | SWE | FIN | CAN | EU-15[3] |
|---|---|---|---|---|---|---|---|---|---|---|---|---|---|---|
| Manufacturing | 17 | 30 | −17 | 17 | 5 | 18 | −4 | −13 | 12 | −6 | 19 | 35 | 18 | 11 |
| R&D-intensive industr. | 8 | 44 | −13 | 18 | −5 | −13 | −17 | −45 | 0 | −19 | 17 | 30 | −2 | 0 |
| Leading-edge techn. | 2 | −45 | 9 | 19 | −23 | −50 | −11 | −69 | −17 | −31 | −28 | 74 | −10 | −38 |
| High-level techn. | 5 | 66 | −24 | 17 | 2 | −1 | −19 | −36 | 7 | −14 | 31 | 3 | 1 | 13 |
| Non-R&D-int. industr. | 9 | 15 | −21 | 17 | 14 | 39 | 6 | 10 | 21 | 5 | 21 | 39 | 34 | 20 |
| Services | 74 | −5 | 4 | −7 | 0 | −5 | −1 | −1 | −1 | −2 | −4 | −12 | −14 | −4 |
| Services excl. Real Estate | 62 | −8 | 5 | −11 | −1 | −5 | 3 | 5 | 5 | −1 | −3 | −13 | −13 | −2 |
| Knowledge-int. serv. | 38 | 4 | 6 | −22 | 4 | −11 | −1 | −1 | −1 | −3 | 0 | −13 | −12 | −4 |
| Excluding Real Estate | 26 | 2 | 10 | −41 | 6 | −13 | 7 | 13 | 13 | −2 | 4 | −16 | −9 | −2 |
| Telecommunications | 3 | −9 | 20 | −61 | −30 | −23 | 12 | −9 | −12 | −31 | −10 | 21 | −6 | −10 |
| Financial Services | 7 | −61 | 21 | −10 | −43 | −19 | −36 | −11 | −36 | −33 | −69 | −67 | −1 | −37 |
| Business Services | 10 | 27 | −5 | −30 | 30 | −7 | 23 | 16 | 37 | −26 | 1 | −40 | −26 | 10 |
| Health/Social Work | 6 | 16 | 16 | 131 | 19 | −13 | 18 | 40 | 23 | 61 | 61 | 38 | 8 | 14 |
| Non-knowl.-int. serv. | 36 | −15 | 1 | 7 | −6 | 1 | −1 | −1 | −2 | −1 | −8 | −11 | −15 | −3 |
| Other industries | 10 | −25 | −3 | 16 | −6 | 3 | 11 | 25 | −13 | 21 | −8 | 12 | 48 | |
| Total | 100 | 0 | 0 | 0 | 0 | 0 | 0 | 0 | 0 | 0 | 0 | 0 | 0 | 0 |

[1]  In trade with non-EU countries

[2]  A positive value indicates that the share of R&D-intensive goods in exports or imports, respectively, of manufacturing goods is larger than on average in all OECD countries combined.

[3]  A positive value indicates that the share of R&D-intensive goods in exports of manufacturing goods is larger than in imports of manufacturing goods.

[4]  A positive value indicates that the R&D-intensive goods positively contribute to the overall balance of trade more than proportionately.

Sources: DIW Foreign Trade Database – calculations of DIW Berlin

The values of exports and imports at the level of commodity groups also reflect the size of the sectors and countries. Moreover, they may fluctuate in line with the overall balance of trade, depending on international business-cycle differences and shifts in exchange rates. The specialisation pattern of a country, therefore, is more appro-

only indicated at the two-digit level such as entire manufacturing plants, or flows not reported in disaggregated form for reasons of secrecy, cannot be classified by industry. Thus, the aggregated figures we have calculated by summing up the detailed data differ from the figures reported by statistical offices.

[7]  The classification follows Grupp et al. (2000: 101).

priately characterised by indicators that are not influenced by the overall balance of trade or by the level of exports and imports. The specialisation pattern allows the evaluation of the relative position of a country in individual commodity groups in comparison over product groups, countries and time. For a description of the indicators, see Box 1. The results for 2002 are compiled in Table 3, the changes over time for Germany are represented in Fig. 4.

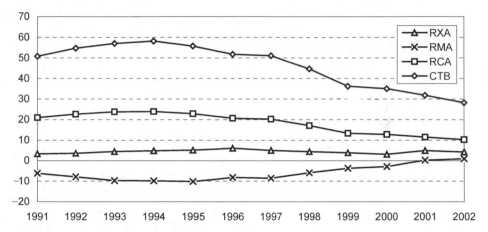

RXA, RMA: A positive value indicates that the share of R&D-intensive goods in exports or imports, respectively, of manufacturing goods in Germany is larger than on average in all OECD countries combined.
RCA: A positive value indicates that the share of R&D-intensive goods in German exports of manufacturing goods is larger than in German imports of manufacturing goods.
CTB: A positive value indicates that the R&D-intensive goods positively contribute to the overall balance of trade in Germany more than proportionately.
Sources: DIW Foreign Trade Database – calculations of DIW Berlin

**Fig. 4.** Foreign-trade specialisation in R&D-intensive goods for Germany, 1991 to 2002

Compared to exports of all OECD countries, the exports of Japan, the USA and Great Britain are most strongly specialised on R&D-intensive goods, followed by Switzerland and Germany (positive RXA values). For leading-edge technology this is true for Great Britain, the USA and Switzerland, followed by Netherlands and France, for high-level technology it only holds for Japan, Germany and Canada. The specialisation of German exports in R&D-intensive goods remained stable since 1991, additional success in Motor Vehicles compensating losses in Basic Chemicals and Pharmaceuticals. Major changes occurred in German imports, which significantly increased. After the mid 1990s the highest growth was in R&D-intensive goods, in leading-edge even more than in high-level technology. The share of R&D-intensive imports in Germany now corresponds to the OECD average, in leading-edge technology it has been above average since 1991 (positive RMA value).[8] The imports

---

[8] The disaggregation of German imports by leading-edge and high-level technology is biased in 2002 as compared to the years before due to changing classification of imports from Ireland in Pharmaceuticals and Basic Chemicals, respectively. In 2002, German imports of leading-edge technology goods are too large while imports of high-level technology goods are too low as compared to earlier years.

of R&D-intensive goods are relatively high in the USA and Great Britain, but they are relatively low in Switzerland and France and extremely low in Japan.

**Box 1.** Indicators of foreign-trade specialisation

It is not the level of trade flows which is important for assessing the technological performance of a country but the structural pattern of exports and imports ('comparative advantage'). The commodity pattern of a country's exports may be compared with the exports of all countries or the imports of the same country. By dividing commodity shares in exports by the commodity shares in exports of all countries combined, we obtain a measure introduced by Balassa (1965) to quantify the specialisation pattern of a country in international trade (RXA). Recalculated in logs, a positive value indicates a commodity group which has a higher share in the exports of that country than in exports of all countries combined, while a negative value indicates that this commodity group has a share in that country's exports which is lower than the average. In an alternative interpretation, a positive (negative) value indicates that an economy achieves a market share in worldwide exports which is above (below) its average export market share. While RXA characterises the specialisation of exports, an analogous calculation comparing the imports gives an indicator of country-specific strong points on the import side (RMA). In a more commonly used measurement, the commodity shares in the exports of a country are divided by the share in the imports of the same country (RCA: revealed comparative advantage). Here, a positive (negative) value in log terms indicates that the share in exports is larger (smaller) than the share in imports or, put alternatively, that the export-import ratio is larger (smaller) than the export-import ratio in total trade. The RCA values describe the pattern of comparative advantages and disadvantages of a country including foreign competition on the domestic market.

The three indicators are the ratio of two ratios and exclude differences between the size of commodity groups and differences between overall exports and imports. We calculate a supplementary indicator which gives the direction of specialisation (which is the same as by RCA) and, additionally, takes the quantitative importance of the commodity groups into account. It compares the actual trade balance in a commodity group with a hypothetical trade balance which involves no specialisation at all (CTB: Contribution to Trade Balance; Lafay 1987; OECD [ed.] 1999). The hypothetical trade balance is calculated by proportionately distributing the overall trade balance to the individual commodity groups according to their share in the overall trade volume (i.e. exports plus imports). The differences between actual and hypothetical trade balance are given in per thousand of the total trade volume, in order to make the figures comparable over countries and over time. A positive (negative) value indicates that the positive contribution to the overall balance of trade is larger (smaller) than it should be according to the size of the commodity group. This indicator is additive and the sum of the values over all commodity groups is zero.

The four indicators are calculated for trade in manufacturing goods of selected OECD countries. The basis of comparison is the foreign trade of all countries which were members of the OECD by 1993.

The comparison of exports and imports confirms the comparative advantage of Germany in R&D-intensive goods (RCA and CTB values). In 2002, Germany ranks fifth behind Japan, Switzerland, Great Britain and USA and in front of France. The other OECD countries considered in the analysis reveal a comparative disadvantage in R&D-intensive trade. The three largest countries provide a large number of high-tech goods in which they have a comparative advantage. While the USA is more specialised in leading-edge technology, intermediate and investment goods, German strength lies in advanced-technology investment goods and consumer durables. In leading-edge technology Germany reveals comparative disadvantages. Japan now follows this pattern as well (see also Germany's 'comparative advantages' in industrial R&D, Chapters 2.1 and 2.2).

Compared to the beginning of the 1990s, the foreign trade position of Germany in R&D-intensive goods deteriorated according to the RCA and CTB values. In 1991, Germany was at the same level as Switzerland and Great Britain, in 2002 it lied significantly behind them and ranked – together with France – at the lower end of the six leading countries having comparative advantage in R&D-intensive goods. The largest parts of the deterioration were due to Basic Chemicals, Pharmaceuticals, Data Processing Equipment, Electronic Circuits and various types of Machinery. The only and very large improvement was in Motor Vehicles. In 2002, by far the largest positive contribution to the trade balance is from this sector. Thus, the German export surplus, which grew considerably since the mid 1990s in absolute value and relative to GDP, depends more and more on Motor Vehicles.

In general, the pattern of comparative advantage and its changes are shaped more by exports and less by imports. The changes in Germany are one of the rare exceptions. They are mainly due to the dynamic imports of R&D-intensive goods after the mid-1990s. An important reason is the increased trade with the transition countries in central and eastern Europe. After the political changes in these countries, large German firms very quickly integrated them into their intra-firm division of labour. The lower wages in these countries stimulated the international outsourcing from Germany and increased intra-industry trade in R&D-intensive industries. On the one hand, the additional division of labour with central and eastern Europe contributed to higher German imports. On the other hand, it improved the German competitiveness on world export markets through cheapening the price of intermediary goods.

In evaluating the changes in the German position in international trade, global macroeconomic conditions must also be taken into account. After 2000, the production related to IT activities was severely hit, resulting in lower international trade in these commodity groups. Germany was less affected directly, given its lower involvement as a supplier in this part of leading-edge technology. Moreover, considerable changes in exchange rates played an important role. They had an effect on the volumes and patterns of trade.

## Exchange Rates and Specialisation Patterns

Since the 1980s, exchange rate movements among high-income OECD countries in a number of years were much larger than would have been necessary to compensate for differences in inflation rates. Thus, currencies strongly devaluated or revaluated in real terms. Consequently, the same foreign trade flows are valued differently in international statistics and, secondly, foreign demand and supply react to the shifts in price competitiveness after a certain time lag. The two consequences of an exchange rate change have an opposite effect on the value of trade flows in US $. If a currency appreciates in real terms, the value of exports increases due to higher valuation in US $ and it decreases due to diminishing export quantities provided negative price elasticity for export goods. In a year of strong real depreciation, the nominal export market share decreases, while national statistics show dynamic increases in exports in absolute terms and in relation to GDP.

The effect of a change in exchange rate on quantities depends on the price elasticity of demand. Empirical analyses suggest that the export quantity reacts negatively with a time lag (of around one year). One may also assume that the price elasticity of exports varies, depending on the type of product. The lower the price elasticity, the more important is competition in terms of quality, which crucially depends on R&D and human-capital-intensity. More recent theoretical and empirical studies conclude that the price elasticity of export demand differs by the R&D intensity of products (see Lucke et al. 2004). The results support the hypothesis that the price elasticity is negative and that it tends to be smaller for R&D-intensive goods than for non-R&D-intensive goods. Thus, exchange rate changes have an impact on the volume and, additionally, on the commodity pattern of trade.

Consequently, the real depreciation of the DM (real appreciation of the US $) in the second half of the 1990s may have been a reason for the deterioration of the RCA and CTB indicators of comparative advantage in R&D-intensive goods in Germany during that period of time. The lower price competitiveness of foreign suppliers had a larger negative effect on non-R&D-intensive products, making them relatively more successful in R&D-intensive products. For firms in Germany, the opposite is true: the higher price competitiveness supported German exports of non-R&D-intensive goods more than the supplies of R&D-intensive goods.

Due to the high weight of exports in the German economy, the exchange rate changes also had an impact on the sectoral pattern of total production (see Fig. 5). The specialisation of the German economy in Manufacturing as a whole and in R&D-intensive industries increased in phases of low valuation of the DM or during the first half of the 1980s in the same way as during the second half of the 1990s. Both periods are characterised in (West) Germany by export-lead structural changes and low growth (see DIW 1988). In the decade between these two periods, the export ratio of German manufacturing remained more or less unchanged. The specialisation indicators for value-added in manufacturing and R&D-intensive industries in (West) Germany in 2002 were very similar to those in 1985. The changes in the specialisation pattern of production in the USA tended to be complementary to those in Germany. Hence, the re-specialisation in several EU countries in Manufacturing after 1995 – as compared with average trends in the large OECD countries – may also be due to changes in exchange rates. The effect was very large in Germany because the German economy is oriented towards exports much more than other comparable economies.

The revaluation of the vis-à-vis the US $ since 2002 may be expected to have the opposite effects on the commodity structures of foreign trade, as € firms now face a lower price competitiveness while it is better for US $ firms. The structural position

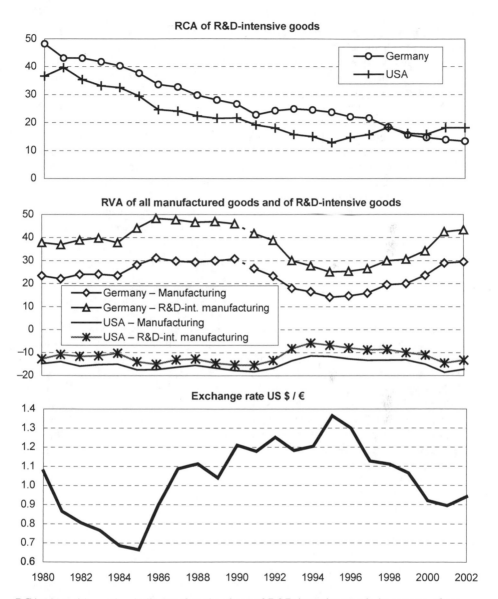

RCA: A positive value indicates that the share of R&D-intensive goods in exports of manu-facturing goods is larger than in imports of manufacturing goods.

RVA: A positive value indicates that the value-added share of R&D-intensive manufacturing in Germany or the USA, respectively, is larger than on average in the six largest OECD countries combined.

Sources: OECD, STAN Database 2004 – OECD, Economic Outlook 2004, No. 75 – calcu-lations by DIW Berlin

**Fig. 5.** Exchange rate and specialisation in R&D-intensive industries in Germany and the USA, 1980 to 2002

of Germany in foreign trade, therefore, should improve in R&D-intensive goods because firms of the US $ area will increase non-R&D-intensive supplies more easily while German exporters are forced to rely more on innovative and less price-elastic products. A highly valued     should also tend to reduce the specialisation of the German economy in manufacturing and R&D-intensive industries.

Movements of the US $ exchange rate, however, only have a limited effect on German exports because half of Germany's foreign trade is with other countries in the €area. At the end of 2004, the US $ value of the € was 36.4 per cent above the 2001 average, whereas the real effective exchange rate for Germany – which is an indicator of price competitiveness of the German economy in total foreign trade – only increased by 6.7 per cent. Moreover, the 'German' € devaluated in real terms vis-à-vis the other countries in the €area because price increases in the other €countries were larger than in Germany after the introduction of the common currency. Thus, the price competitiveness of firms in Germany improved in relation to firms in other € countries during the first years of the new decade.

## Conclusions

During the 1990s and the first years of the new decade, international differences in growth, changes in exchange rates, the integration of the transition countries in central and eastern Europe, the increasing importance of IT technologies and the end of the IT hype had an impact on production and international trade of R&D-intensive goods. Germany only achieved low overall growth and strong increases in exports and imports with growing export surplus. The specialisation patterns in production and in exports indicate a good technological performance of the German economy. However, in terms of production levels, in R&D-intensive goods and knowledge-intensive services combined, the relative position of Germany worsened. At the beginning of the 1990s only the USA had a much higher level, in 2002 a number of other OECD countries achieved or surpassed the German level. Lacking domestic dynamics in the long term also tends to weaken the strong export position in high-tech goods because lead market positions may be lost.

The (re-)specialisation in R&D-intensive manufacturing in Germany after the mid-1990s is due to great success in exports. As the R&D-intensive imports increased even more than exports, Germany's comparative advantage in foreign trade of R&D-intensive goods decreased. Nevertheless, Germany still belongs to the small group of OECD countries that have a comparative advantage in these goods. Germany distinguishes itself in both aspects of foreign trade: it has a high export surplus in R&D-intensive goods, unlike the USA, and also imports such goods on a large scale, in contrast to Japan. Thus, Germany is net exporter of technology in foreign trade on the one hand, and it takes advantage of gains from trade also in the high-tech segment, on the other hand. In international trade, it has a strong position in both supply and demand of R&D-intensive goods, indicating a good performance in the production and application of technologies. The strong German position in exports, however, more and more depends on Motor Vehicles.

To sum up, the empirical evidence on R&D- and knowledge-intensive production suggests that the technological performance of the German economy is strong in terms of sectoral patterns whereas it has fallen behind in terms of levels. On the other hand, the analysis of foreign trade flows suggests that the German position in R&D-intensive goods is strong in absolute terms whereas it weakened in terms of commodity patterns.

In the same way as the real appreciation of the DM or the   contributed to the decrease of the German comparative advantage in R&D-intensive goods during the second half of the 1990s, we may expect that they should be reinforced again after the revaluation of the € in 2002. The development of Germany's foreign trade pattern in 2003 to 2005, therefore, will be a test for the technological performance of the German economy. Owing to lower price competitiveness, German exporters must concentrate more on R&D-intensive goods and can thus contribute to increasing real income by improved terms of trade.

In international comparison the German manufacturing sector is (still) extraordinarily important. The growing dependence of the German economy on exports reinforced the manufacturing sector and slowed down the shift towards the services sector. In Germany, human-capital-intensive production is more oriented towards Manufacturing and less towards Services than in comparable OECD countries. This suggests that the share of R&D-intensive manufacturing in Germany will tend to decrease again. And this will be more pronounced in employment than in value-added because of considerable increases in labour productivity. The growth of knowledge-intensive services, therefore, becomes more and more important.

# 4.2 Technology-based Start-ups

Christian Rammer

**Abstract.** The formation of new firms contributes to the emergence of new sectors, promotes innovation and intensifies competition. This is especially true for firm formation in fields of new technology and for start-ups that commercialise new technologies. Technology-based start-ups are therefore an important dimension to sustain and improve an economy's technological performance. This chapter analyses the dynamics of technology-based start-ups in the time period 1995 to 2003, taking also into account the dynamics of firm closures and stock of firms. Germany shows a rather low share of technology-based start-ups in total new firm formation, and low start-up dynamics in R&D-intensive manufacturing and knowledge-intensive services. Entry rates (new firms as a percentage of firm stock) are among the lowest of all countries considered. At the same time, exit ratios are low, too, resulting in a rather stable stock of technology-oriented firms.

## Introduction

The dynamics of start-ups in an economy's technology sectors is an important indicator of technological performance for several reasons: first, the formation of new firms that focus on the development and introduction of new technology is a major source of innovation and technological advance. Many of these technology-based start-ups transfer new knowledge or new ideas for products and processes into commercial applications. Knowledge and ideas may either originate from public research or from established companies. In the former case, start-ups transfer academic findings into market products (so-called public research spin-offs, see OECD [ed.] 2000a; Egeln et al. 2003). In the latter case, so-called company spin-offs often pick up innovations (or ideas for innovations) that were not fully utilised by their parent firm, partly because their market potential was estimated to be too low, partly because they were outside the market focus of the firm (see Gompers et al. 2003; Cassiman & Ueda 2002).

Secondly, technology-based start-ups spur competition in their markets (see Geroski 1991). Especially for upcoming technologies and when new product markets develop, divergent innovation designs compete with each other. Start-ups are likely to bring in new solutions and challenge established companies that enter these new markets, too. In general, intensifying competition is a relevant function of any new firm foundation which may impel innovation through fierce competition in any product market. Finally, new technology-based firms represent a source for innovative firms that substitute those firms that failed and thus contribute to continuity in the number of technology-developing and innovating firms. Without new market entries, the stock of innovating small firms would likely diminish, restricting the innovative potential of the SME sector.

*U. Schmoch, C. Rammer and H. Legler (eds.), National Systems of Innovation in Comparison, 153–167.*

Altogether, technology-based start-ups will contribute to a shift in industry structure towards more technology-oriented activities. In order to assess this structural change through new firm formation, both start-up activities in non-technology sectors as well as firm closures have to be taken into account. If market entries in non-technology sectors exceed the number of technology-based start-ups, the balanced effect of start-up activity on structural change will be negative. The same is true if the number of market exits of firms in the technology sectors is higher than those of market entries. Moreover, market entries and exits together are measures of market dynamics and intensity of competition. Both may be viewed as a stimulator for innovation, as high dynamics of entries and exits open up new business opportunities, while fierce competition forces established firms to check and adjust their competitive capabilities – including innovation – regularly.

This chapter reports on the significance and dynamics of technology start-ups as well as on firm closures and their change vis-à-vis firm entries in the technology sectors. International comparison is based on data from a number of EU countries as well as the USA and Japan. Several types of indicators are used to assess new firm formation in technology sectors: the share of technology-based start-ups in the total number of start-ups, start-up intensities (i.e. the number of start-ups per labour force), entry and exit rates, the ratio of entries to exits, and the development of the number of start-ups over time.

## Data Sources

There is no internationally uniform database on firm start-ups and closures. A potential source for measuring firm dynamics are business registers that contain all active firms, including basic information on firms such as sector code and size.[1] Provided that business registers accurately record entries and exits of firms, these can be used as a statistical base for analysis. Recently, the European Commission launched a 'Business Demography Project' that collects data on stock, entry and exit of firms for a number of EU countries plus Norway. The first data were released by Eurostat in 2004 (see Eurostat 2004). While this is a significant step forward in statistical analyses of start-up activities, there are still major shortcomings in terms of cross-country and chronological comparability: cross-country comparison is generally complicated by diverging definitions of 'firms' in business registers with respect to lower size limits, coverage of not-registered firms, and sources for compiling data (value added tax declarations, social security declarations etc.). Moreover, national legal settings for establishing or closing firms affect the propensity to start up or close businesses. Comparison over time is aggravated by changes in these legal settings (such as insolvency law, labour law or social security law) that provide incentives or disincentives to open up or close down business at a particular point in time. Moreover, changes in the definition of what constitutes a 'firm' for being considered in business

---

[1] The Global Entrepreneurship Monitor (see Acs et al. 2005) provides data on entrepreneurial attitudes among the labour force in a large number of countries, but contains no data on the number of market entries and exits.

registers, as well as fundamental up-dates and improvements in coverage of business registers may cause implausible changes over time.

Another disadvantage of Eurostat's business demography data is a considerable time lag: In summer 2005, full data are only available for the year 2000, while the most recent data (on 2002) are available for six countries only. For five countries – Austria, France, Germany, Greece and Ireland – data is still missing for all years. Nevertheless, this data source will be used as a starting point for international comparison of the number of technology-based start-ups as well as of entries and exits in other sectors. For Germany, France, the USA and Japan – as well as for Great Britain – national sources will be deployed, in order to obtain more recent information than provided in the business demography data. These sources are described briefly in the following.

In *Germany*, official statistics do not provide any data on exits and entries of firms so far. In order to analyse start-up activities, one depends on inofficial sources. The Institute for SME Research (IfM) collects entry and exit data based on registrations and deregistrations of businesses in the *Gewerbeanzeiger* (see Günterberg & Kayser 2004). The state-owned KfW-Bank conducts a representative survey of the German employable population to identify the number of self-employed and persons actively founding firms (see KfW-Bankengruppe 2004). The Federal Agency of Labour (BA) maintains an establishment data base that can be used to identify exit and entries of establishments (see Weißhuhn & Wichmann 2000). All these data suffer from the fact that they are not comparable to business register data, as they do not strictly refer to firms as legal entities that form an organisational unit to produce goods or services. Another data source which overcomes this lack and thus may be viewed as closest to the definition of firm used in EU statistics, are the ZEW Foundation Panel and the ZEW Enterprise Panel. Both are compiled by the Centre for European Economic Research (ZEW) based on information from Germany's largest credit rating agency, Creditreform (see Engel & Fryges 2002; Almus et al. 2000). The ZEW Foundation Panel contains all start-ups in Germany from 1989 on. Twice a year, firm data such as size, activity (5-digit NACE), shareholding, management, credit rating etc. are up-dated by Creditreform, based on information gathered through their extensive network of regional offices. The ZEW transforms these data into a panel structure and performs several quality controls (identifying doublets, imputing for missing values, identifying firms that are not economically active but founded for legal or financial reasons only). For most current start-up data, extrapolation procedures are used that are based on the time lag between the actual date of firm foundation and the time the firm entered Creditreform's database which could be observed in part years. The ZEW Enterprise Panel is a similar database containing all firms operating in Germany since 2000. Firm information for this total stock of firms is also up-dated twice a year and brought into a panel structure. These data also contain various information on firm closures that allows non-active firms to be identified.

For *France*, a special analysis by the national statistical office (INSEE, database Sirene) was conducted to survey the number of firm entries and the total stock of active firms for 1995 to 2003, broken down by sectors. A few sectors (Agriculture and Forestry, Banking/Insurance, Public Services) are not covered, however.

*USA* data for exits, entries and stock of firms are available from the US Small Business Authority (SBA) for 1990 to 2000, based on a compilation of the County

Business Patterns Survey conducted by the US Census Bureau. Stock data are both available for firms (i.e. legal entities) and establishments, while data of entries and exits are reported for establishments only. By using a correction factor for each year and sector (4-digit SIC or NAICS) one can derive an estimate for the number of firms entering and exiting the market. In 1998, sector classification changed from SIC to NAICS causing a break in series for a number of sectors.

The *Japanese* government conducted establishment censuses in 2000 (covering the time period 1996–1999) and in 2002 (covering 1999–2001). From these censuses, the number of newly founded firms for the years 1995–2001 on a 2-digit level of JSIC can be derived, as well as data on the stock of firms in 1999 and 2001 on a 3-digit level. The number of entries and exits on a more disaggregated sector level is available for establishments only, and is published for the two periods 1996–1999 and 1999–2001 as a total figure. In order to estimate the number of start-ups and firm closures, we use a sector-specific correction factor. Annual figures for more disaggregated sectors are estimated based on the annual figures for 2-digit sectors.

The Small Business Service (SBS) of the *British* government provides data on entries, exits and the stock of firms for 1994–2004 by 3-digit NACE. These data are derived from registration and deregistration data of value added tax (VAT) numbers. VAT numbers have to be registered for firms with an annual taxable turnover of £54,000 (fiscal year 2002/03). This threshold value increases almost annually and was £55,000 in 2004. Data on sectors that are exempted from VAT (Health and Education Services) are only poorly covered.

In order to compare technology-based start-ups across countries, different sector classifications (in particular: NACE, NAICS/SIC, JSIC) were consolidated in order to identify technology-oriented industries. Given constraints in sector disaggregation of Eurostat's business demography data, as well as aggregation needs to merge different sector classifications, a rather broad concept of technology-oriented industries had to be applied, distinguishing two main groups:
- R&D-intensive manufacturing (NACE 24, 29-35);
- knowledge-intensive business services (KIBS; NACE 64.2, 72, 73, 74.1–74.4).

Holding companies (74.15) are neither considered in international comparisons nor in the analysis of German data.

## Share of Technology-based Start-ups

Technology-oriented start-ups accounted for 10 per cent to 27 per cent of all new businesses in 2000 among the countries for which information is available (Fig. 1). The majority of technology-based start-ups are founded in services, while only about one per cent of all firm entries took place in R&D-intensive manufacturing. Somewhat higher shares are reported for Japan (3.5 per cent), Portugal (2.3 per cent) and Italy (1.7 per cent). High-tech start-ups, though often in the focus of public and policy debates when it comes to strengthening new firm foundation, thus represent only a very small fraction of all start-ups. The share of start-ups in KIBS is considerably higher. In most countries, more than 15 per cent – and up to 25 per cent – of all new firm formations occur in this service sector.

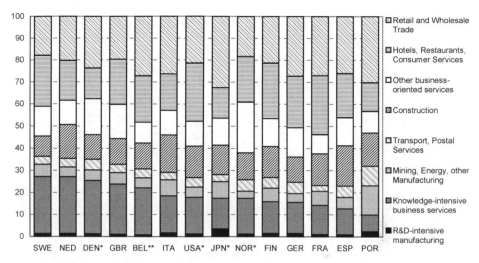

Total: business sector except Banking/Insurance
*   2001 – **   2000
Sources: Eurostat (New Cronos), SBA (USA), INSEE, Statistics Bureau Japan, SBS (GBR),
ZEW – calculation by ZEW

**Fig. 1.** Sector composition of firm entries in 2002 in selected countries (in per cent)

The highest shares of technology-based start-ups are reported for Sweden, the Netherlands, Denmark and Great Britain, while USA, Japan, Norway, Finland, Germany and
France show below average shares. The lowest figures are reported for Spain and
Portugal. Interpretation of this indicator is complicated, however, as it also depends
on the definition of firms and market entries with respect to the threshold values from
which on business activity is covered in business registers. The high threshold value
in Great Britain, for example, ignores a number of start-ups with low resources and a
low level of economic activity (such as self-employed without employees). Such start-
ups are likely to occur in sectors where establishing a business can be done at very
low cost, e.g. in Retail Trade, Construction or Consumer Services. Compared to countries that record all persons that go into business for themselves as start-ups, sector
structure of firm entries is likely to be shifted towards sectors with low entry costs.

The share of technology-based start-ups has increased in the five largest countries –
USA, Japan, Germany, Great Britain and France – since 1995, though the trends are
divergent for R&D-intensive manufacturing and KIBS (Fig. 2). The share of start-ups in
R&D-intensive manufacturing is slightly decreasing over this period except for Japan,
where it increased until 1998, but dropped to the level of 1995 until 2001. On the
contrary, all five countries show a rise in the significance of start-ups in knowledge-
intensive business services since 1995, though their share has fallen in some countries
after 1999/2000, particularly in Great Britain and Germany.

Japan shows a kind of 'specialisation' of start-up activities in R&D-intensive manufacturing, since the share of new firm foundation in this sector is significantly higher
throughout the period covered, while the other four large countries show persistently
low shares. In KIBS, Great Britain is clearly ahead of the other four large countries,
with a share of about 25 per cent of KIBS start-ups in all start-ups.

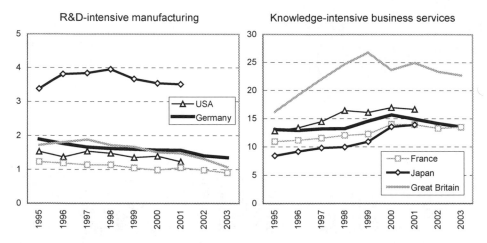

Number of start-ups in R&D-intensive manufacturing and knowledge-intensive business ser-
vices as a percentage of all start-ups (except Banking/Insurance).
Sources: Eurostat (New Cronos), SBA (USA), INSEE, Statistics Bureau Japan, SBS (GBR),
ZEW – calculation by ZEW

**Fig. 2.** Share of technology-based start-ups 1995–2003 in five large countries (in per cent)

An alternative indicator of the quantitative relevance of technology-based start-ups in
an economy is therefore the 'start-up intensity', i.e. the ratio between the number of
start-ups and the labour force (which represents the potential of firm founders). With
respect to firm entries in all sectors, Spain and Italy[2] show the highest start-ups-to-
labour-force ratio while Japan, USA, Germany and Great Britain show the lowest
(Fig. 3). This pattern suggests that new firm formation tends to decrease by income
level and by country size. This corresponds to a similar pattern identified with data
from the Global Entrepreneurship Monitor (GEM), showing the highest entrepreneurial activity in low income countries (Wennekers et al. 2005; Thurik & Grilo 2005)
and Japan with the lowest figure (see Acs et al. 2005). In contrast to firm entry data,
GEM data report a high level of entrepreneurship activity for the USA, however. Here
one may assume a lack in recording very small start-ups (self-employed businesses) in
business registers which will also be true for Japan, Germany and Great Britain.
Nevertheless, the identified pattern is economically reasonable, since high income
levels are associated with high income opportunities for employees and correspondingly a rather low difference between expected income for paid employment and for
self-employment or entrepreneurial activity. This difference may be viewed to be a
main driver for the decision to start a business. Country size positively supports the
emergence of large companies by offering high growth potentials through utilising
scale economies in the home market. A large number of large companies in the
market is likely to act as a barrier to market entries.

---

[2]  In 2000, also Portugal showed a high start-up intensity, but a change in data collection
    methods caused a decline in the total number of start-ups from 2000 to 2001 by 66 per cent,
    and correspondingly low start-up intensities in 2001 and 2002. These figures seem somewhat
    unreliable.

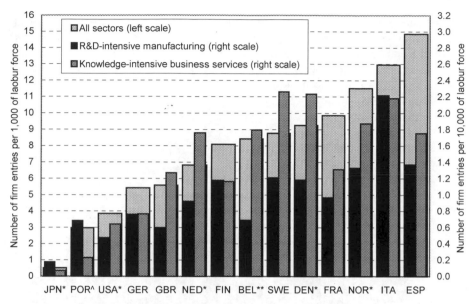

* 2001 – ** 2000 – ^ Portugal likely to be underestimated due to a change in business register recording procedure

Sources: Eurostat (New Cronos), SBA (USA), INSEE, Statistics Bureau Japan, SBS (GBR), ZEW, OECD (MSTI 1/05) – calculation by ZEW

**Fig. 3.** Firm entry intensity in 2002 in selected countries (in per cent)

With respect to technology sectors, high start-up intensities in R&D-intensive manufacturing are reported for Italy, Spain, Norway, Sweden, Denmark and Finland. Germany clearly falls behind, but still has a significantly higher number of start-ups in high- and medium-to-high-tech manufacturing than Japan, the USA and Great Britain. In knowledge-intensive business services, Sweden, Denmark and Italy rank first, followed by Norway, Belgium, the Netherlands and Spain. Germany again ranks at the end of the countries considered and also falls back to the level of France and Great Britain, while the USA and Japan show very low start-up intensities in this sector group, too.

## Entry and Exit of Technology-based Firms

In order to assess the relative dynamics triggered by new firm formation in a market, the ratio of newly founded firms to the stock of firms (firm entry ratio) is a useful indicator. Based on this indicator, the USA shows the highest start-up based dynamics in the firm sector when looking at all sectors, followed by Great Britain, Norway and France (Fig. 4). Start-up based firm dynamics is low in Belgium, Germany and Sweden, and particularly low in Japan. This pattern largely also holds true for R&D-intensive manufacturing, with Germany and Japan showing the smallest figures for firm entry ratio. In KIBS, Denmark and Norway show particularly high ratios: in

2001, the number of new firm entries equalled 15 per cent of the firm stock at the beginning of this year. High market entry dynamics are also reported for the Netherlands, Great Britain, the USA and France, while Germany ranks least (7.5 entries per 100 firms at the beginning of 2002). Interestingly, Japan shows a rather high entry ratio in KIBS of 8 per cent despite low dynamics in most other sectors, including R&D-intensive manufacturing.

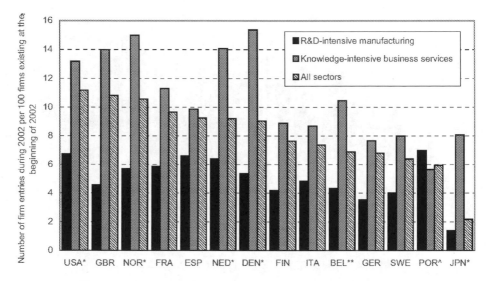

\* 2001 – \*\* 2000 – ^ Portugal likely to be underestimated due to a change in business register recording procedure
Sources: Eurostat (New Cronos), SBA (USA), INSEE, Statistics Bureau Japan, SBS (GBR), ZEW – calculation by ZEW

**Fig. 4.** Firm entry ratio in 2002 in selected countries (in per cent)

Low firm entry rates in Germany are accompanied by low exit rates, indicating generally low dynamics in the firm sector compared to other countries. In R&D-intensive manufacturing, only about 3 per cent of the firms existing at the beginning of 2001 exited the market in 2001, while this ratio is about 10 per cent in many other countries, and 12 per cent in the USA (Fig. 5).[3] The highest exit ratio in R&D-intensive manufacturing is recorded in 2001 for Japan (13 per cent) which contrasted with an entry rate in this sector of 1.5 per cent only, showing a considerably decline in the number of firms. In KIBS, countries with high entry rates also show high exit rates (Norway, Denmark, USA, the Netherlands), pointing to a fierce competition in this sector. The rather high entry ratio in KIBS for Japan is associated with an even higher exit ratio.

---

[3] For some reason, data on firm entries, firm exits and the stock of firms are not consistent for most countries, i.e. the stock of firms at the beginning of the year plus entries minus exits is not equal to the stock at the end. Therefore, a direct comparison of entry and exit rates should be done with caution.

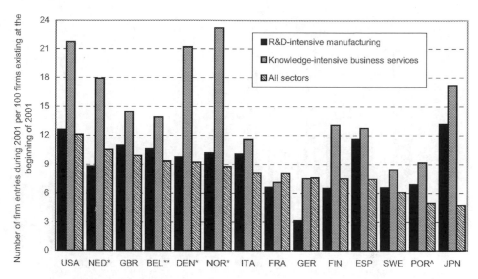

* 2000 – ** 1999 – ^ Portugal likely to be underestimated due to a change in business register recording procedure

Sources: Eurostat (New Cronos), SBA (USA), INSEE, Statistics Bureau Japan, SBS (GBR), ZEW – calculation by ZEW

**Fig. 5.** Firm exit ratio in 2001 in selected countries (in per cent)

For all countries (except entry data for Portugal, which data seem less reliable), entry and exit rates in KIBS are significantly higher than those in R&D-intensive manufacturing, reflecting differences in barriers and incentives for market entry and exit (see Siegfried & Evans 1994; Geroski 1991, Nyström 2005). Barriers particularly refer to the amount of fixed investment needed for starting up a business and the combination of different skills needed, which both are typically higher in Manufacturing where machinery and equipment as well as both technical and managerial skills are required. Incentives refer, among others, to the degree of competition in a certain market that offers young, small firms opportunities to successfully place their products and services, and to find niches not yet occupied by established firms.

The sum of firm entry and firm exit ratios may be called firm turbulence ratio and provides a measure for the speed of change in the stock of firms through the formation and closure of businesses. A high level of exits and entries need not necessarily result in a rapid change of the individual firms active in the market, of course. As long as exits primarily concern firms that entered the market in the same period or in recent periods, the individual firms representing the stock of firms will remain basically the same over a long period of time. There is no information available, however, on the age of exiting firms for the sample of countries considered here. Analyses of firm survival suggest that the probability of firm exit (hazard rate) is indeed highest for young firms (see Prantl 2003; Audretsch & Mahmood 1995), but that there is still a significant portion of firm entries that survive the first 5–10 years (see Wagner 1994; Storey & Wynarczyk 1997; Geroski et al. 2002; Harhoff et al. 1998). One may thus assume that firm turbulence is also a proxy for the dynamics in the firm sector.

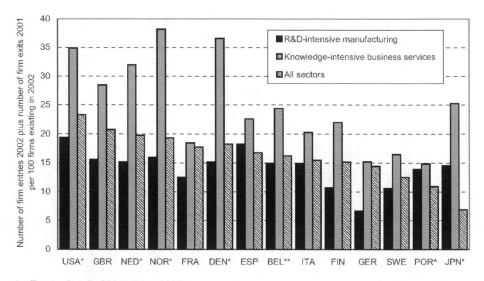

*   Entries/stock: 2001, exits: 2000
**  Entries/stock: 2000, exits: 1999
^   Portugal likely to be underestimated due to a change in business register recording procedure
Sources: Eurostat (New Cronos), SBA (USA), INSEE, Statistics Bureau Japan, SBS (GBR),
ZEW – calculation by ZEW.

**Fig. 6.** Firm turbulence in 2001/2002 in selected countries (in per cent)

Moreover, firm turbulence is likely to be negatively correlated with the existence of
entry and exit barriers and may thus also be viewed as an indicator for the degree of
competition and legal and fiscal incentives to start up new businesses, and to rapidly
close them down in the case of failure. In this respect, the US economy proves to be
highly competition-intensive, facilitating firm entries and exit, followed by Great
Britain and the Netherlands (Fig. 6). In these countries, the number of market entries
and exits together equals 20 to 24 per cent of the total number of firms existing at the
beginning of the year. In Germany, this figure is clearly lower (about 15 per cent),
while Japan shows the lowest firm turbulence (7 per cent).

In the technology sectors, the picture is somewhat different, however: In R&D-
intensive manufacturing, again the USA shows the highest turbulence ratio, but Japan
reports a high level, too, ranking close to Great Britain and the Netherlands. High
numbers of entries and exits with respect to the stock of firms in high-tech manufacturing is also to be found in Spain, Denmark, Belgium and Italy. Germany shows
by far the lowest firm turbulence in R&D-intensive manufacturing.

In KIBS, Norway and Denmark report a particularly high entry and exit dynamic
when compared to the number of active firms in this market, which is even higher
than that of the USA. The Netherlands and Great Britain report a high speed of
change, too, followed by Japan. Germany ranks last again, while the low figure for
Portugal has to be treated with caution due to a possible lack in comparison.

## Dynamics of Technology-based Start-ups

Examining entry and exit of firms for a single year has the main shortcoming of possible distortions due to business cycle effects or changes due to adaptations in the legal setting for new firm foundation and firm closures. For Germany, time series data for 1995 to 2003 are available for both exit and entries, allowing for analysis of the time pattern of firm dynamics. Until 2001, the total firm entry rate fell continuously from 1995 onwards, but slightly increased since then (Fig. 7).[4] In KIBS, the development was somewhat different as entry rates remained constant in 1999 and 2000, but fell in 2001 and 2002. In R&D-intensive manufacturing, the lowest level of firm entry rates was reached in 2002.

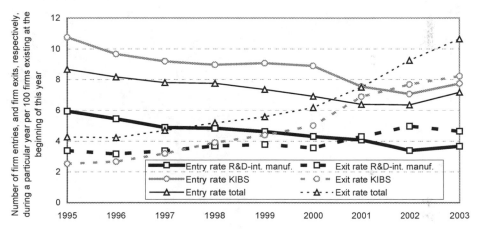

KIBS: knowledge-intensive business services – Total: all sectors except Banking/Insurance
Sources: ZEW Foundation Panel – calculation by ZEW

**Fig. 7.** Firm entry and exit ratios in Germany 1995–2003 (in per cent)

The increase in the number of new firm formations, and consequently in the entry rate, in 2003 was mainly caused by labour market policy efforts to help unemployed start up their own business. Though most of these self-employment projects deploy little activity in terms of the size of market transactions and are thus not covered by the definition of new firm formation used here, there seems to be still a significant number of start-ups out of unemployment that create a considerable amount of economic activity, thus raising entry rates. This effect is clearly larger in non-technology-oriented sectors than in R&D-intensive manufacturing or KIBS.

Exit rates show a reverse pattern: From 1995 on they continuously increased, especially strongly after the year 2000. Here, two effects merged: first, the slow-down in economic growth resulted in greater financial difficulties for many small firms, often followed by market exit. Secondly, a change in the insolvency law in 2001 eased the

---

[4] Data prior to 1995 show even higher entry rates, which are strongly influenced by the establishment of a private firm sector in eastern Germany, causing high numbers of market entries while at the same time the stock of firms was low.

requirements for applying for insolvency, which is likely to have increased the number of insolvencies.

Until 2000, exit rates in Germany were clearly below entry rates both in R&D-intensive manufacturing and KIBS, as well as for the total of sectors. This means that the stock of firms has expanded throughout this period. In 2001, however, exit rates exceeded entry rates. In R&D-intensive manufacturing and in KIBS, this development took place one year later. Both in 2002 and 2003, the number of economically active firms in theses sectors declined also. It is obvious that this is a consequence of the weak macroeconomic development (see Chapter 4.1), with a very low real growth in GDP in 2002 (+0.1 per cent) and a slight decline in 2003 (–0.2 per cent).

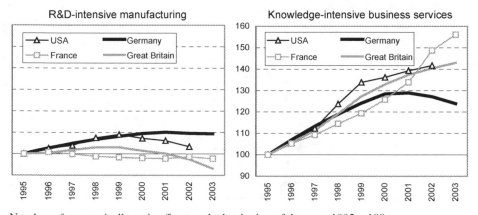

Number of economically active firms at the beginning of the year, 1995 = 100
Sources: SBA (USA), INSEE, SBS (GBR), ZEW – calculation by ZEW

**Fig. 8.** Development of the stock of firms 1995–2003 in selected countries

A positive firm dynamic in the second half of the 1990s is to be seen in most other large countries, too.[5] In R&D-intensive manufacturing, this dynamics was rather restrained, however. The stock of firms did increase until 1999 in the USA and Great Britain, but just to about 5 to 10 per cent above the level of 1995 (Fig. 8). Since 2000, the number of active high-tech firms fell in these two countries, and in Great Britain it reached a level in 2003 clearly below that of 1995. In France, the stock of high-tech firms remained nearly constant over the period covered. Germany experienced an increase in the stock of high-tech firms until 2001 and only a very moderate decrease since then, resulting in a still high level of R&D-intensive manufacturing firms in 2003.

In KIBS, the dynamics are significantly stronger. In 2000, the number of firms in this sector was 25 to 35 per cent above that in 1995. Since then, the dynamics vanished in Germany, slowed down in the USA and Great Britain, and remained very high in France. In 2003, Germany thus significantly lagged behind the other three large countries with respect to the expansion in the number of KIBS firms: compared to 2003, it was 25 per cent above the figure of 1995, while the USA (for 2002) and Great Britain reported +42 per cent and France +57 per cent.

---

[5] Annual stock data from 1995 onwards are available for USA, Great Britain, France and Germany only.

These differences in firm dynamics are also reflected in the development of the number of start-ups in the same period: in R&D-intensive manufacturing, start-up numbers tended to decline since 1995, with increases only in certain years in each country (Great Britain and Japan: 1996, Germany: 1998 and 2003, France: 2001, USA: 2000). In 2003, the number of firms newly entering high-tech manufacturing markets was clearly below the respective number in 1995 in all countries (Fig. 9).

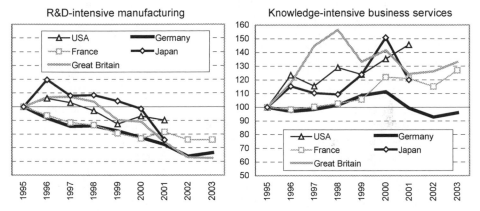

Number of start-ups, 1995 = 100
Sources: SBA (USA), INSEE, Statistics Bureau Japan, SBS (GBR), ZEW – calculation by ZEW

**Fig. 9.** Development of technology-based start-ups 1995–2003 in selected countries

The situation in KIBS is clearly different. Start-up figures tended to rise – although not continuously – in all countries except Germany. In Germany, the increase in the number of market entries remained rather low compared to other large countries in this sector until the year 2000. In 2000, the number of new firms entering the KIBS market was just 10 per cent above the 1995 level, while in this particular boom year of the 'New Economy' the other countries reached levels of 20 per cent (France), 35 per cent (USA), 40 per cent (Great Britain) and 50 per cent (Japan) above 1995. After 2000, start-up figures in KIBS clearly fell in Germany. In the USA, in contrast, start-up figures continued to increase until 2001, although data for 2002 onwards are not available yet. In France and Great Britain they remained on a high level in 2001 and 2002 and even increased in 2003. For Japan, a sharp decline in 2001 is reported, while more current data are not available.

## Conclusion

The propensity to start up new businesses in the technology sector is rather low in Germany, both with respect to the entry ratio, i.e. the number of newly founded firms per stock of firms, and the entry intensity, i.e. the new firm formations per labour force unit. At the same time, those relatively few firms that entered the market are more likely to stay there than start-ups in other countries do. Consequently, firm turbulence in the technology sector – the number of entries and exits per stock of firms – is lowest in Germany among all countries considered. In R&D-intensive manufacturing, the number of economically active firms did increase until 2003 despite a strong downward trend in the number of start-ups. In this particular sector, firm dynamics in Germany exceeded that of other large countries.

In knowledge-intensive business services (KIBS), the situation is worse. After 2001, firm dynamics in Germany turned negative due to a sharp decline in start-up figures and a drastic increase in the number of firm closures. While entry ratios and entry intensities are low in international comparison and clearly fell after 2000, there was a strong increase in the number of market exits in the German KIBS sector from 2001 on. This was certainly caused by the weak domestic demand in Germany. While young services heavily depend on domestic customers as exports are hampered by low tradability of most services and high entry costs to foreign markets, young firms in R&D-intensive manufacturing may more easily escape unfavourable economic conditions in Germany by entering export markets. This may explain the different recent development in firm exits in the two parts of the technology sector.

This development is somewhat alarming as KIBS represent a major segment of an economy's technology sector, both in terms of generating new knowledge (e.g. software, business methods, R&D in new fields) and demanding and applying technology from the manufacturing sector (e.g. telecommunication, technical services, testing). A low dynamics in the KIBS sector may thus also weaken innovation in Manufacturing due to slipping demand for new products used in the service sector.

When looking for the reasons for the low start-up level in the German technology sector, four factors may be stressed in particular: unfavourable macroeconomic environment, lack of financing, bureaucratic burdens, and high opportunity costs:

• Weak domestic demand has been already mentioned as a likely cause for the recent fall in start-up figures and the sharp increase in firm closures. Since new firms only rarely are able to enter export markets shortly after their foundation – even in the high-tech sector their share is rather low (see Fryges 2004; Bürgel et al. 2004) – they are heavily dependent upon domestic demand. Especially in KIBS, where services are only partially tradable, local and regional customers are the main business partners. Weak demand will certainly reduce business prospects of existing firms, and provides little incentives for potential firm founders to start up new businesses.

• Lack of financing refers both to credit financing for young firms as well as to venture capital supply. Credit financing – covering both bank loans and supplier credits – is relevant for the bulk of start-ups, including most technology-based start-ups, in order to set up their business. In the course of Basel-II (which is likely to lead to a stronger consideration of individual risks in the conditions of loans offered to small enterprises), there are reports that German banks became increasingly reluctant to offer start-ups favourable financing conditions. Especially firm founders who do not have collateral at their disposal and those requiring only small credits will find it difficult to obtain bank loans (see VDG 2004). Moreover, supplier credits are difficult to get for start-ups as they lack a track record about their financial capabilities and their business prospects. Venture capital (VC) supply for technology-based start-ups in Germany was very high in 1999 and 2000, but fell sharply since then. In 2003, the absolute amount of VC investment in seed and start-up stages was lower than the respective figures in Great Britain and France (see Rammer 2004), while the German VC only slowly recovered in 2004.

- Bureaucratic burdens are often reported as a main barrier for starting up a business in Germany. Main complaints refer to long duration of registration procedures and a large number of different agencies that have to be approached. The World Bank Doing Business Database indeed shows that establishing a new firm requires both more time and money (World Bank 2004): The average cost for starting up a business are estimated to be about 6 per cent of GDP per capita in 2003, while the USA, Great Britain, France and Scandinavian countries report between almost 0 and 3 per cent. The average time needed for firm start-up was said to be around 45 days in Germany in 2003, while the other countries mentioned allow for starting-up within 5 to 20 days. Moreover, in some fields, starting up a business still demands rather ambitious requirements from the founder, e.g. in the craft sector. The most recent edition of 'Doing Business' (World Bank 2005) reports considerable increases for Germany, however, putting Germany among the top ten reformers in business foundations in 2004. Costs for starting a business dropped to 4.7 per cent, and the average time for firm start-up was 24 days only.

- Finally, for many years employment opportunities for researchers and other highly qualified personnel were manifold in Germany and promised high income levels with high job security. Consequently, incentives to start one's own business, and thus take considerable economic risks, have been low. However, this situation has changed significantly in recent years as a result of the weak economic development and the corresponding rise in unemployment.

In order to increase start-up activities in the German technology sectors, several measures have been undertaken recently by the government. With respect to financing, a reform of public VC programmes took place, including the introduction of an umbrella fund to provide additional financing to private VC companies for seed and start-up financing, and a new public–private high-tech start-up fund that will directly invest in new high-tech start-ups, with special emphasis laid on research spin-offs. Moreover, a number of measures concern dismantling bureaucratic burdens, e.g. by introducing one-stop-shops for firm founders and lifting some formal restrictions for firm founding.

What is still left to do is to improve financing for the vast majority of small technology-based start-ups which do not require VC, but a rather small amount of bank loans. These start-ups often fail to receiving bank loans due to low bankability or lack of collateral. Above all, improving the macroeconomic environment and bringing the German economy back onto a growth path seem to be the most important factors when it comes to improving framework conditions for technology start-ups in Germany.

# 4.3 Diffusion of Information and Communication Technology

Thomas Hempell

**Abstract.** Due to startling and continued technological advances, information and communication technology (ICT) has received major attention in analysing innovation and growth dynamics in industrialised countries over the last decade. Beyond innovation and productivity increases in the ICT-producing sector itself, the diffusion of ICT has enabled not only the deployment of completely new technological domains, such as Biotechnology, but has also fostered process innovations and the reshaping of organisational structures in more established parts of industrialised economies. Due to its character as a *general purpose technology*, ICT diffusion has become an important aspect of the performance of innovation systems. This chapter shows that ICT diffusion varies markedly between industrialised countries, with Germany ranking somewhere in the middle for most indicators discussed.

## Relevance of ICT for Innovation and Productivity Growth

There is arguably no technology that has shaped work environments and business relationships more markedly during the last decades than information and communication technology (ICT). At the heart of the success story of ICT is the general purpose character of ICT (Bresnahan & Trajtenberg 1995), reflected by its wide range and variety of use, as well as its inherent large potential for further technical improvements. Moreover, the particular relevance of ICT for innovation systems accrue from its 'enabling' properties: the use of ICT facilitates innovations in a broad range of business areas, including the generation of new products and services (in particular in Banking and Insurance, but also the manufacturing industries, such as the Car Industry), the reshaping of organisational structures in firms as well as Internet-based business contacts and co-operations (B2B e-commerce, in particular).[1] Pointing to these characteristics of ICT, various theoretical and empirical studies have highlighted the key role of ICT production and use for recent economic growth in industrialised countries.

Over the last years, various studies addressing the economic relevance of ICT for innovation activities and economic growth have emerged. Innovation and productivity growth has been particularly large in the ICT-producing sector itself. However, the economic impacts go far beyond the computer and software industry. In nearly all sectors of industrialised economies, ICT has adopted the role as a key input favouring innovation activities. For example, cars are increasingly equipped with micro-computers that operate navigation systems and monitor operations of car components.

---

[1] See Bresnahan & Greenstein (1998), Licht & Moch (1999), Bresnahan et al. (2002), Bertschek & Kaiser (2004), Hempell (2005a; 2005b).

*U. Schmoch, C. Rammer and H. Legler (eds.), National Systems of Innovation in Comparison, 169–184.*

Similarly, computers have facilitated new kinds of services, with cash machine tellers, online banking, e-commerce, and Internet-based after-sales services being only some examples. Beyond facilitating the introduction of completely new products and processes, ICT is used to improve the quality of existing products and services, in particular service quality, timeliness, and convenience (Licht & Moch 1999).

Comment: balance of negative and positive contributions amounts to average labour productivity growth per year
Source: Jorgenson (2005)

**Fig. 1.** Sources of labour productivity growth 1995–2001

ICT applications foster innovation dynamics also by impacting processes and organisational structures inside firms and administrations (Bresnahan et al. 2002). Firms employ more flexible and more easily programmable manufacturing tools that embody ICT; applications for supply chain management increasingly link the production processes of suppliers and clients; and new tools for customer care, such as customer relationship management, help to recognise changes in demand more quickly (Hammer 1990; Rigby et al. 2002). In various cases, these developments are associated with substantial organisational changes and often entail new skill requirements for workers (Brynjolfsson & Hitt 2000).

The technical advances in ICT production as well as productivity improvements associated with ICT investments have been cited as important drivers of economic growth in industrial countries over the past decade.[2] In a recent empirical analysis, Jorgenson (2005) quantifies the contributions of ICT production and ICT use to labour productivity growth in the G7 countries (see Fig. 1). The results for the period 1995–2001 show that more than one-third of annual labour productivity growth in Germany, which amounted to 1.3 per cent, can be attributed to ICT capital deepening,

---

[2] For a summary of empirical evidence at macro, industry, and firm level, see OECD (2003; 2004a).

i.e. increases in ICT equipment per worker. Moreover, multi-factor productivity increases in the ICT-producing sector account for some further 0.65 percentage points of annual labour productivity growth. This substantial contribution is particularly impressive, given that the ICT sector accounts for only a small proportion of GDP in Germany by international standards.[3]

Even though these ICT contributions in Germany are large, they are even higher in other countries. In Japan and the USA, for example, the contributions of ICT capital deepening to annual labour productivity growth amount to about 0.9 percentage points. In contrast, the contributions of ICT in other economies of continental Europe (France, Italy) are similar to those found for Germany.

The underlying reasons of diverging growth effects of ICT are difficult to identify from aggregate figures. Empirical studies based on firm-level data show, however, that firms that combine ICT use with complementary innovations and organisational changes perform better than firms that pursue isolated strategies (Bresnahan et al. 2002). Moreover, firms with experience from earlier innovation activities have been shown to be more successful in ICT use (Hempell 2005a). Early liberalisation of markets (in particular in services) in the USA may have enhanced competitive pressure and innovation needs of US businesses, contributing to a more productive adoption of ICT in the USA than in more protected European firms.

The following sections provide more detailed indicators on the diffusion of ICT in industrialised countries. Important sources of these indicators are annual statistics released by the European Information Technology Observatory (EITO), the International Telecommunication Union (ITU), as well as figures released by the European Statistical Office. These sources are complemented by own data collections by the Centre for European Economic Research (ZEW), Mannheim, on more recent technologies such as WLAN hotspots.

A major challenge involved in the selection and discussion of ICT-related indicators are the startling and continuing technological advances in ICT technology, which entails trade-offs between data availability and technological state of the art. While more established ICT applications are generally well-documented for international comparisons, data on important but relatively young technologies (such as mobile telecommunications from the so-called third generation or 3G) are difficult to obtain and are often not standardised for international comparisons. This chapter aims to achieve a reasonable solution in this trade-off by providing long-term time series of indicators of important established technologies (such as mobile phone or Internet use) as well as comparisons for younger ICT applications (such as 3G or WLAN hotspots) for more recent years only.

---

[3] According to calculations by OECD (2002b), the share of ICT production in business sector value added in 1999 amounted to about six per cent in Germany compared to an OECD average of about 10 per cent.

# International Indicators of ICT Use

## General Indicators of ICT Markets

Total expenditures on ICT goods and services in Germany amounted to  128.3 billion in 2004, which is a mid-value among industrialised countries. Although international ICT markets worldwide have grown slightly in nominal terms, the proportion of ICT expenses relative to GDP has decreased in nearly all industrialised countries during the years after 2000. This is because economic growth in most economies exceeded growth of ICT markets. According to figures published by EITO, the share of ICT expenses relative to GDP has decreased in all EU countries (see Fig. 2).

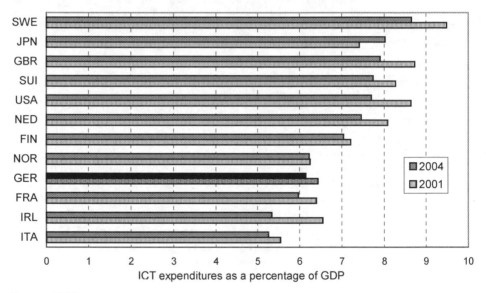

Source: EITO

**Fig. 2.** Shares of ICT markets in GDP

The decline in relative importance of ICT was particularly pronounced in the USA, where the corresponding share decreased by nearly one percentage point between 2000 and 2004. In Germany, ICT expenses amounted to 6.2 per cent of GDP in 2004.

However, taking into account the fact that quality-adjusted prices for ICT products and services have been declining at considerable rates, real ICT expenses relative to real GDP are likely to have increased. Due to the lack of internationally comparable price indices for ICT goods and services, these shares can unfortunately not be exposed for a cross-country comparison. Calculations by the Deutsche Bundesbank (2004) show that in Germany real ICT investment accounts for more than 40 per cent of all investment in plant and equipment compared to only nine per cent at the beginning of the 1970s. In nominal terms, in contrast, the increase was less marked, with an increase from 18 per cent in 1970 to 32 per cent in 2002.

**Table 1.** Glossary of some technical terms

| | |
|---|---|
| e-commerce | Electronic commerce denotes transactions executed via the Internet or other electronic networks. |
| e-government | Electronic government refers to public services available to citizens and businesses via the Internet. |
| B2B | Business-to-business e-commerce refers to orders between firms accomplished via the Internet. |
| B2C | Business-to-consumer e-commerce denotes orders over the Internet placed by consumers. |
| GSM | Global System for Mobile refers to a standard of the so-called second generation (2G) that has prevailed during the 1990s up to present. |
| 3G | Mobile communication services of the so-called third generation (3G) denote mobile applications that allow for a fast transmission of large data packages such as video streams. |
| UMTS | Universal Mobile Telecommunication Systems refer to a particular technological standard of 3G mobile services used predominantly in Europe. |
| ADSL | Asynchronous digital subscriber lines is a technology to separate telephone mainlines into three lines: one for voice phone calls, one for downloading data, and one for uploading data. ADSL is generally associated with download rates of several megabits per second. |
| WLAN | Wireless local area networks allow for wireless high speed data transmission within a limited range of up to some hundred meters. |
| Hotspots | Hotspots are publicly accessible WLANs, predominantly run by airports, hotels, or cafes. |

One reason for the low ICT expenditure in Germany compared to other industrialised countries may be the weak cyclical situation. A large part of ICT expenses consist of investment which is particularly dependent on business cycles.[4] Moreover, replacement investment in ICT can be more readily delayed than other replacement investment since the technical lifetime of computers and software tends to exceed its economic lifetime. However, also ICT investment cannot be delayed arbitrarily, because compatibility problems of new and old equipment may arise due to the fast technological progress in this sector.

A further explanation of the small relative size of ICT markets in Germany may be industry structure. The German economy is traditionally dominated by manufacturing industries (such as the Car Industry and Mechanical Engineering) which dispose of a lower potential for ICT investment than ICT-intensive service industries, such as Banking and Insurances.

Further indicators of ICT diffusion, however, show that the economic recession and industry structure are unlikely to be the only reason for low ICT expenditures in Germany. When it comes to the equipment of firms, public administration, other institutions and households with personal computers, Germany ranks in the middle of the industrialised countries (see Fig. 3). Statistically, there are 390 computers per 1,000 inhabitants in Germany, compared to 800 in the USA. Greece, Spain, Portugal, and Italy rank lowest in this international comparison with values between 120 and 210.

---

[4]  See e.g. Deutsche Bundesbank (2004).

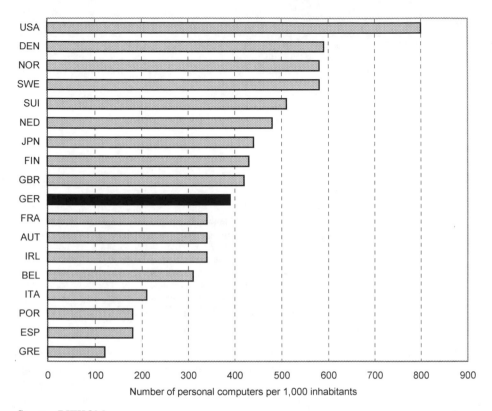

Source: BITKOM

**Fig. 3.** Diffusion of personal computers in 2004

## Internet Use

Even though worldwide ICT expenses do not continue to grow at the same rates as during the 1990s, ICT continue to diffuse rapidly. A most prominent example is Internet use as illustrated in Fig. 4 for the USA, Germany, and the EU-15. Germany ranks above EU average, but is lagging behind US penetration rates by about three years. Compared to industrialised countries more generally, Germany holds a mid-position with respect to Internet use.

Apart from the mere number of Internet users, the speed of data transfer with Internet connections has gained in importance over the last years. Many applications, such as downloads of music, software, films, or newspaper content, require users to have broadband connections to the Internet. The most frequently used technologies for broadband access are asynchronous digital subscriber lines (ADSL) and cable modems connected to cable television infrastructure. In Western Europe, the number of broadband connections more than doubled from 2002 to 2004 to 27 million. In Germany, the number of broadband connections in 2004 amounted to 6.7 million, corresponding to 83 subscriptions per 1,000 inhabitants (see Fig. 5).

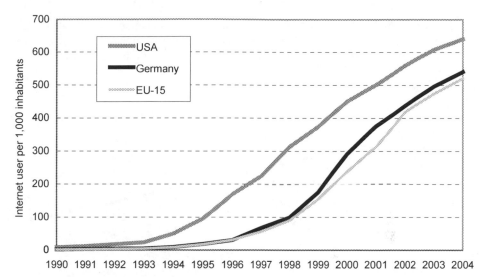

Source: ITU, EITO, Eurostat – own calculations

**Fig. 4.** Development of Internet use 1990–2004

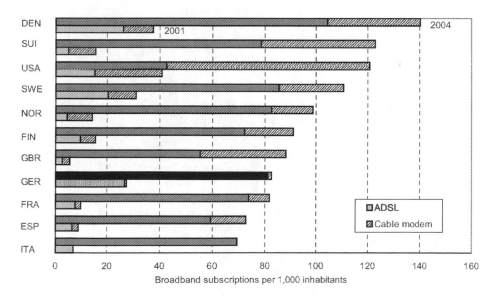

Source: ITU, EITO, Eurostat – own calculations

**Fig. 5.** Broadband penetration 2001 und 2004

When it comes to prices of broadband Internet access, Germany ranks in the middle range of major industrialised countries. With the cheapest German provider charging € 32.90 per month for unlimited broadband access (*flat rate*) in November 2004, prices are higher than in France and the USA (€14.90 and 21.00 respectively), but

about the same as in the United Kingdom and slightly cheaper than in Italy (€35.90).[5]
During the first months of 2005, however, competition in broadband access in Germany
has intensified substantially with some providers offering unlimited broadband access
for less than € 25.

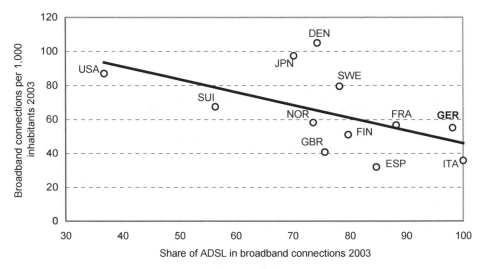

Sources: EITO, Eurostat, GeoHive – calculations by ZEW

**Fig. 6.** Broadband penetration and technology competition

One reason for the middling position of Germany with respect to broadband diffusion
may be the lack of competition between alternative broadband technologies. While
broadband connections are based on ADSL to about 98 per cent in Germany, access
via cable networks is far more widespread in other countries. As Fig. 6 illustrates,
countries with a less dominant role of ADSL for broadband access tend to exhibit
higher diffusion rates of broadband than countries dominated by ADSL. Two aspects
may contribute to understanding this correlation. First, existence of an accepted alternative enhances competition and thus tends to lower prices and to foster innovation of
broadband services. Second, ADSL access continues to be dominated by the former
telecommunications incumbents since ADSL is based on telephone lines. This dominance of established providers with corresponding market power may deter potential
competitors from entering the markets.

Basically, conditions in Germany for a greater relevance of cable networks for
broadband access are excellent. With 260 cable television subscribers per 1,000
inhabitants in 2003, Germany ranks among the top-five with respect to the diffusion
of cable networks (see Fig. 7). The low usage of cable infrastructure for Internet
access is thus primarily a consequence of the prolonged process of Deutsche Telekom
AG's selling its cable networks to investors. Objections by the German Cartel Office
have averted corresponding deals on several occasions in the past. Moreover, the

---

[5]  See Hempell (2004: 15). Surprisingly, broadband diffusion in Denmark in one of the highest
    in international comparison, even though prices for flat rates are about € 48.50.

German cable TV market is highly segmented at the lowest network level, the connection to households. More than 5,000 operators (mainly housing societies) exist at this level. Use of cable networks for broadband access requires investments in technological upgrading at this network level. For cable network providers, however, negotiating and co-ordinating actions with a large variety of partners make upgrading an expensive and time-consuming task. Finally, switching costs are a further deterring factor for competitors offering cable modem technology. With ADSL subscribers having reached a lead in diffusion, it is increasingly hard to convince ADSL users to abandon ADSL for cable modem technology, which requires substantial set-up costs.

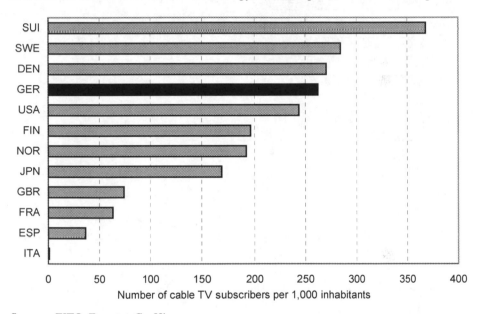

Sources: EITO, Eurostat, GeoHive

**Fig. 7.** Cable TV penetration in 2003

A technology that enables broadband access at public places is wireless Internet use via WLAN routers. This technology allows providers to deploy one fixed broadband access for various simultaneous users within a radius of about 30 meters within buildings and of up to several hundred meters outdoors. As a precondition, PCs and laptops of users must be equipped with corresponding WLAN processors. Apart from private households and enterprises, WLAN has gained popularity at so-called hotspots, such as airports, hotels and cafes. The internet platform *www.jwire.com* collects data on diffusion of these hotspots which allow for international comparisons. According to this source, there were about 70,000 hotspot locations worldwide by July 2005. Diffusion of hotspots relative to population, however, varies substantially by country (see Fig. 8). While Britain, Switzerland, and Denmark disposed of more than 100 hotspots per million inhabitants in November 2004, diffusion in the EU on average amounted to 53 hotspots per million inhabitants. In Germany, there were about 4,500 registered hotspots or 55 per million inhabitants. By July 2005, however, this number has grown substantially to 6,200 hotspots.

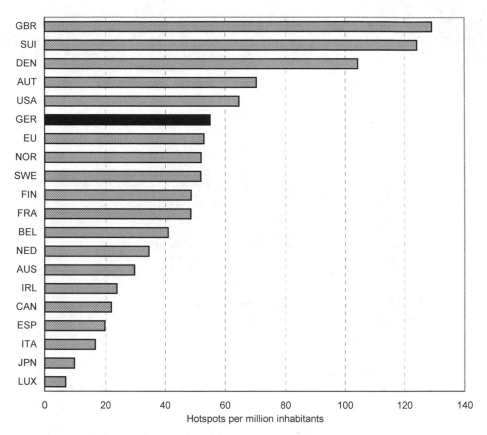

Source: *www.jiwire.com*, Eurostat, GeoHive – calculations by ZEW, date: November 2004

**Fig. 8.** Diffusion of Hotspots

## Mobile Phones

Penetration of industrialised countries with mobile phones continues, albeit at sub-stantially lower speed than in the 1990s, when two-digit growth rates were standard in most countries. Mobile telephony is arguably the only ICT application where Europe has taken and so far preserved its lead compared to the United States. As illustrated in Fig. 9, there were about 84 mobile subscriptions per 100 inhabitants in the EU in 2003 compared to only 54 in the USA. Germany is slightly below EU average with 79 sub-scriptions per 100 inhabitants. One reason for this lag within Europe may be the rela-tively high cost of mobile services in Germany.[6]

The arguably most important reason for Europe's lead in mobile telecommun-ications was the early agreement on the Global System for Mobile Communications (GSM) as a unique standard for mobile communications in Europe. The USA, in con-trast, allowed a variety of standards to compete, which complicated communication

---

[6] For an international comparison of prices for mobile services, see Hempell et al. (2005).

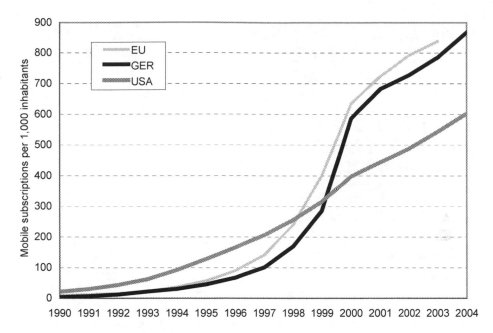

Source: ITU, EITO, Eurostat – own calculations

**Fig. 9.** Long-term diffusion of mobile phones 1990–2004

between these standards and led to smaller network effects and slower diffusion of mobile phones.

Experience from GSM for mobile phones of the so-called second generation (2G) inspired European regulators to pursue a similar strategy for mobile services of the third generation (3G). These services allow much higher data transfer rates than 2G and thus enable transmission of pictures and films. Hoping for similarly beneficial effects as with GSM, European regulators obliged 3G operators to adapt the W-CDMA standard underlying UMTS. This standard, however, entailed a variety of problems which delayed introduction of these services by years.

In the meanwhile, 3G services have been introduced in all West European countries. Diffusion rates 2004 were highest in Italy and the United Kingdom, which were the first European countries to introduce UMTS in 2003. In June 2004, there were nearly one million subscribers in each of these two countries. This corresponds to 16.7 and 16.5 users per 1,000 inhabitants (see Fig. 10). In Germany, in contrast, UMTS started only in spring 2004, and the number of subscribers in June 2004 amounted to some 18,500 or 0.2 UMTS users per 1,000 inhabitants.

However, diffusion of 3G is much higher in parts of Asia, where a different standard (CDMA200-1X) is predominantly used. According to figures published by *www.3gtoday.com*, there were about 128 million users worldwide by the end of July 2004. This number increased to some 184 millions by the end of May 2005. Standards different from UMTS proved to incur less problems in practice and partially allow particularly high data transmission rates of up to 2 Mbits/s compared to a maximum of 384 kbits/s in the case of UMTS.

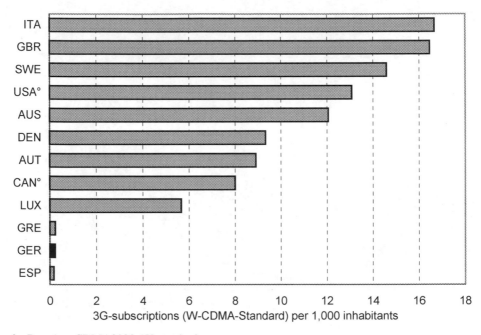

° Based on CDMA2000-1X standard
Sources: EMC, Eurostat, GeoHive – own calculations

**Fig. 10.** Diffusion of UMTS services in June 2004

## Use of E-commerce and E-government

Productive use of ICT in firms requires a variety of adjustments with respect to firm organisation and redesign of processes.[7] A particularly important application requiring such adjustments is the use of the Internet as a sales channel in electronic commerce (e-commerce). Most importantly, business-to-business (B2B) e-commerce helps firms to accelerate acceptance and processing of orders and to deliver intermediates and services more quickly. Moreover, e-commerce helps firms to save costs by delivering digitalised products such as software, music titles or films directly over the web.

According to calculations by EITO (2005), e-commerce transactions in western Europe amounted to a value of €680 billion in 2004. This value is anticipated to grow strongly over the next years and to reach more than €2,200 billion by 2008. B2B e-commerce accounts for the major part of e-commerce (87 per cent).

Germany is not only the biggest market for electronic commerce in Europe, with transactions amounting to a value of €203 billion in 2004 (EITO 2005); it also ranks among top countries when e-commerce relative to GDP is considered (see Fig. 11). E-commerce transactions make up 4.4 per cent in GDP in Germany, compared to an average of 3.5 per cent for the EU. Relative importance is higher only in Sweden, Finland, the United Kingdom, and Austria. Also the share of German consumers buying

---

[7] For microeconomic evidence, see e.g. Bresnahan et al. (2002) and Hempell (2005b).

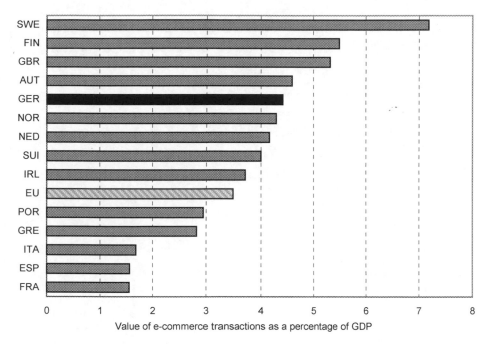

Source: tns infratest, EITO – own calculations

**Fig. 11.** Sales via e-commerce as proportions of GDP, 2004

online is relatively high by international standards, amounting to 210 in 1,000 consumers (see Fig. 12). However, the good position of Germany is not secured for the years to come. Many e-commerce applications make sense only for consumers with broadband access to the Internet. The comparatively low dynamics in broadband diffusion in Germany may thus prove a hampering factor for growth in electronic commerce.

The Internet not only provides new possibilities of services for firms but also for public administration. The provision of corresponding services via the Internet (e-government) allows administrations to improve services for citizens and firms and to improve efficiency and speed of processes. These increases in effectiveness may help to save costs for public administrations which may lead to lowering taxes or reducing governmental borrowing. Moreover, e-government enhances the attractiveness of the Internet for citizens and firms, and is thereby a measure to promote diffusion of Internet use.

A study by Cap Gemini Ernst & Young for the European Commission shows that Germany is lagging considerably behind in terms of a broad application of e-government. Considering the availability of public administration services via the Internet,[8] Germany ranks lower than all other EU countries except Luxembourg (see

---

[8] For calculating the degree of online availability of public administration services, the study by Cap Gemini (2004) assesses to what degree a variety of public services can be made available online theoretically using best practice. Consequently, the study evaluates to what degree this theoretically possible online availability was achieved in each of the countries under consideration.

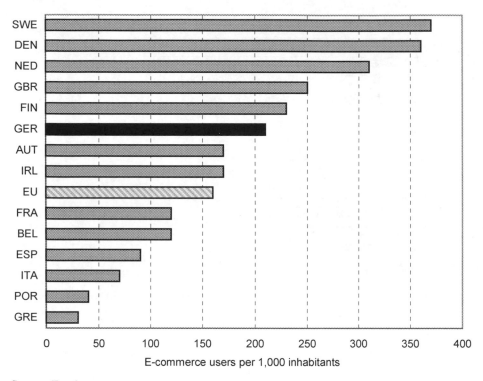

Source: Eurobarometer

**Fig. 12.** Use of e-commerce in 2003

Fig. 13). The position improves only slightly if only those public administration services are considered that can be provided completely online. Under these premises,
Germany ranks among the middle of the West European countries considered.

Assessing the more detailed results of the study, it turns out that Germany performs
particularly poorly when it comes to the possibility of registering start-ups via the
Internet. Many public administrations do not even provide online information about
the registering process required in this context. In contrast, other countries such as
Sweden, Denmark, and Italy allow the registration of new businesses completely via
the Internet.

## Conclusions

Use of Information and Communication Technology (ICT) continues to form an important base for productivity growth and innovation activities in industrialised economies. Empirical studies demonstrate that a substantial part of productivity increases
and economic growth can be attributed to production and use of ICT. Moreover, ICT
has become an indispensable part of innovation systems. The marked advances in
relatively new technologies – such as Biotechnology – would have been impossible

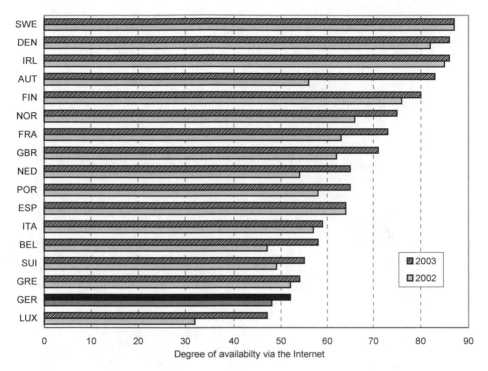

Source: Cap Gemini Ernst & Young – tns infratest

**Fig. 13.** Online-availability of public administration's services

without the enormous progress in computers' capacity of computing and storage power. Also in more established technological domains, such as the automobile or aircraft industry, ICT use creates considerable innovation potentials both in the development of new products and as key intermediate goods such as control and navigation systems.

Relative to its economic size, Germany does not have a strong ICT-producing sector on its own but is a net importer of ICT products and services. In order to benefit from advances in ICT, Germany needs to exploit the potentials of ICT for innovation activities in other technological areas and industries. Considering international indicators of ICT diffusion, however, Germany is far from ranking among the top users of ICT. This discomforting position is currently weakened additionally by the weak cyclical forces that hamper investment in general. After all, ICT expenditures in Germany have recovered again since the marked drop in 2002. However, ICT growth rates in Germany remain considerably lower than in other industrialised countries. Pointing at the weak business cycle to explain this development is not enough. ICT is most frequently used for innovating processes and work organisation. Factors hampering such changes are thus also restraints to a faster diffusion of new technologies.

The mediocre overall importance of ICT in the German economy is reflected also by relative reluctance of private households to make use of ICT. The endowment of consumers with computers and ICT literacy is only average in comparison with other industrialised countries. One positive exception is the use of B2C e-commerce, which is developing particularly well by international standards. As in other countries, however, B2C makes up only about ten per cent of total sales via the Internet. This means that the good position of Germany with respect to e-commerce can be attributed primarily to a well-developed B2B e-commerce between firms.

Considering the future deployment of ICT markets, fast access to the Internet via broadband connections turns out to be particularly important. Broadband access is a key not only to a broader use of e-commerce, but also for exploiting the advantages from division of labour in firms by outsourcing computing capacities and services. Moreover, new cost-saving technological developments in telecommunications, such as voice-over-IP, are based on broadband. So far, Germany ranks in the middle of the major industrialised countries with respect to broadband access. This position, however, is jeopardised by comparatively low growth of broadband connections in Germany. Growth is hampered in particular by the fact that ADSL is nearly the exclusive technology for broadband access. After all, the introduction of resale in 2004 started to undermine the dominant role of the former telecommunications incumbent in this area. Cable modem technology, which uses cable TV infrastructure for fast Internet access, is by far less used in Germany than in other countries despite the fact that cable TV infrastructure is particularly well developed. The main factors hampering the use of this technological platform for broadband connection are the delayed sale of cable networks to private investors and the fragmentation of markets in the domain of connecting of cable networks to households, the so-called 'last mile'.

Finally, online activities of public administrations (e-government) play a decisive role for ICT diffusion. ICT and the Internet are characterised by 'network effects', meaning that the utility and attractiveness of these technologies increase with the number of users and the amount of content provided online. In this context, public administrations hold a key role for fostering Internet use. This is because the provision of public administration services via the Internet not only helps to reduce costs in public administrations themselves, but also to improve service quality and to make access to public services easier for firms and citizens. This raises overall incentives for individuals and businesses to make use of computers and to connect to the Internet.

International comparisons of the online availability of public administration services point to large differences in e-government advances in European countries, with Germany ranking at the bottom. These results suggest that initiatives designed to improve e-government in Germany – such as 'BundOnline' – point in the right direction, but need to be enforced to make the Internet help reduce bureaucratic burdens for firms and individuals and to raise incentives of going online.

# Part 5.   Education as a Base for NSI

# 5.1 Education Structures and Highly Skilled Employment in Europe – A Comparison

Rainer Frietsch, Birgit Gehrke

**Abstract.** Economic structural change and pressure to generate innovation enormously pushed a need for highly qualified personnel, especially for scientists and engineers, which is still increasing. As a consequence, a skill-biased technological change and a rising importance of high formal qualifications can be found all across Europe, with some countries starting to catch up and even overtake the established ones. But demography has put some obstacles in the way towards the European Research Area. The future demand for highly skilled employees might be covered by the increasing supply, due to an on going qualification and knowledge intensification. But a growing share of these individuals will be needed for substitution and a shrinking share will be available for the intended goal of increasing total qualification levels. Shortcomings seem unavoidable, at least at selective and crucial points.

## Introduction and Study Goal

Experiences and analyses of globalisation indicate that the global economy has entered an innovation-oriented phase which is characterised by, firstly, intensifying competition and digitalisation in the global market. Secondly, the crucial role of research and development nationally as well as in enterprises grows, so that, thirdly, human capital is becoming one of the most central factors of competitive and innovative ability, growth, income and employment, not only in manufacturing industries, but also in the service sector.[1]

This makes education and skills of growing relevance, both from an entrepreneurial and from the individual point of view, for higher levels of qualification induce higher productivity and thereby higher earnings and a lower unemployment risk (Reinberg & Hummel 2002; OECD [ed.] 2003d). This trend is commonly summarised under the headings knowledge intensification *or* shift towards knowledge societies. From a labour market perspective it can be called *skill-biased technological change* and is induced by the structural shift towards more knowledge-intensive sectors or branches and by the increasing internationalisation of markets, hence a stronger competition between economies (Kölling & Schank 2002; Machin 2005; Stadler & Wapler 2004).

All industrialised countries follow a similar trend characterised by a kind of double structural change (see Chapter 4.1):

---

[1] See European Council (2004), OECD (ed.) (2001a), de la Fuente and Ciccione (2002), BMBF (2002).

*U. Schmoch, C. Rammer and H. Legler (eds.), National Systems of Innovation in Comparison, 187–204.*

- Knowledge- and research-intensive industries perform much better than others.
- New jobs mainly arise in the service sector, and particularly in those knowledge-intensive fields in which high technologies create new markets. Industry and services are growing closer and closer together via their reciprocal market ties; and service providers mainly act as customers and suppliers to industry (Klodt et al. 1997). One prominent example is the IC sector (Information and Communication Technologies and Services),[2] which had the highest share in productivity and growth during the 1990s and from which many new, mostly highly skilled jobs in and outside the IC sector emerged.

On top of that, due to changes in organisation structures and production processes, advanced services (like R&D, planning, consultancy) become more and more important economy-wide, also in manufacturing industries. This requires new skills for the employees and therefore has immense consequences for the educational system:

- On the one hand, demand for qualified labour is just increasing because knowledge-based industries play an expanding role for economic production.
- On the other hand, pressure to generate innovation is significantly higher in knowledge-based branches. This intensifies the demand for top qualifications like natural or information scientists and engineers (S&E) representing the core competence for technical innovations.

By this means, the technological performance of Germany and other European economies is decisively influenced by the availability of a sizable and continually growing pool of highly qualified employees. Shortages, particularly in S&E, may induce restrictive impacts on innovation, growth and employment – as could be seen in Germany in the late 1990s.

Discussions about these shortages of qualified personnel at the end of the 1990s, closely connected to that, and the establishment of the 'green card' aiming at getting highly qualified people to Germany, plus the bad results of German pupils in the PISA study, raised Germany's eyes across borders and across educational systems. The question, if other countries actually face or formerly faced similar problems and challenges, makes international comparisons even more attractive and more important. The age structure of the population and especially of the employable population plays a special role in this international comparison, as the other nations cannot only be seen as 'suppliers' of highly qualified human capital, but also as 'competitors' on the world market for qualified personnel, if they also show positive human-capital-intensive developments of the economy and the labour market and/or a similar demographic 'misfit' in their age structure leads them to the same intention, namely, covering the demand by international migration.

Section 2 gives an overview of the indicators and data applied in this study. Section 3 analyses the education standards of the European population and workforce in a regional and temporal comparison, focussing on demographic aspects as well as on technical and management occupations. As a supplement to this supply-side approach, Section 4 deals with the sectoral demand for highly skilled (academic) manpower in

---

[2]  On the level of NACE divisions available here, the IC sector encompasses Computers and Electronic Components (30), Radio, Television and Communication Equipment and Apparatus (32), Telecommunication Services (64) and Software Development and Data Processing (72).

European regions against the background of structural change and economic trends in the period from 1995 to 2003. Special attention is thereby paid to Germany. Conclusive remarks are drawn in Section 5 (see in detail Frietsch & Gehrke 2004).

## Methodological Aspects and Data

Two data sources are used for the analyses in this section. The first is the German *Mikrozensus*, which is an annual census that surveys one per cent of all inhabitants and that covers, first and foremost, questions of social structure and labour market participation. The second dataset is the Community Labour Force Survey, provided by Eurostat and covering data on EU-15 countries, the ten new members of the European Union as well as some further candidates and the associated EFTA countries. Both sources used here start in the mid-1990s and point to the most recent past for which data was available (2003).

In a first step of the analyses, the German situation is addressed and the specific educational system is taken into account, focussing exclusively on vocational qualifications, as these are the relevant ones for the labour market. This is not to neglect that especially the secondary school leaving certificates – and here first of all the *Abitur* – have gained importance in the last 30 years. The German system of vocational qualifications is built on several different school types and degrees, which can be aggregated to at least three groups.

First, vocational training in the so-called 'dual system' (*Duales System*), where young people of usually 15 years and more receive a training on the job in a firm or company and in parallel go to school, where they are taught the more theoretical framework of their occupations (see Chapter 5.2). Some occupations and some schools also offer a purely school-based vocational training, which is summarised together with the certificates from the dual system as *vocational training* here (containing groups 3b and 4b of the International Standard Classification of Education: ISCED[3]). Second, master/technician (*Meister/Techniker*) diplomas (ISECD 5b) can be reached by people – mostly in blue-collar, technical occupations and by workmen – who already served a vocational apprenticeship and who have some experience in their job. These qualifications are taught in full-time schools or in part-time schooling. The duration is between six months and three years for full-time schooling. For many occupations it is still mandatory to hold a master craftsman's diploma to run his/her own firm. But it is still a very important qualification also in the German manufacturing sector. Third, academics (ISCED: 5a or 6) in Germany can receive their degrees at universities, where next to diplomas (and comparable degrees) also doctoral degrees can be awarded. Though this degree mostly qualifies directly for some occupation, the universities have a clear and strong theoretical orientation and should also qualify for a scientific career. The universities of applied sciences (*Fachhochschule*) are more practically oriented, but also supply a sound academic qualification. That is why these two grades are summarised as *Academics*.

Based on the Community Labour Force Survey, this national differentiation of educational qualifications cannot be kept. Instead, the ISCED is applied that was created

---

[3] For a description and explanation of the ISCED, please refer to OECD (1999), UNESCO (1997; 1999).

to compare educational programmes between countries. For the purpose of the analysis of the supply, a further aggregation is used that differentiates between low, medium and high levels. Low level in this case means people without any school certificate or only a primary degree (ISCED groups 0–2). High level covers academic and similar degrees (ISCED 5 and 6), whereas medium refers to the other categories of upper secondary and the post-secondary non-tertiary degrees (ISCED 3 and 4).

*Research-intensive industries and knowledge-intensive services*: the analysis is performed on the basis of the definition presented in Chapter 1 and on the basis of employment and occupation data on a two-digit level of the NACE stemming from the Community Labour Force Survey (LFS), which is provided by Eurostat.

*Demand for highly skilled employees*: the presence of research- and knowledge-intensive industries effectively represents a country's or region's industrial innovative potential. To what extent this is ultimately exploited can be measured by the share of highly skilled academic manpower, here determined:

- at first, by the share of employees working in science and engineering professions (group 21 in the International Standard Classification of Occupations: ISCO) being particularly relevant for R&D and technical innovations in Manufacturing but also in the IC sector;
- furthermore, by the share of total academic occupations (ISCO group 2 in total) to allow for the fact that innovations in the service sector are often of non-technical nature and require other than technical or scientific qualifications.[4]

## Educational Structures in Germany

In this section the questions that are addressed concern the distribution of educational degrees and qualifications in European countries and in selected sectoral groups, with a special focus on Germany. These are compared over time and also between countries. In a second part, this section deals with the age structure of the qualified people and the implications that arise for the future development of the European Research Area and by that, for the substitutional demand of highly skilled workers.

### Structures of Educational Supply in Germany and Europe

Since the late 1960s and early 1970s, several reforms of the education system in Germany led to a changed and still changing behaviour of children and their parents in the selection of school types. A clear and steadily increasing trend towards higher education is visible and the effect of all this is called 'educational expansion' (*Bildungsexpansion*), see also Chapter 5.4. Even within the short period of time

---

[4] Thus, this approach forms a compromise between OECD's concept 'Human Resources for Science and Technology by Occupation (HRSTO)' as a whole and its so-called 'core' concept, the first including all people employed in occupations classified in ISCO major groups 2 (professionals) or 3 (technicians and associate professions) even if they do not have a third level education, the second only considering the subgroups 21 (natural and engineering scientists) and 22 (life science and health professions) (OECD 1995).

analysed for the purpose of this study, this development becomes evident. When looking at age cohorts, it can be shown that even between the beginning of the 1990s and the beginning of the new century, the shares of employees with an academic degree increased in Germany from some 12 per cent to more than 15 per cent and together with the masters/technicians, more than 26 per cent are among the highly qualified. And these shares increased more among the employed persons than among all inhabitants, which indicates that the use and application of the higher qualifications in the labour market also increased. At the same time, persons without any formal training are more likely to drop out of the employment system.

Table 1 displays the vocational qualifications in manufacturing and service sectors in Germany for the year 2003. It can be seen that the high-technology sectors are above the average of the total manufacturing sector as well as above the total average concerning academics as well as masters/technicians. In detail, the leading-edge technologies employ a very large share of highly qualified personnel, similar to the knowledge-intensive services and – interesting, though not surprising – the non-industrial economy which is dominated by the public sector also has a high demand for these qualifications. In contrast, the less R&D-intensive and the 'other service' sectors reach very low shares of highly qualified staff and very high shares of people with no formal vocational training. And this latter group has lost ground in the recent past especially in the service economy, whereas the structure in the manufacturing sectors is rather stable, with slight advantages for academics.

**Table 1.** Vocational qualifications in manufacturing and service sectors, 2003 (in per cent)

| | Less R&D-intensive manu-facturing | Lea-ding-edge tech-nology | High-level tech-nology | Total manu-factu-ring | Know-ledge-inten-sive services | Other ser-vices* | Total ser-vices* | Non-indus-trial econo-my | Total** |
|---|---|---|---|---|---|---|---|---|---|
| No formal qualification | 19.3 | 12.2 | 15.1 | 17.3 | 10.3 | 20.8 | 16.5 | 14.0 | 15.8 |
| Vocational training | 63.8 | 51.9 | 58.6 | 61.1 | 51.9 | 65.2 | 59.8 | 48.4 | 57.9 |
| Master/technician | 9.7 | 11.0 | 11.7 | 10.5 | 11.7 | 7.6 | 9.3 | 12.9 | 10.8 |
| Academic | 7.2 | 24.9 | 14.6 | 11.1 | 26.0 | 6.4 | 14.4 | 24.6 | 15.5 |

\*  Commercial business
\*\* Additionally includes the sectors Construction and Energy
Source: Mikrozensus 2003 – Fraunhofer ISI computations

The share of persons with the highest educational degrees in Germany are among the largest in Europe, and the older generations especially reached a higher educational level than the people of the same age in other European countries. This points to the fact that the educational expansion started earlier in Germany (see Table 2). But the trend is the same in all countries; the share of people with low formal qualifications decreases whereas the relative number of medium and highly qualified people increases, especially among the employed. The largest growth rates in the 1990s can be found in the United Kingdom and central Europe, whereas Germany, France and northern Europe reached a high level earlier and therefore show only smooth growth rates. From the German perspective, two results are very interesting. First, Germany has the

**Table 2.** Educational levels in manufacturing and service sectors in Europe, 2003 (in per cent)

| | Less R&D-intensity | High-techno-logy | Total manu-facturing | Know-ledge-intensive services | Other services* | Total services* | Non-industrial economy | Total** |
|---|---|---|---|---|---|---|---|---|
| Germany | | | | | | | | |
| Low | 20.6 | 14.2 | 17.5 | 13.7 | 17.5 | 15.7 | 10.1 | 15.0 |
| Medium | 64.0 | 58.3 | 61.3 | 52.9 | 67.8 | 60.9 | 48.2 | 58.9 |
| High | 15.4 | 27.5 | 21.2 | 33.4 | 14.8 | 23.4 | 41.7 | 26.1 |
| France | | | | | | | | |
| Low | 35.9 | 24.8 | 31.7 | 25.3 | 29.6 | 27.4 | 29.1 | 29.1 |
| Medium | 50.7 | 50.0 | 50.5 | 37.4 | 51.0 | 44.1 | 40.2 | 45.0 |
| High | 13.3 | 25.3 | 17.9 | 37.3 | 19.4 | 28.5 | 30.7 | 25.9 |
| United Kingdom | | | | | | | | |
| Low | 48.6 | 44.0 | 46.6 | 28.8 | 44.6 | 36.9 | 29.2 | 38.7 |
| Medium | 31.0 | 24.1 | 28.0 | 27.2 | 38.9 | 33.2 | 23.5 | 30.0 |
| High | 20.4 | 31.9 | 25.3 | 44.0 | 16.5 | 29.9 | 47.2 | 31.4 |
| Northern Europe (DEN, SWE, FIN, NOR, IRL, excl. ISL) | | | | | | | | |
| Low | 27.9 | 16.6 | 23.4 | 13.1 | 24.3 | 18.0 | 15.9 | 19.0 |
| Medium | 57.2 | 56.4 | 56.9 | 47.5 | 58.3 | 52.3 | 37.8 | 50.9 |
| High | 14.9 | 27.0 | 19.7 | 39.5 | 17.4 | 29.7 | 46.3 | 30.1 |
| Southern Europe (POR, ESP, GRE, ITA, CYP) | | | | | | | | |
| Low | 63.8 | 44.2 | 58.1 | 25.8 | 51.2 | 42.2 | 45.3 | 49.1 |
| Medium | 27.0 | 37.5 | 30.1 | 36.0 | 36.4 | 36.3 | 27.7 | 31.4 |
| High | 9.1 | 18.3 | 11.8 | 38.2 | 12.3 | 21.6 | 27.1 | 19.5 |
| Central Europe (BEL, AUT, SUI, excl. LUX, NED) | | | | | | | | |
| Low | 28.8 | 20.4 | 25.6 | 15.4 | 22.9 | 19.5 | 17.6 | 20.8 |
| Medium | 57.3 | 52.8 | 55.6 | 45.6 | 61.0 | 54.0 | 46.1 | 53.0 |
| High | 13.9 | 26.8 | 18.8 | 39.0 | 16.1 | 26.5 | 36.3 | 26.2 |
| Eastern Europe (BUL, CZE, EST, HUN, LAT, LTU, ROM, SVK, SLO, excl. POL) | | | | | | | | |
| Low | 13.9 | 10.2 | 12.9 | 7.4 | 7.5 | 7.4 | 21.3 | 16.4 |
| Medium | 78.8 | 78.4 | 78.7 | 64.6 | 80.1 | 74.4 | 60.9 | 67.7 |
| High | 7.2 | 11.5 | 8.4 | 28.0 | 12.4 | 18.2 | 17.7 | 16.0 |
| EU-15 | | | | | | | | |
| Low | 43.9 | 28.3 | 37.9 | 22.0 | 36.6 | 30.0 | 29.8 | 33.0 |
| Medium | 42.9 | 46.3 | 44.2 | 39.6 | 48.4 | 44.4 | 34.7 | 41.9 |
| High | 13.2 | 25.4 | 17.9 | 38.4 | 15.1 | 25.6 | 35.4 | 25.2 |

Source: Eurostat, Labour Force Survey 2003 – Fraunhofer ISI computations

lowest shares of people with only a low educational level,[5] which can be explained by high shares of medium-level qualifications. These are, first of all, the result of the

---

[5] Together with eastern Europe, where the medium level qualification is the standard, but which does not have a similarly high share of highly qualified people.

dual system, which emphasises the importance of this kind of training for the still favourite German position and which is a specific German strength (for a closer discussion of the vocational system in Germany, please refer to Chapter 5.2 in this book). Second, the shares of highly qualified persons have been above the European average for a very long time, but the other countries were able to expand massively. This means that Germany was overtaken by many countries, though it is still ahead of the EU-level.

Concerning the highest educational level as defined here, the United Kingdom reaches the highest shares, followed by northern Europe, central Europe, Germany, and France. At the same time, the British also have the largest shares of lowly qualified personnel and only a few middle-range positions. As already stated, only small numbers of the German employees are trained on a low level. This also holds for eastern Europe and to some extent for northern Europe, so that the medium qualifications play a very important role in all of these countries.

The structural differences between the less R&D-intensive and the high-technology sectors are very similar across Europe and can be calculated as being about 12–13 per cent. The knowledge-intensive services reached the highest shares of highly qualified personnel in any country and higher shares than in high-technology sectors, which is consistent with the results we already found for Germany. However, it can be assumed that the leading-edge technologies – which cannot be separated on the basis of this data – also reach high shares of highly qualified degrees, similar to that in the knowledge-intensive services. It is also interesting to note the high qualificational needs of the non-industrial economy that is above the average in nearly all countries, except eastern Europe, where the public sector seems to have lower needs, or – what is more probable – is less attractive for people with medium and high qualifications.

The trends are very similar in all countries or regions and across all sectors: the low qualifications are losing ground, whereas the highly qualified have gained in importance since 1995.[6] This is extremely positive in southern and central Europe, which show an enormous development. While in France, northern and southern Europe, the service sectors profited most from this trend, it is the other way around in the United Kingdom and central Europe, where the manufacturing sector gained higher shares of highly qualified employees. A statement that holds for all countries is that the knowledge-intensive sectors intensified their needs above average since the mid-1990s and thereby became even more knowledge-intensive.

## Age Structure in Technology-oriented Sectors

In the recent past, the present and future influence of the changing age structure of societies on the social and political framework has been broadly discussed. In this context, the impacts of these structural changes for example on the pension and health-care systems play an important role. For the analysis of the technological competitiveness, by contrast, it has to be acknowledged that more and more employees will retire and (at least the largest share) have to be substituted by young people entering the employment system. But as the numerical relation of older and younger

---

[6] For details, please refer to Frietsch and Gehrke (2004).

people has changed, this development also influences the perspective of educational research with respect to economic and technological performance.

The qualification level of the total German population has changed, due to several reforms of the education system in the 1960s and 1970s and by the accompanying relative change of costs and returns of higher education. This awakens the expectation that the older people who end their working life can be replaced by at least equally or even more highly qualified personnel. No immediate shortages should arise. On the other side, the demand for more highly qualified personnel has also increased, due to the already mentioned skill-biased technological change. The good news for Germany is that the demographic change will show a negative effect on the number of students and graduates with a certain delay not before 2010, as until then the increase in the number of entitled students keeps the absolute number on a persistently high level, due to on-going expansions of the number of secondary school leavers. Beyond 2010, it can be assumed that even the total number of people of employable age in Germany will shrink (Buck et al. 2002; Fuchs et al. 2004; Grömling 2004).

Besides, the demographic factor plays a crucial role for the actual and future demand, if in the short- to mid-term perspective the high birth rate cohorts of the postwar period drop out of the labour system due to their age and at the same time in fact more highly educated, but numerically smaller cohorts enter the system.

At least for Germany it can be shown that the qualification level of the pensioners clearly increased since the beginning of the new century, as these are already the foothills of the qualification expansion after the Second World War. And this puts further pressure on the new entrants, as many more people are needed just for substitution and a smaller share can be devoted to skill-biased technological change. Furthermore, the evidence is that the share of working people among the total population grows with an increasing level of education. And this implies that the demographic development shows more favourably in the books of qualified employees than in the books of the total population.

**Table 3.** Share of 57–64 year old employees in manufacturing and service sectors in Germany by vocational qualification, 2003 (in per cent)

|  | Less R&D-intensive manu-facturing | Lea-ding-edge tech-nology | High-level tech-nology | Total manu-factu-ring | Know-ledge-inten-sive services | Other ser-vices* | Total ser-vices* | Non-indus-trial econo-my | Total** |
|---|---|---|---|---|---|---|---|---|---|
| No formal qualification | 9.9 | 9.1 | 10.2 | 9.9 | 11.7 | 9.2 | 9.9 | 12.4 | 10.4 |
| Vocational training | 7.6 | 6.0 | 6.4 | 7.1 | 6.4 | 7.7 | 7.2 | 8.6 | 7.4 |
| Master/technician | 11.5 | 8.0 | 9.8 | 10.5 | 7.2 | 11.6 | 9.3 | 10.1 | 10.0 |
| Academic | 9.3 | 6.0 | 7.6 | 7.9 | 9.7 | 7.9 | 9.3 | 13.2 | 10.5 |

\* Commercial business – \*\* Additionally includes the sectors Construction and Energy
Example: 9.9 per cent of the employees in the less R&D-intensive sectors without a formal qualification are 57–64 years old
Source: Mikrozensus 2003 – Fraunhofer ISI computations

Table 3 displays the shares of 57–64 year old employees in industry and service sectors in Germany by vocational qualification. In the total workforce – depending on their level of education – between 7.4 and 10.5 per cent of the personnel is at least 57 years old. The share of this age group among all employed persons in the leading-edge technologies is lowest, followed by high-level technologies. The less R&D-intensive part of the manufacturing sector shows higher shares, respectively. The respective picture in the service sector is less clear. Whereas people with a vocational training or masters/technicians in the knowledge-intensive services are less often 57–64 years old, the share of academics is rather high at 9.7 per cent. The highest shares of people between 57 and 64 years can be found in the non-industrial economy. This means that in this area, but also in broad areas of the industrial economy, most exits of the workforce due to old age will result in necessary replacements in a mid-term perspective.

In absolute terms, the substitution of working people in the manufacturing sector is about 610,000 people. In the service sector, including the non-industrial economy, even two million people have to be replaced between 2003 and 2010. From these results a necessary number of 890,000 highly qualified people can be derived – on average 110,000 persons per year – of which about 40 per cent hold a master's or technician's degree and about 60 per cent attained an academic degree. In the period 1993–2000 the number of necessary entrants was 500,000 highly qualified people. This means: whereas between 1993 and 2000 1.5 per cent of all employees and 6.7 per cent of all academics had to be replaced, these shares increased to 2.7 per cent and 10.4 per cent, respectively, in the period 2003–2010. This simple comparison emphasises the increasing necessity for substitutional personnel – if productivity is maintained at the same level – and a decreasing share that is available for knowledge intensification.

**Table 4.** Absolute number of 57–64 year old employees in the industrial economy in Germany by occupation and vocational qualification, 2003 (in thousand)

|  | No formal qualification | Vocational training | Master/ technician | Academic |
|---|---|---|---|---|
| Metal and Mechanical Engineering | 19 | 86 | 29 | 2 |
| Occupations in Electronics | 6 | 24 | 19 | 1 |
| Natural Science | 4 | 11 | 2 | 8 |
| Engineers/technicians/master | 16 | 37 | 36 | 72 |
| IC | 3 | 10 | 2 | 6 |
| Consulting and Management | 22 | 68 | 25 | 68 |
| Other occupations | 340 | 862 | 139 | 132 |
| Total | 410 | 1098 | 252 | 289 |

Source: Mikrozensus 2003 – Fraunhofer ISI computations

Looking only at the industrial economy, a need for more than two million people can be calculated, among whom more than 250,000 have an master's/technician's degree and nearly 290,000 hold an academic degree (see Table 4). A further qualification of these results can be reached by the differentiation of occupational groups. More than half of the 540,000 highly qualified persons have technology- and knowledge-oriented occupations. The largest groups are engineers (108,000) and consultants (93,000), whereas natural scientists and IC staff are of limited absolute numbers. In contrast, in the year 1993 these numbers were 359,000 highly qualified people in the industrial economy and about 178,000 in technology- and knowledge-oriented occupations. Also, the number of engineers has increased from 79,000 as well as the number of consultants (64,000), which raises the expectation of high future needs. The substitutional demand is about 37 to 54 per cent higher than ten years ago.

**Table 5.** 50–64 year old employees in manufacturing and service sectors in Europe by qualification level 2003 (in per cent)

| Qualification level | Less R&D-intensity | High-techno-logy | Total manu-facturing | Know-ledge-intensive services | Other services* | Total services* | Non-industrial economy | Total** |
|---|---|---|---|---|---|---|---|---|
| Germany | | | | | | | | |
| Low | 21.4 | 20.8 | 21.2 | 19.7 | 17.5 | 18.4 | 28.9 | 20.1 |
| Medium | 22.6 | 20.7 | 21.7 | 19.3 | 22.2 | 21.0 | 25.7 | 21.8 |
| High | 24.8 | 23.4 | 23.9 | 22.9 | 25.6 | 23.8 | 34.0 | 27.0 |
| France | | | | | | | | |
| Low | 27.4 | 33.8 | 29.3 | 31.8 | 28.0 | 29.8 | 38.0 | 31.8 |
| Medium | 16.9 | 18.9 | 17.7 | 17.8 | 16.3 | 17.0 | 23.8 | 18.9 |
| High | 12.8 | 12.8 | 12.8 | 17.4 | 12.0 | 15.6 | 22.2 | 17.1 |
| United Kingdom | | | | | | | | |
| Low | 33.9 | 34.1 | 34.0 | 31.5 | 24.2 | 27.0 | 32.3 | 29.4 |
| Medium | 14.0 | 15.7 | 14.6 | 19.8 | 12.9 | 15.6 | 21.5 | 16.0 |
| High | 17.8 | 18.1 | 18.0 | 20.5 | 13.5 | 18.5 | 27.6 | 21.2 |
| Northern Europe (DEN, SWE, FIN, NOR, IRL, ISL) | | | | | | | | |
| Low | 37.5 | 37.5 | 37.5 | 36.3 | 30.8 | 33.0 | 46.9 | 36.7 |
| Medium | 23.2 | 21.3 | 22.4 | 25.7 | 19.8 | 22.8 | 31.0 | 23.9 |
| High | 23.5 | 15.0 | 18.8 | 24.5 | 19.2 | 23.2 | 34.0 | 26.0 |
| Southern Europe (POR, ESP, GRE, ITA, CYP) | | | | | | | | |
| Low | 22.1 | 25.6 | 22.9 | 28.0 | 26.7 | 27.0 | 36.6 | 27.3 |
| Medium | 11.6 | 12.9 | 12.0 | 12.7 | 12.4 | 12.5 | 19.8 | 13.9 |
| High | 12.2 | 12.8 | 12.5 | 15.1 | 13.0 | 14.3 | 22.8 | 16.9 |
| Central Europe (BEL, LUX, NED, AUT, SUI) | | | | | | | | |
| Low | 20.7 | 21.8 | 21.0 | 23.4 | 22.0 | 22.5 | 35.6 | 24.4 |
| Medium | 17.5 | 18.8 | 17.9 | 18.5 | 18.1 | 18.2 | 24.8 | 19.3 |
| High | 22.5 | 19.4 | 20.8 | 18.2 | 17.4 | 17.9 | 23.9 | 20.2 |
| Eastern Europe (BUL, CZE, EST, HUN, LAT, LTU, POL, ROM, SLO, SVK) | | | | | | | | |
| Low | 22.7 | 24.3 | 23.1 | 38.1 | 26.4 | 30.6 | 40.8 | 36.8 |
| Medium | 14.4 | 17.7 | 15.4 | 21.2 | 14.5 | 16.6 | 17.1 | 16.8 |
| High | 20.5 | 20.4 | 20.4 | 24.1 | 17.9 | 21.4 | 20.2 | 20.7 |
| EU-15 | | | | | | | | |
| Low | 24.8 | 28.1 | 25.7 | 28.9 | 25.4 | 26.5 | 36.1 | 27.9 |
| Medium | 17.6 | 18.1 | 17.8 | 18.2 | 16.8 | 17.4 | 23.3 | 18.5 |
| High | 18.0 | 18.0 | 18.0 | 19.5 | 16.3 | 18.4 | 27.1 | 21.1 |

* Commercial business – ** Additionally includes the sectors Construction and Energy
Example: 21.4 per cent of the employees in the less R&D-intensive sectors in Germany with a low qualification level are 50–64 years old
Source: Eurostat, Labour Force Survey – Fraunhofer ISI computations

Due to methodological restrictions of the underlying database, similar analyses can not be conducted for European countries. However, Table 5 displays the shares of 50–64 year old employees by educational level in selected European countries and regions. As already discussed, the educational expansion started earlier in Germany than in other European countries. Derived from this observation, a higher substitutional demand can be expected within the next years. The United Kingdom and northern Europe show a similarly high level of highly qualified people among the 50–64 year old employees and this also increased in the recent past. Compared to that, southern Europe shows a large backlog concerning the highest degrees among this age group and also only a slow upward trend.

Looking at Germany, first and foremost, the unfavourable age structure holds for nearly all sectors and branches under observation here. Besides, similar values are partially reached only by northern and eastern Europe, which means that in a mid-term perspective in most of the other European countries no similar substitutional demand will arise. The problem for Germany is even exacerbated by the fact that the shares of 50–64 year old people with medium level degrees in the workforce are above the average values of other countries, too. One exception here is again northern Europe.

Furthermore, the differentiation by occupations reveals that the engineers and natural scientists are much older in Germany than in the other European countries. In France, in contrast, the IC employees – especially in high-technology areas and 'other services' – are older than in other nations. In the United Kingdom, persons with a technical occupation (Metal Engineering, Electronics, Natural Sciences and Engineering, see Table 4) are older than their colleagues in other European countries. For northern Europe it has to be acknowledged that a similarly unfavourable age structure as in Germany exists for nearly all occupational groups, but especially the shares in some technical occupations are clearly above the European average. Whereas southern and central Europe show low shares of older employees in all occupations, people in eastern Europe with occupations in Electronics and Engineering very often belong to this age group. This means for Germany, but also for other European countries with shortages in qualified personnel, that these eastern European countries can hardly be used as a source of human capital to solve the problem of a lack of employees in neuralgic occupations like Engineering and Natural Sciences, as long as they are not attracted simply by higher wages, though the bureaucratic hurdles have been lowered for those who are willing to move to other countries. But the readiness and willingness to emigrate might be reduced against the backdrop of the expectancy of economic impulses for their domestic market due to the recent EU membership.

The just described analysis of the highest formal qualifications revealed that, next to Germany, the demographic pressure on the labour market exists first of all in northern Europe, where the number of people aged 50 and more is five times higher than about ten years ago. Absolutely, this does not mean that other countries will not run into trouble due to age-driven demand for qualified labour. A comparison of the first half of the 1990s and the first half of the new century reveals clearly increasing numbers of persons aged 50–64 in nearly all occupations and in all countries. For example, in France the numbers nearly doubled and in central Europe these figures even tripled (see in detail Frietsch & Gehrke 2004).

As a consequence, the demand for highly qualified personnel will clearly increase all over Europe within the next years, due to retirement. This development first of all hits the social and health-care services, where the respective numbers doubled within the last ten years. Furthermore, natural scientists and engineers as well as consultants and managers are 50 per cent more likely to be in the oldest age group. The clearest effect can be seen in the IC occupations, where the numbers in Europe tripled since 1995. If these shares are converted into absolute numbers, the demographic problem might not become that evident. But it has to be kept in mind that this only reflects the substitutional demand. The room to manoeuvre for a further skill-biased technological change will become narrower at the same time.

## Components of Highly Qualified Employment Growth in Europe

In 2003, about 130 million people were employed overall throughout the *EU-15* in the business sector.[7] Of these, nearly 12 million had an academic profession, nearly one in four of these in a science and engineering (S&E) profession (4.75 million, which means 3.7 per cent of total employment).

European employment patterns follow global trends. Industrial employment is shrinking, new jobs with often higher skill requirements arise in services (see Chapter 4.1). Research and knowledge-intensive branches are gaining in importance, both in manufacturing and in the service sector, to the detriment of those less dependent on highly skilled labour. Thus knowledge-intensive services (at 18 per cent) and research-intensive industries (11.5 per cent) employ much higher shares of academic personnel than less research-intensive industries (4.3 per cent) and non-knowledge-intensive services (2.1 per cent). Beyond this, the pressure to innovate (new products, processes or services) is increasing, giving additional impetus to the demand for academic qualifications, whereas job opportunities for less skilled persons fall short: while total EU-15 employment achieved positive growth rates of above 1 per cent on average per year between 1995 and 2003, the demand for academic graduates grew above 3 per cent, for S&E professions even more sharply (4 per cent). In absolute terms, employment in S&E fields rose from 3.8 million in 1995 to 5.2 million in 2003, being of particular relevance for research-intensive industries (9.3 per cent of total employment) and the IC sector (19 per cent on average, nearly 40 per cent in Software Development and Data Processing).

### Continually Rising Demand for Highly Skilled Staff in Spite of Cyclical Fluctuations

Academic employment increased in all European regions, both in cyclical upturn 1995–2000 as well as during the economic downturn 2000–2003.

During *1995–2000* the number of employees with higher education in the EU-15 totally arose by 2.85 million people, i.e. nearly 17.5 per cent. General employment growth can only explain about 7 per cent of this, whereas the significantly greater impact (each with more than 5 per cent or 860,000 additional jobs) on demand for university graduates came from the fact that knowledge-intensive industries grew faster than others (structural effect), accompanied by increasing sector-specific skill requirements (Table 6).

---

[7] Private, non-farm sector.

**Table 6.** Changes in employment of academics and S&E in Germany and Europe by sectors 1995–2003 (components of changes in percentage of the basic year)

| Regions | | 1995–2000 | | | | 2000–2003 | | | |
|---|---|---|---|---|---|---|---|---|---|
| | | Total | Trend[1] | Struct.[2] | Skill[3] | Total | Trend[1] | Struct.[2] | Skill[3] |
| | | All academic occupations | | | | | | | |
| Germany | Business sector | 12.6 | 1.5 | 5.3 | 5.8 | 7.6 | −1.1 | 4.5 | 4.1 |
| | Manufacturing | 17.2 | 1.5 | −1.6 | 17.3 | 5.8 | −1.1 | −2.9 | 9.8 |
| | Research-intensive | 20.9 | 1.5 | 0.9 | 18.5 | 7.6 | −1.1 | −2.5 | 11.1 |
| | Less research-intensive | 7.9 | 1.5 | −7.8 | 14.2 | 0.7 | −1.1 | −4.1 | 5.9 |
| | Services | 27.0 | 1.5 | 17.6 | 8.0 | 10.9 | −1.1 | 9.4 | 2.6 |
| | Knowledge-intensive | 31.7 | 1.5 | 21.5 | 8.7 | 13.1 | −1.1 | 11.1 | 3.1 |
| | Non-knowledge-intensive | 3.6 | 1.5 | −2.3 | 4.4 | −3.2 | −1.1 | −1.4 | −0.7 |
| | Other sectors | 0.6 | 1.5 | −1.8 | 0.9 | 5.0 | −1.1 | 2.5 | 3.6 |
| | IC sector[4] | 64.1 | 1.5 | 36.4 | 26.2 | 15.6 | −1.1 | 13.0 | 3.7 |
| EU-15 | Business sector | 17.4 | 6.8 | 5.2 | 5.3 | 7.9 | 3.5 | 2.8 | 1.5 |
| | Manufacturing | 16.1 | 6.8 | −3.8 | 13.2 | 6.8 | 3.5 | −7.5 | 10.8 |
| | Research-intensive | 19.3 | 6.8 | −2.6 | 15.0 | 5.2 | 3.5 | −8.3 | 10.0 |
| | Less research-intensive | 11.1 | 6.8 | −5.9 | 10.2 | 9.6 | 3.5 | −6.1 | 12.2 |
| | Services | 31.5 | 6.8 | 15.4 | 9.3 | 8.9 | 3.5 | 5.5 | −0.1 |
| | Knowledge-intensive | 34.6 | 6.8 | 17.8 | 9.9 | 8.9 | 3.5 | 6.2 | −0.8 |
| | Non-knowledge-intensive | 10.1 | 6.8 | −1.4 | 4.7 | 9.2 | 3.5 | −0.1 | 5.7 |
| | Other sectors | 7.3 | 6.8 | −0.3 | 0.8 | 7.1 | 3.5 | 2.7 | 0.9 |
| | IC sector[4] | 73.2 | 6.8 | 42.4 | 24.0 | 12.4 | 3.5 | 4.8 | 4.0 |
| | | Natural or information scientists and engineers | | | | | | | |
| Germany | Business sector | 22.6 | 1.5 | 3.9 | 17.2 | 2.2 | −1.1 | 2.1 | 1.2 |
| | Manufacturing | 16.1 | 1.5 | −1.7 | 16.3 | 2.5 | −1.1 | −2.9 | 6.5 |
| | Research-intensive | 20.7 | 1.5 | 0.7 | 18.5 | 3.8 | −1.1 | −2.7 | 7.6 |
| | Less research-intensive | −1.8 | 1.5 | −11.0 | 7.7 | −3.9 | −1.1 | −4.2 | 1.4 |
| | Services | 36.4 | 1.5 | 19.4 | 15.5 | 8.8 | −1.1 | 12.4 | −2.5 |
| | Knowledge-intensive | 48.3 | 1.5 | 25.9 | 21.0 | 9.7 | −1.1 | 15.5 | −4.7 |
| | Non-knowledge-intensive | −2.2 | 1.5 | −1.6 | −2.1 | 4.4 | −1.1 | −2.5 | 8.0 |
| | Other sectors | 14.2 | 1.5 | −7.9 | 20.6 | −7.8 | −1.1 | −6.2 | −0.5 |
| | IC sector[4] | 73.6 | 1.5 | 41.1 | 31.0 | 14.0 | −1.1 | 14.4 | 0.7 |
| EU-15 | Business sector | 28.9 | 6.8 | 9.9 | 12.2 | 5.9 | 3.5 | 1.5 | 0.8 |
| | Manufacturing | 14.1 | 6.8 | −3.6 | 10.9 | 6.3 | 3.5 | −7.6 | 10.3 |
| | Research-intensive | 18.0 | 6.8 | −2.6 | 13.8 | 4.1 | 3.5 | −8.5 | 9.0 |
| | Less research-intensive | 3.2 | 6.8 | −6.6 | 3.0 | 13.2 | 3.5 | −4.9 | 14.5 |
| | Services | 46.5 | 6.8 | 26.6 | 13.0 | 7.2 | 3.5 | 6.9 | −3.3 |
| | Knowledge-intensive | 54.1 | 6.8 | 31.8 | 15.5 | 7.1 | 3.5 | 7.9 | −4.4 |
| | Non-knowledge-intensive | 6.1 | 6.8 | −0.7 | 0.0 | 7.9 | 3.5 | −0.8 | 5.2 |
| | Other sectors | 15.2 | 6.8 | −4.1 | 12.6 | 2.2 | 3.5 | 0.4 | −1.8 |
| | IC sector[4] | 77.2 | 6.8 | 48.0 | 22.3 | 12.0 | 3.5 | 5.5 | 2.9 |

[1]   Trend effect: change in occupation due to general growth
[2]   Structural effect: change in occupation due to structural change to research- and knowledge-intensive industries
[3]   Skill effect: change in occupation due to increasing sector-specific skill requirements
[4]   IC Technologies (30 + 32) and Services (Post/Telecommunications: 64; Software and Data Processing: 72)
Sources: Eurostat, CLFS – NIW calculations and estimations

**Box 1.**

Changes in the demand for highly skilled employment (here: S&E or all academic occupations) can be divided into three components: the *'trend effect'* describes the part depending on general growth and its impact on employment. The *'structural effect'* is caused by changes in employment patterns in favour of research- and knowledge-intensive industries which induce growing demand for highly skilled labour. Finally, the *'skill effect'* is the result of increasing sector-specific requirements of skills.

In Manufacturing of the EU-15, the structural effect caused a reduction of highly skilled demand by nearly 70,000 people (–3.8 per cent). The less distinct losses in research-intensive industries are ascribed to the high growth of the European automobile industry during this period. Regarding the non-public service sector, its knowledge-intensive services were exclusively and particularly favoured by structural change. This provided nearly 970,000 new jobs for university graduates (18 per cent), most of them in computer and other business activities.

*Sector-specific growing skill requirements* resulted in 575,000 new highly skilled jobs in services (focussed on IC services and financial services) and about 230,000 in manufacturing industries (particularly Transport Equipment and Chemicals/Pharmaceuticals). In Manufacturing, total demand was more strongly influenced by the skill effect than in knowledge-intensive services where structural change had a more distinct impact. This can be seen as the enterprises' answer to growing pressure to innovate, especially and broadly concerning Manufacturing rather than Services and more than ever the non-business sector.

*Europe-wide* employment of scientists and engineers (S&E) rose more sharply (29 per cent) than those of other university graduates (13 per cent, all academics: 17.4 per cent) from 1995 to 2000. Almost 90 per cent of those additional 1.1 million S&E jobs were created in research- and knowledge-intensive industries (Table 6).

Comparing *Germany* to other European regions, one has to consider that general employment growth had the lowest impact on the demand for highly skilled labour (Table 7) during this period. Yet, structural and skill effects on all university graduates were at least as effective in Germany as in the rest of Europe. With reference to S&E, a broad extension of sector-specific requirements of skills compensated for the lack of dynamics in structural change.

In the German manufacturing industry the additional demand for S&E professions was nearly exclusively attributed to sector-specific growing requirements of skills (Table 6) during the upturn. Similar effects could be observed for its neighbour countries (in 'central' Europe) and in the United Kingdom.

Research-intensive industries accounted for nearly one-quarter of additional S&E jobs, on the EU-15 average only for 14 per cent. The small structural effect for Germany was the result of comparably weaker employment growth in knowledge-intensive services, particularly in the IC sector.

During the economic downturn period *2000–2003*, the proportion between additional demand for S&E and other academic graduates decisively changed (Table 6 and 7). In total, throughout the EU-15 the number of S&E employees arose by 290,000 people (nearly 6 per cent) and thus at a lower rate than total demand for highly skilled employment (8 per cent). Unfavourable and insecure market and sales prospects and restricted R&D activities affect S&E more than other academic personnel (see Chapter 2.1). This is particularly obvious in Germany. During the upturn in the second half of the 1990s there was a near-balance proportion between additional jobs for S&E and other academic graduates (1 : 0.9) whereas during the following economic slump only one out of ten additional jobs for academic graduates required S&E competence.

Thus, the trend of an increasing demand for higher qualifications is continuing regardless of cyclical fluctuations. Nevertheless, its composition is different. Downturn and recessive periods hand in hand with unfavourable market prospects induce shrinking R&D activities and a relatively weaker demand for S&E graduates. Provided that market and sales prospects will approve presently, this situation may reverse quickly.

**Table 7.** Changes in employment of academics and S&E in European regions 1995–2003 (components of changes in percentage of the basic year)

| Regions | 1995–2000 | | | | 2000–2003 | | | |
|---|---|---|---|---|---|---|---|---|
| | Total | Trend[1] | Struct.[2] | Skill[3] | Total | Trend[1] | Struct.[2] | Skill[3] |
| All academic occupations | | | | | | | | |
| Germany | 12.6 | 1.5 | 5.3 | 5.8 | 7.6 | −1.1 | 4.5 | 4.1 |
| France | 8.4 | 6.1 | 2.4 | −0.1 | 13.2 | 3.7 | −0.8 | 10.3 |
| United Kingdom | 17.5 | 7.1 | 6.9 | 3.5 | −4.4 | 3.4 | 2.2 | −10.1 |
| North | 27.3 | 12.0 | 7.3 | 8.1 | 11.7 | 2.7 | 5.6 | 3.4 |
| Central | 23.6 | 7.2 | 6.2 | 10.1 | 10.4 | 0.9 | 3.3 | 6.2 |
| South | 20.6 | 10.0 | 4.1 | 6.5 | 12.7 | 8.1 | 2.8 | 1.8 |
| EU-15 | 17.4 | 6.8 | 5.2 | 5.3 | 7.9 | 3.5 | 2.8 | 1.5 |
| Natural or information scientists and engineers | | | | | | | | |
| Germany | 22.6 | 1.5 | 3.9 | 17.2 | 2.2 | −1.1 | 2.1 | 1.2 |
| France | 18.9 | 6.1 | 4.9 | 8.0 | 19.4 | 3.7 | 1.5 | 14.3 |
| United Kingdom | 29.7 | 7.1 | 10.2 | 12.4 | −12.3 | 3.4 | −1.5 | −14.2 |
| North | 38.0 | 12.0 | 22.9 | 3.1 | 13.7 | 2.7 | 0.6 | 10.5 |
| Central | 28.0 | 7.2 | 14.1 | 6.7 | 12.7 | 0.9 | 3.5 | 8.3 |
| South | 46.0 | 10.0 | 17.9 | 18.1 | 23.2 | 8.1 | 5.6 | 9.5 |
| EU-15 | 28.9 | 6.8 | 9.9 | 12.2 | 5.9 | 3.5 | 1.5 | 0.8 |

NORTH: DEN, IRL, SWE, FIN, ISL, NOR – CENTRAL: BEL, LUX, NED, AUT, SUI – SOUTH: ITA, GRE, ESP, POR
[1] Trend effect: change in occupation due to general growth
[2] Structural effect: change in occupation due to structural change to research- and knowledge-intensive industries
[3] Skill effect: change in occupation due to increasing sector-specific skill requirements
Sources: Eurostat, Labour Force Survey – NIW calculations and estimations

## New Challenges from Increasing Skill Competition in Europe

Assessed on its share of S&E employment in industrial economy (4.5 per cent), Germany still enjoys clear advantages over the European average (Table 8). The crucial factor for this is the high weight of research-intensive industries underlying an increasing pressure to generate innovations. However, these advantages evaporate when Germany is measured against its competitors in northern and central Europe. Particularly the northern countries succeeded in catching up during the last decade.[8]

Germany's shrinking headstart is attributed to its characteristic economic structure, i.e. a strong focus on high-level technology, deficits in leading-edge technology and a comparably lower employment contribution and 'innovation orientation' (referring to S&E demand) of knowledge-intensive services (Table 8, see also Chapters 2.2 and 4.1). As a result, Germany disposes of substantial knowledge advantages only compared to southern and eastern Europe.

**Table 8.** Employment of S&E in the business sector in Europe 2003

| | EU-15 | GER | GBR | FRA | North | Central | South | East |
|---|---|---|---|---|---|---|---|---|
| Share of S&E in per cent of all employees | | | | | | | | |
| Business sector | 3.7 | 4.5 | 4.4 | 4.8 | 4.5 | 4.0 | 1.8 | 2.6 |
| S&E share of all employees (EU = 100) | | | | | | | | |
| Research-intensive industries | 100 | 120 | 119 | 136 | 110 | 89 | 42 | 50 |
| Chemicals | 100 | 114 | 98 | 126 | 132 | 95 | 63 | 91 |
| Machinery and Equipment | 100 | 147 | 124 | 150 | 97 | 88 | 29 | 59 |
| Automobiles and Equipment | 100 | 134 | 103 | 90 | 80 | 48 | 51 | 36 |
| Other Motor Vehicles | 100 | 115 | 126 | 151 | 53 | 55 | 41 | 32 |
| IC Technologies $(30 + 32)$[1] | 100 | 108 | 94 | 194 | 119 | 87 | 49 | 35 |
| Electrical Machinery + Apparatus | 100 | 142 | 131 | 62 | 67 | 119 | 53 | 45 |
| Instruments[2] | 100 | 82 | 105 | 215 | 137 | 81 | 19 | 55 |
| *Less research-intensive industries* | *100* | *101* | *163* | *212* | *107* | *101* | *32* | *71* |
| Knowledge-intensive services | 100 | 96 | 111 | 102 | 122 | 120 | 77 | 95 |
| Air Transport | 100 | 142 | 88 | 109 | 138 | 70 | 58 | 141 |
| Post/Telecommunications | 100 | 100 | 112 | 77 | 114 | 113 | 104 | 56 |
| Financial Intermediation | 100 | 88 | 128 | 119 | 160 | 192 | 35 | 69 |
| Real Estate/Renting | 100 | 88 | 191 | 20 | 41 | 175 | 51 | 131 |
| Software and Data Processing | 100 | 87 | 112 | 139 | 141 | 116 | 44 | 90 |
| Research and Development | 100 | 149 | 88 | 64 | 115 | 75 | 95 | 88 |
| Other Business Activities | 100 | 99 | 104 | 93 | 124 | 120 | 93 | 118 |
| Health and Social Work | 100 | 148 | 100 | 14 | 99 | 163 | 72 | 144 |
| Recreation, Culture, Sports | 100 | 119 | 135 | 89 | 60 | 199 | 31 | 203 |
| *Non-knowledge-intensive services* | *100* | *159* | *63* | *232* | *136* | *140* | *26* | *87* |
| *IC sector*[3] | *100* | *94* | *112* | *123* | *150* | *116* | *51* | *55* |

*NORTH*: DEN, IRL, SWE, FIN, ISL, NOR – *CENTRAL*: BEL, LUX, NED, AUT, SUI – *SOUTH*: ITA, GRE, ESP, POR – *East*: CZE, SVK, SLO, BUL, EST, LAT, LTU, HUN

[1]  Office Machinery and Computers; Radio, TV and Communication Equipment
[2]  Medical, Precision and Optical Instruments
[3]  IC Technologies (30 + 32) and services (Post/Telecommunications: 64; Software and Data Processing: 72)
Sources: Eurostat, Labour Force Survey – NIW calculations

Furthermore, the EU average does not seem to be an adequate benchmark for evaluating qualification and knowledge structures of the German industries. Given the

---

[8]  In France S&E demand has risen sharply since the beginning of the new century. Following years of stagnation, this development is a result of expanding R&D activities since then.

current global economic developments, it would be much better to benchmark the European activities and qualification structures in relation to the dynamic regions in America, Asia or Oceania, which, however, do not provide comparable and reliable data. Moreover, one gets the impression that the decisive difference between Germany and other European countries was the restricted economic growth that was also induced by shortages in human capital at the end of the millennium. This particularly concerned domestic small and medium-sized enterprises, either because of missing incentives to generate innovation or because of a lack of highly skilled and affordable personnel.

## Conclusions

In sum, the skill-biased technological change and the rising importance of high formal qualifications can be found all across Europe, with some countries starting to catch up and even overtake the established ones, and eastern and also southern Europe lagging behind, but backed by positive trends. The needs and demands for employees with higher educational degrees and qualifications, particularly for scientists and engineers, will also increase in Europe in the next years. Bottlenecks must be expected here in future, particularly in Germany, which is confronted with a quite unfavourable demographic situation and comparably less young people taking up university studies, especially in fields of relevance for technology.

The countries in Europe grew closer within the European Union, especially since the new Member States joined in 2004. And this even widened the pool of skilled and qualified employees, which is an asset on the way to the European Research Area and to strengthen the competitiveness of Europe, especially with regard to the United States and Japan, but also in relation to the emerging and emerged Asian countries like Korea, Singapore or Taiwan. Furthermore, on the way to becoming the largest research area in the world, Europe also has to face the challenge of ageing societies and unfavourable demographic developments. The future demand for highly skilled employees might be covered by the increasing supply, due to ongoing qualification and knowledge intensification. But a growing share of these individuals will be needed for substitution and a shrinking share will be available for the intended goal of increasing total qualification levels. The fact that some countries within the European Union are lagging behind in their numbers and shares of highly skilled employees even increases the pressure, though this might not immediately result in substitutional demand.

Consistent with these findings, the European Commission and also many national governments laid a new emphasis on the education and qualification of the European population. In fact, the problem can only be solved internally by national and European educational programmes. An external solution, for example by migration, can only be used in addition and in parallel to these efforts. It cannot substitute the necessity of own investments in human capital, though an active, controlled immigration policy and integration will be an important instrument to meet the decreases in the labour force and young age groups. But it is a delusion to believe that this would solve the problem, considering that all other European countries except Ireland and France, but especially the new Member States in middle and eastern Europe, are also confronted with ageing populations, declining birth rates and increasing needs for highly skilled personnel.

# 5.2 Challenges to the German Dual System

Alexandra Uhly, Klaus Troltsch, Günter Walden

**Abstract.** This article analyses the adaptability of the dual system of initial vocational education and training in Germany, particularly with regard to technical training occupations, which have a particular part to play in Germany's technological productivity. Confirmation of the efficiency of the system is demonstrated by the way in which the strong increase in demand for training places since the end of the 1970s has been overcome, as well as by securing the formation of qualified human capital by the modernisation of state-regulated training occupations. Currently, however, serious problems relating to the lack of training places remain to be redressed. If the aim is to provide all young people with the opportunity of qualified training and thus improve the life chances of this generation as well as securing the formation of qualified human capital in terms of society as a whole, training capacities need to be significantly extended, particularly in the new and modernised technical occupations.

## Introduction

Qualified vocational education and training plays a crucial role in determining individual labour market perspectives and life chances in general, as well as having a decisive effect on the available human capital resources and thus the potential performance and competitiveness of a national economy. 'One can even call the twentieth century the Age of Human Capital in the sense that the primary determinant of a country's standard of living is how well it succeeds in developing and utilizing the skills, knowledge, health, and habits of its population' (Becker 1995: 1). Various empirical studies provide evidence for these positive effects of human capital (cf. Tessaring & Wannan 2004: 33ff). Within the process of globalisation and technological change, education is increasingly gaining in significance as a competitive factor: 'Globalisation, the easy movement of capitals – both financial and fixed assets and technological progress have increasingly turned qualified manpower into a crucial comparative edge. At the same time, as a result of technological progress, the most profitable and enduring kind of competitiveness is achieved through quality and value added, rather than abatement of costs' (ILO Cinterfor 2001: 8; cf. here Reich 1993). Vocational education and training is taking on a decisive role in this process (Kutscha 1999: 110). In the following, we will consider the German dual system of initial vocational education and training (VET), which is still held up as a role model within international comparisons, despite signs of crisis. The dual system of vocational education and training in Germany leads to qualified vocational certification below the tertiary qualification level. Within the Standard Classification of Education (ISCED), this is classified as upper secondary level (ISCED 3) (Westerhuis 2001: 16). As in other countries with dual VET systems (Austria, Denmark, Switzerland) the

*U. Schmoch, C. Rammer and H. Legler (eds.), National Systems of Innovation in Comparison, 205–225.*

dual system of vocational education and training is characterised by a combination of practical and theoretical training below the academic qualification level.

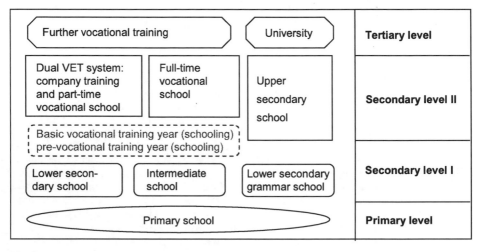

**Fig. 1.** Education and training system in Germany

The adaptability of the system to the challenges posed by development processes related to economic structure, management, economic situation, demographic change and educational requirements will be discussed. Particular emphasis will be placed on the developments in the area of recognised technical occupations. The reason for selecting technical occupations as an example is the particular significance attached to these within the context of Germany's technological performance (cf. Beicht et al. 2003). The fact that these occupations have been affected by considerable pressure for change since the 1980s is an additional reason for choosing those occupations.

The article is structured as follows. Firstly, the institutional characteristics of the Dual VET System in Germany will be outlined and some stylised facts relating to structures and developments in the VET system will be presented. A more in-depth analysis of technical occupations will follow. The delineation of the technical occupations will be commented upon before the supply of training places over the course of time is described. Training participation of companies will be applied as a further indicator of the significance of the Dual VET System for the development of human capital. Subsequently, there will be a description of central developments and their respective varying effects on the supply of in-company training places in technical occupations since 1980. The focus here will be on indicators relating to the requirement for skilled workers and qualifications within the economy. In addition, the influence of training costs on participation in training on the part of companies involved with technical occupations will be examined. Finally, there will be an analysis of the quantitative effects of the increased pace of renewal of training regulations of the recognised technical occupations since the mid-1990s as an indicator of the modernising success of the VET System. Furthermore, the development of the apprentices' previous general school qualifications as indicators of the attractiveness and skill requirements of the recognised technical occupations is analysed. The development in the proportion of women as an indicator of the success of the various measures undertaken to increase the number of women in technical occupations with-in the framework of gender mainstreaming will also be considered.

The article will conclude with an overall evaluation of findings set against the background of the adaptability of the Dual VET System in Germany as a whole and with regard to technical occupations.

## The Dual VET System in Germany

### Key Features and Principles of the German Dual VET System

Germany's Dual VET System represents a progression route from school in the general educational system and is available as a matter of principle to all young people regardless of the school qualifications they have achieved (*no formal entry requirements*). It takes place in vocational schools as well as in-company[1] and is usually of three years' duration.[2] A civil law training contract is concluded between the apprentice and the company, guaranteeing extensive VET in a state-recognised occupation and providing the apprentice with remuneration based on collective wage agreements for the duration of the contract.[3] In the Federal Republic of Germany, comprehensive regulation of the dual system was stipulated in the Vocational Training Act (BBiG) of 1969, last amended in 2005.[4]

The principle of the in-built *duality of training locations and concepts*, a combination of practical in-company training and theoretical training at a vocational school, is seen as one of the major advantages of this system. It is considered to be a pre-requirement of both an exhaustively theoretical qualification and of training relevant to business practice, furthermore as an optimum way of vocational socialisation. The duality of the places and concepts of learning is, finally, viewed as the reason for the comparatively low level of youth unemployment in countries operating dual VET systems. In practice, however, a plurality of places of learning and their combination has resulted (cf. Kutscha 1999), not least due to the lack of in-company training positions. Since the 1970s, full-time vocational schools have been extended, intended either as preparation for dual VET (pre-vocational year), or counting towards it (basic vocational education and training year), or to provide full vocational training. Nevertheless, the combination of theoretical education at school and

---

[1]   Irrespective of participation in training, there is compulsory schooling for young people up to the age of 18. This requirement can be fulfilled within the general educational system as well as at full-time vocational schools or on a part-time vocational basis in combination with in-company training.

[2]   A range of training regulations also provide for training lasting two or three and a half years.

[3]   In Germany, therefore, apprentices with training contracts are thus liable for compulsory social security contributions and form part of the system of general employment, as well as still belonging to the training system.

[4]   Compared to other countries with dual systems of VET, the scope of the regulations, comprising commercial VET in crafts trades, industry, commercial administration, agriculture and domestic services, represents a particular feature of the German system (cf. Stach 1998: 50). For historical development of the VET system in Germany, see Frommberger & Reinisch (2004: 80) and Deissinger (2004).

in-company training at the workplace remains the principle and the ideal of the Dual VET System.

*Competence and responsibility* for VET is also set up in a *dual* way. The federal government's Vocational Training Act regulates in-company VET, the federal states being responsible for vocational schools. In terms of regulative policy, the dual system can be described as a mixed system, combining *elements of the market economy as well as state and corporative control elements* (cf. Kutscha 1999: 3; Deissinger 2004: 29) or as a 'state-controlled market model' (Ertl & Sloane 2007: 3). There are tripartite, corporative arrangements in place between the state, national economic associations and the trade unions (cf. Kutscha 1999: 7). These arrangements are based on consensual, social partnership oriented processes of negotiation. These act as a counterweight to the polarisation of vested interest groups and alleviate the risks of state or market failure even if, to an extent, associated with high transaction costs.

The duality of the training goes hand in hand with *duality of financing* of training. The companies usually bear the costs of in-company training, whereas the vocational schools are publicly financed. As training positions are presently in short supply, however, there are exceptions to this basic principle in the form of special programmes and measures where the costs of practical training are provided by financial grants from the public purse or from the Federal Employment Agency.[5]

A further characteristic of the dual system is the *principle of occupation* (*'Berufs-prinzip'*). Within the framework of dual training, young people can acquire a certified qualification in any of the 350 training occupations which are currently recognised by the state (as of 1 October 2004). Legally stipulated training regulations govern the minimum contents for every training occupation across the whole country. They are structures geared towards fields of activity and functional areas in trade and industry and management, as well as towards vocational and educational stipulations. '[... They] are a package of qualifications enabling occupational action competence independent of any individual company in various positions of employment at the level of a skilled worker or skilled employee. They form the basis of continuing vocational education and training [...] and make a major contribution to personal development and social integration. As qualification standards on the labour market, they represent reliable means of orientation with regard to supply of and demand for qualifications' (Brenner 1997: 55). Development of new training regulations (new training occupations), or the modernisation of existing regulations and their co-ordination with the Standing Conference of the Ministers of Education and Cultural Affairs of the States of the Federal Republic of Germany is a multi-stage procedure, in which the stakeholders in VET, the Federal Institute for Vocational Education and Training (BIBB), employers' associations, trade unions, the federal government and the federal states are all substantially involved (for details, see Westerhuis 2001: 24ff and 35ff).

---

[5] According to estimates of the Federal Institute for Vocational Education and Training (BIBB), training contracts which are predominantly publicly financed account for a total of just under 10 per cent of all training contracts, in eastern Germany nearly 30 per cent (BMBF 2005: 15). Available official statistics relating to training contracts do not currently record any public finance element of such contracts.

### The Empiricism of the Dual System: Stylised Facts

'In fact, the re-occurring discussions surrounding the 'crisis of the dual system' in the inner-German debate of academics and researchers are almost as old as the system itself' (Ertl & Sloane 2004). These discussions all highlight different aspects (cf. Stach 1998). In the 1970s, the emphasis was on more qualitative aspects (training contents, quality of training, democratisation etc.). At the end of the 1970s and beginning of the 1980s, as a result of demographic development, quantitative aspects took centre stage. Current discussions are once again focussing on a shortage of supply of training positions. The following will analyse the adaptability of the dual system to socio-demographic and socio-economic developments, as well as quantitative disparities of supply and demand on the training places market.

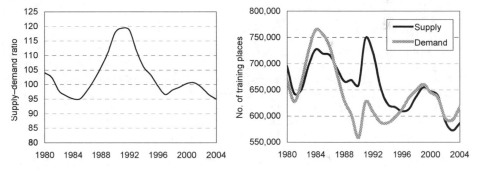

\*   Until 1990 area of the Federal Republic of Germany before October 3, since 1991 including the former GDR; SDR: (S / D) \* 100
Source: Careers guidance statistics of the Federal Employment Agency and a survey of newly concluded training contracts by the Federal Institute for Vocational Education and Training (BIBB), reference date in each case 30 September – calculations of the BIBB

**Fig. 2.** Supply and demand on the training places market, Germany\* 1980–2004

A simple indicator here is the supply–demand ratio (see SDR, Fig. 2). When referring to the training places market, the terms supply and demand are not used in the usual way they are applied to labour markets. Supply is defined as the provision of apprenticeships by companies, and demand as the young people seeking training places. This highlights a 'social demand' approach, with an emphasis on the right to training (Wenger 1997: 392). The supply (S) is measured as the sum of all newly concluded training contracts plus those offered training positions registered as vacant by the Federal Employment Agency;[6] and demand (D) as the sum of all newly concluded training contracts plus those applicants registered by the Federal Employment Agency as not yet placed in a training position or an alternative scheme. The SDR is a simplifying indicator which does not take various aspects into account. The statistically recorded number of training contracts also includes contracts which are predominantly publicly financed within the framework of state support measures. Furthermore, young people who take a sideways step into pre-vocational measures, jobs etc. are no longer recorded in the demand figure. If these aspects are taken into

---

[6]   Each with reporting date at the beginning of a training year on 30 September.

consideration, the current supply–demand ratio is even more unfavourable (Ulrich & Troltsch 2003; Krekel, Troltsch & Ulrich 2004).

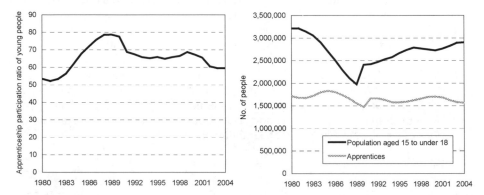

\*   Until 1990 area of the Federal Republic of Germany before October 3, since 1991 including the former GDR
APR: until 1993 percentage of apprentices with new training contract of the $Pop_{15-18}$; since 1993 percentage of apprentices with new training contract of the Pop for every age[7]
$Pop_{15-18}$: resident population aged 15 to under 18
Source: Vocational educational statistics[8] and population statistics of the Federal Statistical Office, reference date in each case 31 December – calculations of the BIBB

**Fig. 3.** Participation in training of young people and companies, Germany\* 1980–2004

The German training places market exhibits market imbalances in specific phases. In the course of time, there have been various factors which have influenced development. At the start of the 1980s, the dual system was faced with the challenge of dealing with the strong increase in demand of young people for in-company training places (Fig. 2) caused by demographics (Fig. 3). Considerable expansion of training capacities on the part of trade and industry coupled with measures taken by the state enabled the increase in demand largely to be met. From the mid-1980s, a lower level of demographic development with regard to the age groups relevant to demand once again led to an easing of pressure on the training places market, meaning that many training places could not be filled. From the mid-1990s, due to a decreasing supply of training places and a significant increase in the number of applicants, the supply–demand ratio in turn deteriorated. 2004 saw a rise once again in the supply of training places by approximately 2 per cent (decreases, some of which were significant, are recorded for the years 2000 to 2003). Due to an increase in demand, however, the SDR

---

[7]   Since 1993, it has been possible to calculate the training participation quota more precisely by recording the ages of apprentices with a newly concluded training contract within the framework of statistics for vocational education and training; $\sum_{i=16}^{24} \frac{AN_i}{POP_i}$ ; i: 16 to 24.

[8]   This data will often be used in what follows, being a total survey of all training contracts in Germany. In contrast to the survey of newly concluded training contracts by the Federal Institute for Vocational Education and Training (BIBB), various characteristics of apprentices and examination data are also recorded.

once again deteriorated to 95 per cent, meaning arithmetically that there are *circa* 95 training places provided for every 100 applicants.[9]

One indicator which measures the provision of young people with training places, and thus also measures the weighting of the dual system, is the apprenticeship participation rate of young people (APR). Over the course of time, there is significant variation in the proportions of young people in the dual system (cf. Table 2). A shortage of supply in the training places market therefore led to a significant decrease in the training participation quota of young people, but this remains, nevertheless, at a high level (60 per cent of young people in the relevant age group in 2004).

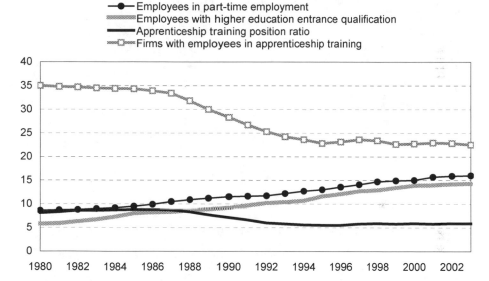

* Until 1990 area of the Federal Republic of Germany before October 3, since 1991 including the former GDR
Source: Employment statistics of the Federal Employment Agency,[10] reference date in each case 30 June – calculations of the BIBB

**Fig. 4.** Training participation of companies, transformation of the occupational structure, Germany* 1980–2003

Various factors can be considered as causes of the decrease in the supply of training places, in the apprenticeship training position ratio or in the participation of companies since the 1990s (Fig. 4). For one thing, the employment system is exhibiting *structural qualification change infavour of  degree-level  employment*, at the expense of low to medium formal qualification levels (cf. Plünnecke & Werner 2004:

---

[9]  In the reasons for its judgment on the 1980 Training Finance Act, the German Constitutional Court defined a training places market in which there was choice (freedom of choice of occupation) as an obligation for the economy as a whole to the effect that it was necessary to ensure that there were 112.5 training places for every 100 applicants.

[10]  A central record for Germany of the total number of employees liable for social security contributions and registered by companies with the relevant social security institutions is maintained here.

37ff). Particularly strong growth was recorded for employees with higher education entrance qualification. Another significant factor is the influence of new forms of employment. Temping, leasing of staff and part-time work, amongst other things, have all led to companies making changes to their employment structures alongside the training of their own skilled workers. One example of these developments is the increasing level of part-time employment.

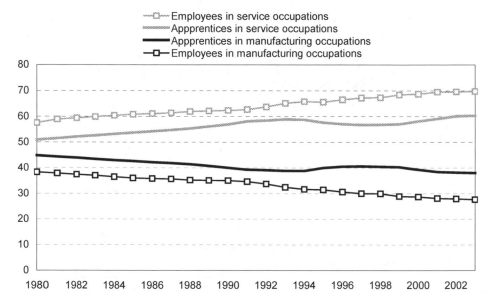

* Until 1990 area of the Federal Republic of Germany before October 3, since 1991 including the former GDR
Source: Employment statistics of the Federal Employment Agency,[11] reference date in each case 30 June – calculations of the BIBB

**Fig. 5.** Transformation of the occupational structure, Germany* 1980–2003

It is further apparent that the change of occupational structures within the dual system does not completely follow the development of the employment system.[12] Shift share analyses have been used to show that structural occupational change has had a negative influence on the supply of training places (cf. Plünnecke & Werner 2004: 37ff). An example of this is the development in the percentage proportions of trainees and employees[13] in service occupations, where, notwithstanding the significant increase in the amount of employment, training provision for young people has not risen to the same extent (Fig. 5).

Overall, a strong connection can be made between the training places market and the labour market. Krekel, Troltsch and Ulrich (2003) establish a strong, negative con-

---

[11] A central record for Germany of the total number of employees liable for social security contributions and registered by companies with the relevant social security institutions is maintained here.
[12] For a structural breakdown of the development in the number of apprentices in technical branches, see Werner (2003: 11ff).
[13] Without apprentices.

nection between the situation on the labour market and the supply of training places. Furthermore, the current economic situation has an effect on the supply of training places. Plünnecke and Werner (2004) establish a macroeconomic connection between economic growth (gross domestic product) and the supply of training places. Hartung and Leber (2004) use a multivariate analysis on the basis of a large scale, representative company survey (company panel of the Institute for Labour Market and Company Research) to establish that turnover has a significant positive influence on company participation in training.

The overall picture shows, therefore, the majority of young people in Germany still embarking upon vocational education and training within the dual system, despite some difficulties in adaptation and the shortage of training places in evidence since the mid-1990s. 'Despite the signs of crisis, the dual system in Germany remains relatively attractive, even for those who have completed general educational qualifications beyond the level of compulsory school attendance. In other European OECD countries, on the other hand, the expansion of 'higher' education has undermined practical, occupational training.' (Schmid & Liebig 2001: 15). The *dual system thus remains a central pillar of vocational education and training in Germany*. In the following, the focus will be placed on technical occupations, which are of particular importance, given their significance for the productivity and competitiveness of the economic location.

## Structures and Developments in Technical Occupations

Although a great deal of attention is paid to technical occupations,[14] there is an absence of a generally recognised *definition*, enabling individual occupations to be allocated to this category. The Federal Statistical Office Classification of Occupations (Federal Statistical Office Germany 1992) provides a systematic overview of occupations which also delineates the group of technical occupations (Occupational Area IV), but this is narrowly limited to engineers, chemists, physicists, mathematicians, technicians and technical specialists. Technical occupations within the large group of manufacturing occupations (Occupational Area III) are, therefore, not recorded within this process and not specifically identified as technical occupations. Neither can the specialist literature offer any concrete definition of technical occupations in the commercial technical sector (manufacturing occupations).

In the following, those manufacturing and service sector occupations were selected which exhibit a high level of technical elements within their activity and knowledge profiles (for example, a high amount of monitoring/controlling of machines, facilities, technical processes etc.).[15] Particularly those occupations which have been accorded a stronger technical orientation via new or updated regulations have also been included. The selection of occupations can be defined in varying levels of detail, depending on the database used. The vocational education and training statistics of the Federal Statistical Office differentiate between all individual training occupations, unlike the

---

[14] The decisive factor governing the future of the German economy and German society is for many young people to deploy their creativity and commitment in technical occupations, in order to develop innovative technology 'made in Germany' (BMBF 2004b).

[15] For information on activity and knowledge profiles in occupations, see Biersack et al. (2001).

data of the employment statistics of the Federal Employment Agency, however. Thus the latter source also includes, to a certain extent, occupations with a lesser level of technical orientation than in the classical technical occupations.

The number of training contracts in technical occupations rose slightly dispro-portionately at the start of the 1980s, before falling from the mid-1980s to the mid 1990s. This is followed by another rise, lasting until 2001, meaning a further increase in the proportion of newly concluded training contracts in these occupations. Since 2002, the number of apprentices in these occupations has also been declining (Fig. 6).

\* Until 1990 area of the Federal Republic of Germany before October 3, since 1991 including the former GDR

Source: Vocational education and training statistics of the Federal Statistical Office, reference date in each case 31 December – calculations of the BIBB

**Fig. 6.** Apprentices in technical occupations, Germany* 1980–2003

To enable a closer analysis of the developments within the technical occupations, the following will consider level of participation of companies in training and the in-fluence of the modernisation of the training occupations on the development and structure of trainees in the technical occupations.

**Training Participation of Companies**

**Company Training Quotas**
The duality of the German system means that structural and actual developments within the economic and employment system have a direct effect on the in-company training system. As briefly outlined in the chapter on stylised facts, this has certainly led to problems of adaptation for the dual system to the various socio-demographic and socio-economic developments. It would, however, be in line with expectations for the area of the technical occupations to be affected to a lesser extent by these general

processes, due to the increasing rate at which technology is being introduced into the economy and into occupational activities.

The *ratio between the numbers of apprentices and the number of employees* in technical occupations and the development of this represents a suitable indicator by which the respective significance of VET and the adaptability of the dual system in the face of the changes in economic and social framework conditions can be described. As shown in Fig. 7, company participation in training in technical occupations fell significantly on the whole between 1985 and 1995, whilst at the same time remaining above the average quota. Not until the period from 1995 onwards was an ongoing improvement in the supply of training places recorded, this lasting until 2003. Training in technical occupations is, therefore, obviously subject to similar influences, as described above.

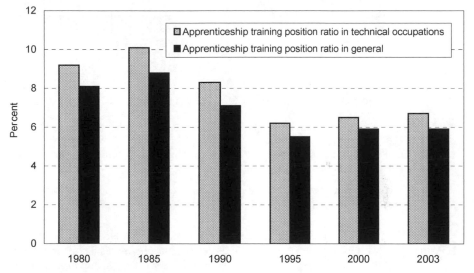

* Until 1990 area of the Federal Republic of Germany before October 3, since 1995 including the former GDR
Source: Employment statistics of the Federal Employment Agency, reference date in each case 30 June – calculations of the BIBB

**Fig. 7.** Training quotas in technical occupations in Germany* 1980 and 2003

The rates of change in the total number of those employed between the various phases (Fig. 8) show a constant decrease in the level of employment for technical occupations, apart from a phase between 1985 and 1990. This falling requirement for employees in manufacturing industry and service sector, a consequence of the economic and technological change taking place in Germany, is inevitably reflected in the falling supply of training places. Nevertheless, there was, at the same time, a prevailing demand within technical occupations for degree level workers, with technical university or university qualifications. The consequence of this was also an increase in the supply of training places for young people educated to university level, either in specialist or general subjects.

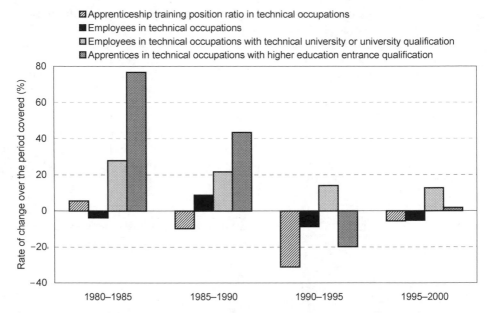

* Until 1990 area of the Federal Republic of Germany before October 3, since 1991 including the former GDR
Source: Employment statistics of the Federal Employment Agency, reference date in each case 30 June – calculations of the BIBB

**Fig. 8.** Phase specific rates of change in the numbers of employees in technical occupations in Germany* between 1980 and 2000 according to selected criteria

As a consequence of economic change and changes in qualification structures in Germany, as well as a result of economic development, there was a shift in the importance of VET between 1980 and 2000. Apprentices in these occupational areas account for a smaller group than they did in 1980, but possess today a higher level of previous general education. To this extent, the Dual VET System in Germany is proving to be an attractive alternative for both companies and young people.

**Costs of Vocational Education and Training**
The dual nature of financing the Dual VET System in Germany means that companies providing training of necessity incur considerable costs in carrying this out. These comprise personnel costs for the apprentices (training remunerations, statutory, wage agreement and voluntary social security contributions), personnel costs for full-time and part-time trainers, material costs and costs of facilities (at the workplace, apprentices; workshops, in-company teaching), as well as additional expenses for teaching and learning materials and media, examination fees etc. According to full costing (cf. Beicht et al. 2004a), which takes into account and evaluates all the costs entailed in producing the company's goods and services, training in technical occupations is in many cases more expensive and cost-intensive than in other occupations (Table 1).

**Table 1.** Average company training costs in technical and other occupations of the VET System in Germany in the year 2000 (full costing in €)

| | Gross costs | Returns | Net costs | Personnel costs | | Material costs | Other costs |
|---|---|---|---|---|---|---|---|
| | | | | Apprentices | Trainers | | |
| All occupations | 16,351 | 8,431 | 7,920 | 8,723 | 5,591 | 306 | 1,732 |
| *Technical occupations* | | | | | | | |
| Total | 16,334 | 5,876 | 10,458 | 7,484 | 5,904 | 1,116 | 1,830 |
| In trade and industry | 20,450 | 6,089 | 14,361 | 9,249 | 6,716 | 2,281 | 2,204 |
| In craft trades | 13,739 | 5,720 | 8,019 | 6,343 | 5,390 | 402 | 1,604 |
| *Individual technical occupations (selected)* | | | | | | | |
| Mechatronics technician | 29,335 | 4,889 | 24,446 | 10,657 | 11,444 | 4,244 | 2,990 |
| Industrial mechanic | 24,244 | 6,018 | 18,226 | 11,122 | 7,82 | 3,632 | 2,407 |
| Chemical laboratory technician | 23,368 | 8,593 | 13,775 | 10,858 | 7,410 | 2,905 | 2,550 |
| IT systems electronic technician | 22,368 | 8,593 | 13,775 | 9,875 | 7,817 | 2,091 | 2,584 |
| Surveying technician | 16,964 | 6,957 | 10,007 | 9,187 | 6,202 | 238 | 1,337 |
| Electrician | 14,897 | 6,316 | 8,580 | 6,999 | 6,112 | 251 | 1,534 |

Source: Costs and benefits survey of vocational education and training by the BIBB

There are scarcely any differences between technical and other occupations in terms of gross costs. Although the fact that it is only possible to produce lower returns during training in technical occupations means that net costs here are at a significantly higher level. There are, moreover, distinct gross and net differences with regard to technical occupations between trade and industry on the one hand, and craft trades on the other. Training costs in relation to individual technical occupations also exhibit high differences. An extrapolation of the data thus gives us a figure for total gross costs incurred by firms and companies in Germany for in-company training in the year 2000 of 27.7 billion, whereby apprentice productivity led to total returns of 13.0 billion being generated. Especially in major industrial companies, technical training for young people needs to take place to a certain extent in company apprentice workshops, leading to high facilities and materials costs and necessitating the deployment of mostly full-time trainers. In addition, as far as technical occupations are concerned, integration of apprentices in productive work processes in the company workplace is frequently very much more difficult than is the case in other occupations, this being reflected in lower training returns. However, the relatively high quotas of apprentices offered permanent employment on conclusion of training and the length of time they spend with the company usually results in overall net benefits for firms, even given the high training costs associated with technical occupations (cf. Walden & Herget 2002). The high costs of technical occupations probably mean that companies tend to exercise a good deal of caution with regard to personnel planning. This means that there is an inherent danger of underinvestment in the case of technical occupations.

Calculations regarding the development of training costs (cf. Beicht et al. 2004b) show that net costs have not risen across the board in recent years. To this extent, reasons of cost cannot be portrayed as the central cause of the decrease in the supply of training places. Changes in company requirements for skilled workers are much more likely to be a significant factor.

## Modernisation of VET by Renewal of Training Regulations

The modernisation of training regulations of the recognised training occupations has been undergoing a process of acceleration since 1996, in order to come to terms with the demands of the employment system (cf. Werner 2003). In this period, 230 training regulations have been renewed, including the 59 new occupations which have been created (as of 1 October 2004). We deal with the *definition and delineation* of occupational groups first. Included in the following summary of non-modernised occupations are all recognised training occupations which have had no new or updated regulation since 1996. Of all occupations with new or updated regulation since 1996, only those not having a predecessor version are categorised as new, all other reclassified occupations being defined as modernised training occupations.

## The Development of New and Modernised Technical Occupations

The quantitative development of training contracts in new and modernised occupations, compared to that in non-modernised occupations, is used as an indicator of the success of modernisation of VET by the process of renewal of training regulations. The decrease in the number of contracts concluded in non-modernised occupations is more than compensated for by the increase in the number of those commencing training in new and modernised occupations.

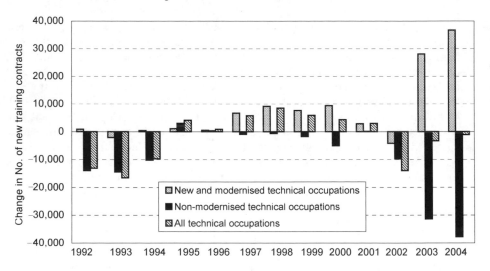

Source: Vocational education and training statistics of the Federal Office of Statistics, reference date in each case 31 December – calculations of the BIBB

**Fig. 9.** Increase of new training contracts in technical occupations with and without renewed training regulations, Germany 1992–2004

Fig. 9 shows overcompensation until the year 2002, thereafter there is a fall in the number of newly concluded contracts compared to the previous year's figures in newly classified technical occupations too. In 2003 and 2004, the numbers rose again, but this failed to cancel out the fall in the number of new apprentices in non-modernised occupations. Taking into account the figures for all occupations, the previous three years had also failed to produce this positive balancing effect. The overall numbers of those commencing training have been in decline since the year 2000. This means that the comparatively favourable development in technical occupations since the mid-1990s can be judged as a particular success of the modernisation process of dual training occupations via more intensive process or renewed training regulations, especially in the technical occupations.

The global development in the number of training contracts does not represent the sole indicator of the future prospects of technical training occupations. In the following, two structural features of apprentices recorded within the framework of official statistics on vocational education and training will be considered. The first point is the previous schooling of those commencing training within the dual system, the development of which should offer some indications as to the development of the *level of requirements and attractiveness of occupations.* Secondly, *representation of women* amongst apprentices in technical occupations will be analysed on the basis of the proportion of women commencing training in those fields.

**Higher General Education Qualification Levels Among Apprentices**
In principle, as is described in the key features of the German Dual VET System, training is available to all young people, regardless of the qualifications they have previously achieved in general schooling. Until the start of the 1990s, there is a recognisable trend in Germany as a whole towards a higher level of qualification of those leaving the general education system. Since then, there has been a relatively low fluctuation in the different types of general education qualification. At present, just under 9 per cent of young people leave general schooling with no qualifications, 26 per cent with secondary general school certificate, about 41 per cent with intermediate general school certificate and nearly 25 per cent with higher education entrance qualification.[16] What have been the developments in the dual system? Since 1993, the vocational education and training statistics of the Federal Statistical Office have recorded the last school attended by young people with a newly concluded training contract, meaning either the highest qualification attained in the general school system or the type of vocational school attended (school-based basic vocational training year (bvt), pre-vocational training year (pvt) or full-time vocational school (vs). No information in respect of the level of qualification attained in the general school system is available for those who have previously attended a vocational school.[17]

---

[16] The figures for 1980 were: 11 per cent without qualifications, 40 per cent secondary general school certificate, 33 per cent intermediate general school certificate and 16 per cent higher education entrance qualification (source: schools statistics of the Federal Office of Statistics).

[17] Since previous schooling at general and vocational schools has not hitherto been recorded separately, information regarding the qualifications of all apprentices in the general school system is, unfortunately, not available. The category 'others' is also used to show previous types of schooling not specified in detail.

220 Alexandra Uhly, Klaus Troltsch, Günter Walden

**Table 2.** Previous general school qualifications of apprentices*, Germany 1993, 1998 and 2004, in per cent[18]

| | 1993 | | 1998 | | 2004 | |
|---|---|---|---|---|---|---|
| | | | Occupations | | | |
| Previous general education qualifications | Technical | All | Technical | All | Technical | All |
| Without secondary general school certificate | 2.0 | 3.5 | 1.4 | 2.5 | 1.1 | 2.5 |
| Secondary general school certificate (sec) | 37.5 | 33.7 | 32.1 | 30.2 | 26.2 | 28.8 |
| Intermediate general school certificate (inter) | 41.0 | 35.6 | 42.9 | 36.9 | 46.1 | 37.5 |
| Leavers with higher education entrance qualification (sec II) | 9.3 | 14.1 | 12.5 | 16.7 | 13.1 | 15.3 |
| Pre-vocational training year (pvt) | 1.0 | 1.2 | 1.2 | 1.8 | 1.3 | 2.2 |
| Basic vocational training year (bvt) | 3.2 | 3.8 | 3.0 | 3.1 | 2.7 | 2.7 |
| Full-time vocational schools (vs) | 5.0 | 6.8 | 5.7 | 7.2 | 7.9 | 8.7 |
| Others | 0.9 | 1.3 | 1.2 | 1.6 | 1.6 | 2.3 |

\* With new training contracts
Source: Vocational education and training statistics of the Federal Office of Statistics – calculations of the BIBB

In 2004, 28.6 per cent of all those commencing training in technical occupations had, before the start of their vocational education and training, either no school qualifications, secondary general school certificate (sec) or had completed a pre-vocational training year (pvt)[19] (Table 2). Compared to 1993, the proportion of these apprentices has decreased by more than 29 per cent, from a figure of 40.5 per cent. In comparison with all apprentices (37.5 per cent), an over-proportionate number of apprentices in technical occupations (46.1 per cent) have an intermediate general school certificate (inter). There is, overall, an under-proportionate number of apprentices with a higher education entrance qualification (sec II) in technical occupations. 59.2 per cent of apprentices in technical occupations with a newly concluded training contract had previously obtained an intermediate general school certificate or a higher education entrance qualification, this proportion having risen by nearly 18 per cent since 1993 from a figure of 50.3 per cent. This trend towards a higher level of general qualifications can also be recognised in all dual training occupations as a whole, but is more marked in technical occupations.

If a differentiation is made between *manufacturing and service sector occupations*, it is possible to recognise in both areas that significantly higher proportions of those commencing training in technical occupations have higher level school qualifications than is the case with those commencing training in non-technical occupations. *Technical occupations in the service sector* in particular *exhibit very high proportions of apprentices with a higher education entrance qualification (sec II)* (cf. Table 3).

This trend towards a higher level of school qualification is especially apparent in the new technical occupations. For example, the training occupation IT specialist ('*Fachinformatiker*') accounts for the greatest proportion of newly concluded training

[18] Not including missing information about previous education, 2003 missing information about previous education 1.7 per cent as a whole and 1.4 per cent in technical occupations.
[19] In the course of a pre-vocational training year, students often obtain a secondary general school certificate.

**Table 3.** Previous general school qualification of apprentices* in technical and non-technical manufacturing and service sector occupations (in per cent), Germany 2004

| | Manufacturing occupations | | Service sector occupations | |
|---|---|---|---|---|
| *Previous general education qualifications* | Technical occupations | Non-technical occupations | Technical occupations | Non-technical occupations |
| Without secondary general school certificate | 1.2 | 4.0 | 0.2 | 0.9 |
| Secondary general school certificate (sec) | 29.8 | 47.1 | 7.5 | 21.6 |
| Intermediate general school (inter) | 47.4 | 28.7 | 39.4 | 39.2 |
| Leavers with higher education entrance qualification (sec II) | 8.5 | 4.4 | 37.1 | 22.1 |
| Pre-vocational training year (pvt) | 1.5 | 3.2 | 0.5 | 1.3 |
| Basic vocational training year (bvt) | 3.1 | 6.3 | 0.8 | 1.0 |
| Full-time vocational schools (vs) | 7.1 | 4.3 | 11.9 | 11.5 |
| Others | 1.4 | 1.9 | 2.7 | 2.5 |

* With new training contracts
Source: Vocational education and training statistics of the Federal Office of Statistics – calculations of the BIBB

contracts in all new technical occupations, with 7,628 commencing training in the year 2004. The proportion of young people in this occupation with a higher education entrance qualification is noticeably high at 48.3 per cent (more than three times greater than the overall figure for all those commencing training and more than 60 per cent higher than in all new occupations as a whole). Thus, since 1993, a significant overall trend towards a higher level of qualification has been exhibited with regard to previous school education of apprentices in technical occupations, this trend being more marked than is the case with occupations in general. This might be an expression of the increase in the level of requirements in technical occupations from the point of view of companies providing training. On the other hand, it can also be interpreted as an indication of a higher level of attractiveness of these occupations from the standpoint of the apprentices, given that increasingly well qualified young people are showing an interest in these occupations, meaning, in turn, that there is a greater probability that companies will select such well qualified individuals amongst the applicants. This especially applies to technical occupations in the service sector.

**Representation of Women in Technical Training Occupations**
With reference to the Amsterdam Treaty of the European Union (Articles 2 and 3), the federal government has committed itself to the promotion of equal opportunity as a cross-section task –'gender mainstreaming'– meaning that equality of opportunity for men and women is now recognised as an integrated guiding principle.

Occupational segregation by sex can be observed at an international level,[20] and is: '[...] extensive in every region, at all economic development levels, under all political systems, and in diverse religious, social and cultural environments' (Anker 1997: 1). Despite various political measures, this segregation remains, defying explanation in terms of rational criteria within the framework of economic theory. Entrenched

---

[20] For occupational segregation of male and female employment in Europe, see European Foundation for the Improvement of Living and Working Conditions (2002: 10).

stereotypes of female and male occupations obviously still prevail (Anker 1997). In this section, the *representation of women in technical occupations* will be investigated. Here it is to be noted, however, that varying distribution of different groups of people across occupations is a result of personal inclinations and interests, influencing selection of occupation as well as of varying opportunities of access. The latter are themselves, in turn, affected by a variety of factors, including, for example, access to qualifications and skills prior to vocational education and training, but also by the preferences of certain young people for the training occupations. The analysis of the varying levels of representation of different groups of people amongst apprentices virtually always only allows the net result of the various influencing factors to be observed, thus not permitting any conclusions to be reached with regard to the effect of individual factors.

**Table 4.** Women as a proportion of all apprentices in occupational groups, Germany* 1980–2003

|                                          | 1980 | 1985 | 1990 | 1995 | 2000 | 2004 |
|------------------------------------------|------|------|------|------|------|------|
| Technical occupations                    | 7.5  | 9.4  | 11.1 | 11.0 | 10.8 | 9.9  |
| Technical manufacturing occupations      | 3.4  | 4.8  | 6.5  | 6.8  | 6.9  | 6.8  |
| Technical service sector occupations     | 50.0 | 53.5 | 53.9 | 48.2 | 35.3 | 28.9 |
| All training occupations                 | 38.2 | 40.6 | 42.6 | 39.8 | 40.9 | 40.1 |

\*   Until 1990 area of the Federal Republic of Germany before October 3, since 1995 including the former GDR
Source: Vocational education and training statistics of the Federal Office of Statistics – calculations of the BIBB

In the course of the 1980s, the proportion of female apprentices increased in the area of technical occupations (cf. Table 4). Since 1992, shares of women have again decreased, accounting for 9.9 per cent in 2004 (1991: 12.0 per cent). Despite the increase seen in the course of the 1980s, these proportions are thus at a significantly lower level than the figure for the dual system as a whole (about 40 per cent). Since it is well known that there is a significant difference in the gender-specific composition of apprentices between manufacturing and service sector occupations,[21] proportions of women are considered separately for both technical and non-technical occupations. As expected, the proportions of women in technical manufacturing occupations are the lowest. Also in line with expectations were the low proportions of women in the technical service sector occupations compared to the non-technical service sector occupations. Surprising, however, is the strong decrease in the proportion of female apprentices commencing training in the technical service sector occupations, falling from a representation level of almost 50 per cent in 1993 to significantly under one-third in the year 2004.

---

[21] For female occupational segregation in vocational training in Germany, see Dorsch-Schweizer (2004), Granato & Schittenhelm (2004) and for the German labour market Biersack (2002); differing opportunities for access to manufacturing and service sector occupations for women and men can also be ascertained independently of the level of their qualifications attained in the general school system (cf. Frietsch 2004b: 25).

Such a decrease can be caused by a corresponding reduction in the proportion of women in all technical service sector occupations, or the reason may be a change in the composition of the occupations (each with a differing proportion of women). Female shares in terms of those commencing training in modernised occupations are roughly in line with those in non-modernised occupations (40–50 per cent). As far as the new occupations are concerned, however, the proportions of women are significantly lower. Female representation is under 30 per cent here, even falling to 24.3 per cent by 2003. When observing the technical occupations, a different picture emerges. In the new and modernised occupations, proportions of women are significantly higher than in non-modernised occupations (4–6 per cent). However, these proportions are in decline in modernised occupations (falling from 37.3 per cent to 13.2 per cent) as well as in new occupations (decreasing from over 20 per cent to 14.8 per cent). Differentiating according to technical *manufacturing and service sector occupations* leads to the result that the reason for the strong decrease in the female proportion in the technical service sector occupations is the *low proportions of women in the new technical service sector occupations*. This figure is only about 17–19 per cent. In the modernised and non-modernised technical service sector occupations, the proportions of women fluctuate only slightly and are at a significantly higher level, about 60 per cent and about 40 per cent respectively. The reason for the strongly decreasing proportion of women in the technical service sector group can be found in the structural changes within this occupational group. In the course of time, there has been a strong increase in the number of newly concluded training contracts, particularly in the IT occupations which exhibit low levels of female participation. The number of those commencing training in the traditional technical service sector occupations (laboratory occupations and draughtsmen) is falling considerably. These occupations have high proportions of women. This means that the new technical service sector occupations are gaining a constant, strongly increasing weighting relative to technical service sector occupations (0 per cent in 1993 and 57.2 per cent in 2003) and the female proportion of those commencing training in the technical service sector occupations is falling. In the case of the technical manufacturing occupations, the proportion of women fluctuates slightly, remaining virtually unchanged in terms of the comparison between 1993 and 2003, since the non-modernised occupations are not losing their relative weight to such an extent in this area (1993: 84.0 per cent, 2002: 65.2 per cent) and due to the fact that although the proportion of women in the modernised and new technical manufacturing occupations is relatively high, the figure is decreasing over the course of time. Low female proportions in the technical occupations are thus caused by the *very low number of female apprentices in the manufacturing occupations*, whereby the proportion of women in the new and modernised occupations in this area is comparatively high. The cause of the decrease in the proportion of women in the the technical occupations is the strong *growth in the number of apprentices in the new technical service sector occupations, which have relatively low proprotions of women.*

## Conclusion

In the past, the Dual VET System in Germany thoroughly demonstrated its adaptability, an example of this being the way in which the rise in demand of young people for training places as a result of demographic change at the end of the 1970s and beginning of the 1980s was easily met. The adaptation of occupational structures in the dual system to underlying developments in the employment system is also a step in the right direction, if not quite going far enough. The more intensive process of renewing training regulations of recognised occupations in the technical occupations is proving a successful strategy. Training opportunities for more highly qualified school leavers in particular have increased in this area. The modernisation of training occupations is a significant process, but the potential to increase training capacities should not be overestimated and the number of newly created training occupations is, in itself, not yet a success indicator of the dual system. In the light of the current problematic situation in the training places market, which has its origins in cyclical and structural problems within the employment system and on the sales markets of companies, the contribution made by the reclassification of training occupations can, in principle, only be very limited.

Nevertheless, problems in adapting to the shortage of training places, which has existed since the end of the 1990s, are becoming apparent. If the aim is to provide all young people with the opportunity of qualified training and thus improve the life chances of this generation[22] as well as to secure the formation of qualified human capital in terms of society as a whole, training capacities need to be significantly extended. There is a particular and considerable deficit in the area of service sector occupations. It is also necessary to provide alternative opportunities by making the system more flexible, without forgoing the basic principles of the dual training system. 'The main problem is how to protect system flexibility from misuse. In this sense 'flexicurity' is the key word to mark a consensus-based pathway to fit out the Dual System as an 'expandable model' for the future' (Kutscha 2000: 16). In this context, the reforms introduced as a result of the Vocational Training Reform Act of 2005 should be judged in a positive light. For example, 190,000 apprentices are thus far taking part in full-time school based training outside the scope of the Vocational Training Act (BBiG), not least because of the tight situation regarding apprenticeships. The new vocational education and training law provides these students with easier access to the so-called Chamber Examination, which until now was only sat by young people undergoing in-company training. The overall result of this will be an easing of the training places market, and there will be positive effects for training in technical occupations. Other innovations in vocational education and training law, such as more rapid modernisation and the creation of (new) training occupations by shortening processing times and reducing the number of statutory committees will also make a contribution to a higher level of adaptability of the dual system.

Another point to be considered in this context is, however, that additional recruitment potential will need to be mobilised in the light of the shortage of training position applicants there will be in the future, due to demographic reasons. In view of

---

[22] For the negative consequences of not having vocational education and training on the life situations of whole cohorts, see the life studies of Max Planck Institute for Educational Research (Blossfeld 1990).

the increase in qualification requirements, particularly in the new and modernised technical occupations, this process is likely to be made more difficult. One possible way may be to increase the proportion of women in technically oriented occupations. Until now, however, this has only been achieved in a few individual technical occupations. Amongst those commencing training in technical occupations, girls are, on the whole, significantly underrepresented. Despite numerous political measures to increase the proportion of women, female proportions have actually started falling again. Obviously, entrenched gender stereotypes are at work here, and it will be scarcely possible to alter these in the short term. If technical occupations are to be accorded an important role in Germany's technological productivity, it will be necessary to tackle the demographically related decrease in the supply of skilled workers in these occupations at an early stage (see Troltsch 2004a: 8ff).

# 5.3 Higher Education Indicators

Jürgen Egeln, Christoph Heine

**Abstract.** A profound change has taken place in the qualificational profile of the working population in Germany. The absolute figure for employment among academics is increasing, while the employment figure for unqualified workers is decreasing. The demand for higher education in Germany is too low to meet the requirements of a knowledge-based economy. The key to this issue is the educational potential of the lower tiers of society. It is important to increase interest in studying in the fields of science and engineering, which are of great importance to Germany's technological preformance. But increasing the demand for higher education alone will not be enough to increase the supply of graduates, the effectiveness of the higher education on offer in Germany has to be improved. To expand higher education while maintaining a high level of course quality, or even improving quality, will not be possible without further financial investment, whatever the sources of this may be.

## Introduction

A profound change has taken place in the qualificational profile of the working population in Germany in recent decades, the main characteristic of which is a trend towards higher levels of qualification. While the proportion of the workforce without an academic qualification who have not completed any form of training has decreased greatly, the proportions both of qualified workers (who have completed vocational training at work or school) and highly qualified workers (with qualifications from higher education) have increased.[1] In particular, the employment of academically qualified workers has shown an above-average growth rate. Fig. 1 shows the increase in the proportion of academically qualified workers in the two main sectors of production and services. It can be clearly seen that the absolute figure for employment among academics even continues to increase when the employment figure for unqualified workers decreases.

Projected figures for the firms' demand for qualifications in the next years suggest that this change in the qualificational structure of employees will continue into the future. However, there are also signs of qualification problems on the supply side of the labour market: the problem of 'dropping out' (leaving education without completing the relevant qualification) has shown an increase in various areas of the educational system, from universities to vocational institutions and even schools. This increase will not be without consequences for the supply of qualified workers within the economy. The overall dynamic of qualification development, generally referred to as 'upgrading', is the result of various changes. First, the development reflects the consequences of a change in sectoral structures, particularly the shift towards the service

---

[1] Bund-Länder Commission for Educational Planning and Research Promotion (BLK) (2002).

*U. Schmoch, C. Rammer and H. Legler (eds.), National Systems of Innovation in Comparison, 227–243.*

sector (see also Chapter 4.1). This development is compared with strong growth of knowledge-intensive services within the tertiary sector. Secondly, the qualification levels of labour demand rise in the other economic sectors as well, particularly in the production sector. This effect is triggered by a move towards service orientation of many activities within this area. International competition increases the pressure on firms to constantly offer new products (with new, technology-intensive production processes) and services. This, in turn, increases the pressure to innovate, which tends to lead to the employment of highly qualified workers, particularly with a quali-fication from higher education.

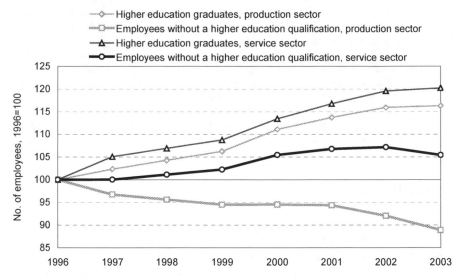

Source: Federal Agency of Labour (BA) (various years) – ZEW calculations

**Fig. 1.** Employees with and without a higher education qualification in Germany, 1996–2003 (index with base year 1996 = 100)

From the demand for expansion alone, which is a product of the structural change and growth in those economic areas that are the most knowledge-intensive, it must be feared that bottlenecks in the provision of highly qualified labour could result in the medium term. These would then act as a restriction to innovation and growth. This will be increased by the fact that a large number of retirements are expected in the next years. The high demand for replacement caused by these will only serve to com-pound the demand for expansion, again particularly in the courses of study that we focus on here. The looming shortage of suitable labour could be far higher than any phenomeon of scarcity that has been experienced in the past for economic or cyclical reasons. This development is taking place against the background of the lack of la-bour supply due to the demographic development which could hardly be compensated by an overproportional growth in the segment of highly qualified skilled workers; all the more so as there is currently no sign of such growth. This development has to be seen in the context of Germany's already noticeable 'lagging behind' in training academically qualified human resources.

It is against this background that this report examines indicators that reveal Germany's position and development with respect to the supply of graduates. The main focus is upon recruitment and the potential for recruitment of workers with a science or engineering qualification, as people with these professional competencies play a key role in technical and economic development. Furthermore, since higher education and labour markets become increasingly internationalised, particularly the market for highly qualified workers, an international comparision seems pertinent.

The German situation in the market for highly qualified labour is analysed by looking at four topics:

- The development of the demand for higher education determining the potential of graduates.
- The development of conditions at universities, study programmes, course quality and effectiveness largely determine how successful higher education institutions are in achieving their task of training and qualifying their students.
- The transition from higher education into employment and the extent to which graduates remain in a profession associated with their education profile.
- Finally, expenditure on and financing of higher education is important since an increase in the volume of higher education graduates is needed to satisfy demand on the labour market. This answered the question of whether higher education is underfunded in Germany.

## Demand for Higher Education Places

The number of persons with an entitlement to higher education entry (due to their attainment of the relevant qualifications) in Germany, both in absolute terms and as a proportion of their age group, has shown a noticeable upwards trend in the long term (see Fig. 2). The highest figure so far was recorded in 2003.

Many factors contribute to this increase. Particularly worthy of mention is the level of participation of young women in courses of education that can lead to higher education, which has increased at an above average rate and remains high. The general increase in relative participation in the relevant schools should not be ignored either. In spite of this most welcome result, particularly in the context of stable or even slightly diminishing entitlement quotas in many other OECD countries, Germany still has one of the lowest entitlement quotas for higher education (see Table 1).

These differences can be partially explained by national peculiarities in how the school system and admission to higher education are organised, particularly as regards the point in a person's education at which a decision is made as to whether or not he or she will follow an educational path that leads to higher education (the 'selection' process). Germany suffers from a considerable narrowing of the paths leading to higher education, which impacts accordingly on the transition into higher education. Furthermore, changes in the nature of work and vocational training in professions that do not require university level qualifications mean that, in all probability, the competition between higher education institutions and vocational training establishments for well qualified school-leavers will only increase. German 'Gymnasien' (establishments for pupils of high-school age, leading to direct qualification for higher education) will find themselves increasingly having to fulfil a 'delivery function', not only for higher education, but also for the more demanding areas of the vocational education system.

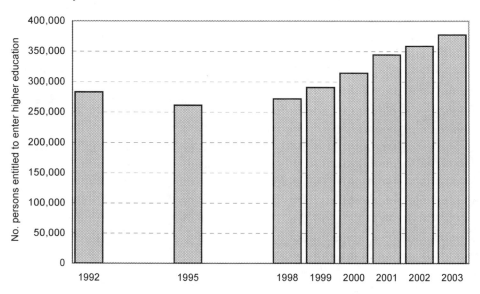

Source: Federal Statistical Office Germany (ed.) (various years)

**Fig. 2.** Development of the number of persons entitled to higher education entry in Germany

**Table 1.** Higher education entitlement quotas in selected OECD countries, 1998–2002

|                 | 1998 |      | 1999 |      | 2000 |      | 2001 |      | 2002 |      |
|-----------------|------|------|------|------|------|------|------|------|------|------|
|                 | 1)   | 2)   | 1)   | 2)   | 1)   | 2)   | 1)   | 2)   | 1)   | 2)   |
| AUS             | 67   | –    | 66   | –    | 67   | –    | 68   | –    | 69   | –    |
| CAN             | 72   | –    | –    | –    | –    | –    | –    | –    | –    | –    |
| FIN             | 89   | –    | 89   | –    | 87   | –    | 91   | –    | 85   | –    |
| FRA             | 54   | 0.3  | 52   | 0.3  | 49   | 0.7  | 51   | 0.7  | 51   | 0.7  |
| GER             | 34   | 10.2 | 33   | 9.9  | 33   | 9.3  | 32   | 9.5  | 34   | 8.6  |
| ITA             | 67   | –    | 71   | –    | 74   | –    | 69   | –    | 72   | –    |
| JPN             | 70   | –    | 69   | –    | 69   | –    | 69   | –    | 68   | –    |
| NED             | 87   | –    | 66   | –    | 63   | –    | 62   | –    | 63   | –    |
| ESP             | 43   | 15.3 | 47   | 12.4 | 46   | 9.5  | 47   | 5.4  | 48   | 3.8  |
| SWE             | 79   | –    | 74   | –    | 74   | –    | 71   | –    | 72   | –    |
| GBR             | -    | –    | –    | –    | –    | –    | –    | –    | –    | –    |
| USA             | -    | –    | –    | –    | –    | –    | –    | –    | 73   | –    |
| Country Average | 57   | 3.6  | 57   | 2.4  | 55   | 2.3  | 54   | 3.0  | 61   | 5.2  |

1) ISCED 3A: Upper secondary education that enables direct admission into tertiary A courses
2) ISCED 4A: Post-secondary non-tertiary education that enables direct admission into tertiary A courses
Source: OECD (ed.) (various years): Education at a Glance 2000 to 2004

Young women already make up more than half of those taking the 'Abitur' examinations, and this proportion stands to increase further. Thus women represent a large and increasing proportion of those with higher education entry qualifications, and therefore of large potential for graduates. Since women show only a low level of interest in technical and scientific subjects at school and only a weak preference for technical and scientific subjects when it comes to applying for higher education, the relative size of these courses of study is likely to diminish further, in spite of their importance for the country's technological performance. Unless, of course, it proves possible to mobilise more young women in the direction of these courses and professions. In addition to this, the importance given to science teaching in the upper years of the 'Gymnasium', measured by the pupils' choice of courses and subjects (for example as a core subject), does not reflect the importance of the sciences for technological and economic development. Because of the close relationship between the choice of a core subject and that of a higher education course, it can be said that the shortage of potential future scientists and engineers takes effect in the upper level of the 'Gymnasium' at the latest. This bottleneck is exacerbated further along the paths from vocational education to higher education. Traditionally, specialised 'Gymnasien' and, more importantly, specialised subject-specific high schools (so-called *Fachoberschulen*, which permit entry to a limited number of university courses) provide a central reservoir of interested and eligible applicants for higher education courses in science and technology subjects. In particular, the figures for pupils in the technologically specialised branches of subject-specific high schools diminished significantly in the 1990s. In spite of a rise in the last few years, they have by no means recovered from this blow. The importance of this stems from the fact that the majority of young engineers in Germany are educated at universities of applied sciences – the proportion of engineering students who study at universities of applied sciences is around 60 per cent, among both new entrants and graduates.

The share of young people starting university was nearly stable in the first half of the 1990s, but then rose, attaining its highest ever level in 2003 (cf. Fig. 3). Again, an interplay of various factors is responsible for this result. These include demographic conditions, an increasing interest in higher education among young women and, last but not least, an increased willingness to attend higher education among those entitled to do so. This last factor is in itself partially a result of the fact that alternative educational and training options to higher education have become relatively scarce in recent years.

The increase in the number of foreign students entering higher education in Germany, particularly in engineering and science subjects, has also contributed to the rise in the number of higher education entrants. Analysing the participation in education by social group reveals that the participation of young people with an academic family background (defined as a family where at least one parent has received a higher education) is so high that it has virtually reached a saturation point, meaning that there is hardly any potential for expansion available. To expand participation in higher education, more efforts are needed to include and encourage both foreign nationals who have been educated in Germany and, more particularly, the lower social strata. Such efforts are also important because 'educational climbers' show more affinity in their choice of course for engineering subjects.

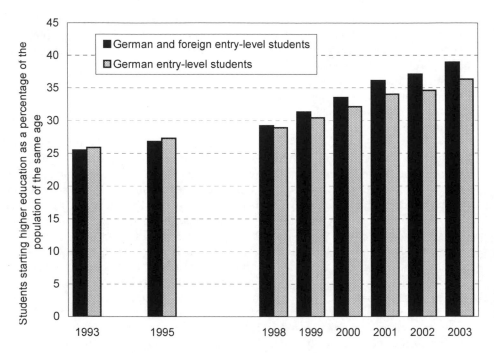

Source: Federal Statistical Office Germany (ed.) (various years)

**Fig. 3.** Higher education entry rates (students in their first semester of higher education) in Germany: students starting higher education (in the summer and following winter semesters) as a proportion of the population of the same age, 1993, 1995 and 1998–2003.

Seen from the point of view of Germany's technological potential and the professional competencies needed to sustain it, the development of the demand for places in engineering courses offers further cause for concern. The decrease in the number of students starting these courses was sharper and more sustained than for other groups of subjects and, in spite of a renewed increase at the start of the new millenium, the ratio of engineering students to all students (see Table 2) in 2003 was still four to five percentage points lower than the level reached in the mid-1980s.

Although the general 'recovery' in demand for higher education is also to some extent apparent within the engineering subjects, it has come later and is more modest than on average.

Compared to other OECD countries, Germany shows a strong increase in higher education entry rates, but this remains well under the level of other countries (see Table 3).

The gap between Germany and most other highly developed countries is so clear that, even bearing in mind the methodical and systemic difficulties in comparing entry rates internationally, caused by the diversity of countries' vocational and higher education systems, it must be seen as a fundamental issue and is not merely the result of structural differences.

**Table 2.** Subject area quota: proportion of students in their first semester of higher education according to subject group and two generalised groupings (Mathematics/Science and Engineering). Figures are shown as a percentage of all first-semester students, for the years 1992, 1995 and 1998–2003

|  | 1992 | 1995 | 1998 | 1999 | 2000 | 2001 | 2002 | 2003 |
|---|---|---|---|---|---|---|---|---|
| Languages and Cultural Studies, Sport | 19.9 | 22.7 | 21.6 | 21.1 | 20.9 | 21.8 | 21.9 | 21.5 |
| Law, Ecomomics and Social Sciences | 33.3 | 35.3 | 35.6 | 35.5 | 34.0 | 33.7 | 34.4 | 33.2 |
| Medicine, Veterinary Science | 4.4 | 4.6 | 4.3 | 4.3 | 4.0 | 3.8 | 3.7 | 3.5 |
| Agricultural Sc., Forestry; Nutritional Sc. | 2.3 | 2.4 | 2.4 | 2.2 | 2.0 | 1.9 | 2.0 | 2.1 |
| Art, Fine Arts | 2.8 | 3.7 | 3.7 | 3.6 | 3.5 | 3.4 | 3.4 | 3.2 |
| Mathematics, Sciences | 14.9 | 13.0 | 14.9 | 16.3 | 18.7 | 18.6 | 17.7 | 18.1 |
| *Biology* | *2.4* | *2.3* | *2.4* | *2.5* | *2.4* | *2.4* | *2.3* | *2.2* |
| *Chemistry* | *2.0* | *1.4* | *1.6* | *1.6* | *1.7* | *2.0* | *2.1* | *2.3* |
| *Computer Science* | *3.5* | *3.2* | *5.3* | *6.5* | *8.6* | *7.7* | *6.4* | *6.1* |
| *Mathematics* | *2.8* | *2.3* | *2.0* | *2.2* | *2.4* | *2.8* | *3.0* | *3.2* |
| *Physics, Astronomy* | *1.8* | *1.1* | *1.1* | *1.2* | *1.3* | *1.5* | *1.6* | *1.7* |
| Engineering | 22.0 | 18.2 | 17.3 | 16.8 | 16.8 | 16.7 | 16.8 | 18.4 |
| *Electrical Engineering* | *5.6* | *3.5* | *3.9* | *4.0* | *4.0* | *4.2* | *4.1* | *4.2* |
| *Mechanical, Chemical, Traffic Engineer* | *9.4* | *6.6* | *6.9* | *7.0* | *7.4* | *7.5* | *7.9* | *8.9* |
| All subjects | 100.0 | 100.0 | 100.0 | 100.0 | 100.0 | 100.0 | 100.0 | 100.0 |

Source: Federal Statistical Office Germany (2002) – HIS calculations

**Table 3.** Higher education entry rates: proportion of the population of a typical age for entering higher education who actually do so[1] in selected OECD countries 1998–2002

| Country | 1998 | 1999 | 2000 | 2001 | 2002 |
|---|---|---|---|---|---|
| AUS | 53 | 45 | 59 | 65 | 77 |
| FIN | 58 | 67 | 71 | 72 | 71 |
| FRA |  | 35 | 37 | 37 | 37 |
| GER | 28 | 28 | 30 | 32 | 35 |
| ITA | 42 | 40 | 43 | 44 | 50 |
| JPN | 36 | 37 | 39 | 41 | 41 |
| NED | 52 | 54 | 51 | 54 | 53 |
| ESP | 41 | 46 | 48 | 48 | 50 |
| SWE | 59 | 65 | 67 | 69 | 75 |
| GBR | 48 | 45 | 46 | 45 | 47 |
| USA | 44 | 45 | 43 | 42 | 64 |
| Country Average |  | 45 | 47 | 51 |  |

German and foreign students starting at universities and universities of applied sciences (*Fachhochschulen*), *Verwaltungsfachhochschulen* excluded, ISCED 5A
Source: OECD (ed.) (various years): Education at a Glance 2000 to 2004

## Choice of Study and Quality of Higher Education

In a situation where the development of the demand for higher education places is already unsatisfactory, the number of potential graduates further diminishes over the course of students' studies in German higher education institutions. At the end of the day, it is the 'output' and not the 'input' of higher education which is relevant for the supply of a highly qualified labour force. This seems to be made even scarcer by the German higher education system's ineffectiveness in achieving its aims.

Germany is still one of the countries in which students require the most time in higher education before successfully attaining a qualification. In relation to the number of students entering higher education, the final number of graduates is reduced to a considerable extent, varying by the course of study being followed. This is due to high dropout rates (students leaving higher education prematurely or changing their course).

From a subject-specific point of view, the 'loss' suffered by a subject comes not only from students dropping out – leaving higher education permanently without a qualification – but also from students changing to another subject. Even taking into account the fact that courses of study and subjects do not simply lose students to other subjects, but also gain a number of students from other subjects, the majority of science and engineering subjects at universities still suffers a noticeable loss from what was already a low total demand. This loss amounts to around half of the total students who start a course. Only at the universities of applied sciences do the figures look better. Against this background, it seems reasonable to ask whether the core problem, in terms of higher education fulfilling its function of serving the labour market, might in fact lie not so much with the development of demand, but instead primarily with the low success rates and the low effectiveness of the higher education system that accompanies them.

The unfavourable success quota in Engineering and the Sciences contrasts with the by no means unfavourable conditions of study in these subjects at universities. Particularly positive are the student-faculty ratios, which are not only much lower than those of many 'boom subjects' because of demand development, but which also decreased appreciably in the 1990s, before rising again slightly around the turn of the millenium, particularly in the subject group Mathematics/Sciences (this was largely due to an increase in the number of students in computer science). The available data on capacity utilisation of different courses points in the same direction. While the subject groups for Languages and Cultural Studies, Law, Economics and Social Sciences use more of their capacity than the average, capacity utilisation among subjects in the group for Mathematics/Sciences and Engineering (apart from Computer Science) lies far under the maximum theoretical capacity (see Table 5).

In current debates about the politics of higher education in Germany, much hope is being placed on the new Bachelor/Master's courses of study. As well as the international aim of establishing a standard European framework for higher education with comparable course structures, it is hoped that this reform will promote an increased demand for higher education (through the introduction of shorter courses of study) and increase success rates through more 'user-friendliness' and higher effectiveness. As expected, the supply of new courses has increased sharply in the last five years, but the current state of implementation is such that there are large differences between

**Table 4.** Balance of dropout rates for selected subject groups and areas of study at universities and universities of applied sciences (Fachhochschulen) (in per cent). Based on graduates for 1999 and 2002

| Subject group | Year of gradu- ation | Drop- out quota | + | Losses due to chang- ing course | = | Total losses | – | Gains due to chan- ging course | = | Balance of losses |
|---|---|---|---|---|---|---|---|---|---|---|
| | | | | At Universities | | | | | | |
| Mathematics, Sciences | 2002 | −26 | + | −20 | = | −46 | – | 7 | = | −39 |
| | 1999 | −23 | + | −22 | = | −45 | – | 6 | = | −39 |
| Mathematics | 2002 | −26 | + | −39 | = | −65 | – | 13 | = | −52 |
| | 1999 | −12 | + | −45 | = | −58 | – | 7 | = | −51 |
| Computer Science | 2002 | −38 | + | −19 | = | −57 | – | 8 | = | −49 |
| | 1999 | −37 | + | −16 | = | −53 | – | 10 | = | −43 |
| Physics, Earth Science | 2002 | −30 | + | −25 | = | −55 | – | 6 | = | −49 |
| | 1999 | −26 | + | −25 | = | −51 | – | 7 | = | −44 |
| Chemistry | 2002 | −33 | + | −25 | = | −58 | – | 3 | = | −55 |
| | 1999 | −23 | + | −32 | = | −56 | – | 4 | = | −52 |
| Pharmacy | 2002 | −12 | + | −11 | = | −23 | – | 16 | = | −7 |
| | 1999 | −17 | + | −7 | = | −24 | – | 18 | = | −6 |
| Biology | 2002 | −15 | + | −17 | = | −32 | – | 8 | = | −24 |
| | 1999 | −15 | + | −21 | = | −35 | – | 16 | = | −19 |
| Geography | 2002 | −19 | + | −25 | = | −44 | – | 18 | = | −26 |
| | 1999 | −36 | + | −22 | = | −58 | – | 38 | = | −20 |
| Engineering | 2002 | −30 | + | −17 | = | −47 | – | 10 | = | −37 |
| | 1999 | −26 | + | −17 | = | −43 | – | 6 | = | −37 |
| Mechanical Engineering | 2002 | −34 | + | −18 | = | −52 | – | 4 | = | −48 |
| | 1999 | −25 | + | −17 | = | −43 | – | 6 | = | −37 |
| Electronic Engineering | 2002 | −33 | + | −18 | = | −51 | – | 2 | = | −49 |
| | 1999 | −23 | + | −20 | = | −43 | – | 1 | = | −42 |
| Civil Engineering | 2002 | −30 | + | −24 | = | −54 | – | 6 | = | −48 |
| | 1999 | −35 | + | −25 | = | −61 | – | 10 | = | −51 |
| Average of all subject groups | 2002 | −26 | + | −13 | = | −39 | – | 10 | = | −29 |
| | 1999 | −24 | + | −16 | = | −40 | – | 12 | = | −28 |
| | | At Universities of Applied Sciences (*Fachhochschulen*) | | | | | | | | |
| Mathematics, Sciences | 2002 | −40 | + | −6 | = | −46 | – | 24 | = | −22 |
| | 1999 | −34 | + | −7 | = | −41 | – | 22 | = | −19 |
| Computer Science | 2002 | −39 | + | −6 | = | −45 | – | 24 | = | −21 |
| | 1999 | −36 | + | −7 | = | −42 | – | 19 | = | −23 |
| Engineering | 2002 | −20 | + | −6 | = | −26 | – | 8 | = | −18 |
| | 1999 | −21 | + | −5 | = | −26 | – | 9 | = | −17 |
| Mechanical Engineering | 2002 | −21 | + | −7 | = | −28 | – | 4 | = | −24 |
| | 1999 | −25 | + | −6 | = | −31 | – | 10 | = | −21 |
| Electrical Engineering | 2002 | −32 | + | −8 | = | −40 | – | 11 | = | −29 |
| | 1999 | −20 | + | −4 | = | −24 | – | 8 | = | −16 |
| Civil Engineering | 2002 | −20 | + | −4 | = | −24 | – | 16 | = | −8 |
| | 1999 | −24 | + | −6 | = | −30 | – | 14 | = | −16 |
| Average of all subject groups | 2002 | −22 | + | −4 | = | −26 | – | 11 | = | −15 |
| | 1999 | −20 | + | −5 | = | −24 | – | 13 | = | −11 |

Source: Heublein et al. (2005): HIS-Studienabbruchuntersuchung 2004

the different subject groups. The basic quantity of new-style courses on offer is still very low, at only 16 per cent of all courses. The situation is considerably better in the area of post-graduate programmes, which incidentally are also highly attractive for universities. 63 per cent of these courses already lead to a Master's degree. Engineering subjects are among those where the educational reform towards Bachelor and Master's programmes is the most advanced. In most subjects, potential applicants are offered the alternative between the old and new degree courses. The number of students taking up a Bachelor course has risen markedly in the last few years, pointing to a strong increase in the acceptance of such courses, though their share in the total number of students entering higher education is still very low, at 8 per cent.

This growth comes primarily from two subject groups, Mathematics/Sciences – with Computer Science causing most of the growth – and Agricultural Science, Forestry and Nutritional science. The most important motive for not choosing to pursue a Bachelor course is the fact that applicants cannot estimate their employability and chances on the labour market.

**Table 5.** Capacity utilisation (as of 2002) universities/faculties (in per cent)

| Subject groups (excluding Medicine) | 1998 | 2000 | 2002 |
|---|---|---|---|
| Languages and Cultural Studies | 85 | 89 | 108 |
| Sport | 101 | 108 | 127 |
| Law, Economics and Social Sciences | 89 | 95 | 112 |
| Mathematics. Sciences | 61 | 69 | 91 |
| of which … | | | |
| *Computer Science* | *63* | *95* | *126* |
| *Physics. Astronomy* | *44* | *46* | *66* |
| *Chemistry* | *46* | *55* | *81* |
| Agricultural Science, Forestry, Nutritional Science | 75 | 84 | 78 |
| Engineering | 42 | 63 | 71 |
| of which … | | | |
| *Mechanical/Traffic Engineering* | *38* | *60* | *84* |
| *Electronic Engineering* | *30* | *44* | *53* |
| Art, Fine Arts | 82 | 99 | 106 |

Source: HIS-Ausstattungs-, Kosten- und Leistungsvergleiche (AKL) 1998, 2000 and 2002. Results for 2002 are provisional. Universities from the following states are included: Bremen, Hamburg, Mecklenburg-Vorpommern and Schleswig-Holstein; Berlin included from 2000 on

## Higher Education Graduates and the Entry into Employment

Because the new programmes of study naturally take time to complete, their graduates are still very modest in number, at 1.4 per cent of all graduates in 2003. A first study of graduates carried out by HIS (Higher Education Information System) shows a high transfer rate from Bachelor to Master's programmes (77 per cent for universities and 58 per cent for universities of applied sciences). For those who chose to enter employment after their first degree, statistics show a high success rate for transtion and integration into the labour market. As such, the very pessimistic scenarios that have all too often been painted in discussions about higher education, regarding the employment chances of Bachelor graduates compared to graduates from traditional programmes of study, have proved to be untrue, at least according to the first set of results. It should be noted, however, that information on the consequences of the reform for success and drop-out rates is not yet available at this early stage. Therefore it is not yet possible to judge the effectiveness of the reform, as compared to the high expectations it inspired.

Even though the number of graduates and their proportion in their age group rose for all types of degree in 2003 for the first time in many years (see Fig. 4), the development in the 'output' of graduates as a whole is clearly unsatisfactory. Even the very optimistic estimates of the German Standing Conference of the Ministers of Education and Cultural Affairs of the Länder (Kultusministerkonferenz – KMK) show that the number of graduates in engineering subjects will not regain its mid-1990s level even by 2010 (see Fig. 4).

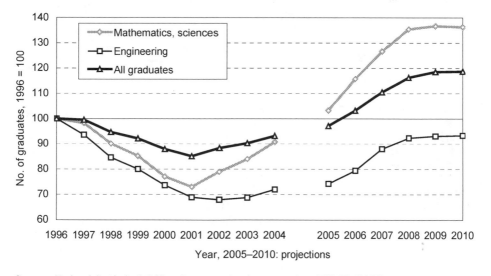

Source: Federal Statistical Office Germany (various years) and KMK (2003)

**Fig. 4.** Number of graduates – overall total and totals for selected courses of study 1996–2010; prognosis from 2005 onwards (index, with base year 1996 = 100)

The graduate quota in Germany is not only very low when compared internationally, but the gap to other OECD countries is even increasing. The proporation of engineers among all graduates has decreased sharply, from 25.7 per cent (1993) to 18.1 per cent (2003).

It is true that the proportion of science and engineering graduates out of all graduates (subject area quota) is lower still in many other countries. However, the low proportion of all graduates in the German population of the same age means that Germany ends up with a lower proportion of all young people qualified in the Sciences and Engineering than most other industrialised countries (see Table 6).

**Table 6.** Graduates in engineering and science subjects* per 100,000 persons in the labour force between the ages of 25 and 34 (1998 to 2001)

|           | 1998  | 1999  | 2000  | 2001  | 2002  |
|-----------|-------|-------|-------|-------|-------|
| AUS       | 1,262 | 1,303 | 1,253 | 1,365 | 1,659 |
| CAN       | 776   | 822   | 855   | n.a.  | n.a.  |
| FIN       | 1,266 | 1,363 | 1,579 | 1,540 | 1,785 |
| FRA       | 1,435 | 1,464 | 1,507 | 1,567 | 1,609 |
| GER       | 720   | 732   | 715   | 707   | 721   |
| ITA       | n.a.  | 629   | 633   | 663   | 676   |
| JPN       | 1,062 | 1,048 | 1,037 | 1,052 | 1,074 |
| NED       | 668   | 571   | 530   | 597   | 653   |
| ESP       | 833   | 919   | 885   | 970   | 935   |
| SWE       | 783   | 902   | 1,050 | 1,150 | 1,267 |
| GBR       | 1,309 | 1,353 | 1,401 | 1,666 | 1,727 |
| USA       | 850   | 878   | 877   | 901   | 928   |
| Average** | 962   | 961   | 965   | 1,020 | 1,053 |

\* Courses of study at ISCED levels 5A and 6: Biology (Life Sciences), Physics, Mathematics/
Statistics, Computer Science, Engineering, Civil Engineering
\** Average of the named countries, 1998 value without Italy, 2001 without Canada
Source: OECD Online Labour Database, OECD Education Online Database – calculations by
HIS

This picture will change slightly since the supply of graduates will increase in the next few years, as the increased number of students starting higher education work their way through the system. Yet it is exactly the two groups of subjects that are most important for the country's technical performance, Mathematics/Sciences and Engineering, that are underrepresented in the increased entry (with the exception of Computer Science). The 'dry spell' in the relationship between supply and demand for engineers in particular is likely to last for some years to come.

    The overall success of the transition process from higher education to employment for scientists and engineers, and their integration into their chosen profession, is a clear sign of a high demand in the relevant parts of the labour market for employees with suitable qualifications and competencies in these subjects. The number of engineering graduates going straight on to a regular job is very high. The figure is only lower for science graduates because of the high numbers going on to further study. The results of an HIS graduate study show that the employment situation for these graduates has clearly improved for those who graduated in 2001 compared to those who graduated in 1993. All of the indicators for employment and the particular job attained (e.g. unemployment, type of job, appropriateness of the position) point in the direction of a smoothly running process of finding and starting a job. Also worthy of note is the high, above average success of graduates of hybrid subjects in the workplace, at least when they start a new job. Such subjects, for example, combine technical and economic competence.

## Higher Education Expenditure and Funding

Higher education expenditure is often used as an indicator of the relevance a nation ascribes to its higher education establishments as institutions for the production and distribution of knowledge. It is a widely spread belief in Germany that the higher education system is underfunded and that government expenditure on higher education does not reflect the importance of higher education as a centre of competence in the emerging knowledge society. In any case, objective criteria for a reasonable level of finance for higher education have proved illusive. Establishing reference points by which to judge the level of funding for higher education can only be achieved by comparisions over time (for example, the development in higher education expenditure compared to the development in student numbers) or by the use of international benchmarks. Public and private spending on higher education as a proportion of GDP (on the basis of OECD data up to 2001) has not changed in Germany in recent years (see Table 7).

**Table 7.** Higher education expenditure* as a proportion of GDP (in per cent) for selected countries (1998–2001)

| Country | Year | | | |
|---|---|---|---|---|
|  | 1998 | 1999 | 2000 | 2001 |
| AUS | 1.4 | 1.3 | 1.4 | 1.4 |
| CAN | 1.3 | 1.4 | 1.4 | 1.5 |
| FIN | 1.5 | 1.7 | 1.7 | 1.7 |
| FRA | 0.9 | 0.9 | 0.9 | 0.8 |
| GER | 1.0 | 1.0 | 1.0 | 1.0 |
| ITA | 0.8 | 0.8 | 0.9 | 0.9 |
| JPN | 0.9 | 0.9 | 1.0 | 1.0 |
| NED | 1.2 | 1.3 | 1.2 | 1.3 |
| ESP[1] | 1.1 | 1.0 | 1.1 | 1.1 |
| SWE[2] | 1.7 | 1.7 | 1.7 | 1.7 |
| GBR[2] | 1.1 | 1.1 | 1.0 | 1.1 |
| USA[3] | 1.9 | 1.7 | 1.7 | 1.8 |
| Average[4] | 1.23 | 1.24 | 1.25 | 1.28 |
| Average[4] (without USA) | 1.17 | 1.19 | 1.21 | 1.23 |

\*   Higher education expenditure for 1998 include ISCED Levels 5A and 6, for subsequent years only ISCED Level 5A
[1]   The expenditure in 1998 includes ISCED Level 5B as well as 5A and 6
[2]   Expenditure include ISCED Level 5B as well as ISCED Levels 5A and 6
[3]   OECD data for the USA originally included post-secondary non-tertiary education, as well as ISCED Levels 5A, 5B and 6
[4]   Unweighted mean for the countries listed
Source: OECD (ed.) (2004d: Table B.2.1c)

The proportion for Germany is well below the average that other countries, such as the USA, Canada, Australia and the Scandinavian countries, spend on higher education. However, it is about the same level as can be found in other highly populated industrialised countries. However, in none of the countries observed here, is the proportion of private households' budgets spent on higher education (excluding living costs) lower than in Germany (see Table 8).

**Table 8.** Public and private expenditure on higher education as a proportion of GDP (in per cent) for selected countries 1998–2001

| Country | 1998 Public | 1998 Private[1] | 1999 Public | 1999 Private[1] | 2000 Public | 2000 Private[1] | 2001 Public | 2001 Private[1] |
|---|---|---|---|---|---|---|---|---|
| AUS | 1.1 | 0.5 | 0.8 | 0.7 | 0.8 | 0.7 | 0.8 | 0.7 |
| CAN | 1.5 | 0.3 | 1.6 | 1.0 | 1.6 | 1.0 | 1.5 | 1.0 |
| FIN | 1.7 | n.a. | 1.8 | n.a. | 1.7 | n.a. | 1.7 | n.a. |
| FRA | 1.0 | 0.1 | 1.0 | 0.1 | 1.0 | 0.1 | 1.0 | 0.1 |
| GER | 1.0 | 0.1 | 1.0 | 0.1 | 1.0 | 0.1 | 1.0 | 0.1 |
| ITA | 0.7 | 0.2 | 0.7 | 0.1 | 0.7 | 0.1 | 0.8 | 0.2 |
| JPN | 0.4 | 0.6 | 0.5 | 0.6 | 0.5 | 0.6 | 0.5 | 0.6 |
| NED | 1.2 | 0.0 | 1.0 | 0.3 | 1.0 | 0.2 | 1.0 | 0.3 |
| ESP | 0.8 | 0.3 | 0.9 | 0.3 | 0.9 | 0.3 | 1.0 | 0.3 |
| SWE | 1.5 | 0.2 | 1.5 | 0.2 | 1.5 | 0.2 | 1.5 | 0.2 |
| GBR | 0.8 | 0.3 | 0.8 | 0.3 | 0.7 | 0.3 | 0.8 | 0.3 |
| USA[2] | 1.1 | 1.2 | 1.1 | 1.2 | 0.9 | 1.8 | 0.9 | 1.8 |
| Average[3] | 1.1 | 0.3 | 1.0 | 0.3 | 1.0 | 0.3 | 1.0 | 0.5 |

[1]   Net value: i.e. less public subsidies received by educational establishments
[2]   Figures for post-secondary non-tertiary education included in tertiary
[3]   Average according to OECD data
Source: OECD (ed.) (2004d: Table B.2.1c)

Through the use of other indicators, which relate higher education expenditure to the number of students starting a course, currently studying and graduating, the following picture emerges: expenditure on higher education in Germany did indeed increase slightly up to the year 2000, but this was primarily due to the decline in student numbers. When the number of students and the economic potential (GDP) per head of population are brought into consideration, then it is still true to say that Germany invests less – in some cases far less – than the USA, Canada, Australia and Sweden, but invests roughly the average for an OECD country. The indicator 'higher education expenditure per new entrant' in Germany even turns out to be more postive than for all other countries except the USA, which is far ahead. This figure is, however, decreasing for Germany as a consequence of the increasing number of entry level students. On the other hand, the indicators 'expenditure per graduate' and 'expenditure per course of study', which take into account the average length of a course, do not give such a positive account of Germany. They reveal that Germany spends the second-most per graduate, after the USA, and the highest amount per course of study (the USA being excluded in this criterion). An explanation for these findings lies with the high dropout rates and long courses that characterise higher education in Germany.

There is no single clear interpretation of these findings. On the one hand, international comparison shows that Germany invests relatively large amounts of resources in higher education. At the same time, the higher education entry rate is relatively low. Countries with higher entry rates spend greater amounts of money on their higher education system. The only conclusion is that the political target of increasing participation in higher education in Germany will require additional funds to be made available in considerable quantity if the increase is to be realised without a reduction in quality. On the other hand, certain indicators – such as the high cost per student and per course of study – show that the German higher education system has a great deal of unused potential. However, it is impossible to make a clear statement in this case, since the high costs could also have been caused by other factors, such as a larger share of higher education funding going into research in Germany than is the international norm, or a higher quality of education. Owing to the limitations of the data available, it is impossible to test for these factors.

## Conclusions

Based on the findings presented in this report, four conclusions may be drawn:
- First, the demand for higher education in Germany is too low to meet the requirements of a knowledge-based economy. The key to this issue is the educational potential of the lower tiers of society, which is currently scarcely used.
- Secondly, it is of particular importance to increase interest in studying in the fields of Science and Engineering, which are of great importance to Germany's technological preformance. It will fall to young women to play a key role in achieving this.
- Thirdly, increasing the demand for higher education alone will not be enough to increase the supply of graduates. Clear improvements in the effectiveness of the higher education on offer in Germany are also needed.
- Fourthly, it must be assumed that to expand higher education while maintaining a high level of course quality, or even improving quality, will not be possible without further financial investment, whatever the sources of this may be.

In the future, particular attention will have to be paid to the consequences of demographic change – i.e. the decline in births and an ageing working population – for higher education establishments, further education and the labour market. These processes could permanently alter the function of higher education within society in the course of an enduring socio-economic shift towards knowledge-intensive products and services and higher pressure for innovation.

It takes a long time for an education system to react to changes and reforms. For this reason it is important to start the necessary reforms soon. Important starting points for reform are:
- The school system should be conceived in such a way that high quality in school education is attained mainly by effectively encouraging and supporting individual pupils, so that selection and elimination play a less important role.

- The flexibility of the school system in permitting pupil mobility must be clearly increased, to allow 'late developers' the chance to attain school-leaving qualifications, or another form of certificate that would permit entry into higher education.
- All organisational measures for schools that have been proven in an international context should be examined to see if they could help with the targets mentioned in the above points. Examples of such measures include: compulsory preschool *education* (not preschool care) with suitably qualified staff; a clear rise in the number of teaching hours over a pupil's entire school career (all day *school,* not all day supervision); clear and common standards of attainment (for example, through central examinations or making schools' budgets dependent on their performance); meaningful further training programmes for working teachers that would offer them the opportunity to incorporate new subject-specific and social developments into their teaching; or the introduction of additional school subjects (to allow, for example, for the addition of a 'technology' subject, which would act as a precursor while in school for the study of an engineering subject when in higher education).
- As the above-mentioned reforms can only affect the number of students in the long term, short-term possibilities to increase the number of students should be considered. One such possibility would be to open up higher education to persons who have completed vocational training or similar but who have not attained the German 'Abitur' or 'Fachhochschulreife' examinations. Instead, aptitude or acceptance examinations could be used. Included in this measure could be the acceptance of the 'Fachhochschulreife' exam for university entrance.
- The restructuring of higher education through the introduction of Bachelor and Master's courses, which has already begun, should be carried forward swiftly and consistently. The option of being able to leave higher education with a qualification after three or four years changes the basis of an individual's 'human capital investment decision' considerably. In the past, opting for higher education meant either a qualification or nothing at all at the end of four to six years. Those less willing to take risks, especially when the decision had to be reached amidst high uncertainty, would tend, in great numbers, to choose the 'no higher education' option. This calculation has been changed dramatically by the restructuring.
- It is necessary to promote technically relevant courses of study in a targeted manner, in order to raise the number of students in these subjects by a considerable number. At present, numbers for these subjects are trailing behind the overall upwards trend. To achieve this increase, economic incentives should be considered, such as increased grants or a reduction in the proportion of a grant that has to be paid back after graduation, or, in case they are introduced, reduced tuition fees.
- The task of further academic education should be placed firmly in the hands of the education system. German higher education establishments have up to now shown little activity in this area, as international comparison shows. Firms should call upon their long-standing employees to make appropriate efforts to participate in further education (supporting them if necessary), instead of relying on hiring and firing to update their stock of qualifications.

Even when such efforts are quickly and effectively implemented by the relevant policy-makers, there are many areas where a shortage of qualified staff, which would limit the possibilities for economic development, can only be avoided by companies competing internationally for academically qualified personnel. Politicians should improve and extend the possibilities of doing so. Any worsening of German firms' positions in the international race for innovation caused by the fact that qualified staff available internationally could not be recruited for political reasons, can only mean bad news for Germany as a whole.

# 5.4 Germany's Education System in an International Perspective – An Analysis in Relation to Innovation

Dieter Dohmen

**Abstract.** The paper investigates the performance of the German education system by referring to output qualification levels and international comparative studies, such as the Third International Math and Science Study (TIMSS) and the Programme for International Student Assessment (PISA), as well as the OECD's 'Education at a Glance' which presents an important sample of internationally comparable input indicators. In addition, it presents some data on the development of some core age cohorts of the labour force and analyses some data on the private and social returns to education and their relation to innovation. Finally, it provides a different approach to calculating the overall expenditure for education in Germany at the macro level and its distribution between public and private sources.

## Introduction

The first international comparison of students' performance was conducted in the early 1960s. However, apart from the first round in Maths and Science, respectively, Germany did not participate in such studies until the early 1990s. At the same time, roughly 15 years ago, the OECD started to establish its studies on educational indicators, now called 'Education at a Glance', where Germany participated from the early beginnings. Such time series on performance and education input should theoretically allow us to investigate how input indicators and the performance of German students developed over time.

However, it should be noted that this is more wishful thinking than practical, for several reasons. Firstly, the first studies were marred by several methodological problems and, although state-of-the-art at that time, not comparable to today's studies, which themselves are often criticised. Some critical issues will be touched later on. Secondly, these 'benchmark studies' often provide a picture that may be misleading if differences at the system level are not taken into consideration adequately. For example, while a dual vocational education and training system is unknown in many OECD countries, apart from Germany, Austria and Switzerland, its existence may result in different public and private spending patterns for these countries. For example, since dual training systems are linked to a 'training salary' for the trainees, an opportunity cost is incurred for students who intend to remain enrolled in general education schools and their parents. This, in consequence, may finally affect (and possibly explain the comparatively low) participation rates in Germany's higher education system (for more detail see Chapter 5.3).

Thirdly, different modes of financial involvement affect the overall level and, thus, the indicators. For example, some countries, in particular the Scandinavian ones

*U. Schmoch, C. Rammer and H. Legler (eds.), National Systems of Innovation in Comparison, 245–262.*

support students independent of parental income by a mixture of grants and loans, while other countries, as for example Germany and many Mediterranean countries expect a parental contribution, which is partially 'reimbursed' via the tax system and/ or childcare benefits.[1] Since tax exemptions are not included in the official expenditure statistics, those countries which incorporate part of their public subsidies to education in income taxation spend less for education than other countries. In addition, it might also affect the distribution between funding sources.[2] Similar problems arise with respect to tuition fees and student support schemes, where grants and loans are provided in different ratios and under diverging conditions etc.[3] These comments are not intended to criticise the OECD's methodology, but request some caution concerning the interpretation of 'benchmarks'.

In the next section, this paper shortly investigates the development of qualification levels among the highly industrialised OECD countries which are considered a better 'benchmark' for an assessment of the status of Germany's education system than the OECD average, which also includes some less advanced countries. Section 3 investigates how the performance of German students has evolved over time on the output and the input side (Section 4), taking into consideration such systemic differences. Section 5 provides an extended approach on the public and private net expenditures for education that intends to calculate the marginal (opportunity) expenditure of the government, companies, and parents and students. The final section refers to the private and social returns to education and their relation to innovation before the results are summarised and some conclusions are drawn.

## Development of Qualifications – Some Indicators

It seems useful to provide a few indicators on the development of qualification levels over the last decade first, since there are important and interesting differences between Germany and other industrialised countries.

Figure 1 reveals that nearly all industrialised countries have greatly increased the share of university graduates within an age cohort over the last decades; some have more than doubled their share. In contrast, Germany's (and Austria's) increase is very modest. Furthermore, while the share of university graduates of the 55 to 64 year olds was above the average of the OECD countries, though slightly below that of the highly developed countries, it is now slightly more than half of the latters' average and

---

[1] Germany has a long tradition in lawsuits involving the constitutional court on how tax deductions for child care are to be considered and which minimum amount would be required to respond to the constitution (for an overview in relation to the financing of education, see e.g. Dohmen 1999).

[2] Although the OECD has adapted its methodology to respond to such differences, it is probably impossible to account for all of them. Thus, it can be expected that differences remain which are not accounted for.

[3] Not accounting for such differences, in fact, favors countries with interest-bearing loans since their final public spending is lower than presented and thus over-estimated in relation to that of countries which support their students by grants. In this case, the ratio between public and private is different from that presented.

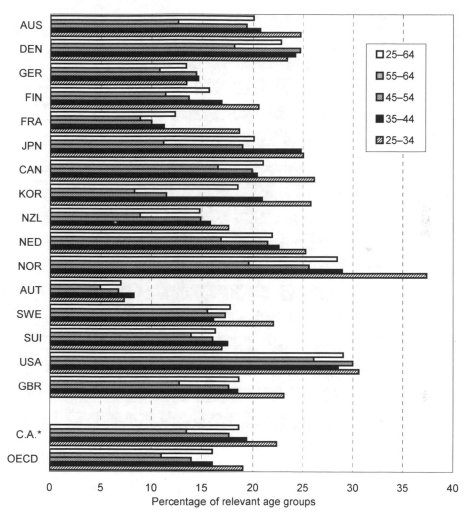

\*  Country average

**Fig. 1.** Development of university graduates in relation to the relevant age cohorts

one-third less than the OECD average. While Germany stood still, the other countries have rapidly increased the share of highly qualified younger people; important is also the indication that the share of the youngest cohort is even decreasing.

That this picture is not only valid for university graduates, but for the whole generation becomes evident when looking at Fig. 2 which compares the level of qualification of the 25 to 64 year old generation with that of the 25 to 34 year olds who form the youngest age cohort that has almost completely passed through the education system.[4]

---

[4]  However, it should be noted that some countries, among them Germany and Denmark, for example, have a particularly extensive length of studying which may distort the picture to

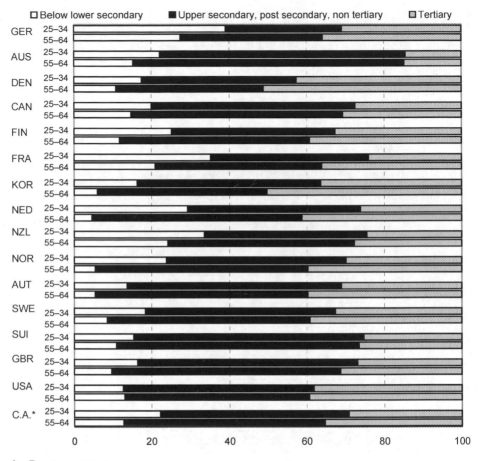

* Country average

**Fig. 2.** Education level of the 25–34 and 55–64 year old population in comparison (2002)

The share of higher education graduates of Germany's youngest cohort is even slightly less than that of the whole labour market cohort. Furthermore, the increase in the share of secondary graduates is also relatively modest (+3 percentage points), compared to other countries. Complementarily, the share of low or unqualified people is also slightly decreasing.

This, in fact, means that the level of highly qualified people in Germany is the lowest of all but one (Austria) of the highly developed countries. The opposite is valid for people with middle level qualifications where only Austria has a higher share than Germany, while Switzerland has the same share as Germany. However, since the share of higher education graduates is higher in Switzerland, its share of lowly qualified people is less than for Germany, whose share is similar to Austria, whose improvement, in fact, is much more dynamic than Germany's.

---

some extent. Yet Germany would have to increase its share by far to arrive at an internationally comparable level.

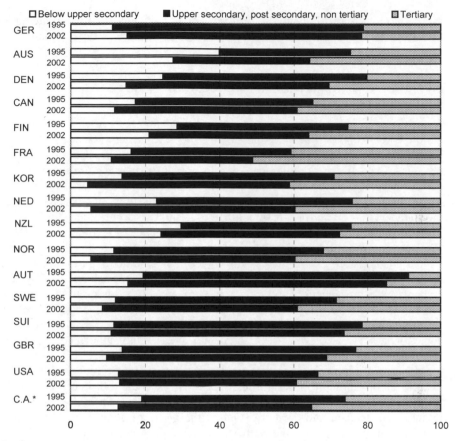

* Country average

**Fig. 3.** Development of education levels of the 25–34 year old population 1995 and 2002 in comparison

Due to the dynamics in other countries which have increased their qualification level by far, the share of unqualified people in Germany is now slightly above the average of highly developed countries, while it is clearly below average for the whole working force. Thus, again, all other countries show a much faster skill upgrading and, thus, Germany is losing ground in the qualification of the labour force. It seems highly realistic that this is one important factor that hampers economic development. However, the picture is even more dramatic, when comparing the qualification levels of the 25 to 34 year olds in 1995 and 2002 (see Fig. 3).

In all countries the increase in higher education graduates is stronger than in Germany (see also Chapter 5.3). On the other hand, Germany is the only country which has increased its share of lowly qualified people among the youngest labour market cohort. Since most countries reveal either an increase in higher and secondary graduates or the increase in tertiary graduates over-compensates decreasing secondary graduates' rates, it follows that Germany is the only country whose qualification level of the 25 to 34 years olds has decreased between 1995 and 2002.

The next section will review the performance of Germany's pupils in international student performance tests and reveal that the emerging picture is very similar.

## German Students in International Comparisons

Approximately 40 years ago, Germany participated in the so-called 'First International Mathematics Study', followed by the science study in 1970. Although German students performed relatively well to some extent, these studies should not be over-valued for methodological reasons. An important feature concerning the performance of *German* students is that only students from the two states of Hesse and Schleswig-Holstein participated, leaving the question unanswered, whether their students are better or worse compared to students from other German states. Thus it is neither possible to assess the final performance of German students in the 1960s nor to answer the question, whether they performed better than today's students.

It was not before the early 1990s that Germany's students participated in such comparisons again. IAEP II investigated the reading performance of 14-year old students, who are generally in grade 8 in Germany but in grade 9 and sometimes even in grade 10 in many other countries. Furthermore, the average age of participating students per country differed. Both issues may have affected the outcomes of the study. However, German students scored slightly, though not significantly, below average.

Although students from eastern Germany scored slightly higher than students from western Germany, no significant differences could be identified. Students from Finland, France, Sweden and New Zealand scored much higher, followed by Switzerland, Iceland and the USA. Out of the group of economically advantaged countries, only Norway and the Netherlands scored below average.

Furthermore, some systematic differences could be identified between eastern and western Germany at that time. While inter-school differences were relatively small in eastern Germany (10 per cent), intra-school differences, i.e. differences in the performance of students of the same school, were larger (90 per cent). The opposite applied to western Germany, where students within one school were by far more homogeneous than between schools, which is no surprise considering that the western school system sorted students according to performance, while the eastern did not. However, this study did not receive much public attention, in contrast to the 'Third International Mathematics and Science Study' (TIMSS) and particularly PISA some years later.

In TIMMS, more than one million students in grade 7 and 8 in 38 countries participated. While Germany's seventh graders performed below average (484 points), the eighth graders scored 509 points, which is only seemingly, but not significantly, above the average of 500 points. In Science, both seventh and eighth graders scored significantly above average. Out of the group of highly industrialised countries, Germany belongs to the low performers; in this group of countries, only students from Norway, Denmark and France scored worse in some points.

The PISA study, conducted in the year 2000, targeted 15-year old students. However, even this approach resulted in differences between countries, since in many countries these students are at least one grade higher than in Germany, where school enrolment starts often only at the age of seven while most other countries start at the age of six and sometimes even younger. Another issue is class repetition, which is unknown in many other countries. Thus, there may be some critical issues regarding methodology, however, this does not really affect the outcome of this study.

German students performed below average in all three subjects, Reading, Maths and Science. It turns out that from the group of highly developed countries, only the US students scored comparably weaker than German students, while Swiss students did in two subjects and the Norwegians and Belgians in one. In contrast, only students from less developed countries scored lower than German students, except Luxemburg.

Comparing TIMSS and PISA, some indications point to an improved performance in a number of countries, while the performance of German students remained more or less unchanged. However, due to methodological reasons, such as a different selection of countries etc., such a conclusion cannot be drawn without caution.

Combining the previous sections, the emerging picture seems not very promising concerning Germany's future. The qualification level of the working force is clearly below the average of highly developed countries and the performance of its students is average, at best. This picture remains even if the slight improvement in the latest PISA study is taken into account. Thus, the question remains whether the slight improvement between PISA 2000 and 2003 will continue in the future.

However, the major question, to what extent this will affect economic performance and the German innovation system in the future cannot be answered yet. But if there is a link between quality of education and economic development, as many studies suggest (see e.g. Gundlach & Wößmann 2003), the expectation is not very promising.

The next sections will turn to an analysis of input indicators.

## Benchmarking Germany's Educational Inputs

It is common practice to compare the macro-economic spending for education by relating the expenditures to Gross Domestic Product (GDP). Although this is not without some distorting effects, we will follow this approach and combine it with the development of public and private spending figures over the last decade.

Again, among the highly developed countries Germany reveals one of the lowest spending levels; only Japan's overall spending is less than Germany's. In both countries, public spending is clearly below the averages, whether that of the OECD countries or of the highly developed countries. In contrast, private spending in both countries is slightly above both averages.

However, structural differences in private contributions should be taken into account. While private spending for 'traditional' education in other countries usually comes from parents and students themselves, it should be noted that private spending in Germany includes contributions from companies for dual VET and from child-care providers. While companies contribute by far the biggest share in VET, the parents' share in pre-primary education is approximately two-thirds, while providers bear the remaining one-third (Dohmen & Hoi 2004).

**Table 1.** Public and private expenditure for education in relation to GDP 1995–2001

|  | 1990 | | | 1995 | | | 2001 | | |
|---|---|---|---|---|---|---|---|---|---|
|  | Public | Private | Total | Public | Private | Total | Public | Private | Total |
| AUS | 4.2 | 0.8 | 5.0 | 4.5 | 1.2 | 5.7 | 4.5 | 1.4 | 6.0 |
| DEN | – | – | – | 6.1 | 0.2 | 6.3 | 6.8 | 0.3 | 7.1 |
| GER | – | – | – | 4.5 | 1.0 | 5.5 | 4.3 | 1.0 | 5.3 |
| FIN | – | – | – | 6.2 | – | 6.3 | 5.7 | 0.1 | 5.8 |
| FRA | 5.1 | 0.5 | 5.7 | 5.9 | 0.4 | 6.3 | 5.6 | 0.4 | 6.0 |
| JPN | – | – | – | 3.5 | 1.1 | 4.6 | 3.5 | 1.2 | 4.6 |
| CAN | – | – | – | 6.2 | 0.8 | 7.0 | 4.9 | 1.3 | 6.1 |
| KOR | – | – | – | – | – | – | 4.8 | 3.4 | 8.2 |
| NZL | – | – | – | 4.8 | – | – | 5.5 | – | – |
| NED | – | – | – | 4.5 | 0.4 | 4.9 | 4.5 | 0.4 | 4.9 |
| NOR | 8.1 | – | – | 6.8 | 0.4 | 7.1 | 6.1 | 0.2 | 6.4 |
| AUT | – | – | – | 5.9 | 0.3 | 6.2 | 5.6 | 0.2 | 5.8 |
| SWE | 5.1 | – | 5.1 | 6.1 | 0.1 | 6.2 | 6.3 | 0.2 | 6.5 |
| SUI | – | – | – | 5.4 | – | – | 5.4 | – | – |
| USA | 4.9 | 2.2 | 7.1 | 5.0 | 2.2 | 7.2 | 5.1 | 2.3 | 7.3 |
| GBR | 4.2 | 0.1 | 4.3 | 4.8 | 0.7 | 5.5 | 4.7 | 0.8 | 5.5 |
| C.A.* (reference countries) | – | | – | – | – | – | 5.2 | 0.9 | 6.1 |
| C.A.* (OECD countries) | – | | – | – | – | – | 5.0 | 0.7 | 5.6 |
| OECD | – | – | – | – | – | – | 4.8 | 1.4 | 6.2 |
| C.A.** | 4.9 | 0.7 | 5.5 | 4.3 | 0.7 | 5.6 | 4.9 | 0.7 | 5.6 |

\* Country average
\*\* Country average for countries with data for 1990, 1995 and 2002
'Public' includes public subsidies to private households attributable for educational institutions from international sources, 'private' without public subsidies attributable for educational institutions

When looking at the development over time it appears that some countries have increased their spending levels for education in relation to GDP, while others, including Germany, Finland, Canada, and Norway have reduced particularly public spending. However, it should be noted that in some cases the reduction may be due to stronger increases in GDP than reduced spending levels.

However, as already mentioned, the mere consideration of macro spending levels may be distorted, e.g. for demographic reasons.[5] Therefore, it seems useful to have a look at the spending levels per student in relation to GDP per capita.

---

[5] For example, it seems plausible to expect that countries with a higher share of students will spend more than countries with a lower share.

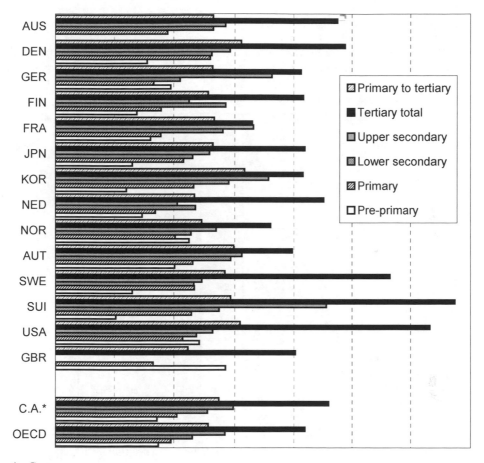

*   Country average

**Fig. 4.** Expenditure per participant in relation to GDP per capita

And, in fact, Fig. 4 and Table 2 reveal a different picture, at least to some extent. While spending levels in Germany remain below average for primary education, it is above average in elementary education – although only due to comparatively high private spending levels – and, though only slightly, in tertiary A levels, i.e. for higher education programmes of more than three years' duration. However, higher education spending clearly falls below average when the high share for research and development (approximately 40 per cent in Germany) is excluded.

In this case, expenditure per student decreases to 25 per cent of per capita GDP instead of 41 per cent, and, thus, below the average ratio of 32 and 34 per cent, respectively.

In contrast, Germany's spending for upper secondary education is clearly above average, partially due to high private spending levels for dual VET, as already mentioned. When considering the education sector from primary to tertiary education, the German spending level is average, though only if spending for R&D at universities is incorporated. Otherwise, when eliminating R&D expenses, as seems appropriate from our point of view, it falls to around five percentage points below the international average.

Finally, when comparing Germany to the most advanced countries it turns out that most of them invest far more in primary and secondary education than Germany.

**Table 2.** Educational expenditures per student in relation to per-capita GDP

| | Elementary (3 years and older) | Primary | Secondary | | | Post secondary, non tertiary | Tertiary (incl. R&D activities) | | | Tertiary total excl. R&D activities | Primary to tertiary |
| | | | Lower secondary | Upper secondary | Secondary total | | Tertiary total | Tertiary B | Tertiary A & research programmes | | |
| | (1) | (2) | (3) | (4) | (5) | (6) | (7) | (8) | (9) | (10) | (11) |
|---|---|---|---|---|---|---|---|---|---|---|---|
| AUS | m | 19 | 26 | 28 | 27 | 23 | 48 | 29 | 51 | 34 | 26 |
| DEN | 16 | 26 | 26 | 29 | 28 | x(4,7) | 49 | x(7) | x(7) | 37 | 31 |
| GER | 19 | 17 | 21 | 36 | 26 | 37 | 41 | 22 | 44 | 25 | 26 |
| FIN | 14 | 18 | 28 | 23 | 25 | x(5) | 42 | 16 | 42 | 27 | 26 |
| FRA | 16 | 18 | 28 | 33 | 30 | 24 | 33 | 35 | 32 | 26 | 27 |
| JPN | 13 | 22 | 23 | 26 | 25 | x(4,7) | 42 | 33 | 43 | m | 26 |
| KOR | 12 | 23 | 29 | 36 | 32 | – | 42 | 27 | 52 | m | 32 |
| NED | 15 | 17 | 24 | 21 | 22 | 19 | 45 | 26 | 45 | 28 | 23 |
| NOR | 23 | 20 | 23 | 27 | 25 | x(5) | 36 | x(7) | x(7) | m | 25 |
| AUT | 20 | 23 | 29 | 31 | 30 | 29 | 40 | x(7) | x(7) | 26 | 30 |
| SWE | 13 | 23 | 23 | 25 | 24 | 14 | 56 | x(7) | x(7) | 31 | 28 |
| SUI** | 10 | 23 | 27 | 46 | 36 | 20 | 67 | 23 | 73 | m | 29 |
| USA*** | 24 | 21 | 24 | 26 | 25 | x(7) | 63 | x(7) | x(7) | 57 | 31 |
| GBR | 28 | 17 | x(5) | x(5) | 22 | x(5) | 40 | x(7) | x(7) | 30 | 22 |
| C.A.* | 17 | 20 | 26 | 30 | 27 | 24 | 46 | 26 | 48 | 32 | 27 |
| OECD | 17 | 20 | 23 | 28 | 26 | 16 | 42 | 28 | 43 | 34 | 26 |

x    Means that the data are included in another column (reference column in brackets)
m    Missing data
*    Country average: mean of countries listed above
**    Public institutions only
***    Public and independent private institutions only

Although expenditure per student increased between 1995 and 2001, the distance to other OECD countries has increased too, as all but Sweden and Norway increased their expenditures even more. This development becomes even clearer when looking at the relationship between educational expenditures and GDP per capita. In this case, it turns out that Germany belongs to those countries that decreased their spending in relation to their economic development, along with Finland, Sweden and the United Kingdom. Thus, if Germany wants to keep up with other countries it will have to increase its financial (and qualitative) effort.

Looking, finally, at the changes in educational spending for general and tertiary education between 1995 and 2002, it becomes evident that the increase in spending is very modest in Germany; only Sweden reveals the same picture and Norway even reduced its expenditures per student. From a German perspective, it seems worth mentioning the high share of private spending for dual VET which increases the overall spending levels to some extent.

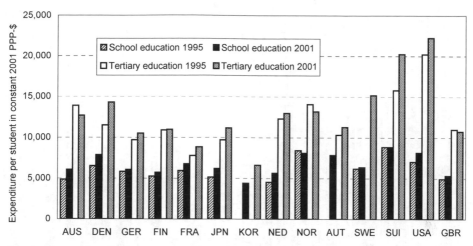

**Fig. 5.** Changes in spending per student between 1995 and 2001

In contrast, the increase in spending for tertiary education is somewhat bigger, though not comparable to Switzerland, Denmark and the USA. On the other hand, several countries, such as Australia, Norway and the United Kingdom reveal decreased spending levels.

Furthermore, when comparing changes in per-student expenditures for education in relation to GDP per capita, it turns out that Germany, Finland, Sweden and the United Kingdom belong to those countries which reduced their spending levels in general and higher education in relation to their economic performance. In contrast to Germany, in general education this is mainly due to increased GDP per capita and less to reduced spending levels. This is also different from the higher education sector where Germany increased its spending level while the other countries reduced it.

If we finally take a look at the nominal spending levels, educational expenditure in Germany is above average in pre-primary education ($5,000 in 2001), though only due to a very high share of private spending (38 per cent), financed by parents and providers.[6] In primary and lower secondary education, Germany's spending is below OECD average while it is above average in upper secondary education, again due to relatively high private spending in dual VET, which is company-financed to a large extent. Spending for higher education is average. Thus, in those education sectors where expenditure per student is above OECD average, this is only due to private spending by parents, providers or companies. Public financing is usually below OECD averages and particularly below the average spending figures of the highly developed countries, which form the more appropriate 'benchmarking' group. Even the modest increases in recent years cannot change this picture really.

Furthermore, it seems worth commenting on the financial situation in higher education, where annual expenditure per full-time student ($10,500) is close to the OECD average, while expenditure per graduate is among the highest ($73,500), topped only by Switzerland ($118,950) whose annual spending per student is $20,000

---

[6] The distribution of private funding between parents and providers is unknown. A rough estimate arrives at approximately two-third to one-third.

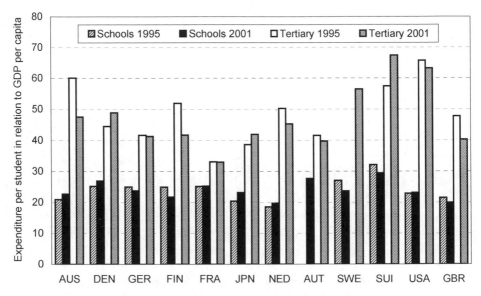

**Fig. 6.** Expenditure per student in relation to GDP per capita 1995 and 2001

and, thus, roughly twice as high as the German figure. This highlights the exceedingly long duration of studying in Germany, and indicates the inefficiency of the higher education system, wastage of time and private and public (opportunity) costs. Furthermore, dropout rates are at about 25 per cent.[7]

In the school system, the picture seems even worse for Student–Staff Ratio (SSR) and class size, due to relatively high teacher salaries. In pre-primary education, Germany's SSR is the highest of all countries, apart from the United Kingdom, while it is only slightly higher than the OECD average from primary to upper secondary education. In contrast, SSR is among the lowest (12.1) in longer lasting higher education programmes (*Fachhochschulen* and universities), which is surprising given the common complaints that SSR is said to be too high in Germany. Furthermore, it should be noted that the 'real' relationship might be even better, since every university student is counted as full-time equivalent, although, in fact, many students study part-time (see footnote 8). Thus, SSR in German universities is even smaller than presented in the OECD statistics, in contrast to many, though by far not all other OECD countries.

---

[7] A difficulty in assessing the 'final' expenditure per student in Germany, and probably in other countries as well, arises by calculating the number of full-time equivalent student numbers, which is impossible to identify since such a distinction neither exist statistically nor formally. Thus, all students in Germany are counted as full-time equivalents, while many (probably most) are studying part-time. A more realistic figure would arrive at expenditure per student that is 50 per cent to nearly 100 per cent higher than presented, which in turn would mean that Germany's expenditure is among the highest in the world. Consequently, expenditure per graduate would be even higher. Furthermore, expenditure per student in higher education is possibly also distorted by different ratios that are spent for R&D, which is according to OECD figures, for example, relatively high in Germany and (surprisingly) low in the United States.

An interesting feature with respect to innovation is the number of contact hours in Maths, Technical Studies and Science. Here, the picture for 12 to 14 year old pupils changes to some extent, depending on the group of countries considered. For example, the number of hours in technical studies in Germany (33) is OECD average (31) but far below the average of highly industrialised countries (59). Furthermore, the number of science hours (91) is below the average of the OECD (110) and highly industrialised countries (101); physics hours are in between. Looking at the relative figures, the share of maths and physics hours in relation to total number of contact hours is beyond country average and in technical studies as well as in science below it. In combination with other issues, as for example, the fact that these lessons are often perceived as uninteresting and demotivating by pupils, this may explain to some extent why German students scored unsatisfactorily in TIMSS and PISA.

## Public and Private Spending for Education – An Extended Approach

In another study, Dohmen and Hoi (2004) intended to gain a deeper insight into public and private spending for education and its net distribution between the stakeholders. In addition to the calculations of the Federal Office of Statistics (FOS), which refer to direct public and private expenditure, we included also those disbursements that are spent indirectly, e.g. as tax exemptions and reimbursements, or are considered an 'opportunity expense' from the payer's perspective. For example, while tuition fee is a direct expense from the student's perspective, maintenance and accommodation is not, since they occur in any case, i.e. whether studying or working. This is distinct from the financier's perspective. If parents have to finance their child's maintenance while studying they incur an opportunity cost, since this amount of money is not available for their own consumption, nor would they have to finance it if their child did not study, but earns its own income. The idea of this approach is to identify the marginal private and public contribution for education, whether direct or indirect. Inevitably, these result in different figures compared to FOS data. However, this extended approach might allow us to understand the decision-making process within families (see also Dohmen 1999).

The first finding is that total expenditure for education is higher than presented in official statistics, which was to be expected. While the FOS figure amounts to €128.5 billion, our figure arrives at €167.2 billion; an increase of 30 per cent. The second effect refers to the distribution between public and private sources. While the FOS reports a share of 74 per cent public spending and 26 per cent private, our calculation changes the distribution to 66 respectively 34 per cent. Thirdly, we calculate that private households (parents, students), spent 20 per cent, companies 13 per cent and child-care providers 1 per cent. Finally, according to our calculations, process-related spending is €122 billion, while €45 billion is spent additionally, e.g. for travel, maintenance, accommodation etc.[8] Table 3 reveals the overall picture.

---

[8] The FOS does not report any figure for private indirect expenditures for education, although it includes public spending for student support, which is mainly for indirect purposes. According to our estimates, this refers to €6.6 billion or about 5 per cent.

**Table 3.** Total public and private spending for education in Germany

| Education sector | Total | Public | | Total | | Companies/private non-profit organisations | | Private households | | Expenditure | Share of public spending |
|---|---|---|---|---|---|---|---|---|---|---|---|
| | | | | | | | | | | Official budget for education | |
| | Bn € | Bn € | % | Bn € | % | Bn € | % | Bn € | % | Bn € | % |
| *Educational process* | | | | | | | | | | | |
| Pre-primary education | 11.3 | 7.1 | 63% | 4.2 | 37% | 1.8 | 16% | 2.4 | 21% | 11.3 | 63% |
| Primary and secondary education | 48.9 | 45.3 | 93% | 3.6 | 7% | 0.0 | 0% | 3.6 | 7% | 46.3 | 98% |
| Vocational education and training | 24.7 | 14.6 | 59% | 10.1 | 41% | 9.0 | 36% | 1.1 | 4% | 23.2 | 42% |
| Higher education | 12.8 | 10.9 | 85% | 1.9 | 15% | 0.0 | 0% | 1.9 | 15% | 11.5 | 95% |
| Further and adult education | 21.2 | 9.8 | 46% | 11.4 | 54% | 5.5 | 26% | 5.9 | 28% | 9.3 | 2% |
| Others | 3.0 | 3.0 | 100% | 0.0 | 0% | 0.0 | 0% | 0.0 | 0% | 9.6 | 97% |
| Total | 122 | 90.7 | 74% | 31.2 | 26% | 16.3 | 13% | 14.9 | 12% | 115,8[1] | 73% |
| *Accomodation and maintenance etc.* | | | | | | | | | | | |
| Pre-primary education | 0 | 0.0 | 0% | 0.0 | 0% | 0.0 | 0% | 0.0 | 0% | | |
| Primary and secondary education | 8.5 | 1.9 | 22% | 6.6 | 78% | 0.0 | 0% | 6.6 | 78% | 2.1 | 100% |
| Vocational education and training | 4 | 3.9 | 98% | 0.1 | 3% | 0.0 | 0% | 0.1 | 3% | 2.3 | 44% |
| Higher education | 15.6 | 3.5 | 22% | 12.1 | 78% | 0.0 | 0% | 12.1 | 78% | 5.2 | 100% |
| Further and adult education | 17.2 | 10.4 | 60% | 6.8 | 40% | 6.8 | 40% | 0.0 | 0% | | |
| Others | 0 | 0.0 | 0% | 0.0 | 0% | 0 | 0% | 0 | 0% | (3,1)[2] | (100%) |
| Total | 45.3 | 19.7 | 43% | 25.6 | 57% | 6.8 | 15% | 18.8 | 42% | 12.6 | 90% |
| *Total* | | | | | | | | | | | |
| Pre-primary education | 11.3 | 7.1 | 63% | 4.2 | 37% | 1.8 | 16% | 2.4 | 21% | 11.3 | 63% |
| Primary and secondary education | 57.4 | 47.2 | 82% | 10.2 | 18% | 0.0 | 0% | 0.0 | 18% | 48.4 | 98% |
| Vocational education and training | 28.7 | 18.5 | 64% | 10.2 | 36% | 1.8 | 31% | 9.0 | 4% | | |
| Higher education | 28.4 | 14.4 | 51% | 14.0 | 49% | 0.0 | 0% | 3.7 | 49% | 13.8 | 86% |
| Further and adult education | 38.4 | 20.2 | 53% | 18.2 | 47% | 9.0 | 32% | 13.2 | 15% | | |
| Others | 3.0 | 3.0 | 100% | 0.0 | 0% | 6.8 | 0% | 1.9 | 0% | | |
| Total | 167 | 110.4 | 66% | 56.8 | 34% | 19.4 | 14% | 30.2 | 20% | 128.4 | 74% |

Bn €: billion €
[1]  Incl. €4,6 billion private expenditure
[2]  Child care allowance which cannot be assigned to a certain sector
Source: Dohmen and Hoi (2004)

This extended approach has some consequences for education. For example, our estimate arrives at 18 per cent of private funding for primary and secondary school education, while the 'official' share is 2 per cent. This figure is even more important as it
is completely incurred at the upper secondary level, where dual VET is a serious option. This means that particularly parents incur a serious opportunity cost if their child
enrols in school-based upper secondary education instead of moving into the dual
VET system. The monthly difference may add up to €400 for the parents and €500
(net) for the young person. Another interesting picture shows up in VET, where the
governmental share is 64 per cent, the companies finance 31 per cent and private
households 4 per cent, mainly for fees in school-based VET. The core implication of
these figures is that parents have a very strong incentive to motivate their child to
move into dual VET instead of enrolling in school-based upper secondary education.

This may explain why enrolment figures in tertiary education in Germany, as well as in Austria and Switzerland are far below the rates of other OECD countries.

Finally, in higher education the 'official' share of private spending arrives at 14 per cent out of €13.8 billion. Our calculation reveals a public-private distribution of 50 per cent each and a budget of €28.4 billion. Thus, parents and students pay roughly €14 billion; the government spends the same amount.

If we sum up, the private expenditure for upper secondary school education only amounts to €18,000 on average for the student, while the parents calculate their share to be €13,300 on average for three years. Private households, and here mainly the parents, have to bear another €26,500 for studying at the university. From the parents' perspective, this expenditure is a real opportunity cost, since this is not available for their personal consumption or savings. Traditional economic analysis usually neglects such differences, since accommodation and maintenance is largely irrelevant for an economic analysis from the student's perspective; both items occur independently from study or employment. This opportunity cost does not arise in many other OECD countries, where VET is usually school-based and not related to an income and may be able to explain inter-country differences.

## Private and Social Returns to Education and Innovation

The private and social returns to education are usually considered to indicate whether and to what extent an investment in education pays off. The higher the private and/or social return, the higher the incentive. Furthermore, if there are differences between the returns of different subjects, young people might become motivated to study certain subjects, particularly those which are more important for innovation than others, i.e. Science etc. The same could apply to countries, if a correlation between innovation and social returns to (higher) education exist, i.e. more innovative countries should have higher rates of returns. Therefore, Ammermüller and Dohmen (2003) aimed at identifying a correlation between the returns to education and selected indicators on innovation.

Figure 7 reveals that the private returns to education are very high in some countries. For example, the returns in the United Kingdom, the United States and France are double that of Germany and Canada or Japan. However, Fig. 8 clearly indicates that several factors affect the final outcome and differences of such international comparisons when adjustments are made. The gross salary is only one of them. Unemployment, taxation and the existence and amount of tuition fees can strongly affect the net return to graduates. Furthermore, if we look at the differences between countries, no clear link between the returns to education and indicators on innovation appears to exist.

Finally, if we try to identify a correlation between the returns to certain subjects and their relevance for innovation, it turns out that evidence is very limited at best. Firstly, there are only very few studies which try to establish some correlations or indications in this respect. Secondly, a closer look at German studies trying to calculate the rates of return on a subject basis clearly identifies that they are hampered by methodological constraints. Neglecting such weaknesses, in general it may seem that such a correlation exists, but the evidence is very mixed.

Thus, for the time being, one has to confess that the empirical evidence concerning the linkage is limited.

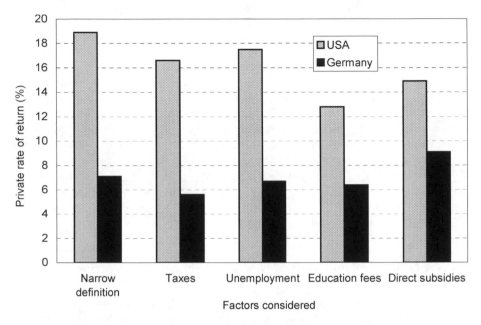

**Fig. 7.** Private rates of return to tertiary education 1999–2000

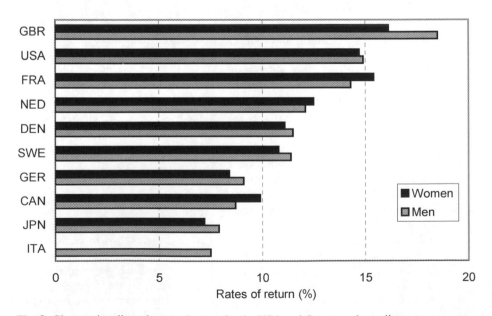

**Fig. 8.** Changes in adjusted rates of return for the USA and Germany depending

## Summary and Conclusion

When summarising the three sections investigating the output and input of the education system in Germany, there appears to be evidence that Germany's economic future is at risk. Firstly, the increase in the share of highly qualified young people is only very modest. In contrast, all other industrialised countries reveal far more dynamic patterns. Secondly, there is evidence that is also relevant concerning the overall increase in educational qualifications. Thirdly, even more striking is that the level of qualification of 25 to 34 year olds in 2002 is lower than that of 1995. While the share of higher education graduates in 2002 is only marginally higher than in 1995, the share of secondary graduates has decreased and – in contrast – the share of lowly qualified people increased. This development needs careful consideration. In an international perspective, the German pattern differs strongly from that of other comparable countries which are very dynamic in increasing the educational qualification of their younger cohorts while Germany's improvements are very modest, at best.

Fourthly, the performance of German students in international comparisons is average, and sometimes even less. One-quarter of students at the end of lower secondary education have to be considered as 'students at risk', i.e. their reading and writing performance is very limited. Among the industrialised countries, Germany reveals the strongest correlation between socio-economic background and student's performance; comparable to countries as, for example, Turkey and Mexico.

When considering some selected input indicators, such as spending for education in relation to GDP, spending levels per student nominally and in relation to GDP per capita, Germany is, again, average, at best, and often even below – particularly when public spending indicators are considered. Thus, it spends less than one should expect according to its economic performance. In those areas where Germany's spending level is above average, this is usually due to comparatively high private contributions, i.e. public spending is far below the level of any other comparable country.

Finally, for different reasons, rates of return to higher education are below those of some other countries. However, in this case, international comparisons should be considered with some care, since they often consider gross income and wages and are, from my viewpoint, limited in their relevance for suggesting policy measures. For example, some countries favour higher differences in salary levels which sometimes over-compensate even very high tuition fees (see, for example, Fig. 8). In contrast, in some other countries, such as Germany or the Scandinavian countries, differences in salaries are less on the one hand, while tax rates are higher and social security contributions are (high and) obligatory, while this is largely voluntary in other countries. If such differences are not taken into consideration adequately, what is the advice for policy – introducing fees and reducing social security and taxes? Although some of these measures might be suitable for Germany to some extent, some caution might be appropriate.

For example, even without paying tuition fees, the share of university students and graduates is below the average of comparable countries, which may be due to relatively high opportunity costs which are linked to the dual system and high discount rates for future income compared to present income.

In this respect, one question is what to expect from the introduction of fees in several German states. From our viewpoint, much will depend on the amount to be paid and the concrete model to be implemented. Thus, there is no general answer, such as 'yes' or 'no' to tuition fees. Instead, it depends on the particular model and on the way of introduction.

For the time being, the fee levels as specified in the particular laws are moderate and should be acceptable for most students. However, given the low enrolment rates in Germany, the question is less how the average or median student might respond but how the marginal student will. Such 'marginal' students may be female or come from socially disadvantaged backgrounds and have to take out another loan of up to €10,000 to finance their maintenance already. Here, to be noted positively, most laws limit the additional burden to €15,000 for fees and student support. Although this may seem acceptable for many people, particularly those who have a different socio-economic background or longer life experience than students, it may cause another barrier. Thus, it must be carefully observed what the effect on (prospective) students will be. Recent studies and decreasing rates of university enrolment in recent years suggest caution and point to some possible negative effects of tuition fees, although experience from other countries, such as Austria, for example, may also suggest that this is a temporary effect. Thus, this suggests a careful analysis of the particular approaches and an evaluation of the effects of the models introduced.

# Part 6.   Policies for Improving NSI

# 6.1 Trends in Innovation Policy: An International Comparison

Christian Rammer

**Abstract.** Innovation policy (IP) is a rather new emerging field of government intervention in favour of R&D, new technologies, and the diffusion of new products and processes. In contrast to science and technology policy, IP stresses the interrelation of various policy areas in order to fully exploit human capital, public science and firm R&D capacities for productivity gains, international competitiveness and growth. This chapter analyses major trends in this cross-sectional policy area in recent years, focussing on five large industrial econo-mies (USA, Japan, Germany, Great Britain, France) and Finland as a case of a small and highly R&D-oriented country. It shows that objectives and basic strategies of IP tend to merge across countries, but heterogeneity in the par-ticular measures employed to achieve these goals is still high. Since around 2000, most governments started to substantially increase their investment in R&D and technology relative to GDP, except Germany. Mission-oriented IP has received increasing attention again, Life Sciences and military-related re-search experiencing the highest increment. More and more governments use in-direct measures (such as tax incentives) to stimulate private R&D investment, and adjusting the regulatory environment in favour of innovation is also be-coming a main priority.

## Introduction[1]

Research and innovation are increasingly being perceived as central policy areas for growth and employment. Pertaining to this background, the question of international trends in policies that attempt to promote research and innovation activities is gaining in significance. A proper design of theses policies – which we call innovation policy (IP) for reasons of simplicity – is critical in order to sustain a country's technological performance. While successful IP has first of all to react to challenges stemming from changes in markets, institutions and the business environment, considering new policy developments in other countries has become more important, too. First, national IP may learn from other countries' experiences and approaches in tackling new chal-lenges. Secondly, IP may be regarded as an independent determinant of a country's innovation performance as it provides financial resources for innovative activities of public and private actors as well as incentives – and maybe disincentives – for deci-sions on performing research and innovation. The way national IP is shaped may thus

---

[1] This chapter summarises main findings of a study conducted by ZEW and Joanneum Research (Vienna) in 2003/2004 (see Rammer et al. 2004). This study was co-authored by Wolfgang Polt, Jürgen Egeln, Georg Licht, Andreas Schibany, Andreas Fier, Günter Ebling and Franziska Steyer. The author thanks Alexis Develett for help in translating into English.

*U. Schmoch, C. Rammer and H. Legler (eds.), National Systems of Innovation in Comparison, 265–286.*

attract – or detain – private investment in research and experimental development (R&D) and innovation.

An international comparison of developments in IP may serve as reference in the debate on the current state and perspectives of national efforts in Germany in IP. In this chapter, main results of such a comparative exercise are reported. They rest on a study commissioned by the German Federal Ministry for Education and Research in Germany (BMBF) that attempted to identify central trends in various areas of IP in five countries (USA, Japan, Great Britain, France, and Finland) and to draw conclusions for German IP. The analysis concentrates on recent developments (i.e. from ca. 1998 onwards) in IP, paying particular attention to shifts in aims and thematic orientation of IP priorities, the government funding of R&D in firms, stimulation of technology-oriented firms start-ups and R&D in small and medium-sized enterprises (SMEs), management and promotion of knowledge and technology transfer, the coordination of national IP, and the role of the EU as an actor in IP. The state of information, from which this chapter departs, is that of mid-2003.

Innovation policy is used here to cover all government activities aiming at promoting and accelerating technical progress, creating and disseminating new findings, technologies and skills through public and private R&D, and effectively using them in economy and society in order to increase wealth (see Jaffe et al. 2002; Larédo & Mustar 2001). This broad definition implies that IP is a cross-section policy area that covers main parts of traditional policy fields such as science, education and technology policy, but also touches competition policy, regional policy, sector policies, and regulatory policy. For an overview on the different action lines in IP, see the 1995 EU Innovation Action Plan (European Commission 1995).

## Current Directions in the Development of National IPs

Six main trends may characterise the current development of IP in the countries considered. These trends largely correspond to those identified by the OECD (2002c) in recent developments in science and technology policy in industrial countries.

Challenges to which national IP has to respond tend to converge across countries. Increasing internationalisation of economic activities result in changes in R&D and innovation activities of firms, notably a reduced local embeddedness of innovation processes and increasing international competition in technology development (see Archibugi et al. 1999). The emergence and diffusion of new general purpose technologies (Information and Communication Technologies – ICT, Biotechnology, Nanotechnology) demand new approaches to promote these technologies and to regulate and develop markets (Cowan & van de Paal 2000). Internationalisation contributes to parallel developments of factor markets, including a synchronisation of shortages or oversupply in risk-taking capital or highly qualified labour. At the same time, large companies have changed their global innovation strategies and reorganised their R&D activities (e.g. global sensing, short-term perspectives, closer ties with marketing). Internal innovation capacities of firms are increasingly complemented by overarching structures ('strategic R&D alliances') and new forms of co-operation between businesses and science, having impacts on other actors such as SMEs and public research

organisations. Technological changes render the distinguishing features of fundamental and applied research less obvious, calling for changes in the division of labour
in R&D and innovation between public and private research, and new forms of co-
operation. This also changes the role of public science in innovation, and may demand
reforms in public research organisations. Furthermore, international co-ordination of
IP, and a systematic exchange of IP-relevant information, has gained increasing
attention in international organisations such as the EU and OECD, contributing to a
common understanding of challenges and ways to respond to them.

As a result of converging challenges, the canon of policy objectives and approaches of IP becomes more and more similar across countries. At the beginning of
the 21st century, six strategic directions of IP can be found in almost all industrial
countries: increasing public financing of R&D; focussing R&D promotion on certain
fields of science and technology, notably Life Sciences (incl. Health), ICT, Nanotechnology, environmental technologies and 'security-related' research; improving the
general (regulatory and market) framework for innovation in firms (incl. the effectiveness of intellectual property rights – IPRs); stimulation of technology-based start-
ups and innovation in SMEs; intensifying technology transfers at public research
organisations, including institutional reforms in these organisations; and administrative reforms to better co-ordinate IP activities among government agencies.

The demand for co-ordination in IP has become more important since IP is developing as a cross-section policy area that incorporates elements of a large number of
traditional policy fields, including, among others, education, science, technology,
competition, sector, corporate, social, legal, defence, foreign and migration policy.
A primary objective is to interlock these policy fields with respect to innovation-
related aspects and to form a sound and coherent integrated IP.

Intervention by IP is increasingly oriented towards improving the functioning of
innovation systems by creating favourable conditions for research and innovation
with respect to markets, institutions/regulations, and organisations. In this respect,
direct government promotion of new technology and innovation become less important though still occupying a prominent position. Indirect measures, the promotion of
SMEs, and various activities to facilitate interaction among innovation actors (firms,
public research, and government agencies) gain in relevance.

The primary objective of IP – strengthening the production and diffusion of knowledge in order to increase wealth – has become a priority among government objectives in most countries. Increasing policy attention to IP issues is reflected in growing
government budgets for research and innovation, the introduction of separate 'innovation units', 'innovation councils' or even 'innovation ministries' within public administration, and the publication of White Papers on innovation.

IP is responsive to new insights from innovation analysis, and regularly adjusts its
set of instruments to incorporate new conceptual approaches to innovation policy. The
main rationale for IP intervention is basically the same in all countries, relying on the
notion of market and systemic failure (see Audretsch et al. 2002). Among the new
conceptual approaches that have influenced IP worldwide, one may mention the national innovation system approach (see Edquist 1997; Lundvall 1992; Nelson &
Rosenberg 1993) which stresses the role of interaction and co-operation of various
actors and institutions. As a result, measures targeting co-operation, technology transfer, SME involvement, and regional and sectoral clustering have received increasing

attention. During the 1990s, trust in market forces as the most appropriate mechanism to find an optimal path of technology development has risen among policy-makers and consultants, contributing to a relative gain in importance of indirect and often non-financial measures (such as designing an appropriate legal setting and fostering competition in markets).

These trends led to a rather uniform set of goals and strategies of IP in the vast majority of industrial countries. On the level of individual measures and their relative weight, significant differences prevail. This heterogeneity at the instrument level reflects different institutional settings, policy traditions and legal frameworks. On the one hand, this offers a large body of policy experiences with different instruments and policy mixes from which other countries may learn. At the same time, learning has to take into account the country-specific settings which often restrict a direct transfer of IP measures from one country to another (see Lundvall & Tomlinson 2001).

In the remainder of this chapter, we will analyse five particular aspects of IP development and assess the respective activities of IP in Germany:

- trends in public financing of R&D, including shifts in thematic priorities;
- the system of public R&D financial support for R&D in firms;
- support for technology-based start-ups and innovation in SMEs;
- promoting technology transfer from public research and reforming public research organisations; and
- the role of the EU in innovation policy.

These five themes are of course just an extract of the relevant trends in today's IP. Important policy areas such as education and training, IPRs, innovation management practices, and co-ordination among IP actors are not considered here due to space limitations. The final chapter summarises the main conclusions from this international comparison for IP in Germany.

## Trends in Public Funding for R&D

Until the mid-1990s, government spending for R&D declined in the countries considered, with Japan being a notable exception. In the late 1990s, this trend came to a halt, and more emphasis was given again to the multiplier effect of public research. The time period 1998 to 2005 saw a significant *increase in public financing of R&D* (sum of funding to public and private organisations) (Fig. 1):

- In the USA, the government's civil and military R&D expenditures are both massively increasing. In 2005, the level of public R&D funding in real terms was almost 60 per cent above that of 1998. The increase of civil R&D was thereby primarily addressed to scientific research in the area of Life Sciences. This expansion was clearly larger than economic growth, resulting in an increase in the ratio of government R&D spending per GDP from 0.85 per cent in 1998 to more than 1.1 per cent in 2005 (Fig. 2).
- Japan has followed a steady expansion path in government R&D financing since the early 1990s. Despite unfavourable macroeconomic conditions, this path was followed until 2004. In 2005, the level of government R&D funding was 33 per cent above that of 1998. Additional R&D funding is almost entirely flowing into the

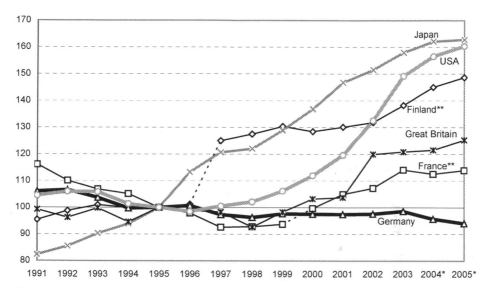

Constant prices figures were calculated using the implicit price index for GDP.
\* 2004 and 2005 figures according to budget plans. USA: 2005 figures based on AAAS estimates which are based on OMB data and agency budget planning; Japan: R&D expenditures for Science and Technology in Fiscal Year 2004 and 2005; Finland: budget plans as per Statistics Finland, Febr. 17th, 2005; France: budget planning for 2005: +4 per cent for civil R&D and +2 per cent for military R&D; Great Britain: CSR Plan of R&D expenditures Fiscal Years 2004/2005 and 2005/2006 (OST SET Statistics, Oct. 4th, 2004), Germany: budget plans by federal government and ZEW estimates on changes in R&D expenditures by federal states
\*\* Finland: strong increase 1996–1997 basically due to changes in accounting method; France: increase 1999 to 2000 overemphasised due to changes in basic definitions of governmental R&D spending
Source: OECD (MSTI I/05), national budget planning – calculations by ZEW

**Fig. 1.** Development of government spending for R&D in real terms, 1991–2005 (1995 = 100)

university system. This expansion has to be seen against the background of a very low level of government R&D funding in international comparison. In 1991, the share of this spending in GDP was only slightly above 0.4 per cent, while all other large industrial countries spent 0.8 per cent or more. In 2005, Japanese public funding for R&D reached almost 0.8 per cent.

- In Great Britain, the starting point for the rise of public expenditures for R&D beginning in 1998 (until 2005: +35 per cent in real terms) was the impending erosion of the traditionally highly performance prone British scientific landscape. Accordingly, the expansion focused on research funding programmes and the institutional funding of research organisations. Government R&D spending as a percentage of GDP increased from a historically low level of 0.67 per cent in 1998 to 0.75 per cent in 2005, which is, however, still below the level of the early 1990s.

- Despite serious budget restraints, France as well extended its governmental spending on R&D over the past years, experiencing a real increase of 23 per cent from 1998 to 2005 (though some of this increase may be attributed to changes in definition of what falls under government R&D spending). The main focus is on R&D

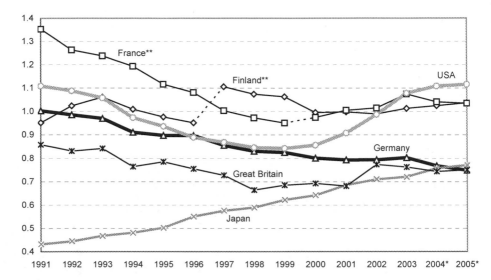

\*    2004 and 2005 figures according to budget plans (see Fig. 1 for sources)
\*\* Finland: strong increase 1996 to 1997 basically due to changes in accounting method;
France: increase 1999 to 2000 overemphasised due to changes in basic definitions of govern-
mental R&D spending
Source: OECD (MSTI I/05), national budget planning – calculations by ZEW

**Fig. 2.** Government budget outlays and appropriations for R&D as a percentage of GDP, 1991–
2005

in new priority fields, promoting technology transfer from public research, and
technology-oriented start-ups. Government R&D spending as a percentage of
GDP, which is traditionally rather high in France, recovered from 1998 on, after
sharply falling for a decade or so.

- In Finland government R&D expenditures were significantly raised during the
  1990s, which came to benefit both the public research organisations (through a rise
  of institutional and project-based financing) as well as the firm sector (mainly
  through technology programmes). Collaborative research and participation of
  SMEs were increased in particular. The overall dynamics of public R&D funding
  was relatively moderate compared to the other countries considered, with a real increase from 1998 to 2005 of 17 per cent. This was slightly less than the real GDP
  growth, thus public R&D spending in GDP insignificantly fell in this period, but
  remained at a high level of above 1 per cent.

- Germany clearly does not follow this trend. Total government expenditure for
  R&D remained constant in real terms from 1998 to 2003, and is likely to fall in
  2004 and 2005, reflecting the fierce situation of public budgets both at the federal
  and the state level. Government R&D spending as a percentage of GDP kept falling since the early 1990s, the only exception being 2003 when economic recession
  caused a minor rise in this indicator. Over the period 1998 to 2005, government
  budget appropriations and outlays for R&D fell by 2 per cent in real terms. Cuts in
  R&D budgets primarily concerned government funding of R&D in firms.

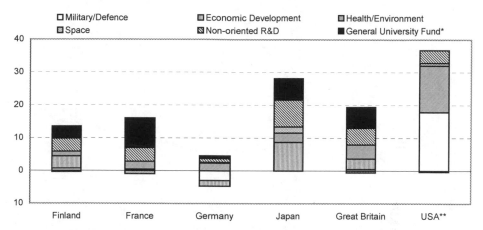

Constant prices figures were calculated using the implicit price index for GDP. 1996/1998: average of years 1996, 1997 and 1998; 2001/2003: average of years 2001, 2002 and 2003
\*   Including other objectives not covered by any of the six categories listed
\*\* USA: except institutional funding of R&D at universities by the states (no data available)
Source: OECD (MSTI I/05) – calculations by ZEW

**Fig. 3.** Changes in government spending for R&D by objectives 1996/1998 to 2001/2003 (in per cent, based on constant prices)

Enlarged government budgets for R&D accompanied shifts in thematic orientation of R&D (Fig. 3). Based on OECD compilation of socio-economic objectives targeted with government R&D budgets, the European countries (Great Britain, France and Finland) as well as Japan particularly increased funds for institutional funding of university research and for funding non-oriented R&D, which is most often R&D for academic research projects delivered through research councils, foundations are other competitive mechanisms. Japan also increased R&D spending for economic development, which basically refers to governmental labs performing R&D related to specific sectors or technologies.

Stagnating government R&D spending in Germany resulted from cuts in military-related R&D (which is largely focussed on R&D in the defence industry) and in research for economic development, a category that also covers R&D subsidies to firms outside thematic programmes. Increases for research in universities were very small, while the only area with some noteworthy gain in public funding was Health and Environment.

The USA clearly followed different thematic priorities when expanding its public R&D financing (see AAAS 2003). Additional funds have overwhelmingly been allocated to R&D for *Military Purposes and for Life Sciences* in the field of civil research. Public spending for military R&D rose from US $40 billion in 2000 to $52 billion in 2003 (both figures expressed in 1996-$), topping the level of defence-related R&D reached in the late 1980s in real terms (Fig. 4). The vast majority of this R&D is devoted to technological development for new weapon systems. A small but still significant fraction in absolute term is basic research into new technologies with future potential applications in security, defence and military funded through DARPA (Defense Advanced Research Projects Agency). In 2005, this financing source for

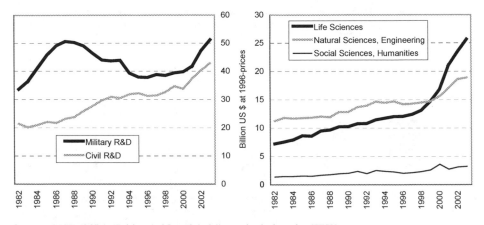

Source: NSF (2004: Tables 4–28 and 4–34) – calculations by ZEW

**Fig. 4.** US federal government spending for R&D 1982 to 2003 by military and civil purpose, and for total research by field (billion constant US $)

fundamental research will amount to US $2.7 billion, which is coming close to the to-tal volume of direct R&D funding by the German Federal government through thematic programmes (2004: €3.4 billion).

Even more pronounced is the increase in R&D funding for Life Sciences (see Omenn 2003). Between 1998 and 2003, financing for research in this particular field of science, which covers Medical Sciences, Biology and Agriculture, doubled from US $13 billion to 26 billion. The overwhelming majority of additional funds was dis-tributed through the National Institutes of Health (NIH) and strengthened research on a large number of diseases. Research in Biotechnology also profited a lot from higher NIH founding sources. Other science and engineering fields also experienced a broa-dening of their funding, but at a clearly slower pace. Most recent data from mid-2005 indicate that R&D budget increases will not continue beyond 2005, since high gov-ernment deficit and still increasing military expenditure is calling for cuts in govern-ment spending, although it is likely that the high level of R&D spending will be sustained.

The dramatic shift in focus and the provision of enormous additional funding sour-ces to particular areas of research in the USA are likely to cause several effects in the US innovation system as well as in those other countries, not all of them being neces-sarily positive:

- In the short term, absorption capacities of the scientific sector are limited. A supply-shock in research funding is thus likely to lead to inefficiencies such as enlarging the costs of research projects without any significant increase in new findings. Anecdotal evidence suggests that such inefficiencies have occurred.
- The concentration of funds on the Life Sciences works as incentive for the rearrangement of research activities, and may also influence decisions of students on which field to study. Other areas – e.g. Engineering – become relatively less attractive, and their capacity for producing new knowledge and new technologies decreases. Unbalanced, short-term changes to the science and innovation system

may thus undermine effective structures that have evolved over a long time (see Clough 2003).

- Due to its significant expansion of funds in the field of Life Sciences, the USA is quite attractive for internationally mobile stellar researchers since considerably better working and income conditions are to be found there, compared to other countries. To retain the according know-how, other countries reacted by upgrading and improving on research in the Life Sciences. The undesirable effects are equally applicable to these countries.
- A strengthening of military R&D is currently only taking place in the USA. In France, Great Britain and Japan the growth since 2000 in funding for military R&D is modest, and in Germany it is clearly decreasing. The US government's additional R&D funds are directed primarily at the development of new weapons. Spillovers into civil fields of application are hardly to be expected; an immediate dual use is in most cases usually not feasible.
- The budget expansion does, however, also reach technologies with potentials for civil use, especially concerning the DARPA technology programmes. For smaller high-technology firms these programmes have great significance since they make, next to R&D funding, also some initial demand available from the military sector (as e.g. in the development of Silicon Valley).
- The greatest proportion of funds for military R&D is drawn by large firms in the aviation, electronics, automotive, computer and manufacturing industries. These are usually active both in civil as well as military production. A short-term expansion of R&D for military purposes leads to a crowding out of civil (privately financed) R&D over the short term.

IP in Germany did not seem to have reacted to these developments. First of all, budget restrictions due to the unpropitious condition of public budgets had prevented German IP from following a similar path. But even in case of less fierce budget constraints, one has to envision that the amount of R&D budget *increase* realised by the US government in recent years is far beyond the R&D capacity of large European countries. From 1998 to 2004, US federal R&D budget increased by almost US $50 billion, which is close to the total annual R&D spending of the German economy, and three times the annual R&D budget of the German government (federal plus states). Secondly, there are also some good reasons not to follow the way of US research policy. A main strength of the German innovation system may be seen in its broad, though little distinctive and specialised, spectrum of competencies in science, research and innovation, including a balanced thematic orientation of IP priorities and R&D funding. This diversified knowledge base facilitates one of the most prominent comparative advantages of German firms in the innovation business, i.e. the integration of several technologies into new products.

One should also bear in mind that productivity gains and wealth do not originate from spending on research, but from the commercial use and diffusion of new technologies and new knowledge. With regard to Life Sciences and Military Research, priority in German innovation policy should be given to rapidly absorb and apply new findings generated by increased R&D efforts in the USA.

## Public Financing of R&D in Firms

Measured in terms of firms' total internal R&D expenditures, a marked *decrease of government R&D funding of private R&D* took place in the 1990s (Fig. 5). The drawback was most pronounced in the USA, Great Britain and France and affected primarily the area of Military Research. In Japan and Finland the share of public financing in businesses' R&D remained widely constant on a low level.

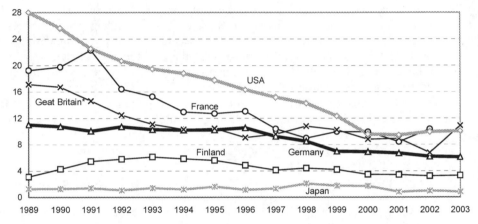

* Great Britain: increase in 2003 due to the privatisation of former DERA (Defence Evaluation and Research Agency), resulting in a re-classification of public funding to this organisation

Source: OECD (MSTI I/05) – calculations by ZEW

**Fig. 5**. Share of direct government funding in total R&D expenditures of firms 1989 to 2003 (in per cent)

Germany followed this trend in the second half of the 1990s, with a notable reduction in government funding shares of private R&D between 1996 and 1999. In this period, R&D expenditures in firms grew rapidly while public funding more or less stagnated in real terms.

Since 2000, this trend seemed to have stopped, at least temporarily. In the USA, the government funding share in total business R&D expenditures is even slightly increasing, which is basically a result of the rise in military R&D. In most other countries, public funding shares of private R&D remained rather stable. The highest share of public financing in business R&D expenditures is exhibited by countries with high significance of military R&D. Governments in Great Britain, France and the USA finance about 10 per cent of the business sector's R&D expenditures. In Germany this share amounts to a little below 7 per cent. Japan has the smallest share of government financing at 1 per cent.

Government funding of business R&D does not take into account indirect measures, however, such as *tax credits for R&D* or allowances on social security fees of researchers. Such indirect measures produce costs for the government (through a loss in taxes or social security contributions), but do not generate a flow of money from the government to the firm. Nevertheless, the firm's savings in taxes and charges due to R&D-related tax credits and allowances should be viewed as an equally relevant way of government financing of business R&D.

Figure 6 shows that the total subsidy ratio of R&D increases to almost 15 per cent for France, and 12 per cent for the USA and Great Britain when taking indirect measures into account. For Japan, the very low share of direct government funding is complemented – at least from 2004 on – by a generous R&D tax credit, the costs of which equal about 4 per cent of total business R&D in Japan. What is more, many countries have recently broadened tax-related R&D support, including all four large countries considered here (see European Commission 2002; 2003a; van Pottlesberghe 2003; OECD 2002d; Warda 2002). Germany, in contrast, has not applied such indirect measures since 1991, and there are no government plans to introduce such types of instruments. Among the group of countries considered, Finland follows the German way.

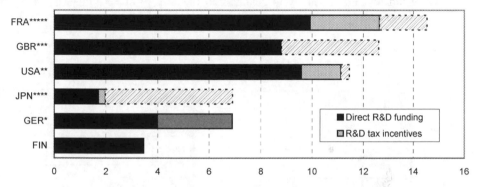

*       Hatched: non-thematic R&D project subsidies (R&D programmes for eastern German firms, collaborative R&D programmes, R&D programmes by states)
**      Costs of R&D tax credits by states estimated, hatched: estimated costs of changes to the Alternative Incremental Credit in Fiscal Year 2002/2003
***     Hatched: estimated effect of newly introduced tax incentives for SMEs (2000) and large firms (2002)
****    Estimated costs of change in R&D tax credits to a volume-based scheme in 2003
*****   Hatched: estimated costs of changes to the Crédit d'Impôt Recherche in 2004
Source: National statistics and compilations (see Rammer et al. 2004: 84ff), OECD (MSTI 2/03) – calculations by ZEW

**Fig. 6.** Share of direct and indirect government funding in total business R&D 2000/2004 (in per cent)

In fact, tax incentives for R&D have advantages and disadvantages. While tax incentives may cause less market distortions, are technology-neutral, are able to address a very large number of firms with rather little administrative costs, and eases planning for firm, serious concerns refer to a low level of additionality, increasing complexity of tax systems, increasing budgetary uncertainty at the side of treasury, and potential pro-cyclical effects. Nevertheless, there is a very large variety of different types of tax incentives and ways to design such measures so that disadvantages can be minimised and effectiveness ensured (see Hall & van Reenen 2000).

In order to assess the role of government support for firm R&D in more detail, a differentiation by delivery mode is useful. For this purpose, we distinguish three types of direct civil R&D funding for firms: through technology programmes, through other types of thematic R&D subsidies, and through not thematically focussed R&D subsidies (including cash equivalent of interest subsidies for loans, which are a rare IP instrument, however). Furthermore, R&D grants and contracts for Military Research are treated as a separate part of direct support. Indirect support through tax credits and the like form a fifth category.

The USA, Great Britain and France deliver the majority of governmental R&D support through *military research grants and contracts*, while Japan and Finland hardly apply this type of funding at all. This mainly reflects priorities and strategies of defence policy and is very loosely related to IP. Germany ranks between these two extremes. Tax incentives for R&D play a major role today in Japan, France and Great Britain. One should note, however, that figures on R&D tax credit costs are rather rough estimates and are likely to change considerably from year to year. Thus, the shares shown in Fig. 7 are to be read as reference points only.

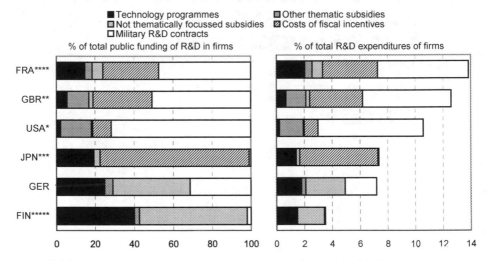

For definitions of various delivery modes, see Rammer et al. (2004: Table 3)
\*        2000, including estimates on costs of R&D tax credits offered by states (2000: approx. US \$400 million) and R&D subsidies by states (2000: approx. US \$450 million)
\*\*       2000, except for estimated costs of R&D tax credits for non-SMEs: 2002
\*\*\*      2000, except for estimated costs of R&D tax credits: 2003 (based on the new volume-based tax credit scheme)
\*\*\*\*     2000
\*\*\*\*\*    2001
Source: National statistics and compilations (see Rammer et al. 2004: 84ff), OECD (MSTI I/03) – calculations by ZEW

**Fig. 7.** Composition of government funding for R&D in firms by delivery mode (in per cent)

Germany and Finland offer a significant amount of government funding for R&D projects in firms without focussing on specific technologies or thematic areas. These non-oriented R&D programmes may be viewed as substitutes to tax incentives, though they are associated with higher administrative costs at government agencies for dealing with project proposals, and generate significant compliance costs at firms.

Such a type of funding is thus less likely to reach the same number of firms compared to tax incentives. Especially for small firms and for firms that intend to enter into R&D activities, barriers to access R&D funding through delivering project proposals to government agencies are likely to be higher than asserting R&D costs in tax declarations.

When looking at the share of government support in total business R&D expenditures (right part of Fig. 7), Germany shows the highest ratio with respect to civil direct support, which is basically a result of a high significance of non-thematic R&D schemes such as subsidies for R&D projects in eastern Germany and subsidies for collaborative R&D. With regard to thematic civil R&D support (technology programmes plus other thematic schemes), country differences are small, all countries reporting about two per cent of total business R&D stemming from this source.

*Technology-specific R&D programmes* have gained in significance in recent years again, while during the 1990s, a drawback in 'mission-oriented research policy' was observed. Such programmes typically target both firms and public research organisations and deliver funds through tenders on a competitive base. The greatest allotment of such thematic R&D funds (sum of funding to firms and non-profit organisations, incl. universities) is found in Japan (0.37 per cent of GDP) and in the USA (0.3 per cent). Both countries deliver civil R&D funding typically through agency specific research programmes which have a technology or thematic focus. In Europe, France in particular uses this form of funding with special intensity (0.22 per cent) while Great Britain exhibits a relatively moderate emphasis (0.08 per cent). Finland and Germany share the same proportion (0.15 per cent).

In all countries a shift in thematic priorities can be observed, though to a varied extent, in favour of Biotechnology, Genetic Engineering, Health Research and Medical Technologies, ICT, Nanotechnology, New Materials and Environmental Technologies. The characteristics of technology programmes have significantly changed in the past decade. Besides the development of new technologies, further objectives concerning innovation and research have come into place, such as the co-operation between science and businesses, the promotion of sector networks and regional clusters, the preferential funding of SMEs (e.g. through the SBIR programme in the USA; which has also been adopted by Great Britain and Japan) or the strengthening of diffusion and commercialisation of new technologies, including the evolvement of technology users in technology development. From this resulted, among other things, new ways of funding or access and greater differentiation of this instrument in general.

## Support for Technology-based Start-ups and Innovative SMEs

The European countries under comparison devised a similar set of policy instruments for the promotion of *technology-based start-ups*. In general, concentration on early stages of firm development ('seed' and 'start-up') is increasingly taking place. Public venture capital (VC) programmes aim to broaden the equity base of young firms. Assuming liability for private investors reduces the risk of default for their investment. Preferential tax treatment of VC funds and investments raise the attractiveness of investing in such funds and encourage business angels in their involvement. Further measures address the efficiency in the matching of investors and VC-seeking firms.

The main challenge for IP in recent years in this area was the slump in VC markets, especially in new investments in the early stages, after 2000. While the extent of VC market contraction varied, the challenge was fierce in each country (Fig. 8). In the USA, for example, VC investment equalled up to 1.0 per cent of GDP in 2000, but fell to 0.12 per cent in 2003. In Great Britain, the peak was less pronounced in 2000 (0.4 per cent of GDP) and the decline until 2003 was more moderate (0.17 per cent in 2003). In France and Germany, VC markets did not gain a similar economic relevance, but the relative shrinking of VC investment was serious and significant, too. It fell from 0.2 per cent in 2000 to 0.1 per cent (France) and 0.05 per cent (Germany) in 2003. In 2004, VC investment recovered slowly.

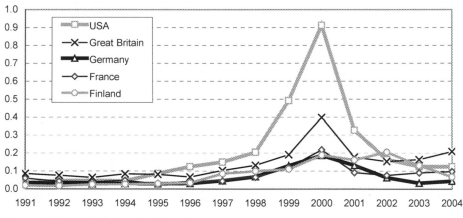

Source: EVCA, NVCA – calculations by ZEW

**Fig. 8.** VC investment (seed, start-up, expansion) as a percentage of GDP, 1991–2004

A possible cause for such heterogeneous development is a varying degree of government intervention in the VC market. In Germany, the government stepped in as co-investor in private initial investments and provided funds for the refinancing and the safeguarding of private VC investments (BTU scheme). Finland applied a similar strategy of VC market intervention. In France and Great Britain, in contrast, government concentrated on establishing publicly financed umbrella funds that provide VC to private funds, and they offered (fiscal) subsidisation of capital supply to private VC funds. Moreover, some public funds performed direct (lead) investment in young technology firms. In the USA, the federal government neither provided any direct funding of VC companies nor did it act as investor, but focussed on offering a favourable legal and tax environment for VC investors.

VC policy in Germany and Finland resulted in a strong pro-cyclical provision of public VC while the instruments at hand were not able to compensate for shrinking private VC investment from 2002 on (Fig. 9). Nevertheless, public VC funding as a percentage of total VC investment increased until 2003 in Germany, though this primarily reflects the need for financing failed investment and did not contribute to a stabilisation of the German VC market. In Great Britain and France, public VC provision peaked in 2002 and largely served as a substitute for falling private investment. In 2004, after a recovery of private VC funding, government intervention was significantly reduced to the level of 2000.

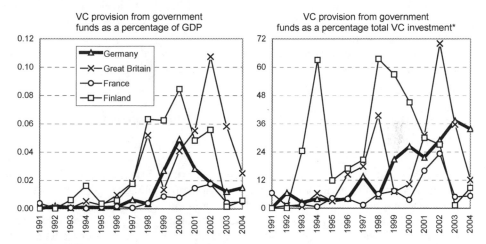

* One should note that VC provision from government funds related to funds raised in a particular year, and not investment. In 2002, for example, Great Britain and France provided public VC funds with additional funding, the investment out of these will take place in consecutive years.
Source: EVCA – calculations by ZEW

**Fig. 9.** Government VC funding, 1991–2004 (in per cent)

The German government reacted to the limited suitability of its VC programmes for periods with low private investment propensity. In 2004, it established a new umbrella fund, and in summer 2005, a new government VC fund (including some money from private companies) was introduced that will directly invest in technology-based start-ups without demanding a private lead investor.

The promotion of *spin-offs from public research institutions* has become a focus of policy measures for the stimulation of the business formation and the commercial application of scientific results or competencies. The different innovation policy designs thereby correspond with different forms of organisation of the scientific apparatus and different barriers in the exploitation of research results through start-up businesses. Main foci of innovation policy activities have recently been addressed at legal adjustments, intended to facilitate firm start-ups by public employees or partnerships among public research institutions and firms, changes to intellectual property rights, extension of consultation services and awareness measures at public research institutions, including the establishment of incubation institutions, provision of seed capital, direct R&D subsidies as well as the inception of specific investment funds for scientific spin-offs.

As regards the promotion of the innovation potential of SMEs in general, an internationally uniform trend cannot be identified. Among the developments which are given emphasis in the different countries are the increased promotion of innovation competencies rather than mere R&D funding, greater support in the accession of public scientific institution's competencies and capacities, the grouping of competencies in SME-related IP to so-called 'one-stop shops', and the improvement of human capital reservoirs in SMEs. In addition, SMEs were able to benefit well above average from the introduction, respectively reform of fiscal R&D subsidisation (Great Britain, Japan, France) and from preferential treatment specific to SMEs in the scope of public R&D funding (as in the SBIR programme in the USA). Finland focuses, similar to Germany, on the integration of SMEs in collaborative projects between SMEs and large firms, respectively between SMEs and scientific institutions.

## Technology Transfer and Reform of Public Research Organisations

In recent years, IP was increasingly concerned with harnessing the full economic potential of research performed at universities and other public research organisations. Governmental activities centred around two main approaches (see Polt et al. 2001): First, organisational reforms at public research that improve the conditions for commercialising research results, and secondly, measures to directly promote technology transfer activities. The individual measures applied in the various countries in order to achieve these goals differ considerably, however, as they are arranged conforming to the respective institutional regime, with regard to highly varying barriers for closer co-operation between science and business, and according to the existing funding system. Typical activities concern:

*   extending the mission of public research institutions in terms of technology transfer as one key component beside education and basic research;
*   providing separate funds for applied research and university–industry collaborative R&D projects;
*   introducing new incentives for researchers to engage in technology transfer, including the incorporation of technology transfer indicators in evaluations;
*   adapting organisational procedures and regulations to allow research organisation to act more flexibly and more professionally in collaboration with firms;
*   stimulation of labour mobility between science and business, including the founding of technology-based start-ups by academics (so-called 'spin-offs');
*   establishment of collaborative research centres for science and business and the founding of 'centres of excellence';
*   establishment of professional offices for the exploitation of technology at the research institutions (Technology Transfer Offices – TTOs, see Siegel et al. 2003);
*   setting up science parks in close proximity to universities and public research organisations to offer space and co-operation opportunities to spin-offs and other high-tech companies (see Link and Scott 2003);
*   facilitating co-operation between different public research organisations, notably between universities and governmental labs; and
*   extension of the research institutions R&D services for SMEs, and of further education and training activities in favour of firm employees.

The efficiency increase of public research is primarily being pursued by the adjustment of the institutional and legal framework conditions as well as incentive schemes. Continuous, mandatory evaluations, the transformation of institutional funds provision into programme- and project-based financing, increased competition among the institutions, and additional decision-making competencies for individual institutions are widespread instruments. This will even lead to privatisation of government-run research organisations, a policy especially followed by the British government (see PREST 2002).

As regards the *evaluation* of public research based on performance indicators, Great Britain is most advanced, using the Research Assessment Exercise (RAE). The RAE is basically a quality concerned rating of scientific publications of academic staff members of university departments, allowing each department to name a selected number of researchers to RAE. Its results grant the research institutions an additional endowment per researcher submitted to RAE, with only the top representatives receiving the financial bonus. 15 years of experience with the RAE show that improved quality orientation and increased productivity (in terms of a greater number of publications) are contrasted by several drawbacks, such as regarding the incentives for science-business collaborations or unconventional and interdisciplinary research (see Roberts 2003). The RAE philosophy has been adopted by a number of other countries for evaluating public research, although no country applied it in the same strict way as Great Britain did (see Tunzelmann & Kraemer Mbula 2003). In France and Finland, for example, evaluations take place within the context of perennial funding contracts between the government and research organisations. Essential to the evaluation in the latter countries are the instruments of self-evaluation and peer review.

Japan focused on reforms of the organisational status of research organisations, giving them a high degree of autonomy. State universities and governmental labs are becoming 'independent administrative institutions' which gives them significantly more freedom with respect to budgeting and external relations. The US federal government is still pursuing a policy towards a more efficient system of technology transfer from large governmental research labs, which started in 1980 with the Bayh-Dole Act on university patenting (see Nelson 2001; Mowery et al. 2001). In Germany, reform of IPRs at universities, changes in career paths of university researchers (e.g. introduction of 'young professorships'), and introducing programme budgeting at large governmental labs are the most prominent activities in this area of IP. In 2002, a comprehensive Action Programme to promote industry–science links was launched, emphasising the role of this policy area for IP in Germany.

The effectiveness of the various activities in the field of technology transfer and organisational reform are not easy to evaluate on a cross-country basis, using the quantitative indicators at hand. One may expect that one result of these policies may be an increased co-operation between public research and the business sector, which may be indicated by a rise in the share of R&D expenditures in public research that is being financed by industry. Available data do not show a clear trend, however. With respect to universities, Germany is the only country showing a clear upwards trend, while the USA, Great Britain and France report shrinking industry shares in university research budgets after 2000, while they too have been rising in the second half of 1990s. In Finland, a slight increase from a very low level can be observed in recent years. At non-university research organisations – which are here called 'governmental labs' for simplicity, though they comprise a very heterogeneous set of institutions varying from country to country – no clear trend can be identified, which is partially caused by changes in the population of non-university research institutions caused by privatisation and restructuring.

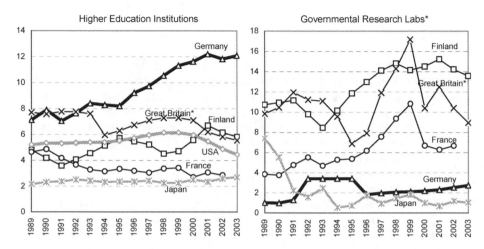

Note that several breaks in series restrict comparison over time.
*   No US data available
Source: OECD (MSTI I/05)

**Fig. 10.** Share of R&D expenditure at public research organisations funded by the business enterprise sector, 1989–2003 (in per cent)

## The EU as Agent in IP

EU activities in IP have undergone significant changes during the past decade. Until the Maastricht treaty, EU activities were mostly restricted to framework programmes as well as to R&D funding as part of structural policy, irrespective of the engagement in specific technology areas (Space Aviation, Nuclear Research). EU research policy was primarily justified by its objective regarding cohesiveness. Since the Maastricht treaty and the Lisbon resolutions, the EU possesses an independent mandate in the field of IP. This underscores the trend of expanding EU activities (see European Commission 2003b; 2003c; Sapir 2003):

*   The Framework Programmes (FP) were extended in both their volume and their thematic scope. The significance of the FP in relation to the Union's budget and to national R&D expenditures has increased steadily. FP budgets as a share in the EU total budget increased from 2.41 per cent for FP1 to 4.15 per cent for FP5. The share of FP budget in total government budget appropriations and outlays for R&D was 3.4 per cent for FP1 and increased to 5.9 per cent for FP5.
*   As part of the Open Method of Co-ordination (OMC), benchmarking initiatives which intend Europe-wide comparative assessment of national programmes and a Europe-spanning technology foresight are gaining in significance.

- IP objectives are increasingly being defined on the European level – the three per cent goal from Barcelona setting the pace. From the Member States' (self-imposed) obligations regarding the fulfilment of the objectives result far-reaching consequences regarding the process of national IP.
- Research policy activities are more and more complemented by firm-oriented innovation measures, thus enlarging the scope of EU policy intervention. The new Competitiveness and Innovation Programme (CIP) is a major step in this respect.
- As a result of cohesiveness as primary justification for EU research policy, participation in FPs tends to follow a country's research potential, as figures for FP4 and FP5 show (Table 1). Large countries tend to be represented below their research potential, while small and southern European countries show higher participation ratios compared to their share in total R&D personnel. Research institutions and firms from Germany have thus far been engaged in FPs only below average. Measured in terms of its potential (number of researchers), Germany exhibits – despite a small increase in its involvement – the lowest participation intensity in FPs of all EU countries.

**Table 1.** Participation in EU Framework Programmes and size of research capacity by member state

|      | Share in R&D 1996 | Personnel 2000 | Share in submitted FP4 | proposals FP5 | Share in successful FP4 | proposals FP5 |
|------|------|------|------|------|------|------|
| AUT  | 1.8  | 1.9  | 2.6  | 3.2  | 2.2  | 2.8  |
| BEL  | 2.7  | 3.0  | 4.5  | 4.2  | 4.8  | 4.3  |
| GER  | 28.4 | 27.8 | 17.1 | 16.2 | 15.9 | 16.6 |
| DEN  | 2.0  | 2.2  | 2.7  | 2.7  | 3.2  | 3.1  |
| ESP  | 5.5  | 6.9  | 8.0  | 9.9  | 7.6  | 8.7  |
| FIN  | 2.3  | 3.0  | 2.8  | 2.6  | 2.7  | 2.7  |
| FRA  | 20.1 | 18.8 | 14.4 | 12.7 | 14.5 | 14.1 |
| GBR  | 16.3 | 15.3 | 15.2 | 14.6 | 17.2 | 15.9 |
| GRE  | 1.2  | 1.5  | 5.7  | 6.3  | 4.2  | 4.6  |
| IRL  | 0.6  | 0.7  | 2.2  | 1.6  | 2.0  | 1.5  |
| ITA  | 8.9  | 8.6  | 11.9 | 13.0 | 10.5 | 11.6 |
| NED  | 5.1  | 5.1  | 6.1  | 6.2  | 7.6  | 7.4  |
| POR  | 1.0  | 1.3  | 2.6  | 2.7  | 2.8  | 2.2  |
| SWE  | 4.0  | 4.0  | 4.2  | 4.0  | 4.6  | 4.4  |

FP4: only sub-programmes ACTS, BRITE EURAM, ENVIRON, ESPRIT, JOULE, TRANSPORT, TSER – FP5: all sub-programmes
Source: Provisio, OECD (MSTI I/03) – calculations by Joanneum Research and ZEW

The thematic structure of Germany's involvement as well as that of other countries in the FP mostly conforms to thematic 'supply' of research funding by the EU (Fig. 11). National specialisation in science and technology can hardly be discerned. This can be attributed primarily to the design of the FP as transnational collaborative projects.

Concerning the influence of EU-IP on national research policies, the following general assessment may be made:

- For the large Member States in particular, the European level of IP has thus far not played a significant role in the orientation of national IP – neither conceptually, nor financially. This is different for those less R&D-intensive and/or smaller countries, in which both cases apply, that EU funds present a significant share of overall

R&D expenditures and the conceptual orientation of national policy issues towards the EU is clearly observable.

- With respect to the FP, national policy-making in many countries was primarily concerned with achieving substantial participation in the submissions scheme as precondition to high returns from the framework programme.
- The reaction to the Barcelona goal has thus far been quite mixed: while many EU Member States have integrated the Barcelona goal into their national objectives, a large gap is evident between the goal and respective actions.

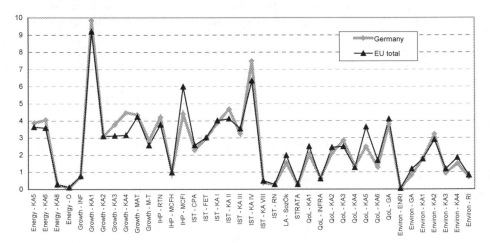

Source: Provisio – calculations by Joanneum Research

**Fig. 11.** Participation in EU-FP5 by sub-programmes: Germany vs. EU total (in per cent)

The EU Commission views the continuing existence of the so-called '15 + 1' situation and the as yet low participation of the Member States in EU-IP as the definitive problem in realising the Lisbon goal and for the inception of a uniform European Research Area. However, the approaches suggested by the EU (e.g. OMC) for increased policy co-ordination appear unsuitable to tackle this situation.

Developments utilising other perspectives will more strongly affect the coherency of national and European IP: on the one hand, IP is tied into other policy areas, in which policy is increasingly being conducted on the European level (Environment, Transportation, Communication, Energy, National Security, in future possibly Defence) and where the connection to infrastructure investment and public procurement is granted. On the other hand, concepts around genuinely European institutions, such as a 'European Research Council' or a European Growth and Innovation Fund, are becoming more and more apparent.

## German IP in International Perspective: A Summary

IP in Germany has followed most of the international trends in research and innovation. The basic aims, strategies and priorities in IP – at least at the federal level – correspond to those of most other industrial countries: creating a framework conducive to innovation, supporting upcoming fields of technology, strengthening technology transfer and co-operation between firms and public research, reforming public research organisations, promoting innovation in SMEs, fostering high-tech start-ups, and ensuring supply of highly qualified labour. The set of instruments employed are largely similar to those found in other countries, including a large number of different financing instruments targeting a variety of different innovation activities in firms, the provision of an extensive public research infrastructure, various non-financial measures to stimulate innovation, ranging from IPRs to innovation management and clustering, and education-oriented activities (see Rammer 2005 for an overview of IP measures in Germany at the federal level). Co-ordination among different IP actors has received increasing attention, too. Initiatives such as the 'Partners for Innovation' have led to more intense co-operation among policy-makers from the federal and the state level.

A main substantial difference to other countries is the low general dynamics in the German innovation system, however. While most governments accompanied the shift of policy priority towards research and innovation with markedly increasing budgets for science and research from the late 1990s on, the German government (sum of both federal and state activities) lagged behind. Public R&D expenditures stagnated in real terms during the 1990s and early 2000s, especially affecting resources for R&D at universities and other public research organisations. Though the private sector in Germany has managed to provide more resources for R&D and innovation in the second half of the 1990s, the speed of expansion was lower than in most other countries (see Chapter 2.2). This low dynamics may threat Germany's position as one of the world's leading locations for science, research and innovation. High supply of R&D funding in other countries may attract researchers from Germany who are looking for versatile and ample funding conditions. Firms' R&D activities may also be attracted by a dynamic environment, providing incentives to allocate additional R&D resources to such locations. Stagnating investment in education and science in Germany bears the threat to restrict the future supply of highly qualified labour, causing scarcity in human capital, given the secular trend to increasing demand for qualified labour. Finally, weakening public research may underpin one of the main comparative advantages of the German innovation system, i.e. the close and fruitful ties between public research and innovation in firms.

The findings of our comparative analyses of IP in six countries suggest some general conclusions on the state of German IP and current challenges:

- German federal policy has paid increasing attention to IP in recent years, which runs parallel to an international trend. While most countries accompanied this rhetoric with marked increases in government spending, Germany clearly lags behind. In order to keep pace with the international development, significant increases in real terms of government R&D spending will be needed.

- German IP follows a broad thematic focus, addressing a large number of techno-logy fields and sectors by R&D programmes and other IP measures. This policy suits the specialisation pattern of the German innovation system and should be kept. Concentration of public resources on a few thematic fields – as was done by the US government in recent years, focusing on Life Sciences and Military R&D – does not seem to be an appropriate path for German IP: unintended effects (decreasing marginal returns of R&D, crowding out of other thematic areas) are likely to be high, while a main comparative advantage of innovation in Germany is to integrate new technology from various sources and fields into customer-oriented new products.
- Government support for R&D in firms in Germany is today strongly based on direct subsidies, whereas indirect measures such as tax incentives are not applied. Since indirect measures might be a particularly attractive way to stimulate R&D in small firms, IP in Germany should think of introducing such an instrument in order to provide incentives for a large number of SMEs to perform R&D in-house. Designed as a base incentive for SMEs, it could complement the existing R&D programmes.
- Promoting technology-based start-ups in high-tech areas is strongly related to the development of the VC market, since the main barrier to innovation in such high-tech start-ups is lack of financing for risky R&D projects. German IP was highly successful in accelerating the provision of private VC during boom phases of the market (i.e. until 2000), while the instruments used were less effective to serve as substitute for the shrinking investment propensity of private VC companies. The redesign of public VC programmes in 2004 and 2005 reacted to this shortcoming.
- Technology transfer from public research, and effective ways of co-operation bet-ween universities, governmental labs and private companies in R&D are certainly one of the strengths of the German innovation system. Reform of public research organisations plus a Federal Action Programme to safeguard effective technology transfer contribute to maintaining this comparative advantage. A major threat may result from restricted funding of scientific research and education, however, since they provide the basis for co-operation and transfer of knowledge.
- The European Commission has become a main agent in IP. The EU influences both the basic strategic orientation of IP and the available funds for R&D. The EU Framework Programme, as well as the new Competition and Innovation Program-me, should be regarded as complements to national funding, focussing on inter-national co-operation. To fully leverage these instruments, adequate institutional settings for active participation, own initiatives to define thematic areas and a com-petitive R&D infrastructure are key instruments at a national level. Moreover, the Barcelona process, i.e. the EU activities towards increasing R&D expenditures to three per cent in GDP by 2010, should be perceived as an opportunity for German IP to adjust policy structures towards an improved support for research and inno-vation.

# Part 7.   Annex

# 7.1 References

AAAS (2003): Research and Development FY 2004. In: AAAS Report, 28, Washington: American Association for the Advancement of Science.

Acs, Z., Audretsch, D. (1990): Innovation and Small Firms. Cambridge: Cambridge University Press.

Acs, Z.A., Arenius, P., Hay, M., Minniti, M. (2005): Global Entrepreneurship Monitor. 2004 Executive Report. Babson Park, MA and London: Babson College and London Business School.

Almus, M., Engel, D., Prantl, S. (2000): The Mannheim Foundation Panels of the Centre for European Economic Research (ZEW). Mannheim: Centre for European Economic Research.

Amable, B., Verspagen, B. (1995): The Role of Technology in Market Shares Dynamics. In: Applied Economics, 27, pp. 197–204.

Amable, B., Barré, R., Boyer, R. (1997): Les Systèmes d'Innovation à l'Ere de la Globalisation. Paris: Economica.

Ammermüller, A., Dohmen, D. (2003): Individuelle und soziale Renditen von Bildungsinvestitionen. Studien zum deutschen Innovationssystem, 1–2004, Köln.

Anker, R. (1997): Theories of Occupational Segregation by Sex. An Overview. In: International Labour Review, 136 (3).

Archibugi, D., Howells, J., Michie, J. (1999): Innovation Policy in a Global Economy. Cambridge: Cambridge University Press.

Arundel, A., Patel, P. (2003): Strategic Patenting. Background Report for the Trend Chart Policy Benchmarking Workshop 'New Trends in IPR Policy'.

Arvanitis, S., von Arx, J., Hollenstein, H., Sydow, N. (2004): Innovationsaktivitäten in der Schweizer Wirtschaft. Eine Analyse der Ergebnisse der Innovationserhebung 2002. In: Strukturberichterstattung, 24, Bern: Staatssekretariat für Wirtschaft.

Arvanitis, S., Hollenstein, H., Marmet, D., Sydow, N. (2005): Forschungs- und Technologiestandort Schweiz: Stärken-/Schwächenprofil im internationalen Vergleich. Strukturberichterstattung No. 32, Bern: State Secretariat for Economic Affairs – Economic Policy Directorate.

Audretsch, D.B., Mahmood, T. (1995): New Firm Survival: New Results Using a Hazard Function. In: Review of Economics and Statistics, 77, pp. 97–103.

Audretsch, D.B., Bozeman, B., Combs, K.L., Feldman, M., Link, A.N., Siegel, D.S., Stephan, P., Tassey, G., Wessner, C. (2002): The Economics of Science and Technology. In: The Journal of Technology Transfer, 27, pp. 155–203.

Australian Bureau of Statistics (2005): Innovation in Australian Business. Melbourne: ABS.

Balassa, B. (1965): Trade Liberalization and Revealed Comparative Advantage. In: The Manchester School of Economic and Social Studies, 33, pp. 99–123.

Becker, G.S. (1995): Human Capital and Poverty Alleviation. Working Papers HROWP (World Bank, Human Resources Development and Operations Policy), 52.

Beicht, U., Walden, G., Herget. H. (2004a): Costs and Benefits of In-Company Vocational Education and Training in Germany. Bielefeld: Bundesinstitut für Berufsbildung.

Beicht, U., Walden, G., Herget, H. (2004b): Kosten und Nutzen der betrieblichen Berufsausbildung in Deutschland. Berichte zur Beruflichen Bildung, H. 264, Bielefeld.

Beicht, U. et al. (2003): Technische Berufe im dualen System der Berufsausbildung – Stellenwert und Entwicklungstendenzen. Studien zum deutschen Innovationssystem, 3–2003. Bonn (http://technologische-leistungsfaehigkeit.de/pub/3_2003.pdf).

Beise, M. (2001): Lead Markets: Country-Specific Success Factors of the Global Diffusion of Innovations. Heidelberg: Physika-Verlag.

Beise, M., Belitz, H. (1999): Internationalisation of R&D in Multinational Enterprises: The German Perspective. In: Barrell, R., Pain, N. (eds.), Innovation, Investment and Diffusion of Technology in Europe. German Direct Investment and Economic Growth in Postwar Europe. Cambridge: Cambridge University Press, pp. 89–119.

Beise, M., Belitz, H. (1998): Trends in the Internationalisation of R&D – the German Perspective. In: Vierteljahrsheft des DIW, 2, Berlin: DIW, pp. 67–85.

Belitz, H. (2004a): Forschung und Entwicklung in multinationalen Unternehmen. Studien zum deutschen Innovationssystem, 8–2004. Berlin.

Belitz, H. (2004b): Foreign Companies Expand Research and Development in Germany. In: Economic Bulletin, 41 (6), 2004, pp. 199–204.

Belitz, H. (2002): Germany as a Location for Research and Development by Multinational Companies. In: Economic Bulletin, 39 (5), pp. 175–180.

Belitz, H. (2000): German Companies Intensify their Research and Development Activities Abroad. In: DIW Economic Bulletin, 37 (6), June 2000, pp. 175–182.

Bertschek, I., Kaiser, U. (2004): Productivity Effects of Organizational Change: Microeconometric Evidence. In: Management Science, 50 (3), pp. 394–404.

Biersack, W. (2002): Überblick zur Beschäftigung und Arbeitslosigkeit von Frauen nach Berufen. In: Engelbrech, G. (ed.): Arbeitsmarktchancen für Frauen. Nürnberg, BeitrAB 258, pp. 127–144.

Biersack, W. et al. (2001): Arbeitssituation, Tätigkeitsprofil und Qualifikationsstruktur von Personengruppen des Arbeitsmarktes. Ergebnisse der BIBB/IAB-Erhebung 1998/1999 im Überblick. Nürnberg, BeitrAB 248.

Blind, K., Frietsch, R. (2003): Sector-Based Multidimensional Forecasting Model (SEFORM). Report to the European Patent Office Within the Research Programme: Improvement of Methods for Forecasting Patent Filings. Karlsruhe: Fraunhofer ISI.

Blind, K., Edler, J., Frietsch, R., Schmoch, U. (2004): The Patent Upsurge in Germany: The Outcome of a Multi-motive Game Induced by Large Companies. Working Paper presented at the 8th Schumpeter Conference in Milano. Karlsruhe: Fraunhofer ISI.

Blind, K., Edler, J., Frietsch, R., Schmoch, U. (2003a): Erfindungen kontra Patente. Schwerpunktstudie 'Zur technologischen Leistungsfähigkeit Deutschlands'. Karlsruhe: Fraunhofer ISI.

Blind, K., Edler, J., Schmoch, U., Andersen, B., Howells, J., Miles, I., Roberts, J., Hipp, C., Green, L., Herstatt, C., Evangelista, R. (2003b): Patents in the Service Industries. Final Report. Brussels: European Commission (ed.).

Bloningen, B.A., Davies, R.B., Head, K. (2002): Estimating the Knowledge-Capital Model of the Multinational Enterprise: Comment. NBER Working Paper, No. 8929, May.

Blossfeld H.-P. (1990): Changing Educational Careers in the Federal Republic of Germany. A Longitudinal Study of Three Birth Cohorts. In: Sociology of Education, 63, pp. 165–177.

BMBF (2005): Berufsbildungsbericht 2005. Bonn, Berlin: BMBF.

BMBF (2004a): Bundesbericht Forschung 2004. Berlin: Federal Ministry of Education and Research, Germany.

BMBF (2004b): Zukunftsnavigation. Jugend und Ausbildung. Broschüre zum Jahr der Technik. Bonn, Berlin: BMBF

BMBF (ed.) (2002): Germany's Technological Performance 2001. Bonn: BMBF.

BMBWK; BMVIT; BMWA (eds.) (2005): Österreichischer Forschungs- und Technologiebericht 2005. Vienna: Federal Ministry of Education, Science and Culture.

BMWA (2004): Wirtschaftsbericht 2004. Zukunftsfaktor Innovation. Berlin: Federal Ministry of Economics and Labour.

Borga, M., Mann, M. (2003): U.S. International Services, Cross-border Trade and Sales Through Affiliates in 2001. In: Survey of Current Business, October, pp. 58–118.

Boskin, M.J., Lau, L.J. (1992): Capital, Technology, and Economic Growth. In: Rosenberg, N., Landau, R., Mowery, D.C. (eds.): Technology and the Wealth of Nations. Stanford: Stanford University Press, pp. 17–55.

Boutellier, R. et al. (1999): Managing Global Innovation. Uncovering the Secrets of Future Competitiveness. Berlin et al.: Springer-Verlag.

BPM5 (1993): Balance of Payments Manual 1993. 5th edition. International Monetary Fund.

Brenner, H. (1997): Entwicklung anerkannter Ausbildungsberufe. Fortschreibung überkommener Regelungen oder Definition zukunftsbezogener Ausbildungsgänge? In: Euler, D., Sloane P.F.E. (eds.): Duales System im Umbruch. Eine Bestandsaufnahme der Modernisierungsdebatte. Pfaffenweiler, pp. 53–69.

Bresnahan, T.F., Brynjolfsson, E., Hitt, L.M. (2002): Information Technology, Workplace Organization, and the Demand for Skilled Labor. Firm-Level Evidence. In: Quarterly Journal of Economics, 117 (1), pp. 339–376.

Bresnahan, T.F., Greenstein, S. (1998): Technical Progress and Co-Invention in Computing and in the Uses of Computers. In: Brookings Papers on Economic Activity: Microeconomics, pp. 1–77.

Bresnahan, T.F., Trajtenberg, M. (1995): General Purpose Technologies: 'Engines of Growth'? In: Journal of Econometrics, 65 (1), pp. 83–108.

Brynjolfsson, E., Hitt, L.M. (2000): Beyond Computation: Information Technology, Organizational Transformation and Business Performance. In: Journal of Economic Perspectives, 14 (4), pp. 23–48.

Buck, H., Kistler, E., Mendius, H.G. (2002): Demographischer Wandel in der Arbeitswelt. Stuttgart: IRB Verlag.

Bund-Länder Commission for Educational Planning and Research Promotion (BLK) (2002): Zukunft von Bildung und Arbeit – Perspektiven von Arbeitskräftebedarf und -angebot bis 2015. Bonn: Bericht der BLK an die Regierungschefs von Bund und Ländern.

Bürgel, O., Fier, A., Licht, G., Murray, G. (2004): The Internationalisation of Young High-tech Firms. Heidelberg, New York: Physica.

Cantwell, J. (1995): The Globalisation of Technology: What Remains of the Product Life Cycle model. In: Cambridge Journal of Economics, 19 (1), pp. 155–174.

Cantwell, J., Kosmopoulou, E. (2001): What Determines the Internationalisation of Corporate Technology. In: Forsgren, M. et al. (eds): Critical Perspectives on Internationalisation. mimeo.

Cantwell, J., Janne, O. (1999): Technological Globalisation and Innovation Centres: the Role of Corporate Technological Leadership and Locational Hierarchy. In: Research Policy, 28, pp. 119–144.

Cantwell, J., Harding, R. (1998): The Internationalisation of German Companies R&D. In: National Institute Economic Review, 163, pp. 99–124.

Cap Gemini (2004): Online Availability of Public Services: How Does Europe Progress? Web-Based Survey on Electronic Public Services. Report of the Fourth Measurement. October 2003 (http://europa.eu.int/information_society/eeurope/2005/index_en.htm).

Cassiman, B., Ueda, M. (2002): Optimal Project Rejection and New Firm Startups. mimeo, IESE Business School.

Cefis, E., Marsili, O. (2004): A Matter of Life and Death: Innovation and Firm Survival. mimeo, Utrecht School of Economics, Utrecht University.

Clough, G.W. (2003): National Priorities for Science and Technology: A View from the Academic Sector. In: AAAS (ed.), Science and Technology Policy Yearbook 2003. Washington, pp. 23–42.

Cohen, W.M., Levinthal, D.A. (1990): Absorptive Capacity: A New Perspective on Learning and Innovation. In: Administrative Science Quarterly, 35, pp. 128–152.

Cohen, W.M., Levinthal, D.A. (1989): Innovation and Learning: The Two Faces of R&D. In: Economic Journal, 99, pp. 569–596.

Cohen, W.M., Goto, A., Nagata, A., Nelson, R.R., Walsh, J.P. (2002): R&D Spillovers, Patents and the Incentives to Innovate in Japan and the United States. In: Research Policy, 31, pp. 1349–1367.

Coombs, R. (2003): The Changing Character of 'Service Innovation' and the Emergence of 'Knowledge-Intensive Business Services'. In: Dankbaar, B. (ed.): Innovation Management in the Knowledge Economy. London: Imperial College Press, pp. 83–96.

Cowan, R., van de Paal, G. (2000): Innovation Policy in a Knowledge-Based Economy. Brussels and Luxembourg: ECSC-EC-EAEC.

Criscuolo, P., Narula, R., Verspagen, B. (2001): Measuring Knowledge Flows Among European and American Multinationals: A Patent Citation Analysis. Eindhoven: Eindhoven Centre for Innovation Studies (Ecis).

Curzio, A.Q., Fortis, M., Zoboli, R. (eds.) (1994): Innovation, Resources and Economic Growth. Berlin, Heidelberg: Springer.

Dalton, D.H., Serapio, M.G. (1999): Globalizing Industrial Research and Development. U.S. Department of Commerce, Technology Administration. Washington D.C.: Office of Technology Policy.

Deissinger, T. (2004): Apprenticeship Systems in England and Germany: Decline and Survival. In: Greinert, W.D.; Hanf, G. (eds.): Towards a History of Vocational Education and Training in Europe in a Comparative Perspective. Luxembourg: Cedefop Panorama Series, 103, pp. 28–45.

Dernis, H., Kahn, M. (2004): Triadic Patent Families Methodology. Paris: OECD.

DEST (2003): Mapping Australian Science and Innovation. Canberra: Department of Education, Science and Training.

Deutsche Bundesbank (2004): The Significance of Information and Communication Technology. In: Monthly Report April, pp. 45–55.

DIHK (ed.) (2005): FuE-Verlagerung: Innovationsstandort Deutschland auf dem Prüfstand, Berlin: DIHK.

DIW (1988): Exportgetriebener Strukturwandel bei schwachem Wachstum. Analyse der strukturellen Entwicklung der deutschen Wirtschaft – Strukturberichterstattung 1987. In: DIW-Beiträge zur Strukturforschung, Heft 103.

Dohmen, D. (2005): Deutschlands Bildungssystem im internationalen Vergleich vor dem Hintergrund der technologischen Leistungsfähigkeit. Auswertung der OECD-Studie 'Bildung auf einen Blick'. Studie für den Bericht zur technologischen Leistungsfähigkeit, 2–2005, Köln.

Dohmen, D. (1999): Ausbildungskosten, Ausbildungsförderung und Familienlastenausgleich (Educational Cost, Student Support and Family Allowances). Eine ökonomische Analyse unter Berücksichtigung rechtlicher Rahmenbedingungen. Berlin.

Dohmen, D., Hoi, M. (2004): Bildungsaufwand in Deutschland – eine erweiterte Konzeption des Bildungsbudgets. Studien zum deutschen Innovationssystem, 3–2004, Köln.

Dohmen, D., Abraham H. (2003): Die Entwicklung der bildungspolitischen Situation Deutschlands im internationalen Vergleich. Gutachten im Auftrag des Bundesministeriums für Bildung und Forschung. Studien zum deutschen Innovationssystem, 19–2003, unpublished, Köln.

Dorsch-Schweizer, M. (2004): Die Ambivalenz moderner Beruflichkeit für Frauen. In: Berufsbildung in Wissenschaft und Praxis (BWP), 33 (5), pp. 43–46.

Dosi, G., Pavitt, K., Soete, L. (1990): The Economics of Technical Change and International Trade. New York: Harvester Wheatsheaf.

DTI (2003): Innovation Report. Competing in the Global Economy: the Innovation Challenge. London: Department of Trade and Industry.

Dunning, J. (1979): Explaining Changing Patterns of International Production. Defence of the Eclectic Theory. In: Oxford Bulletin of Economics and Statistics, 41 (4), pp. 269–295.

Dunning, J., Wymbs, C. (1999): The Geographical Sourcing of Technology-Based Assets by Multinational Enterprises. In: Archibugi, D. et al. (eds.): Innovation Policy in a Global Economy. Cambridge: Cambridge University Press.

Edler, J. (2004): International Research Strategies of Multinational Enterprises: A German Perspective. In: Technological Forecasting and Social Change, 71, special issue 'Science Policy and Innovation Systems', ed. by Heitor, M. et al., pp. 599–621.

Edler, J. (2003): Germany and the Internationalisation of Industrial R&D. New Trends and Old Patterns. In: Canwell, J., Molero, J. (eds.): Multinational Enterprises, Innovative Strategies and Systems of Innovation. Cheltenham, UK, Northampton, USA: Edward Elgar, pp. 105–128.

Edler, J., Kuhlmann, S. (2005): Towards One System? The European Research Area Initiative, the Integration of Research Systems and the Changing Leeway of National Policies. In: Technikfolgenabschätzung – Theorie und Praxis, 14 (1), pp. 59–68.

Edler, J., Döhrn, R., Rothgang, M. (2003): Internationalisierung industrieller Forschung und grenzüberschreitendes Wissensmanagement. Eine empirische Analyse aus der Perspektive des Standortes Deutschland. Fraunhofer ISI Series No. 54. Heidelberg: Physica.

Edler, J., Meyer-Krahmer, F., Reger, G. (2001): Managing Technology in the Top R&D Spending Companies Worldwide – Results of a Global Survey. In: Engineering Management Journal, 13 (1), special issue of the 'Managing High Technology Research Organizations', pp. 5–11.

Edquist, C. (ed.) (1997): Systems of Innovation. Technologies, Institutions and Organizations. London: Pinter.

Egeln, J., Gottschalk, S., Rammer, C., Spielkamp, A. (2003): Public Research Spin-offs in Germany. ZEW Documentation 03–04, summary report, Mannheim: Centre for European Economic Research.

EITO (2005): European Information Technology Observatory 2005. Frankfurt: EITO.

EITO (2004): European Information Technology Observatory 2004. Frankfurt: EITO.

Engel, D.; Fryges, H. (2002): Aufbereitung und Angebot der ZEW Gründungsindikatoren. ZEW Dokumentation Nr. 02–01. Mannheim: Centre for European Economic Research.

EPO (2005): Annual Report 2004. Munich: EPO.

EPO, JPO, USPTO (2004): Trilateral Statistical Report – Edition 2003. Munich, Tokyo, Alexandria, VA: EPO, JPO, USPTO.

Ertl, H., Sloane, P.F.E. (2004): The German Training System and the World of Work: The Transfer Potential of the Lernfeldkonzept. In: bwp@, issue 7 (http://www.bwpat.de/7eu/ertl _sloane_de_bwpat7.pdf).

European Commission (2005): European Innovation Scoreboard. http://trendchart.cordis.lu.

European Commission (2004): European Innovation Scoreboard 2004. Comparative Analysis of Innovation Performance. Brussels: Commission of the European Communities, pp. 1475.

European Commission (2003a): Raising EU R&D Intensity. Improving the Effectiveness of the Mix of Public Support Mechanisms for Private Sector Research and Development. Fiscal Measures. Brussels: European Commission.

European Commission (2003b): Commission Staff Working Paper. Investing in Research: An Action Plan for Europe. Brussels: European Commission, p. 489.

European Commission (2003c): Science and Technology Policies in Europe: New Challenges and New Responses. Final report from the STRATA Consolidating Workshop. Brussels: European Commission.

European Commission (2002): Corporate Tax and Innovation. In: Innovation Papers, 19, Brussels: European Commission.

European Commission (2000): Towards a European Research Area – Communication from the Commission to the Council. The European Parliament, the Economic and Social Committee and the Committee of the Regions. Brussels: European Commission.

European Commission (1997): Second European Report on Science & Technology Indicators. Luxemburg, Brussels: European Commission.

European Commission (1995): Action Plan for Innovation in Europe. Innovation for Growth and Employment. Brussels: European Commission.

European Council (2004): Allgemeine und berufliche Bildung 2010 – Die Dringlichkeit von Reformen für den Erfolg der Lissabon-Strategie. Brussels: European Council, pp. 1–43.

European Foundation for the Improvement of Living and Working Conditions (2002): Quality of Women's Work and Employment. Tools for Change. Foundation Paper No. 3, December 2002, Luxembourg.

Eurostat (2004): Business Demography in Europe. Results for 10 Member States and Norway. Data 1997–2001. Luxembourg: Office for Official Publications of the European Commission.

Eurostat (ed.) (2003): High Tech Industries and Knowledge Based Services. Doc. ESTAT/A4/ STI/-May 03/4.4. To be presented in Luxembourg on 7 and 8 May 2003.

Fagerberg, J. (1997): Competitiveness, Scale and R&D. In: Fagerberg, J., Hansson, P., Lundberg, L., Melchior, A. (eds.): Technology and Trade. Cheltenham: Edward Elgar.

Fagerberg, J. (1988): International Competitiveness. In: Economic Journal, 98, pp. 355–374.

Federal Agency of Labour (BA) (various years): Statistik der sozialversicherungspflichtigen Beschäftigten.

Federal Statistical Office Germany (2002): Studentenstatistik 2002.

Federal Statistical Office Germany (various years): Hauptberichte 1993–2002.

Federal Statistical Office Germany (1992): Klassifizierung der Berufe. Systematisches und alphabetisches Verzeichnis der Berufsbenennungen. Stuttgart: Metzler-Poeschel.

Federal Statistical Office Germany (various years): Nicht-monetäre hochschulstatistische Kennzahlen 1980–1997 und 1980–2000. In: Bildung und Kultur, Fachserie 11, Reihe 4.3.1, Wiesbaden.

Florida, R. (1997): The Globalization of R&D: Results of a Survey of Foreign-Affiliated R&D Laboratories in the USA. In: Research Policy, 26; pp. 85–103.

Freeman, C. (1987): Technology Policy and Economic Performance: Lessons from Japan. London: Pinter.

Freeman, C. (1982): The Economics of Industrial Innovation. London: Pinter.

Freeman, C., Soete, L. (1997): The Economics of Industrial Innovation. London: Pinter.

Frier, A., Czarnitzki, D. (2004): Zum Stand der empirischen Wirkungsanalyse der öffentlichen Innovations- und Forschungsförderung. Mannheim: ZEW, unpublished manuscript.

Frietsch, R. (2004a): Combining Databases for Forecasting Purposes. Patents and Further Economic Data. Paper presented at the WIPO-OECD Workshop on the Use of Patent Statistics, 11th/12th October 2004, Geneva.

Frietsch, R. (2004b): Intensivierung von Bildungsabschlüssen zwischen 1970 und 2000, Analysen im Rahmen der jährlichen Berichterstattung zur technologischen Leistungsfähigkeit Deutschlands. Studien zum deutschen Innovationssystem, 4–2004, Bonn.

Frietsch, R., Gehrke, B. (2004): Bildungs- und Qualifikationsstrukturen in Deutschland und Europa. Studien zum deutschen Innovationssystem, 3–2005. Karlsruhe, Hannover: Fraunhofer ISI, NIW.

Frommberger, D., Reinisch, H. (2004): Development of Disparate Structures of Dutch and German Vocational Education. In: Greinert, W.D., Hanf, G. (eds.): Towards a History of Vocational Education and Training in Europe in a Comparative Perspective. In: Cedefop Panorama Series, 103, Luxembourg, pp. 28–45.

Fryges, H. (2004): Stepping In and Out of the International Market: Internationalisation of Technology-Oriented Firms in Germany and the UK. ZEW Discussion Paper 04–65, Mannheim: ZEW.

Fuchs, M. (1994): Forschungslinien im Maschinenbau. Relevanzstrukturen der technikwissenschaftlichen Forschung an Hochschulen. In: Zeitschrift für Soziologie, 23 (1), pp. 41–55.

Fuchs, J., Söhnlein, D., Weber, B. (2004): Konsequenzen des demografischen Wandels für den Arbeitsmarkt der Zukunft. Herausforderung demografischer Wandel! Wiesbaden: VS Verlag für Sozialwissenschaften, GWV Fachverlage GmbH, pp. 122–139.

Fuente de la, A., Ciccione, A. (2002): Human Capital in a Global and Knowledge-Based Economy. Luxembourg: European Commission.

Gallouj, F. (2002): Innovation in Services and the Attendant Old and New Myths. In: Journal of Socio-Economics, 31.

Gallouj, F. (1997): Towards a Neo-Schumpeterian Theory of Innovation in Services? In: Science and Public Policy, 24 (6), pp. 405–420.

Geroski, P.A. (1991): Market Dynamics and Entry. Oxford: Blackwell.

Geroski, P.A., Mata, J., Portugal, P. (2002): Founding Conditions and the Survival of New Firms. mimeo.

Glänzel, W., Schubert, A. (2004): Analysing Scientific Networks Through Co-authorship. In: Moed, H.F., Glänzel, W., Schmoch, U. (eds.): Handbook of Quantitative Science and Technology Research. The Use of Publication and Patent Statistics in Studies of S&T Systems. Dordrecht, Boston, London: Kluwer Academic Publishers, pp. 257–276.

Glänzel, W., de Lange, C. (2002): A Distributional Approach to Multinational Measures of International Scientific Collaboration. In: Scientometrics, 54, pp. 75–89.

Gokhberg, L., Kouznetsova. I. et al. (2004): Indicators of Innovation. Data Book. Moscow: State University – Higher School of Economics.

Gompers, P., Lerner, J., Scharfstein, D. (2003): Entrepreneurial Spawning: Public Corporations and the Genesis of New Ventures, 1986–1999. NBER Working Paper No. 9816.

Gomulka, S. (1990): The Theory of Technological Change and Economic Growth. London, New York: Routledge.

Granato, M., Schittenhelm, K. (2004): Junge Frauen: Bessere Schulabschlüsse – aber weniger Chancen beim Übergang in die Berufsausbildung. In: Aus Politik und Zeitgeschichte, B28, pp. 31–39.

Grandstrand, O. (1999): Internationalisation of Corporate R&D: A Study of Japanese and Swedish Corporations. In: Research Policy, 28; pp. 275–302.

Granstrand, O., Patel, P.; Pavitt, K. (1997): Multi-technology Corporations: Why they have 'Distinctive Core' Competencies. In: California Management Review, 39, pp. 8–25.

Greinert, W.D., Hanf, G. (eds.) (2004): Towards a History of Vocational Education and Training in Europe in a Comparative Perspective. In: Cedefop Panorama Series, 103, Luxembourg.

Grenzmann, Chr. (2004): Forschung und Entwicklung in der Wirtschaft - Die FuE-Statistik des Wirtschaftssektors. In: Legler, H., Grenzmann, Chr. (eds.): Forschung und Entwicklung in der deutschen Wirtschaft. Materialien zur Wissenschaftsstatistik, 13, Essen: SV Wissenschaftsstatistik, pp. 7–17.

Grömling, M. (2004): Weniger Volk, weniger Wohlstand? Die Auswirkungen des demographischen Wandels auf das Wirtschaftswachstum. In: Wirtschaftswissenschaftliches Studium, 11, pp. 640–646.

Grupp, H. (1998): Foundations of the Economics of Innovation – Theory, Measurement and Practice. Cheltenham: Edward Elgar.

Grupp, H., Jungmittag, A. (1999): Convergence in Global High Technology? A Decomposition and Specialisation Analysis for Advanced Countries. In: Jahrbücher für Nationalökonomie und Statistik, 218 (5+6).

Grupp, H., Schmoch, U. (1992): Wissensbindung von Technik. Panorama der internationalen Entwicklung und sektorales Tableau für Deutschland, Heidelberg: Physica.

Grupp, H., Schmoch, U., Hinze, S. (2001): International Alignment and Scientific Regard as Macro-indicators for International Comparisons of Publications. In: Scientometrics, 51 (2), pp. 359–380.

Grupp, H., Legler, H., Jungmittag, A., Schmoch, U. (2000): Hochtechnologie 2000. Neudefinition der Hochtechnologie für die Berichterstattung zur technologischen Leistungsfähigkeit Deutschlands. Karlsruhe and Hannover: Fraunhofer-ISI and NIW.

Gundlach, E., Wößmann, L. (2003): Bildungsressourcen, Bildungsinstitutionen und Bildungsqualität: Makroökonomische Relevanz und mikroökonomische Evidenz. Kiel.

Günterberg, B., Kayser, G. (2004): SMEs in Germany. Facts and Figures 2004. In: IfM-Materialien, 161, Bonn: Institute for SME Research.

Gustavsson, P., Hansson, P., Lundberg, L. (1997): Technical Progress, Capital Accumulation and Changing International Competitiveness. In: Fagerberg, J., Hansson, P., Lundberg, L., Melchior, A. (eds.): Technology and Trade. Cheltenham: Edward Elgar.

Hall, B.H., Ziedonis, R.M. (2001): The Patent Paradox Revisited: An Empirical Study of Patenting in the U.S. Semiconductor Industry, 1979–1995. In: The Rand Journal of Economics, 32 (1), pp. 101–128.

Hall, B.H., van Reenen, J. (2000): How Effective Are Fiscal Incentives for R&D? A Review of the Evidence. In: Research Policy 29, 449–469.

Hammer, M. (1990): Reengineering Work: Don't Automate, Obliterate. In: Harvard Business Review, 68 (4), pp. 104–112.

Harhoff, D., Stahl, K., Woywode, M. (1998): Legal Form, Growth and Exit of West German Firms – Empirical Results for Manufacturing, Construction, Trade and Service Industries. In: Journal of Industrial Economics, 46, pp. 453–488.

Hartung, S., Leber, U. (2004): Betriebliche Ausbildung und wirtschaftliche Lage. Empirische Ergebnisse des IAB-Betriebspanels. In: Krekel, E., Walden, G. (eds.): Zukunft der Berufsausbildung in Deutschland. Ergebnisse der BIBB-Fachtagung am 4./5. November 2003 in Bonn. Bielefeld: BIBB, pp. 111–129.

Hatzichronoglou, T. (1997): Revision of the High-technology Sector and Product Classification. In: STI Working Paper, 1997 (2), OECD/GD(97)216, Paris: OECD.

Hempell, T. (2005a): Does Experience Matter? Innovation and the Productivity of ICT in German Services. In: Economics of Innovation and New Technology, 14 (4), pp. 277–303.

Hempell, T. (2005b): Computers and Productivity – How Firms Make a General Purpose Technology Work. In: ZEW Economic Studies, 33, Heidelberg: Physica.

Hempell, T. (2004): Einsatz von Informations- und Kommunikationstechnologien 2003. Studien zum deutschen Innovationssystem, 13–2005, Mannheim: Centre for European Economic Research.

Hempell, T., Vanberg, M., Schäfer, A., Ohnemus, J. (2005): Benchmark 'Internationale Telekommunikationsmärkte'. Report for the Federal Ministry of Economics and Labour (BMWA), Mannheim: ZEW (ftp://ftp.zew.de/pub/zew-docs/gutachten/ Benchmark_Telekommunikation.pdf).

Heublein, U., Schmelzer, R., Sommer, D. (2005): Studienabbbruchstudie 2005. Die Studienabbrecherquoten in den Fächergruppen und Studienbereichen der Universitäten und Fachhochschulen. Hannover: HIS-Kurzinformation A 1 /2005.

Heublein, U., Spangenberg, H., Sommer, D. (2003): Ursachen des Studienabbruchs. Analyse. Hannover: HIS-Hochschulplanung, Bd. 163.

HIS (2000): HIS-Workshop OECD-Bildungsindikatoren. Methoden und Ergebnisse des internationalen Bildungsvergleichs. Hannover: HIS-Kurzinformation A4/2000.

Ietto-Gillies, G. (2000): What Role for Multinationals in the New Theories of International Trade and Location. In: International Review of Applied Economics, 14 (4), pp. 413–426.

Ijichi, T., Iwasa, T., Odagiri, H., Keira, H., Koga, T., Goto, A., Tawara, Y., Nagata, A., Hirano Y. (2004): Statistics on Innovation in Japan. Report on the Japanese National Innovation Survey 2003 (J-NIS 2003), selected tables, Tokio: National Institute of Science and Technology Policy.

ILO Cinterfor (2001): Decent Work and Vocational Training. Montevideo: ILO Cinterfor (http://www.cinterfor.org.uy/public/english/region/ampro/cinterfor/publ/sala/dec_work/index.htm).

Jaffe, A.B., Lerner, J., Stern, S. (eds.) (2002): Innovation Policy and the Economy. Vol. 3, Cambridge: MIT Press.

Janz, N., Ebling, G., Gottschalk, S., Peters, B., Rammer, C., Schmidt, T. (2002): Innovationsverhalten der deutschen Wirtschaft. Indikatorenbericht zur Innovationserhebung 2001. Mannheim.

Janz, N., Licht, G., Doherr, T. (2001): Innovation Activities and European Patenting of German Firms: A Panel Data Analysis. Paper presented at the Annual Conference of the European Association of Research in Industrial Economics.

Jorgenson, D. (2005): Accounting for Growth in the Information Age. In: Aghion P.; Durlauf, S. (eds.): Handbook of Economic Growth. Amsterdam, North-Holland (forthcoming).

Kash, D.E., Kingston, W. (2001): Patents in a World of Complex Technologies. In: Science and Public Policy, 28 (1), pp. 11–22.

Katz, J.S., Martin, B.R. (1997): What is Research Collaboration? In: Research Policy, 26, pp. 1–18.

Kazemzadeh, F., Teichgräber, M. (1998): Europäische Hochschulsysteme. Ein Vergleich anhand statistischer Indikatoren. Hannover: HIS Hochschulplanung, Bd. 132.

KfW-Bankengruppe (2004): KfW-Gründungsmonitor 2004. Gründungen aus der Arbeitslosigkeit gewinnen an Bedeutung. Frankfurt/M.: KfW-Bankengruppe.

Klodt, H., Mauer, R.; Schimmelpfenning, A. (1997): Tertiarisierung der deutschen Wirtschaft. Kiel: Mohr Siebeck.

KMK (2003): Fächerspezifische Prognose der deutschen Hochschulabsolventen. In: KMK Statistische Veröffentlichungen, 168.

Kölling, A., Schank, T. (2002): Skill-Biased Technological Change, International Trade and the Wage Structure. Discussion papers No. 14. Friedrich-Alexander-Universität Erlangen-Nürnberg.

Koopmann, G., Münnich, F. (1999): National und International Developments in Technology. In: INTERECONOMICS, 34 (6), pp. 267–278.

Kortum, S., Lerner, J. (1999): What is Behind the Recent Surge in Patenting? In: Research Policy, 28, pp. 1–22.

Krekel, E.M, Troltsch, K, Ulrich J.G. (2003): Betriebliche Ausbildungsbeteiligung bei schwieriger Wirtschaftslage. BIBB startet neues Forschungsprojekt. In: Berufsbildung in Wissenschaft und Praxis (BWP), 32, special edition 'Jugendliche in Ausbildung bringen', pp. 13–16.

Krekel, E.M., Troltsch, K., Ulrich J.G. (2004): Keine Besserung in Sicht? Zur aktuellen Lage auf dem Ausbildungsstellenmarkt. In: Berufsbildung in Wissenschaft und Praxis (BWP), 33 (3), pp. 11–14.

Kuhlmann, S., Arnold, E. (2001): RCN in the Norwegian Research and Innovation System. Synthesis Report in the Evaluation of the Research Council of Norway. Karlsruhe: Fraunhofer ISI.

Kumar, N. (2001): Determinants of Location of Overseas R&D Activity of Multinational Enterprises: The Case of US and Japanese Corporations. In: Research Policy, 31, pp. 159–174.

Kutscha, G. (2000): General Education and Initial Vocational Training in Germany. The 'Flexicurity Route' of Modernization under Aspects of Flexibility, Transferability and Mobility. A contribution to COST A11, working group 1: VET policy (Draft Ku-COST1, Ver2).

Kutscha, G. (1999): Pluralisierung der Berufsbildung als Innovationsstrategie. Modernisierung der Qualifikationsentwicklung im Spannungsfeld von Regulierung und Deregulierung. In: Senatsverwaltung für Arbeit, Berufliche Bildung und Frauen (ed.): Expertisen für ein Berliner Memorandum zur Modernisierung der Beruflichen Bildung. Berlin, pp. 101–125.

Laafia, I. (1999): Beschäftigung im Hochtechnologiebereich. In: Statistik kurz gefasst, Thema 9: Wissenschaft und Technologie, 1/1999. Luxembourg: Eurostat.

Lafay, G. (1987): La Mesure des Avantages Comparatifs Révélés. In: Économie prospective internationale, 41.

Larédo, P., Mustar, P. (eds.) (2001): Research and Innovation Policies in the New Global Economy. An International Comparative Analysis. Cheltenham: Edward Elgar.

Laudel, G. (2002): What Do We Measure by Co-authorship? In: Research Evaluation, 11, pp. 3–15.

Legler, H. (1987): Zur internationalen Wettbewerbsfähigkeit der westdeutschen Wirtschaft. NIW-Forschungsbericht No. 3. Hannover: NIW.

Legler, H., Grenzmann, Chr., Marquardt, R. (2003): Forschungs- und Entwicklungsaktivitäten der deutschen Wirtschaft. Studien zum deutschen Innovationssystem, 10–2004, Han-nover, Essen: BMBF

Les Bas, Ch., Sierra, Ch. (2002): Location Versus Home Country Advantages in R&D Activities: Some Further Results on Multinationals Locational Strategies. In: Research Policy, 31, pp. 589–609.

Licht, G., Moch, D. (1999): Innovation and Information Technology in Services. In: Canadian Journal of Economics, 32 (2), pp. 363–383.

Link, A.N., Scott, J.T. (2003): U.S. Science Parks: The Diffusion of an Innovation and Its Effects on the Academic Missions of Universities. In: International Journal of Industrial Organization, 21, pp. 1323–1356.

Lockett, A., Wright, M., Franklin, S. (2003): Technology Transfer and Universities' Spin-out Strategies. In: Small Business Economics, 20, pp. 185–200.

Lucke, D., Schröder, P., Schumacher, D. (2004): R&D and Price Elasticity of Demand. In: DIW Discussion Paper No. 430, Berlin.

Lundvall, B.-Å. (1990): National Systems of Innovation: Towards a Theory of Innovation and Interactive Learning, London: Pinter.

Lundvall, B.-Å. (1988): Innovation as an Interactive Process: From User-Producer Interaction to the National System of Innovation. In: Dosi, G., Freeman, C., Nelson, R., Silverberg, G., Soete, L. (eds.): Technical Change and Economic Theory. London: Pinter, pp. 349–369.

Lundvall, B.-Å., Tomlinson, M. (2001): Learning-by-Comparing: Reflections on the Use and Abuse of International Benchmarking. In: G. Sweeny (ed.): Innovation, Economic Progress and the Quality of Life. Cheltenham: Edward Elgar, pp. 120–136.

Lundvall, B.-Å. (ed.) (1992): National Systems of Innovation: Towards a Theory of Innovation and Interactive Learning. London: Pinter.

Machin, S. (2005): Skill-Biased Technical Change and Educational Outcomes. In: Johnes, G.; Johnes, J. (eds.): International Handbook on the Economics of Education. Cheltenham: Edward Elgar, pp. 189–210.

Marklund, G. (2000): Indicators of Innovation Activities in Services. In: Boden, M., Miles, I. (eds.): Services and the Knowledge Based Economy. London: Continuum, pp. 86–108.

Markusen, J.R. (2001/2002): Integrating Multinational Firms into International Economics. In: NBER Reporter, winter 2001/2002, pp. 5–7.

Mataloni, R.J. (2004): U.S. Multinational Companies, Operations in 2002. In: Survey of Current Business, July, pp. 10–29.

Mataloni, R.J. (2003): U.S. Multinational Companies, Operations in 2001. In: Survey of Current Business, November, pp. 85–105.

Mataloni, R.J., Yorgason, D.R. (2002): Operations of U.S. Multinational Companies. Preliminary Results from the 1999 Benchmark Survey. In: Survey of Current Business, March, pp. 24–54.

MED (2003): Growth and Innovation Framework. Benchmark Indicators Report 2003. Wellington: Ministry of Economic Development.

Mendonca, S., Pereira, T.S., Godinho, M.M. (2004): Trademarks as an Indicator of Innovation and Industrial Change. LEM Working Paper Series No. 2004/15, Pisa: Laboratory of Economics and Management, Sant'Anna School of Advanced Studies.

Meyer-Krahmer, F., Reger, G. (1997): Konsequenzen veränderter industrieller FuE-Strategien für die nationale Forschungs- und Technologiepolitik. In: Gerybadze, A., Meyer-Krahmer, F., Reger, G.: Globales Management von Forschung und Innovation. Stuttgart: Schäffer-Poeschel, pp. 196–215.

Moed, H. (2005): Citation Analysis in Research Evaluation. Berlin et al.: Springer.

Mowery, D.C., Rosenberg, N. (1989): Technology and the Pursuit of Economic Growth. Cambridge: Cambridge University Press.

Mowery, C.D., Nelson, R.R., Sampat, B., Ziedonis, A.A. (2001): The Growth of Patenting and Licensing by U.S. Universities: An Assessment of the Effects of the Bayh-Dole Act of 1980. In: Research Policy, 30, pp. 99–199.

Narula, R. (2002): The Implications of Growing Cross-border Interdependence for Systems of Innovation. Maastricht: Maastricht Economic Research Institute on Innovation and Technology (MERIT).

Narula, R. (2000): Explaining Inertia in R&D Internationalisation: Norwegian Firms and the Role of Home Country Effects. MERIT Research Memoranda, 2000–021.

Nelson, R.R. (2001): Observations on the Post-Bayh-Dole Rise of Patenting at American Universities. In: The Journal of Technology Transfer, 26, pp. 13–19.

Nelson, R.R. (1988): Institutions Supporting Technical Change in the United States. In: Dosi, G., Freeman, C., Nelson, R., Silverberg, G., Soete, L. (eds.): Technical Change and Economic Theory. London: Pinter, pp. 312–329.

Nelson, R.R., Rosenberg, N. (1993): Technical Innovation and National Systems. In: Nelson, R.R. (ed.): National Innovation Systems. A Comparative Analysis. Oxford: Oxford University Press, pp. 3–21.

Nelson, R.R. (ed.) (1993): National Innovation Systems: A Comparative Analysis. Oxford: Oxford University Press.

Nesta, L., Patel, P. (2004): National Patterns of Technology Accumulation: Use of Patent Statistics. In: Moed, H.F., Glänzel, W., Schmoch, U. (eds.): Handbook of Quantitative Science and Technology Research. The Use of Publication and Patent Statistics in Studies of S&T Systems. Dordrecht: Kluwer Academic Publisher, pp. 531–551.

NSF (2004): Science and Engineering Indicators 2004. Washington: National Science Foundation.

Nyström, K. (2005): Interdependencies in the Dynamics of Firm Entry and Exit. In: CESIS Electronic Working Paper Series No. 28.

OECD (2005a): Science, Technology and Industry Scoreboard 2005. Paris: OECD.

OECD (2005b): Main Science and Technology Indicators. Paris: OECD.

OECD (2004a): The Economic Impact of ICT – Measurement, Evidence and Implications. Paris: OECD.

OECD (2004b): Handbook for Internationally Comparative Education Statistics: Concepts, Standards, Definitions and Classifications. Paris: OECD.

OECD (2003): ICT and Economic Growth – Evidence from OECD Countries, Industries and Firms. Paris: OECD.

OECD (2002a): Frascati Manual 2002: Proposed Standard Practice for Surveys on Research and Experimental Development. Paris: OECD.

OECD (2002b): Measuring the Information Economy. Paris: OECD.

OECD (2002c): Science, Technology and Industry Outlook 2002. Paris: OECD.

OECD (2002d): Tax Incentives for Research and Development: Trends and Issues. Paris: OECD.

OECD (2002e): Investment in Human Capital Through Post-Compulsory Education and Training: Selected Efficiency and Equity Aspects. Economics Department Working Paper No. 333, Paris: OECD.

OECD (1999): Classifying Educational Programmes. Manual for ISCED-97 Implementation in OECD Countries. Paris: OECD.

OECD (1989): The Measurement of Scientific and Technical Activities. R&D Statistics and Output Measurement in the Higher Education Sector – Supplement to the Frascati Manual. Paris: OECD.

OECD (ed.) (2005): OECD Handbook on Economic Globalisation Indicators. Paris: OECD.

OECD (ed.) (2004a): Science, Technology and Industry Outlook. Paris: OECD.

OECD (ed.) (2004b): Compendium of Patent Statistics 2004. Paris: OECD.

OECD (ed.) (2004c): Patents and Innovation: Trends and Policy Challenges. Paris: OECD.

OECD (ed.) (2004d): Education at a Glance 2004. Paris: OECD.

OECD (ed.) (2003a): Science Technology and Industry Scoreboard. Paris: OECD.

OECD (ed.) (2003b): Main Science and Technology Indicators. Vol. 2003/1. Paris: OECD.

OECD (ed.) (2003c): Turning Science into Business. Patenting and Licensing at Public Research Organisations. Paris: OECD.

OECD (ed.) (2003d): Education at a Glance 2003. Paris: OECD.

OECD (ed.) (2002): Education at a Glance 2002. Paris: OECD.

OECD (ed.) (2001a): The Well-Being of Nations. The Role of Human and Social Capital. Paris: OECD.

OECD (ed.) (2001b): Education at a Glance 2001. Paris: OECD.

OECD (ed.) (2000a): Fostering High-tech Spin-offs: A Public Strategy for Innovation. In: STI Review, 26, Paris: OECD.

OECD (ed.) (2000b): Education at a Glance 2000. Paris: OECD.

OECD (ed.) (1999): Science, Technology and Industry Scoreboard 1999. Benchmarking Knowledge-Based Economies. Paris: OECD.

OECD (ed.) (1995): The Measurement of Scientific and Technological Activities. Manual on the Measurement of Human Resources Devoted to Science and Technology 'Canberra Manual'. OECD/GD(95)77. Paris: OECD.

OECD (ed.) (1993): The Measurement of Scientific and Technological Activities. Proposed Standard Practice for Surveys of Research and Experimental Development. Paris: OECD.

OECD: Online Bildungs-Datenbank 2002, 2004.

OECD; Eurostat (1997): Oslo-Manual. Proposed Guidelines for Collecting and Interpreting Technological Innovation Data. Paris: OECD.

Oerlemans, L.A.G., Pretorius, M.W., Buys, A.J., Rooks, G. (2003): Industrial Innovation in South Africa 1998-2000. Report on the South African Innovation Survey for the Period 1998–2000. Pretoria: University of Pretoria, Department of Engineering and Technology Management.

Omenn, G.S. (2003): Science and Technology Policies Concerning the Life Sciences. In: AAAS (ed.): Science and Technology Policy Yearbook 2003. Washington: AAAS, pp. 145–167.

Patel, P., Pavitt, K. (2000): National Systems of Innovation under Strain: The Internationalisation of Corporate R&D. In: Barré, R. et al. (eds.): Productivity, Innovation and Economic Performance. Cambridge: Cambridge University Press.

Patel, P., Vega, M. (1999): Patterns of Internationalisation of Corporate Technology: Location Versus Home Country Advantages. In: Research Policy, 28 (2/3), pp. 145–155.

Pearce, R. (1999): Decentralised R&D and Strategic Competitveness: Globalised Approaches to Generation and Use of Technology in Multinational Enterprises (MNEs). In: Research Policy, 29, pp. 157–178.

Pearce, R., Singh, S. (1997): Motivation and Organization of Decentraliced R&D. In: Pearce, R. (ed.): Global Competition and Technology. Houndmills, Basingstoke, Hampshire: Palgrave Macmillan.

Petersen et al. (1993): Die Bedeutung des internationalen Dienstleistungshandels für die Bundesrepublik Deutschland. DIW-Beiträge zur Strukturforschung, No. 145, Berlin.

Plünnecke, A., Werner, D. (2004): Das duale Ausbildungssystem. Die Bedeutung der Berufsausbildung für die Jugendarbeitslosigkeit und Wachstum. Beiträge zur Ordnungspolitik des Instituts der deutschen Wirtschaft, 9, Köln.

Polt, W., Rammer, C., Gassler, H., Schibany, A., Schartinger, D. (2001): Benchmarking Industry–Science Relations: The Role of Framework Conditions. In: Science and Public Policy, 28, pp. 247–258.

Porter, M.E. (1998): The Competitive Advantage of Nations. New York: The Free Press.

Pottelsberghe van, B. et al. (2003): Improving the Effectiveness of Fiscal Measures to Stimulate Private Investment in Research. Brussels: Expert Working Group for the EC Research DG.

Prantl, S. (2003): Bankruptcy and Voluntary Liquidation: Evidence for New Firms in East and West Germany after Unification. ZEW Discussion Paper 03-72. Mannheim: ZEW.

PREST (2002): A Comparative Analysis of Public, Semi-Public and Recently Privatised Research Centres. Manchester: PREST.

Raan van, A.F.J. (2004): Measuring Science. Capita Selecta of Current Main Issues. In: Moed, H.F., Glänzel, W., Schmoch, U. (eds.): Handbook of Quantitative Science and Technology Research. The Use of Publication and Patent Statistics in Studies of S&T Systems. Dordrecht, Boston, London: Kluwer Academic Publishers, pp. 19–50.

Rammer, C. (2005): European Trend Chart on Innovation. Country Report Germany, Covering Period October 2004 – September 2005. Luxembourg: European Commission.

Rammer, C. (2004): Unternehmensdynamik in Deutschland 1995–2003: Die Rolle forschungs- und wissensintensiver Branchen und eine Einordnung im internationalen Vergleich. Studien zum deutschen Innovationssystem, 11–2005. Berlin: BMBF.

Rammer, C., Peters, B., Schmidt, T., Aschhoff, B., Doherr, T., Niggemann, H. (2005a): Innovationen in Deutschland. Ergebnisse der Innovationserhebung 2003 in der deutschen Wirtschaft. ZEW-Wirtschaftsanalysen, 78, Baden-Baden: Nomos.

Rammer, C., Aschhoff, B., Doherr, T., Peters, B., Schmidt, T. (2005b): Innovation in Germany. Results of the German Innovation Survey 2004. Mannheim: ZEW.

Rammer, C., Aschhoff, B., Peters, B., Schmidt, T. (2005c): Kurzbericht zur Innovationserhebung 2004. Auswertung der Schwerpunktfrage 'Aufnahme/Ausweitung von Innovationsaktivitäten'. Mannheim: ZEW.

Rammer, C., Polt, W., Egeln, J., Licht, G., Schibany, A. (2004): Internationale Trends der Forschungs- und Innovationspolitik – Fällt Deutschland zurück? ZEW-Wirtschaftsanalysen 73, Baden-Baden: Nomos.

Rammer, C., Schmidt, T. (2003): Innovationsverhalten der Unternehmen in Deutschland. Studien zum deutschen Innovationssystem, 15-2004. Berlin: BMBF.

Reger, G., Beise, M., Belitz, H. (1999): Innovationsstandorte multinationaler Unternehmen. Heidelberg: Physica.

Reich, R. (1993): The Work of Nations. Buenos Aires.

Reinberg, A., Hummel, M. (2002): Zur langfristigen Entwicklung des qualifikationsspezifischen Arbeitskräfteangebots und -bedarfs in Deutschland. Empirische Befunde und aktuelle Projektionsergebnisse. In: Mitteilungen aus der Arbeitsmarkt- und Berufsforschung, 35 (4), pp. 580–600.

Revermann, C., Schmidt, E.M. (1999): Erfassung und Messung von Forschungs- und Entwicklungsaktivitäten im Dienstleistungssektor. Essen: RWI, Wissenschaftsstatistik.

Ricardo, D. (1996): Principles of Political Economy and Taxation. In: Great Minds Series. Amherst: Prometheus Books.

Rigby, D.K., Reichheld, F.F., Schefter, P. (2002): Avoid the Four Perils of CRM. In: Technology Review, 80 (2), pp. 101–109.

Rip, A. (1992): Science and Technology as Dancing Partners. In: Kroes, P., Bakker, M. (eds.): Technological Development and Science in the Industrial Age. New Perspectives on the

Science-Technology Relationship. Dordrecht, Boston, London: Kluwer Academic Publishers, pp. 231–269.

Roberts, G. (2003): Review of Research Assessment. Report by Sir Gareth Roberts to the UK Funding Bodies, London.

Sapir, A. et al. (2003): An Agenda for a Growing Europe. Making the EU Economic System Deliver ('Sapir-Report'). Brussels: European Commission.

Schaan, S., Anderson, F. (2001): Innovation in Canadian Manufacturing: National Estimates. Survey of Innovation 1999. Ottawa: Statistics Canada.

Schmid, H., Liebig, T. (2001): Quo vadis, duales System? Das neue Berufsbildungsgesetz und die Berufsbildungsreformen in der Europäischen Union. Diskussionspapiere, 71, St. Gallen: Forschungsinstitut für Arbeit und Arbeitsrecht an der Hochschule St. Gallen

Schmoch, U. (2005): Leistungsfähigkeit und Strukturen der Wissenschaft im internationalen Vergleich, 2004. Studien zum deutschen Innovationssystem, 6–2005. Bonn, Berlin: BMBF (accessible by: www.technologische-leistungsfaehigkeit.de).

Schmoch, U. (2003a): Hochschulforschung und Industrieforschung – Perspektiven der Interaktion. Frankfurt, New York: Campus.

Schmoch, U. (2003b): Service Marks as Novel Innovation Indicator. In: Research Evaluation, 12 (2), pp. 149–156.

Schmoch, U., Hinze, S. (2004): Opening the Black Box. In: Moed, H.F., Glänzel, W., Schmoch, U. (eds.): Handbook of Qualitative Science and Technology Research. The Use of Publication and Patent Statistics in Studies of S&T Systems. Dordrecht: Kluwer Academic Publishers, pp. 215–235.

Schmoch, U., Grupp, H., Mannsbart, W., Schwitalla, B. (1988): Technikprognosen mit Patentindikatoren. Köln: Verlag TÜV Rheinland.

Schultz, S., Weise, Ch. (1999): Der deutsche Dienstleistungshandel im internationalen Vergleich. DIW-Beiträge zur Strukturforschung, 180, Berlin: DIW.

Schumpeter, J. (1911): Theorie der wirtschaftlichen Entwicklung. Eine Untersuchung über Unternehmergewinn, Kapital, Kredit, Zins und den Konjunkturzyklus. Berlin: Duncker & Humblot.

Siegel, D., Waldman, D., Link, A. (2003): Assessing the Impact of Organizational Practices on the Productivity of University Technology Transfer Offices: An Exploratory Study. In: Research Policy, 32, pp. 27–48.

Siegfried, J.J., Evans, L.B. (1994): Empirical Studies of Entry and Exit: A Survey of the Evidence. In: Review of Industrial Organization, 9, pp. 121–155.

Stach, M. (1998): Die Krise des Dualen Systems – Phasen, Symptome, Gründe, Reformen. In: TNTEE Publications, 1 (1).

Stadler, M.; Wapler, R. (2004): Endogenous Skilled-biased Technological Change and Matching Unemployment. In: Journal of Economics, 81, pp. 1–24.

Statistics New Zealand (2004): Innovation in New Zealand 2003. Wellington: Statistics New Zealand.

Stifterverband für die Deutsche Wissenschaft (2004): FuE-Datenreport 2003/04. Forschung und Entwicklung in der Wirtschaft. Bericht über die FuE-Erhebungen 2001 und 2002. Essen: Wissenschaftsstatistik GmbH im Stifterverband für die Deutsche Wissenschaft.

Storey, D., Wynarczyk, P. (1997): The Survival and Non Survival of Micro Firms in the UK. In: Review of Industrial Organization, 11, pp. 209–229.

Strack, G. (2003): Hightech- und wissensintensive Sektoren schaffen Arbeitsplätze in Europa. In: Statistik kurz gefasst, Thema 9: Wissenschaft und Technologie, 10/2003. Luxembourg: Eurostat.

Tae, Y.S. et al. (2002): Korean Innovation Survey 2002: Manufacturing Sector. Seoul: Science & Technology Policy Institute.

Tessaring, M., Wannan, J. (2004): Vocational Education and Training – Key to the Future, Lisbon–Copenhagen–Maastricht: Mobilising for 2010. CEDEFOP Synthesis of the Maastricht Study, Luxembourg.

Thurik, R., Grilo, I. (2005): Determinants of Entrepreneurial Engagement Levels in Europe and the US. Discussion Papers of Entrepreneurship, Growth and Public Policy, 20–2005, Jena: Max Planck Institute of Economics.

Tidd, J., Hull F.M. (eds.) (2003): Service Innovation. London: Imperial College Press.

tns infratest (2004): Monitoring Informationswirtschaft 7. Faktenbericht 2004, Munich.

Troltsch, K. (2004a): Strukturen und Entwicklung der dualen Ausbildung in Technikberufen und Trends im Fachkräfteangebot bis 2015. Studien zum deutschen Innovationssystem, 6–2004, Bonn.

Troltsch, K. (2004b): Berufsbildung und Strukturwandel. Zum Einfluss wirtschaftsstruktureller Veränderungen auf das betriebliche Ausbildungsstellenangebot seit 1980. In: BIBB (ed.): Der Ausbildungsmarkt und seine Einflussfaktoren. Ergebnisse des Experten-Workshops vom 1. und 2. Juli 2004 in Bonn, Bonn: BIBB.

Tunzelmann von, N., Kraemer Mbula, E. (2003): Changes in Research Assessment Practices in other Countries since 1999. Final report, Brighton: SPRU.

Uhly, A. (2005): Die Zukunftsfähigkeit technischer Berufe im dualen System. Empirische Analysen auf der Basis der Berufsbildungsstatistik. Gutachten im Rahmen der Berichterstattung zur technologischen Leistungsfähigkeit Deutschlands. Studien zum deutschen Innovationssystem, 5–2005, Bonn (http://technologische-leistungsfaehig-keit.de/pub/sdi-05-05.pdf).

Ulrich, J.G., Troltsch, K. (2003): Stabilisierung des Lehrstellenmarktes unter wirtschaftlich schwierigen Rahmenbedingungen? Aktuelle Analysen der Berufsberatungsstatistik zur Lage auf dem Ausbildungsstellenmarkt. Forschung Spezial, 5, Bielefeld: Bertelsmann.

Um, M.-J. et al. (2004): Korean Innovation Survey (KIS) 2003: Service Sector. Seoul: Science & Technology Policy Institute.

UNESCO (1999): Operational Manual for ISCED 1997. Paris: UNESCO.

UNESCO (1997): International Standard Classification of Education – ISCED 1997. Paris: UNESCO.

VDG (2004): Bedarfslücke in der Gründungsfinanzierung schliessen! Press information, 27 September 2004, Berlin: Verband deutscher Gründungsinitiativen (VDG).

Voßkamp, R. (2005): Die Beiträge von Forschung, Entwicklung und Innovation zu Produktivität und Wachstum. Berlin: DIW.

Wagner, J. (1994): The Post-Entry Performance of New Small Firms in German Manufacturing Industries. In: Journal of Industrial Economics, 62, pp. 141–154.

Wakelin, K. (1997): Trade and Innovation. Theory and Evidence. Cheltenham: Edward Elgar.

Walden, G., Herget, H. (2002): Nutzen der betrieblichen Ausbildung für Betriebe. Erste Ergebnisse einer empirischen Erhebung. In: Berufsbildung in Wissenschaft und Praxis, 31 (6), pp. 32–37.

Warda, J. (2002): A 2001–2002 Update of R&D Tax Treatment in OECD Countries. Report Prepared for the OECD Directorate for Science, Technology and Industry, Paris: OECD.

Weißhuhn, G., Wichmann, T. (2000): Beschäftigungseffekte von Unternehmensgründungen. Berlin: Berlicon Research.

Wenger, L. (1997): Forschungsrahmen zukünftiger Qualifikationsforschung. In: Zeitschrift für Berufs- und Wirtschaftspädagogik (ZBW), 4 (93), pp. 384–404.

Wennekers, S., van Stel, A., Thurik, R., Reynolds, P. (2005): Nascent Entrepreneurship and the Level of Economic Development. In: Small Business Economics, 24, pp. 293–309.

Werner, R. (2003): Die Bedeutung der neuen Ausbildungsberufe für den Strukturwandel des dualen Systems. In: Beicht, U. et al.: Technische Berufe im dualen System der Berufsausbildung – Stellenwert und Entwicklungstendenzen. Studien zum deutschen Innovationssystem, Nr. 3–2003, Bonn, pp. 6–25.

Westerhuis, A. (2001): European Structures of Qualification Levels. Reports on Recent Developments in Germany, Spain, France, the Netherlands and in the United Kingdom (England and Wales). Vol. II. Luxembourg.

World Bank (2005): Doing Business in 2006: Removing Creating Jobs. Washington: The World Bank.

World Bank (2004): Doing Business in 2005: Removing Obstacles to Growth. Washington: The World Bank.

Youtie, J., Shapira, P., Brice, K., Hegde, D., Changeau, D., Wang, J. (2002): Manufacturing Needs, Practices, and Performance in Georgia, 1999–2002. GaMEP Evaluation Working Paper E 200201, Atlanta: Georgia Institute of Technology.

## 7.2 Abbreviations

| | |
|---|---|
| € | Euro |
| $ | Dollar |
| | |
| 2G | Second generation |
| 3G | Third generation |
| | |
| AAAS | American Association for the Advancement of Science |
| ACTS | Advanced Communications Technology and Services programme |
| ADSL | Asynchronous Digital Subscriber Lines |
| AKL | Ausstattungs-, Kosten- und Leistungsvergleiche |
| ANBERD | Analytical Business Enterprise Research and Development |
| ANOVA | Analysis of Variance |
| APR | Apprenticeship participation ratio of young people |
| AUT | Austria |
| | |
| B2B | Business to Business |
| B2C | Business to Consumer |
| BA | Federal Agency of Labour, Germany |
| BBiG | Vocational Training Act (Berufsbildungsgesetz) |
| BEL | Belgium |
| BIBB | Federal Institute for Vocational Education and Training |
| BITKOM | German Association for Information Technology, Telecommunications and New Media (Bundesverband Informationswirtschaft, Telekommunikation und neue Medien e.V.) |
| BLK | Bund-Länder Commission for Educational Planning and Research Promotion (Bund-Länder-Kommission für Bildungsplanung und Forschungsförderung) |
| BMBF | Federal Ministry of Education and Research, Germany (Bundesministerium für Bildung und Forschung) |
| BMBWK | Federal Ministry of Education, Science and Culture, Austria (Bundesministerium für Bildung, Wissenschaft und Kultur) |
| BMVIT | Federal Ministry of Transport, Innovation and Technology, Austria (Bundesministerium für Verkehr, Innovation und Technologie) |
| BMWA | Federal Ministry of Economics and Labour (Germany/Austria) (Bundesministerium für Wirtschaft und Arbeit) |
| BPM5 | Balance of Payments Manual, fifth edition, International Monetary Fund |
| BRITE EURAM | Basic research in industrial technologies for Europe – European research in advanced materials |
| BTU | Venture Capital for small Technology Enterprises (Beteiligungskapital für kleine Technologieunternehmen) |
| BUL | Bulgaria |

bvt                      School-based vocational training year

CDMA                     Code-Division Multiple Access
CHN                      China
CIP                      Competitiveness and Innovation Programme
CIS                      Community Innovation Surveys
CLFS                     Continuous Labour Force Survey
COMPENDEX                International database of engineering sciences, provided by STN
CSR                      Comprehensive Spending Review
CTB                      Contribution to trade balance
CWTS                     Centre for Science and Technology Studies, Leiden
CZE                      Czech Republic

DARPA                    Defense Advanced Research Projects Agency
DEAR                     Defence Evaluation and Research Agency
DEN                      Denmark
DERA                     Defence Evaluation and Research Agancy
DEST                     Department of Education, Science and Training
DIHK                     German Chamber of Commerce (Deutscher Industrie- und
                         Handelskammertag)
DIW                      German Institute for Economic Research (Deutsches Institut für
                         Wirtschaftsforschung)
DOMA                     (TEMA) German database of mechanical and process engine-
                         ering literature
DPMA                     German Patent and Trade Mark Office
DTI                      Department of Trade and Industry

EAG                      Education at a Glance
e-commerce               Electronic commerce
EFTA                     European Free Trade Association
e-government             Electronic government
EITO                     European Information Technology Observatory
ENVIRON                  The EU Environment and Climate Programme
EPAT                     Patent database containing European patent filings, provided by
                         Questel-Orbit
EPAPAT                   Patent database containing European patent filings, provided by
                         Questel-Orbit
EPC                      European Patent Convention
EPO                      European Patent Office
ERA                      European Research Area
ESA                      European Space Agency
ESP                      Spain
ESPRIT                   The EU information technologies programme
EST                      Estonia
EU                       European Union
Eurostat                 European Union statistical information service
EVCA                     European Venture Capital Association

| | |
|---|---|
| FIN | Finland |
| FOS | Federal Office of Statistics |
| FP | Framework Programme for Research and Technological Development |
| FRA | France |
| Fraunhofer ISI | Fraunhofer Institute for Systems and Innovation Research |
| | |
| GBR | United Kingdom |
| GDP | Gross Domestic Product |
| GDR | German Democratic Republic |
| GEM | Global Entrepreneurship Monitor |
| GeoHive | Global statistics website with geopolitical data, statistics on the human population, earth and more |
| GER | Germany |
| GERD | |
| GRE | Greece |
| GSM | Global System for Mobile |
| | |
| HIS | Higher Education Information System GmbH (Hochschulinformations-System GmbH) |
| HLT | High-level Technology |
| HRST | Human Resources for Science and Technology |
| HRSTO | Human Resources for Science and Technology by Occupation |
| HT | High-technology |
| HUN | Hungary |
| | |
| IA | International Alignment |
| IAEP | International Assessment of Education Progress |
| IC | Information and Communication technologies and services |
| ICT | Information and Communication Technology |
| IFM | Institute for SME Research (Institut für Mittelstandsforschung) |
| ILO | International Labour Organisation |
| IND | India |
| INSEE | National Institute for Statistics and Economic Studies (Institut National de la Statistique et des Études Économiques) |
| IP | Innovation Policy |
| IPC | International Patent Classification |
| IPR | Intellectual Property Right |
| IRL | Ireland |
| ISCED | International Standard Classification of Education |
| ISCO | International Standard Classification of Occupations |
| ISI | Fraunhofer Institute for Systems and Innovation Research |
| ISIC | International Standard Industrial Classification |
| ISL | Iceland |
| ISR | Israel |
| ITA | Italy |
| ITU | International Telecommunication Union |

| JOULE | The EU non-nuclear energy programme |
| JPN | Japan |
| JPO | Japanese Patent Office |
| JSIC | Japanese Standard Industrial Classification |
| | |
| KfW | Kreditanstalt für Wiederaufbau |
| KIBS | Knowledge-intensive Business Services |
| KMK | Standing Conference of the Ministers of Education and Cultural Affairs of the Länder in the Federal Republic of Germany (Kultusministerkonferenz) |
| KOR | Korea |
| | |
| LAT | Latvia |
| LFS | Labour Force Survey |
| LT | Leading-edge Technology |
| LTU | Lithuania |
| LUX | Luxembourg |
| | |
| M&As | Mergers & Acquisitions |
| MED | Ministry of Economic Development |
| MIP | Mannheim Innovation Panel |
| MNEs | Multinational Enterprises |
| MSTI | Main Science and Technology Indicators |
| | |
| NACE | Statistical Classification of economic Activities in The European Community (Nomenclature statistique des Activités économiques dans la Communauté Européenne) |
| NAICS | North American Industry Classification System |
| NATO | North Atlantic Treaty Organisation |
| NED | Netherlands |
| NIH | National Institutes of Health |
| NIW | Institute for Economic Research Lower Saxony (Niedersächsisches Institut für Wirtschaftsforschung) |
| NOR | Norway |
| NSF | National Science Foundation |
| NSI | National System Of Innovation |
| NVCA | National Venture Capital Association |
| | |
| OECD | Organisation for Economic Co-operation and Development |
| OLS | Ordinary Least Square |
| OMB | Office of Management and Budget |
| OMC | Open Method of Coordination |
| OST | Office of Science and Technology |
| | |
| PATDPA | Patent file containing the bibliographic data and legal status for all kinds of patent documents and utility models published by Deutsches Patent- und Markenamt (German Patent and Trade- |

|       | mark Office) as well as all kinds of patent documents of the European Patent Office and the WIPO designated for the Federal Republic of Germany |
|-------|------|
| PCT   | Patent Cooperation Treaty |
| PISA  | Programme for International Student Assessment |
| POL   | Poland |
| POP   | Population |
| POR   | Portugal |
| PPP   | Purchasing power parity |
| pvt   | Pre-vocational training year |
|       |      |
| R&D   | Research and experimental Development |
| RAE   | Research Assessment Exercise |
| RCA   | Relative export-import ratio |
| RIA   | Relative Innovation Advantage |
| RLA   | Revealed Literature Advantage |
| RMA   | Relative share in imports |
| ROM   | Romania |
| RPA   | Revealed Patent Advantage |
| RTA   | Relative Technological Advantage |
| RUS   | Russia |
| RVA   | Relative share in value added |
| RXA   | Relative share in exports |
|       |      |
| S&E   | natural or information Scientists and Engineers |
| SBA   | Small Business Authority |
| SBIR  | Small Business Innovation Research Program |
| SBS   | Small Business Service |
| SCI   | Science Ciatation Index |
| SDR   | Supply-Demand-Ratio |
| sec   | Secondary general school certificate |
| sec II | Leavers with higher education entrance qualification |
| SET   | Science, Engineering, and Technology |
| SIC   | Standard Industrial Classification |
| SIN   | Singapore |
| SITC  | Standard International Trade Classification |
| SLO   | Slovenia |
| SME   | Small and Medium-sized Enterprise |
| SR    | Scientific Regard |
| SSR   | Student–Staff Ratio |
| STAN  | Structural Analysis Database (OECD) |
| StBA  | Federal Statistical Office of Germany (Statistisches Bundesamt) |
| STC   | Selected Threshold Countries |
| STN   | Scientific & Technical Information Network |
| SUI   | Switzerland |
| SVK   | Slowakia |
| SWE   | Sweden |

| TIMMS | Third International Mathematics and Science Study |
| TPE | Taiwan |
| TRANSPORT | The EU common transport policy programme |
| TSER | The EU Targeted Socio-economic Research Programme |
| TTO | Technology Transfer Office |

| SBS (GBR) | United Kingdom Small Business Service |
| SBA (USA) | United States Small Business Agency |
| UK | United Kingdom |
| UMTS | Universal Mobile Telecommunication System |
| UNESCO | United Nations Educational, Scientific and Cultural Organization |
| USA | United States of America |
| USPTO | United States Patent and Trademark Office |

| VAT | Value Added Tax |
| VC | Venture Capital |
| VDG | German Association for Start-up Initiatives (Verband deutscher Gründungsinitiativen) |
| VET | Vocational Education and Training |
| vs | Full-time vocational school |

| W-CDMA | Wideband Code Division Multiple Access |
| WIPO | World Intellectual Property Organization |
| WLAN | Wireless Local Area Networks |
| WOPATENT | Patent database containing PCT filings, provided by Questel-Orbit |

| ZEW | Centre for European Economic Research (Zentrum für Europäische Wirtschaftsforschung) |

# 7.3 About the Authors

**Heike Belitz** is a research associate at the German Institute for Economic Research Berlin, Department Innovation, Manufacturing, Services. She entered the institute in 1991 and has conducted several studies related to technology policy, R&D of multinational companies, innovation systems, innovation indicators, and evaluation of selected R&D promoting programmes. From 2000 to 2002 she worked as secretary of the evaluation commission of the System of Industry-Integrating Research Assistance at the Federal Ministry of Economics and Technology. She studied mathematical economics at the University of Economics in Berlin, where she graduated in 1981 and completed her PhD thesis in 1986.
E-mail address: hbelitz@diw.de

**Dieter Dohmen** is director of the Institute of Education and Socio-Economic Research in Cologne; he founded this private research and consulting institute in 1993. He is an education economist and his major areas are education financing and management, demographic change and international comparative research. He studied economics at the University of Cologne, graduating in 1991 and completed his PhD thesis in the economics of education at the Technical University of Berlin in 1998.
E-mail address: d.dohmen@fibs-koeln.de

**Jakob Edler**, born in 1967, studied at the University of Mannheim (Germany) and Dartmouth College (USA), receiving a Diploma in Business Administration as well as a Degree as Master of Arts in Political Science and Economic History. He wrote his dissertation on European research policy. From 1996 to 1999 he worked at the University of Mannheim and at the Mannheim Centre for European Social Research on European technology policy; in 1997/98 he worked for six months as administrative assistant within the European Commission, GD XII, AP (Framework Programme). Since May 1999 he has been working as a senior researcher at the Fraunhofer Institute ISI in Karlsruhe. His main research areas include: national innovation systems, knowledge supply and technology transfer; comparative research on internationalisation strategies in science and technology policy; innovation strategies of multi-national companies; as well as European technology policy and modes of governance.
E-mail address: jakob.edler@isi.fraunhofer.de

**Jürgen Egeln** has been a researcher at the Industrial Economics and International Management Department of the Centre for European Economic Research (ZEW) Mannheim since 1992 and is now vice head of department. He has carried out several studies related to firm location, the development of regions and the dynamics of firms and markets. From 1998 to 2000 he was one of the team of authors of the summary report on Germany's technological performance. His current research agenda concerns the birth and diffusion of new technologies, the role and interaction of regional innovation structures, the evaluation of instruments of technology policy and the role of academically qualified human capital.
E-mail address: egeln@zew.de

**Rainer Frietsch** finished business training in wholesale and import/export trade and studied social science at the University of Mannheim. Since October 2000 he has been employed as a research scientist at the Fraunhofer Institute for Systems and Innovation Research (ISI), Karlsruhe, in the department Innovation Systems and Policy. His main work focuses are: patent statistics, bibliometrics, economic and social indicators, qualifications and education in the innovation process, technology foresight, and methodological foundations of empirical research.
E-mail address: rainer.frietsch@isi.fraunhofer.de

**Birgit Gehrke** studied economics at the University of Hanover. She completed her doctorate in 1988 with a theoretical and empirical study on 'Entrepreneurial adjustment in structural change'. Since 1989 she has been working as a researcher at the 'Niedersächsische Institut für Wirtschaftsforschung (NIW)' in Hanover with the special topics of international trade, educational and regional economics and policy. She has been a member of the research team analysing indicators of Germany's technological performance since 1991 with particular interests in questions of education and qualification.
E-mail address: gehrke@niw.de

**Christoph Grenzmann** is head of Wissenschaftsstatistik GmbH (Stifterverband für die Deutsche Wissenschaft). He studied mathematics and economics at Cologne University, graduating in 1972. For his PhD thesis in economics he studied at Pennsylvania State University and Cologne, where he completed his thesis in 1975. Between 1975 and 1983 he worked for different consulting and auditing companies. Since 1983 he has been with Wissenschaftsstatistik GmbH and responsible for the monitoring and indicator system of research and development in the German business enterprise sector. He takes part in various international working groups (S + T-Indicators Working Party; EUROSTAT/National Experts on Science and Technological Indicators; OECD).
E-mail address: grenzmann@stifterverband.de

**Christoph Heine** is a senior researcher at HIS Hochschul-Informations-System GmbH Hanover, Germany. His main tasks are research on access to higher education, longitudinal studies on the study paths and training of school leavers entitled to access higher education and indicator systems on higher education training in international comparison. He studied sociology, economics und economic and social history at the Universities of Münster and Hamburg.
E-mail address: heine@his.de

**Thomas Hempell** was a senior researcher in the Research Group "Information and Communication Technologies" at the Centre for European Economic Research (ZEW), Mannheim, Germany. His major research interests are the effects of new technologies on productivity, innovation and management in firms. Dr Hempell has received a Master's degree in Economics and in Philosophy from the University of Hamburg, as well as a Master's degree in Economics from the Universitat Pompeu Fabra, Barcelona. In December 2004 he finished his PhD at the University of Ulm on 'Computers and Productivity: How Firms Make a General Purpose Technology

Work'. Dr Hempell worked at ZEW from November 2000 until September 2005. In October 2005 he accepted a research position at AXA Insurances.
E-mail address: thempell@gmx.de

**Olaf Krawczyk**, born in 1969, studied geography at the Universities of Hanover, Toulouse/France and Fort Hare/South Africa and gained his degree in 1998. Until 2001 he worked at the Mull & Partner Ingenieurgesellschaft mbH (Hanover) in the risk assessment of contaminated sites, conversion and revitalisation planning. In 1999 he had a short-term assignment at CIMEC in East London/South Africa as an expert for local economic development with GTZ. He joined the NIW Institute for Economic Research Lower Saxony in Hanover in 2001. His main research areas are innovation and technology research, sectoral analyses and regional economics.
E-mail address: krawczyk@niw.de

**Harald Legler** studied economics at the Ruhr University of Bochum. He completed his doctorate in 1982 with a theoretical and empirical study on "International Competitiveness of West German Chemical Industry". Since 1971 he has worked as a researcher at the 'Institut für Weltwirtschaft' (Kiel), 'Institut für Systemtechnik und Innovationsforschung der Fraunhofer-Gesellschaft' (Karlsruhe) and 'Niedersächsisches Institut für Wirtschaftsforschung' (Hanover). Currently his special research topics are innovation research, international trade, structural and regional economics and policy. He has been the coordinator of the working group 'innovation indicators' analysing Germany's technological performance since 1985.
E-mail address: legler@niw.de

**Christian Rammer** is a senior researcher at the Department of Industrial Economics and International Management of the Centre for European Economic Research (ZEW), Mannheim, Germany. His major research interests are innovation economics and technology transfer. Among other tasks, he coordinates the annual German Innovation Survey conducted by the ZEW (Mannheim Innovation Panel). Dr Rammer studied regional science at the University of Vienna (MA in 1991, PhD in 1997). After having worked as a research assistant and assistant professor at the Vienna University of Economics, and as a researcher at the Austrian Research Centre Seibersdorf, he moved to ZEW in 2000.
E-mail address: rammer@zew.de

**Ulrich Schmoch** is head of department at the Fraunhofer Institute for Systems and Innovation Research, Karlsruhe, Germany. His major research interests are innovation indicators, IPR issues, university-industry interaction, and performance of scientific research. He studied mechanical engineering at the Universities of Hanover and Grenoble, graduating in 1977. He completed his PhD thesis in social science at the University of Hanover in 1993, and his habilitation thesis in sociology at the University of Karlsruhe in 2002. From 1983 until 1985 he worked at a patent attorney's office in Wuppertal, Germany, and joined the Fraunhofer Institute in 1986.
E-mail address: ulrich.schmoch@isi.fraunhofer.de

**Dieter Schumacher** is professor of international economics at the Europe University Viadrina in Frankfurt (Oder) and senior research fellow at the German Institute of Economic Research (DIW) in Berlin, Germany. His major research interests are determinants and effects of international trade flows. He studied economics, graduating in 1969 and completed his PhD thesis at the Free University in Berlin in 1971. He entered the DIW in 1971. In 1978, he worked as Industrial Development Officer at UNIDO in Vienna, Austria. In 1983 and 1986, he was visiting fellow at the Department of Economics, St. Andrews University, Scotland.
E-mail address: dschumacher@diw.de

**Klaus Troltsch**, born 23 February 1955, studied politics, sociology and law at Stuttgart Technical University and at the University of Bonn. After obtaining his M.A. in politics 1981, he was an academic assistant in the School of Politics at the University of Koblenz-Landau, taught at the University of Mainz in the field of methods and techniques of empirical social research and philosophy of science, and since December 1989 at the Federal Institute for Vocational Education and Training in Bonn, Germany as an academic researcher in the Department for "Sociology and Economics of Vocational Education and Training". Main areas of research: company training provision, disparities on the training places market, employment statistics, economic, occupational and qualifications structure developments on the training places market and in the employment system.
E-mail address: troltsch@bibb.de

**Alexandra Uhly**, born 18 April 1967, studied economics at the University of Trier, obtaining a degree in economics 1995, and completed her PhD thesis in 2000 at the University of Trier. Until 2003 she was an academic researcher/assistant at the Chair of Personnel Economics in the Faculty of Economics at the University of Trier. She has been an academic researcher in the department for 'Sociology and Economics of Vocational Education and Training' at the Federal Institute for Vocational Education and Training in Bonn, Germany, since September 2003. Main areas of research: vocational education and training statistics, developments relating to occupational structure, gender-specific structures and developments within the dual system of vocational education and training, foreign trainees in the dual system.
E-mail address: uhly@bibb.de

**Günter Walden**, born 13 April 1952, studied economics at Berlin Technical University, obtaining a degree in economics 1977, and completed his PhD thesis in 1988 at the University of Bremen. After working in the area of market and social research he has been employed at the Federal Institute for Vocational Education and Training in Bonn, Germany, since 1981, most recently as head of the department for 'Sociology and Economics of Vocational Education and Training'. Main areas of research: cost, benefit, financing of vocational education and training, place of learning cooperation, company training policy, continuing vocational education and training.
E-mail-address: walden@bibb.de